THE JEWISH PEOPLE

HISTORY • RELIGION • LITERATURE

THE JEWISH PEOPLE

HISTORY • RELIGION • LITERATURE

MODERN JEWISH THOUGHT

Selected Issues, 1889-1966

New Introduction
by
LOUIS JACOBS

ARNO PRESS
A New York Times Company
NEW YORK • 1973

Reprint Edition 1973 by Arno Press Inc.

The Idea of Humanity in Judaism by Kurt Wilhelm
was reprinted by permission of Raphael Loewe

The Psychoanalytic Study of Judaism was reprinted
from a copy in the University of Illinois Library

THE JEWISH PEOPLE: History, Religion, Literature
ISBN for complete set: 0-405-05250-2
See last pages of this volume for titles.

Manufactured in the United States of America

Publisher's Note: The selections in
this volume were reprinted from the
best available copies

Library of Congress Cataloging in Publication Data
Main entry under title:

Modern Jewish thought; selected issues, 1889-1966.

(The Jewish people: history, religion, literature)
Collection of reprinted journal articles.
Includes bibliographical references.
CONTENTS: Agus, J. B. Mitzvot, yes; averot, no.--Brickner, B. R. Religious education: the God-idea in the light of modern thought and its pedagogic implications.--Cronbach, A. The psychoanalytic study of Judaism. [etc.]
1. Judaism--Addresses, essays, lectures. I. Arno Press. II. Title. III. Series.
BM40.M58 296 73-2221
ISBN 0-405-05283-9

CONTENTS

INTRODUCTION

The essays in this anthology of *Modern Jewish Thought* first appeared (with the exception of the Wilhelm essay) in well-known Jewish learned journals. As in all anthologies, there is a strong element of subjectivity and possibly arbitrariness in the choice of what to include. Our aim has been to present the reader with complete arguments, of some length rather than mere snippets, in English on some of the main issues Jews have to face in the modern world. Important topics, such as the holocaust and the implications of the State of Israel as a central factor in Jewish life, have not been included since these are at the forefront of Jewish concern so that discussions of them are easily available in present-day Jewish writing. The choice of essays in English has been determined by the nature of the series to which this volume belongs, though one is conscious of the fact that many of the more significant statements on the themes mentioned are in German and, latterly, in Hebrew. There is gain, nonetheless, in that essays in good clear English, as these all are, will reach a wider public than works in other languages.

These essays cover many different aspects of modern Jewish thought. The term 'modern thought' is somewhat nebulous. It is applied to these essays either because the topics considered or the method of treatment would have been impossible in mediaeval times, it being recognized, as Zunz has said, that the Jewish middle ages did not come to an end until the French Revolution and the Emancipation of the Jews. Preference was given to essays which break new ground, at least so far as writing in English is involved.

The first essay in the volume is an overlooked piece by the most outstanding Jewish historian, Heinrich Graetz. Graetz hardly qualifies as a philosopher or a theologian. It would not be difficult to pick holes in his argument, especially where it is coloured by 19th century rationalism. For all that, the bold investigation, by a scholar with Graetz's vast knowledge of the Jewish past, of what Judaism means for the present and future is bound to be stimulating. In Graetz's view the abiding power of Judaism consists in its rational character, in its stern refusal, as he saw it, to surrender to any kind of superstition or trace of idolatry.

Schechter's essay on the dogmas of Judaism is now a classic of Jewish thought. No examination of what it is that Judaism expects of its adherents in terms of belief can proceed without taking into account Schechter's admirable survey of the role dogma has played in the Jewish past. The more the pity that Schechter leaves the reader with a profound sense of disappointment. Having argued convincingly that beliefs are indispensable for the Jewish religion, Schechter refuses to be drawn on the question of which beliefs the modern Jew can entertain without sacrificing his intellectual honesty and integrity. A Jewish theology must obviously advance beyond Schechter if it is to succeed, but this in no way detracts from the value of Schechter's pioneering effort.

Liberal Jewish theology has generally abandoned any belief in the doctrine of the resurrection of the dead conceived of in physical terms, substituting for it some version of the immortality of the soul. This latter belief was subjected to severe attack at the beginning of the century not alone on philosophical but on psychological grounds. At the dawn of the century, before the storm-clouds had gathered and when confidence in a roseate future for man here on earth seemed assured, the axiom that man has an innate desire to live forever was challenged, notably, in the English speaking world, by writers of the calibre of G.B. Shaw and H.G. Wells. It is to this question that Montefiore addresses himself with customary urbanity.

It will come as no surprise to those acquainted with theological tendencies among Jews in the thirties that these frequently anticipated the agitation in the sixties among Protestant theologians around the 'death of God' question. The Brickner and Heller essays discuss what content can be given to the God idea in the light of modern thought, with Brickner taking a more radical, Heller a more conservative, stance. More recent discussions of the whole question have been more concerned with linguistic analysis of religious propositions, of how talk about God can be 'cashed'.

Cronbach's account of psychoanalytic theories of the Biblical narratives and the Jewish rituals together with a critique has been republished in full, very long though it is, since this is one of the few detailed examinations of psychoanalysis from the standpoint of Judaism. Reference should be made to Cronbach's follow-up in a later issue of the same journal (*Hebrew Union College Annual*, Vol. XIX, 1945-6, pp. 205-273).

In none of the earlier essays is there discernible the note of crisis and *angst* which began to emerge among Jewish thinkers in the post-war period, an age which saw the increasing popularity in philosophical circles of existentialist theories, and, on the Jewish scene, a keen interest in the writings of men like Buber and Rosenzweig. The 'gloomy Dane' Kierkegaard became a new hero in the realm of thought, captivating many Jews as well as Christians. Milton Steinberg, while acknowledging some of Kierkegaard's insights and the failure of liberal thinkers to grapple with the more burning problems of human existence, comes down uncompromisingly, in the name of Judaism, against the Kierkegaardian 'teleological suspension of the ethical'. Other Jewish thinkers have been more ready to accommodate Kierkegaard to Judaism. At all events the problem has been adequately summarized by Steinberg and can serve as source material for the existentialist debate from the point of view of Jewish thought.

Leon Roth's essay seeks to demonstrate that at certain periods and among some Jewish teachers the strong Jewish emphasis on sound ethical conduct has tended to become obscured through an excessive preoccupation with the needs and interests of Jews. It has been remarked more than once that in times of stress there has been a tendency for Jews to retreat into their own world with the corollary that in times of greater ease a much wider view has prevailed. Roth appeals for the implications of this to be followed in the Jewish world of today.

Wilhelm treats of the universalistic aspects of Judaism. While a good deal of Wilhelm's material is known to Jewish scholars and thinkers, there is advantage in his acute presentation based on careful analysis without undue apologetics.

Kohn's essay seeks to defend the role of reason in Judaism in face of the challenges presented by logical positivism on the one hand and existentialism on the other. He is especially severe with the existentialist allure for some Jewish thinkers.

Finally, Agus, as a distinguished Conservative thinker, discusses how to convey to the young the idea of Halakhah — the Jewish legal system — as dynamic, that is, binding upon Jews but subject to change. His solution is for teachers to stress that there is great merit in observance but they should avoid creating traumas among their charges by implying that less observant parents are sinners.

In conclusion it need hardly be said that a volume such as this cannot provide, nor was it intended to provide, the reader with a blueprint or with final answers to the questions raised. Its more modest aim is to convey something of the flavour of modern Jewish thought and to encourage further investigation into these and kindred themes. An anthology is not a textbook. At best it can only hope to serve as a not too inadequate guide.

LOUIS JACOBS
London, England

Biographical Notes on the Essayists

Biographical Notes on the Essayists

1. Heinrich Graetz (1817-1891), historian, author of *Geschichte der Juden* (English trans. *History of the Jews*).
2. Solomon Schechter (1847-1915), scholar, president of the Jewish Theological Seminary of America.
3. Claude Goldsmid Montefiore (1873-1942), modernist theologian, leader of Liberal Judaism in England.
4. Barnet Robert Brickner (1892-1958), American Reform Rabbi, President Central Conference American Rabbis 1953-1955.
5. Bernard James Heller (1896-), American Reform Rabbi.
6. Abraham Cronbach (1882-1965), American Reform Rabbi, Professor of Jewish Social Studies at Hebrew Union College 1922-1950.
7. Milton Steinberg (1903-1950) American Conservative Rabbi and theologian.
8. Leon Roth (1896-1963), philosopher, rector of Hebrew University 1940-1943.
9. Kurt Wilhelm (1900-1965), Chief Rabbi of Sweden 1948-1965.
10. Jacob Kohn (1881-1968), Professor of theology at the University of Judaism from 1947 until his death
11. Jacob B. Agus (1911-), leading American Conservative Rabbi and thinker.

LOUIS JACOBS
London, England

MITZVOT—YES; AVEROT—NO

by

JACOB B. AGUS

"Mitzvot--Yes;

Averot--No"

By JACOB B. AGUS

HOW shall we teach our children about the *mitzvot* of our faith? This is a problem which concerns Conservative congregations and schools far more than those identified either with Reform or with Orthodoxy. To Reform Jews ritual observances are of minor consequence, and the residual ceremonies which they retain are practiced largely in the Temple. To the Orthodox, there is officially no problem, since, in theory, the laws summarized in the *Kitzur Shulhan Arukh* and the *Mishnah Berurah* are as valid today as ever they were. To be sure, the lines of demarcation in Judaism are not as rigid as they appear to be on the organizational plane. Some Reform rabbis place increasing emphasis on the observance of *mitzvot* at home. For them, the educational problem is not essentially different from the one faced in the Conservative school. On

---

DR. JACOB B. AGUS is rabbi of Beth El Congregation, Baltimore, Md., and has written many books and articles on Jewish religious and philosophical themes.

the other hand, many Orthodox rabbis are painfully aware of the contradiction between law and life; consequently, they refrain from teaching the Law, as it is stated in the authoritative books, relying on the arts of improvisation and circumlocution to solve all difficulties. To the extent to which they appreciate that the Law, in its authentic fullness, cannot be taught to the children of their members, they, too, sense the dilemma that we face. This question is, therefore, one which the Conservative movement must solve boldly and imaginatively, though the two other movements may be expected to embrace the Conservative solution in part and by degrees.

The Problem Analyzed

Let us begin with an analysis of the problem. As a movement, we favor the observance of *kashrut,* yet we know, from the last survey of the United Synagogue, that only 37 per cent of our lay leadership observe the Dietary laws scrupulously, while another 33 per cent observe some *kashrut* laws. We may, therefore, assume that a good half of the children in our schools come from homes where *kashrut* is honored more in the breach than in the observance. How, then, can we instruct our teachers to teach the children that it is sinful to eat pork or anything else that is *trefah?* To ignore the hard facts of reality and to spell out the law, in bland defiance of life, is to make the child feel that his parents are sinners. And what is true of *kashrut* applies with equal force to the institution of the Sabbath and the Festivals, the daily prayers, the *tallit* and the *t'fillin.* Thus, a painful contradiction is imbedded in the consciousness of the child at his most impressionable age.

Apart from the festering nature of the "guilt" feelings thus sown, the inner essence of religion is denied to the child. For we know now that it is through the love of his parents that the child is taught to experience the healing grace of love for God, society and the realm of ideals. The Book of Proverbs echoes this profound insight when it asserts, "Hear, my son, the teaching of your father and do not forsake the Torah of your mother." The assertion in the Midrash that the voice of God sounded to Moses like the voice of his father is further proof of this observation. The child's attitude to his father is "the gateway to piety"; the child's attitude to his mother is "the highway to society." It is the function of religious education to call attention to these roads and to cultivate them, not to disregard or barricade them.

It must be understood that we think of religion, in psychological terms, as the feeling of closeness to the Supreme Being, achieved by directing one's energies to ideal ends and consecrating onself to His service. Religion is, for us, not the performance of so many *mitzvot,* but the spirit in which they are performed and the effect of that spirit on personal and social life. It is love, loyalty and exertion directed to the Creator and Father of mankind. It is both the expression and the source of the affirmative, outgoing feelings of the human personality. If all the emotional and volitional reactions of our being are classified in accordance with their being oriented toward life and mankind, or away from them, then religion is the projection of those feelings which relate the individual in positive centripetal terms to his environment, to the ideal world and to God. It is not so much fear as reverence, not so much obedience as dedication, not so much surrender as trust. It is the extension of love and loyalty, the yearning for inner purity and harmony, and the search for beauty and truth in all the relations of life. Thus understood, religion cannot possibly be furthered by implanting "guilt-feelings" in the child through the teaching of ritual laws that are flouted so generally. "Guilt feelings" will find expression in fear, anxiety and in the authority-subjection complex that is so characteristic of the tight-laced and thoroughly unhappy "authoritarian personality."

The Problem for Other Conceptions of Religion

We should recognize, however, that other conceptions of religion are possible. From the fundamentalist viewpoint, the more "guilt-feelings" are built up in regard to ritual observances the better, since they are potentially capable of leading to a re-acceptance of the Law either on the part of the parents of the children or on the part of some future generation. Also, in the closed world of *Halakhah,* feelings of guilt, in themselves, are desirable, since they serve to atone, in part, for the sins of the individual, falling in the category of *hirhurei t'shuvah* (thoughts of repentance). The fundamentalist cycle of guilt and "compulsive obsession" is precisely the kind of religion that Freud described and condemned. But, if the growth and happiness of the individual do not concern us, then a strong case can be made out in behalf of teaching the Law in all its logical rigor. We might then expect to raise up two types—embittered cynics, violently despising all forms of religion, and loyal literalists, practicing "religion" in the Freudian sense of the term. Judging by the state of affairs in Israel, we may conclude that the people there are disposed to choose this road with all its ramifications. And the sad split in Israeli Jewry between self-enclosed fundamentalists and defiant atheists is proof of the tragic operation of this formula.

What is the alternative to this approach? We know now that the answer of Classical Reform, disavowing the worth of all ritual observances, is religiously sterile. The experience of the last century has demonstrated the psychological need for ritual acts that transcend all purely rational explanation, appealing to the hidden depths of human nature. Essentially, religious ceremonies are "depth-symbols," and it is remarkable, indeed, that the genius of the *Mussar* movement, Rabbi Israel Lipkin of Salant, recognized this fact in his teaching about the effects engendered by the performance of *mitzvot* upon the unconscious feelings within a person (*hargashot kehot*). Furthermore, ritual observances transmit the impact of the stream of tradition, which is a powerful aid in the evocation of the sense of eternity. Hence, the total repudiation of the Law and the tradition in Classical Reform could not but result in a shallow, rationalistic faith, cold and artificial.

The Mitzvot as Standards of Piety

In other essays, I have suggested that we teach the precepts of *Halakhah* as collectively formulated and voluntarily accepted standards of piety, not as the rigid molds of faith. The *mitzvot,* in their totality, do not constitute a "straight and narrow path," but a multitude of different "ways of pleasantness," or better still —a treasury of good works. We are to encourage all children to grow into the fullness of their God-given stature, and we ought to demonstrate to them how the *mitzvot* of Judaism can serve as so many aids to their ascent on the ladder of spiritual growth. This ladder, we know, is of a threefold nature, consisting of Torah (learning), *avodah* (worship) and *gmilut hasadim* (deeds of loving kindness). A good Jew should ascend simultaneously on all three ladders, but perfection in all three domains of Judaism is well-nigh impossible. All Jews are required to rise above the first rung on each of the three ladders. Some will climb high on one ladder, others on another ladder, but "all Israel is one fellowship." In helping one another to maintain Judaism on its highest level we share in the achievements of the community as a whole.

With this interpretation we can teach *kashrut* as a traditional Jewish way of maintaining the feeling of being part of the covenant-people, dedicated unto God. Even the one who does not sense this feeling in his personal experience cannot but recognize that the public honoring of this *mitzvah* strengthens the religious tone of the community. At the same time, the teacher should make clear that some Jewish People prefer other means of expressing their identification with the Jewish tradition. In the garden of Judaism there are many and diverse flowers and plants. Every Jew is responsible only to his own conscience as to the extent to which he rises on any one of the three sides of the ladder of Judaism, but all Jews are duty-bound to continue climbing throughout their lifetime. Thus, the minimum standards in any one domain will vary for different individuals. Congregations should consist of like-minded individuals who accept, for themselves, standards which are clearly defined. Beyond the congregational level, circles should be formed of those who set for themselves standards that are far above those prevailing in the general community.

In effect, we suggest that the Law be placed in the category that "going beyond the law" previously occupied. The pietists of all ages took as their slogan the maxim, "Sanctify yourself by means of that which is permitted to you." The great moralist, Moses Hayim Luzzatto, urged that every Jew add a new *mitzvah,* conceived and created by himself, to those which the law obliges him to perform. For us of this generation, the *mitzvot* of *Halakhah* constitute the ways whereby we voluntarily sanctify ourselves individually and communally. And the command to be ever on the lookout for new ways of serving God is richly meaningful in our day.

In thus teaching *Halakhah* as a description of the standard Jewish way of encouraging personal growth and communal solidarity, we shall be appealing to a sense of obligation, without resorting to any suggestion of compulsion or sinfulness. The performance of a *mitzvah* is in the category of a contribution to a charitable cause, not in the nature of the payment of a tax. The amount and nature of a tax are specified, but an act of charity cannot be legislated in the same manner. To give a charitable contribution is a *mitzvah,* but it is no sin to refrain from participating in any specific philanthropic enterprise. There is tremendous psychical potency in the concept of sin, and it should be reserved for the area of moral conduct. Thus, we affirm the supremacy of moral aims within our hierarchy of values. But, just as it is unworthy of our human dignity to have no share at all in the collective efforts of the community to offer help to our fellow man, so it is unworthy of our dignity as Jewish People to refrain from participating in any and all observances of our tradition.

Is this approach tenable? Can we teach observances as *mitzvot,* without insisting that their neglect or violation constitutes an *averah* (transgression)? Not only is this attitude possible, but eminently reasonable, if ritual acts are evaluated in accordance with their effect upon the worshipper. I know of no one today who would suggest that a renewed Sanhedrin should reinstitute the system of punishments provided in the Talmud for the infraction of the Law. In the sixteenth century, the *semikhah*-ordination was renewed and a Sanhedrin almost brought into being in Safed for this very purpose of reestablishing the Torah-itic penalty of flagellation. Yet, today, even the proponents of the Sanhedrin shy away from the consequences of their logic, in the realization that the structure of ideas and sentiments behind the facade of the Law has been transformed radically.

The Reasons for the Mitzvot

Essentially, there were three sets of reasons for the observances (*ta-amei hamitzvot*). The first classification is the express Will of God. The second is a presumed automatic connection between human acts and physical and cosmic consequences. The third is the effect of *mitzvot* upon the mind of the individual worshiper and the mentality of the community. The first category reflects the thinking of non-philosophical or naive Judaism; the second is that of Kabbalah, the roots of which are struck deep in the soil of Judaism; the third category is that of philosophical Judaism. To be sure, these categories of *ta-amei hamitzvot* rarely came in pure and unmixed forms.

Thus, the assumption of the laws' being the clear and unmistakable Will of God needed to be reconciled with the proto-philosophy of thoughtful people, the knowledge which we, as human beings, have of God—His universal compassion, His concern for the growth of His creatures, His revelation in deeds of love, justice and holiness. Hence, the Torah is not content to represent the Law as the sheer first fiat of His inscrutable Will. Many reasons are given for the *mitzvot,* so as to demonstrate that His Will is in accord with human reason and experience. They are described as marks of, or steps toward, holiness, as expressions of the love of God, and as reminders of His acts of redemption; as consequences of His goodness and righteousness or of his hostility to ritual acts connected with the worship of other gods, or of the abomination in His sight of immoral acts. God's Will, then, is understandable, even though it cannot be deduced altogether from the principles of human reason and experience.

In the form which Jewish piety assumed in later centuries under the influence of Kabbalah, the various ritual prohibitions were understood to be of a quasi-magical efficacy. The laws were not debased altogether into magical exercises, since intention in thought and devotion in feeling were required; yet, within these limitations, the doctrine prevailed that prohibited acts affected the substance of the universe, with dire consequences for society in general and the offending individual in particular. According to the Zohar, for instance, the prohibited foods cause the "spirit of uncleanliness" to enter a person, insulating his heart against the influence of the Divine Spirit (*Zohar-"Sh'mini"*). The Italian commentator, Seforno, similarly affirms that *trefah* food coarsens a person's character and disposition, making it impossible for his body to be a "dwelling place for the *Shekinah*" (*"Sh'mini"*). This mixture of theosophy and magic was elaborated at great length in the Hasidic movement. Thus, we read in the *Tanya* that *trefah* food draws its "sustenance" from the three absolutely evil "shells" whence, too, the souls of the Gentiles are derived. The words *muttar* (permitted) and *asur* (prohibited), are assigned the secondary meanings of "untied" and "tied" respectively—i.e., the permitted food, even if not consumed with the intention of serving the Lord, is not "tied" to the "shells," whereas the prohibited foods are "tied" or imprisoned, so that if consumed, even with the best of religious motives, the energy resulting from them cannot but serve the malignant purposes of "the other side" (*Tanya* 6, 7, 8). The impetus of Kabbalistic thought persisted even when its intricate, theosophic fantasies were ignored. Thus, Rabbi Samson Raphael Hirsch maintained that *trefah* foods possess the quasi-chemical property of intensifying a person's animal lusts and rendering his soul insensitive to the experience of holiness (*Horeb II,* Hebrew trans. p. 113).

The Conservative interpretation of Judaism is an extension into modern life and into the modern realm of discourse of the philosophical current of thought. According to Maimonides, the reasons for the *mitzvot* are the effect of certain actions upon the individual and society. "Every one of the 613 Commandments is motivated either by the purpose of importing true ideas, or counteracting wrongful opinions, or the establishment of a just order, or the correction of injustice, or the training in good virtues, or the correction of evil practices" (*Guide* III,

31). In other words, all ritual actions are so many symbols, the effectiveness of which may be expected to vary with the times. Thus, Albo infers that a "divine faith" will be adaptable to variations of social conditions. Moreover, he argues that even one commandment, properly performed, is capable of insuring eternal bliss in the hereafter, thus placing the accent almost exclusively on the positive effects of *mitzvot* and ignoring the dire results of any failure to abide by the numerous prohibitions in the Torah (*Ikkarim I,* 23).

The view herein advocated is, therefore, an extension of the basic conception of the *mitzvot* as it was developed in the tradition of philosophic Judaism.

Religious Motivation for Observance

Does this interpretation of the ritual commandments fail to capture the essential motivations of religious acts? By no means. To be sure, by breaking out of the narrow confines of naive literalism, we lose a great deal of intensity of feeling. For enthusiasm runs generally in direct proportion to narrowness, even as the waters of a stream must be dammed up to provide energy. However, all the roots of religious motivation are retained in this interpretation. Briefly, piety derives in part from fear and in part from love—fear of the outside world, in all its imponderable terror, and fear of unknown, dark and dangerous forces within our being; love of all that is good, true and noble in the external universe, and love for the unfolding of the totality of our being in all its complexity and mystery.

The two forms of fear that enter into the pattern of piety are better served in a fundamentalist pattern of piety. Every religious act is then performed as a means of warding off the wrath of the Master, and the tension of inner fear is released by the certainty with which the laws are laid out and applied. On the other hand, it requires the genius of a mythical *Hasid* to allow full scope for the impulses of love and universality within the confines of a fundamentalist faith. In any liberal view of religion, the major sources of piety are the two forms of love; yet, fear, too, plays its part,—fear of the emptiness and loneliness of a loveless life.

In the case of liberal Judaism, the motives of personal piety are reinforced by the obdurate reality of the Jewish community. In love, we cannot but sense the charm of the values and sentiments of our tradition, and in fear, we cannot but contemplate the sad specter of a naked Jewish community disintegrated by neglect and paralyzed by indifference. Even children can understand that our duties are determined for us in large measure by the particular historical situation in which we are placed. As Jews, our tradition is our collective treasure. And those who are more gifted in mind and heart will accept for themselves greater responsibilities, for the sake of their own spiritual growth and for the sake of the community of which they are part.

To have faith in human nature does not mean that we must cherish illusions concerning it.

On the contrary, only open-eyed awareness of the evil that mars human nature is what makes faith in its latent goodness and greatness necessary.

* * *

We have to know the ultimate goals of human life in order to know how to set our compass in trying to attain proximate goals.

* * *

The fact that democracy, as government by the people, has to resort to representation, implies that it begins and ends with compromise.

RELIGIOUS EDUCATION
THE GOD-IDEA IN THE LIGHT OF MODERN THOUGHT
and
ITS PEDAGOGIC IMPLICATIONS

by

BARNET R. BRICKNER

H

RELIGIOUS EDUCATION

THE GOD-IDEA IN THE LIGHT OF MODERN THOUGHT AND ITS PEDAGOGIC IMPLICATIONS

BARNET R. BRICKNER

I

The aim of this paper, as proposed by the Committee on Religious Education, is twofold.

Firstly, to outline a God-idea that is in consonance with modern thought; and secondly, to indicate its implications for our religious schools.

Let me say at the outset that the God-idea of modern thought is not so very different from the God-idea developed by the Jewish mind at its highest, as so many so-called modernists imagine.

The God-idea of modern thought does, however, come into conflict with the popular idea of traditional theism and which is the prevalent idea taught in our Reform religious schools.

The popular God-idea is so well established, and defended, that I hardly see the need for exposing it in this paper. Neither do I deem it worth our while to get into polemic with those who believe in it. I am more concerned with those of us for whom the popular God-idea as expounded in the traditional theism has become unsatisfactory, and who seek to inspire the children under our spiritual leadership with a conception of God that they can live with; a conception that will grow on them and with them as they mature intellectually and spiritually.

The truth has, unfortunately, become apparent to us that the God-ideas inculcated into the minds of many of our most intelligent children in the religious school, clash powerfully with their own clear thinking in later years. This is also true of other theological conceptions which grow out of the God-idea.

The conflict between intellect and traditional belief becomes disastrous for religion.

No matter what may be the policy of other types of religious education, the Jewish Reform Religious School cannot afford to be characterized by evasion, or depend upon the theory that the infantile notions will be outgrown in later life.

Too few people take the trouble to reshape their religious philosophy, once they have outgrown the notions taught them in childhood. What seems to take place is that the child, grown to intellectual adulthood, turns against religions when he discovers that he has been "cheated" by the intellectual evasion practiced by his Sunday School teachers who knew better, but who, instead of imparting their own genuine religious convictions, felt called upon to be simply transmitters and phonograph records for the traditional in religion.

It is our duty, if we wish to save our children for Judaism, that we share with them such doubts and affirmations as we honestly hold, assuming of course that they are mentally ripe for such confidences. But above all, we must impart to them a God-idea in which we actually believe and which lives for us, even if it represents a departure from the God-idea of popular theism.

Personally, I see nothing un-Jewish, ultra-modern or "irreligious" about this attempt which some of us are making, to recast our God-idea. Those acquainted with the development of religious thought among the Jewish prophets and philosophers know that the God-idea in Israel has never been a fixed concept, and that it has always been fluid. Throughout Jewish history, fundamentally different conceptions of God existed side by side, without creating a corresponding fundamental differenece in the practice of Judaism. Witness the priestly and prophetic conceptions of God in the Bible, or the varied names for God to be found in Jewish literature, which are an indication of differences in God-conception—*Jehovah, Elohim, Shekina, Memra, Makom, Logos, Rachmana.*

In the Middle Ages, Maimonides and Ibn Daud held fundamentally different conceptions of God, whilst in practical Judaism they differed only in some legal minutiae.

The principle of a changing theology within the framework of the Jewish people has always been the basis on which historically-minded Jews have stood since the inception of our Reform movement.

Reform Jews, such as we are, have an intellectual obligation to keep our faith a progressive faith, for we realize that when Jewish theology becomes static, not only is our faith endangered, but the survival of the Jewish people is threatened with death. The secret of the survival of the Jewish people seems to me to lie in the fact that within its framework, freedom of belief was always tolerated. This was the principle which saved us from becoming a church like the Catholic Church. We remained a people because we kept alive the principle of development and of growth, touching our faith.

In the relation between God and Israel, Israel was the constant—God the variable.

In the light of Jewish historic development, it is somewhat amusing, to say the least, to charge Jewish Liberals who seek to revitalize their religious conception with "un-Jewishness". Personally, I am more concerned with testing any theological ideas that I hold, not by the question: "Are they Jewish?" but "Are they true?" In the history of Judaism, I find that the development of the idea of God was a continual quest for the truth. "The seal of God is truth," say our sages.

For what concerns me vitally is to have a faith that will function for me, and by which I can live, rather than one that needs to live through me.

Edmond Fleg hits it off very strikingly when he says: "I am a Jew because the faith of Israel demands no abnegation of my mind. I am a Jew because for Israel the world is not yet finished; men will complete it." May I add that I am a Jew because for Israel the God-idea is not yet finished; men are still creating it.

II

Now wherein does the God-idea, according to modern thought, differ from traditional theism? In the first place, it differs in respect to content, and secondly in respect to the method by which the God-idea is reached.

How does a modern intellectual go about building up his God-idea?

It is a simple observation that human beings do not live in a vacuum, but in a world. Hence our life is conditioned upon a certain behavior in the universe. Our life consists in interaction between our own behavior, and the behavior of the universe. To experience life's values, we must constantly be making adjustments among ourselves and our total environment. Some of these life values which we experience are more important to us than others. The highest values that we experience are our sense of security, of well-being, of increasing richness of life, and of its worthwhileness—its sanctity or what our prophets and sages referred to as its *Kedushah.*

It now becomes a fair question to ask: to what mode of behavior in the environing world must we adjust ourselves, in order to possess these highest values?

The answer which the modern religious philosopher gives to this question is: that whatever the mode of behavior in the cosmos may be, that upon which we depend and to which, when we react, gives us the sense of security, of well-being and the increasing richness and worthwhileness of life which we seek—that is God. Now that something may be completely known to us, or simply sensed. It may be either singular or plural, personal, mechanical, or even chemical. It may be a Some One, a Some Thing, or a complex of things. Or to put it in other words, God is that Something that renders the individual and the world significant and worthwhile, and which, when we relate ourselves to it, elicits from us the highest kind of thinking, the deepest kind of emotion, and leads us to the noblest kind of living.

If I understand the concept of *Kedushah*—holiness, aright, then it seems to me that the Jewish prophets and sages insinuated this modern affirmation of God, of which Prof. Rudolph Otto, in his book *The Idea of the Holy* has been the leading modern exponent. "Without the sense of holiness," says Prof. Otto, "no religion would be worthy of the name."

"The Jewish concept of *Kedushah* is the analogue of the modern conception of God. Implied in it also is the idea that life is worthwhile and has a purpose. Furthermore, they looked upon anything that is an end in itself, as *Kedushah.* The idea of holiness personified was to the Jewish sages and prophets, God. To them the experience of the worthwhileness of life as an end in itself was as ultimate as the experience of beauty, truth and goodness was to the Greeks," says Prof. M. M. Kaplan.

Modern thought proceeds on the quest for further knowledge of an *Empiric God,* by the method of scientific technique, by observation and analysis, inference and experimentation—all of which lie in the realm of actual experience. It holds that we cannot find this God by abstract logic, but by concrete living. We begin with the highest values which our hearts long to possess, we seek experimentally to adjust ourselves to our environments so as to secure these values.

It is a process of *through* man *to* God.

Let this not be confused with Humanism, for even though I believe in the need for humanizing religion, that is, making it apply and grow out of all phases of human experience, and even though I accept the protest of Humanism against traditional theism, and use the scientific method, the difference between the Humanists and this point of view I am presenting lies in the fact that the Humanist stops with man, whereas I follow through man to God. It is for this reason that I call this point of view religious Humanism, in counter-distinction to secular Humanism.

In the process of experimentation, we discover certain specific adjustment by which we come into actual possession of life's highest values. We reach certain convictions as to the nature and character of that mode of behavior in the universe, which we call God, and which leads out into ethics. That is why morality becomes from this point of view, the heart of Religion, and goodness and God become almost identical.

In this connection it is important that we do not confuse the scientific method which I have stressed, with the findings of science.

The modern intellectual appreciates that it is fallacious to justify one's God-idea on the basis of this or that scientific theory, for he knows something about the high mortality rate of scientific theory. His God-idea is not based on this or that theory in biology or in physics, but is the outgrowth of the same scientific methodology that the physicists and the biologists use. The God-idea to which the modern religious thinker attains, he regards not as something fixed, but as something just as tentative as any theory in the field of scientific research. The quest of God is perpetual, just as the quest for truth is.

Experience—the experience of the race and the experience of the individual—has for modern thought become the new approach to Religion, replacing the theophanies and the miracles and the doctrine of revelation and supernaturalism that were the bases for religious belief in the past.

In modern thought we have reversed the process of finding truth. Formerly truth was regarded as something given—now it is regarded as something discovered. Once it was something disclosed miraculously by God, now we think of it as something discovered by the intellect of man. I do not want to be understood as saying that the universe has ceased to be mysterious and that the scientists have penetrated all mystery. Firstly, this does not happen to be true, and secondly, I realize how essential it is for those of us who stress socialized religion and who keeps our eyes fixed on scientific knowledge, that we do not forget to provide for another side of man's nature beside his rationalistic side.

The psychologist tells us that man is not primarily a thinking animal who sometimes feels, but a feeling animal who sometimes thinks. We must, therefore, not neglect to provide in our reconstruction of faith for a "sense of mystery" a "feeling of reverence" "the will to self-surrender"—call it as you may—which the religion of our fathers took care of in the avenues of escape which they provided.

The movement for the reconstruction of religion, I believe to be the most vital and hopeful tendency in contemporary life. We must not let it fall by being short-sighted on the side of mysticism. But what I would like to insist on is that whatever we know and can know about God, has come to us by experience and not by revelation—that there is nothing which passes the sphere of experience. I believe that the world is knowable though not yet known, in contradistinction to theology that insists that the universe is forever unknowable and eternally mysterious, and that by the supernaturalism religion gives us a glimpse into this unknowable world.

For it seems to involve a contradiction to believe that the world is unknowable and mysterious, and then to postulate that by the miraculous revelations of religion, we can come to know it. If the mystery of the world can be known, then it can only be known through the scientific method and not through supernaturalism. And the scientific method insists on experience for its datum. And by experience may I say that I do not mean simply the knowledge which comes to us by contact with the outside material world, for experience can be both active and passive, outward and inward, and both types of experience are valid, each in its respective field. The outward for the physical sciences, the inner for religion and kindred fields like art, music and literature.

"The seeker who pursues significance and values is often," according to Prof. Eddington, "compared unfavorably with the scientist who pursues atoms and electrons. The plain matter-of-fact person is disposed to think that the former is wandering amid shadows and illusion, whilst the latter is coming to grip with reality. But it is this matter-of-fact person who is mistaken. It is the scientist, and not the poet, or the seer, who is wandering amid shadow and illusions, for it is consciousness alone that can determine the validity of its convictions.

"It is what we feel that is alone competent to guide and keep us amid the confusions of physical sensation and reaction. Not our sensitivity to sense impressions," says Prof. Eddington, "but the reaching out of a spirit from its isolation to something beyond. A response to beauty and nature and art, an inner light of conviction and guidance—this is what we know; this is reality."

And it is on this basis that we are creating a new religious content. But some will ask: are we destroying religion when we operate on this basis? In a sense yes. We are through with the sort of religion whose essential nature was miraculous and mysterious, and that sought to explain the universe in terms of a supernatural person known as God.

But in a higher sense we are leaning toward another religion which is the outgrowth of the deepest experience that man has, namely: his attempt to identify himself with his world. It is man's inner consciousness of his spiritual life reaching forth into the world to interpret its values, discover its ends, fulfill its ideals in the light of its own reality, and seek its worthwhileness.

In this sense, Religion becomes identical with Life—the universal life force which, as Prof. Whitehead puts it, concretizes in terms of the world as we know it—natural and spiritual. It is the spirit that rolls through all things, come at last to spiritual consciousness and purpose in the human soul.

But it is not alone through the scientific method, that is, the method of experience, by which we come to God. The trend of theoretical development in modern physics and philosophy is also leading us to the same goal; to be sure, not the God of traditional theism, and to the religion based on it, but God and Religion nevertheless. Let me illustrate.

It has always remained an unanswerable riddle of theism to explain how a God who is pure Spirit could have created a world of matter, and from which, from its very nature, God must be divorced. Philosophers, from Plato and Aristotle to Whitehead, have struggled in an attempt to reconcile this dichotomy. In Jewish philosophy, too, this problem existed, especially for Maimonides who, being an Aristotelean and a Dualist, felt the need to bridge the gulf between a spiritual God such as the Judaism of his day believed in, and a material world. But modern Idealistic philosophy with its emphasis on meaning and value, and modern Science, especially the recent trends in physics, which reduces all matter to spirit, and everything to mind, have all come as a powerful ally to Religion.

Recently, Prof. Arthur Compton of the Physics Department of the University of Chicago, a Nobel prize winner, was asked the question: "What has science, particularly the new physics, to say about the old problems of free will, immortality and God?" He replied that it had some astonishing things to say, and mentioned first "a new principle of uncertainty" which Prof. Heisenberg of the University of Leipzig has announced. It is based on Prof. Compton's discoveries in light particles. The Heisenberg-Compton theory, he explained, disputed the uniformity of the physical world, which is the basis for the mechanistic view of man's consciousness, and construed an effective intelligence behind the phenomena of nature. "The new physics," continued Prof. Compton, "admitted the possibility of mind acting on matter, and suggested that the thoughts of men were perhaps the most important things in the world." "This conception," he said, "threw new light on the evolutionary process and gave meaning to human life." In this view, the world and mankind were not developing at random out of atomic chaos. On the contrary he believed that he had found evidence, strongly suggestive of a directive intelligence or purpose back of everything, with the creation of intelligent minds as its reasonable goal.

The corner has been turned. Modern physics, instead of leading to skepticism and to materialism and a mechanistic conception of the universe, is now leading to the renaissance of religious conviction.

Few people realize what a revolutionary effect the discovery of radium played in overthrowing materialism and mechanism. The speck of radium, isolated by the Curies, sufficed to obliterate the barrier that separated matter from energy and opened up the until then hermetically sealed atom to the astonished eyes of physicists. Suddenly man discovered himself as a kind of average-sized unit between the two infinities—the vast solar system of the sun and planets and the minute solar system of the atom.

Here was the filter of the intellect cleaned by Descartes, purified by Kant, and set by Henry Poincare, on the three pin points of certitude. Here was the filter of reason, letting through the most perfect and gorgeous of dreams. Matter, a painted veil, vanished away at the penetrating gaze of science, and in its stead, a firmament of solar systems, as awe-inspiring in their infinite smallness as is the Milky Way and its infinite vastness, is revealed, not to the wild imagination of the poet but to the sober and cold judgment of the physicist.

Let me try to sum up the position of the modern physicist. A table is made of wood. Wood is cellulose. Cellulose is made up of hydrogen, carbon and oxygen, all of which are made up of atoms. An atom is a system made up of one proton, around which electrons whirl, under laws which satisfy the mind. (For that is what we call mathematics.) As for protons and electrons, they are mere centers of phenomena which occur in regular wave-like fashion according to laws which satisfy the mind. Therefore, a table is nothing but movement and mind—i.e., nothing but intelligent energy.

The theory of relativity has also led in the direction of God.

Relativity is the source of the idea that our physical observations can possess no absolute and essential value since they are made by means of material instruments—including our eyes and ears—the atoms of which follow the same laws as those of the objects observed, and therefore may be suspected of conspiring with the whole material world to keep from us the secret of their nature. This, a kind of modesty *apriori,* comes to reinforce the modesty *aposteriori,* which the breakdown of the astronomic theory of the atom has fostered among the one-time proud physicists. And this twice-established modesty is bound to prepare the mind for a divine revelation.

Further, the theory of relativity leads to two all-important observations as to the world and its creation. The first is that space time, or the universe, while unlimited, is not infinite. This notion is in deep harmony with the idea of a transcendent God as opposed to an immanent God, since God is an infinite and not merely an unlimited notion. Such a conclusion is further strengthened by the second observation to which we are led by relativity, i.e., the solidarity among space, time, energy and mass. For, since it is a new law of physics that energy is constantly being degraded along the line of time, it follows—which indeed was obvious to our intuition—that the world was at the top of its energy or, in other words, that the world was all energy precisely at the origin of time, i.e., when it was created. And moreover, since the idea of time has no scientific meaning apart from the ideas of space, mass and energy, there is no sense in inquiring what was there before the zero hour struck. All this obviously points to creation by a transcendent God, of whom nothing can be known and who thus produces an immanent God sending Him forth on a career of gradual disintegration down the slope of time.

It is obvious that such a body of ideas constitutes a favorable ground for the development of a new religion. Nothing is lacking. The high priests have their esoteric dogmas and their sacred secret language (calculus, algebraic formulas). There are abundant mysteries, of course, of an intelligent order, such as the nature of electricity. There are miracles, in the only way in which miracles interest a crowd, i.e., not as violations of the laws of Nature, but as marvelous performances—for instance, wireless telephony or aviation. There are prophets who speak of strange things, true yet incomprehensible, such as the mystery of Creation, I mean, of relativity. And this explains, perhaps, why Einstein, a sentimental-looking scientist, of a modest, retiring and musical disposition, should have become one of the most popular men in the world on the strength of a few pages of abstruse mathematics, which only a few thousands of men have read and only a handful have understood.

For me it is clear that not only the scientific method, but the content of modern philosophy and science makes God an intellectual and spiritual necessity. The question now is: What is this God like, and whither will He lead?

When I think of God, then, I think of Him in terms of Mind, of Spirit. He is for me the expression and synthesis of the Force of Life, in terms of all the laws and stable principles, all the permanent form and order of the world. I find Him in the quiet testimony of truth, beauty, love, goodness, peace, joy, self-sacrifice and consecration which point to another kind of world within the one we see and touch—a world of Spirit, of Intelligence, of Order, of Organizing Power.

God is for me the Spirit of life, moving through order, to the fulfillment of some purpose; though as yet we may not know what that purpose is. God is not only the source from which we spring, but a goal toward which we move. In the light of the theory of creative evolution, He is the Spirit of life in the process of unfolding, evolving from consciousness to consciousness, from instinct to reason, from chaos to order, full of yet uncomprehended possibilities, but fulfilling itself in the creatively evolutionary processes of the world. And the testimony of God's evolution is to be found in the spiritual development of mankind.

God is the Ideal which strives to objectify itself in Reality, and Reality endeavors to perfect itself by reaching out toward the goal. The former is the principle of concretion; the latter is *Imitatio Dei*. This conception of God, in some respects, reflects the older Jewish idea of God as an exemplar of all the moral virtues. According to Jewish ethics we are enjoined to link ourselves to God, *v'atem hadvekim*. For all that man is, God is; all the vision and all the idealism, the impulse for the better and higher life, all the aspiration in the human breast, the heroism that is simply the courage and the faith to hold on to life one minute longer, because one perceives in it a sense of worthwhileness, and believes in its improvability; all of this spiritual nature in man is a concretization of that life force which is cosmic in the universe.

For even as these qualities constitute the soul of the individual and make him unique when compared to all other living creatures, so I believe that regnant in the universe are those spiritual forces which take shape and are formulated in terms of men's values and ideals as man relates himself to the Soul in the universe, which I call God.

Now, if you want to designate what I call the soul of the universe and God, in terms of personality, then you may do so, being cognizant constantly, that what you are speaking about is simply mind, idea, soul, which is, in reality, known only to us in qualitative terms, not as something finished, set, pattern-like in its nature, but something fluid, living, developing, that is in us because it is in the universe.

We speak of personality in the individual, yet it defies us to lay hold on it, or to accurately describe it. All that we can say scientifically about human personality is, *That it is* and this It, so far as we know and have been able to observe, is made up of certain ethical and spiritual qualities that inhere in our human natures.

I have become, in my philosophical thinking, a thorough-going Idealist, which is, I venture to say, the only possible philosophy for one who is a religionist. Now, I do not find it objectionable to formulate God in terms of personality, as we conceive personality in human terms. But when we do this, as sometimes we do, let us remember that it happens not when we are rigorously rational and intellectual, but when we are under the stress of some overwhelming and emotional strain. In the former instance, we are careful not to permit our thought and language to overreach our logical formulations, but in the latter instance, we do, and when we do, we ought to know that it is poetry—imagery and nothing else.

The question will be asked: how can one pray to such a God, and here too I must state that for me prayer is not theological at all. It is principally psychological and social in its meaning and value. It is for me *Tehillah*, and not *Tephillah*. And I am equally intent upon a reinterpretation of prayer and the other theological notions, such as soul, immortality, sin and free will, as I am about the need for recasting the God-idea in terms of modern thought. When the latter has been done, the former will follow inevitably. Personally, I have found myself a much more prayerful person since I have ceased to regard prayer in the traditional theological sense.

For me, prayer has become meditation upon the best we know, communion with the noblest that we understand, and reaching out of what we are to what we yearn to become. In my prayers I do not barter with God or seek to persuade God to do anything, but rather to persuade myself and those whom I can stimulate to cultivate spiritual kinship with the highest in life, which the world tempts us to forget. The purpose of prayer is not to change the will of God, but to make us fulfill it. When we reach out our hands and pray, it is as if we were reaching up and out of ourselves, to that larger life upon our own impinging, and which, if we contact, will help us to do everything that is true and honest and just and pure and lovely and of good report.

The reason so many people do not pray is the same as the reason why so many people have given up their ardent belief in a personal God. It is not because they do not have a need for God or are not prayerful. It is simply that their conceptions of prayer and of God have changed, whereas those of the Synagog and the Church have not kept pace, and in many instances remained stationary.

I confess that the vocabulary and the form of prayer, the order of service, the kind of prayer—in a word, the whole institution of prayer as we now have it in the Synagog and as we teach it to our children is, to say the least, outmoded, and will have to be recast by Liberals who accept, as I do, the protest and the challenge to traditional theology that is voiced in Humanism, but who are not satisfied with the agnosticism of Humanism.

Nothing is more essential in these days of religious unrest, and it behooves religious Liberals, as yet unorganized, and in the main inarticulate in a literary way, to give voice and shape to their point of view which is radically different from that of the secular Humanist. The philosophy of the religious Humanists needs to be systematized, because people are demanding to know what they believe about God, prayer, immortality, and sin. And this new formulation whenever it comes, and it should come soon, must translate itself in terms of service and ritual. And what is even more important is that such a reconstruction of theology is essential for the sake of formulating a curriculum for our religious schools and the training of our religious teachers in these schools.

II

In the main, the curriculum of our Reform Jewish religious schools are up to the Confirmation class, not much different from those in the Conservative and Orthodox schools. It is only in the Confirmation class, when the rabbi meets personally with the young people, to prepare them for confirmation, that he has an opportunity of conveying to them his own reconstructed philosophy of Judaism.

In many congregations I find that the pulpit utterances touching theology are radically at variance with those taught in the religious school and it is most essential that the pulpit and the school teachings be harmonized.

An investigation conducted by Dr. A. H. MacLean to discover what concepts are being taught in Protestant Sunday Schools and to find out what children think about God reveals that the liberal Protestants have exactly the same problems as we have but they have become more self-conscious about it.

I refer you to his doctor's dissertation prepared for Teachers College, Columbia University, and recently published under the title "The Idea of God in Protestant Religious Education." The data brought together by him through his investigation of Protestant Sunday School curriculum textbooks and classroom instruction leads him to the conclusion that though the children in Protestant Sunday Schools differ in their opinion of God and prayer and the meaning of Religion, most of them view "God as a Man." In other words, the anthropomorphic God-conception prevails. He also finds that "children are not being prepared to meet religious difficulties through reliance upon personal judgment, nor are they being provided with an adequate system of religious thought. Issues which should be of interest to those who have the religious problem at heart," he charges, "are being evaded instead of being approached in a scientific spirit." He finds that the textbooks used in the elementary grades inculcate ideas in the children which will have to be unlearned, and that religious instruction ignores the scientific method of modern pedagogy, namely to stress experience as the basis for the child's concepts whether they be religious or other concepts. A child's religious knowledge must grow out of his experiences in life even as does his geography or arithmetic knowledge.

He furthermore states that most of the religious teaching about God and theology is based upon the assumption of the child's incapacity to grasp religious meanings, with the result that an anthropomorphic God-conception, which is the easiest to teach, is imparted, even though it inevitably must get into the way of the religious development of the child grown to maturity.

For the specific findings, I refer you to Dr. MacLean's book, but at this point I hazard the opinion that with the exception of the Christological portion of Dr. MacLean's study, I feel reasonably certain that if Dr. MacLean had subjected an equal number of children in our own Reform religious schools to tests similar to those in the Protestant schools, that the outcome would have been no different. The ideas of our own children concerning God are, I believe, very similar to those of the children in the Protestant religious schools. It is unfortunate that we have not been conducting investigations along this and similar lines. We are taking much for granted that should be open to serious question, especially if the results of our Sunday Schools are judged in terms of our failure to have inculcated a religious attitude of life, and a loyalty to the temple in our graduates, during the past half century.

III

How then should the teaching about God be improved? Someone has well said, all other things that we do are secondary and provisional. Character only is ultimate and final. But the development of character is a most difficult task. For life is made up of tension points and it should be the aim of religious education to prepare the individual to meet the resulting conflict adequately, and to prevent the child from succumbing to the frustrations to which life subjects us. How can we do this with children? Are children instinctively religious?

The psychologist answers that in the whole category of instincts, there is not one listed as religious, but there are instincts such as curiosity which are at the basis of all learning, and which also form the basis of religious education.

Then why not start where the child starts? With experience. The paradox which I find about all religious instruction is that, on the one hand, theology presents a ready-made and finished system to be transmitted to the child from the kindergarten through Confirmation, whereas modern pedagogy insists on experience and experimentation as the only method through which children learn. It is futile to try to spoon-feed theology to children. What we must determine by pedagogic experimentation is, firstly, how much theology and what portion of theology can be given to children of certain ages with promise of better results than have been discovered. Theological teaching has not been graded in terms of child's experience but rather in terms of the historic development of theological ideas.

The question is still open as to whether the teaching about God and the experience of personal relations with Him are essential to childhood. Those who say it is and therefore it is necessary to begin such habit formation early in childhood, have produced nothing as yet that is backed up by careful pedagogic experimentation.

There is still the question of what experience children are capable of having that might be interpreted in terms of man's relation to God. Personally, I am all for starting where the child starts—and where is that?

Does the child form ethical or religious concepts first?

From my study of children I believe that manners precede morals and that the child forms ethical ideas first. Instead of teaching the child the theory of divine nature, why not start with human nature, with the ethical customs which he has already begun to use, and wants to understand?

If you attempt to transmit the God-idea to him at once, he will probably come to have a very naïve and unsatisfactory conception. If you leave the teaching concerning God until later, it will have more significance and worth.

Why not start with the child himself? His relations with his family group and his wider social relations? Why not develop the idea of the brotherhood of man and a sense of social responsibility in terms of concrete problems which the child experiences or which can be brought within the range of his experience? About which he reads in the papers and hears discussed at the family table? The questions on social justice and righteousness and the correct way in which the society in which we live, practices or fails to practice these virtues? Why not let the children in on the hard facts of social conditions? In this way, through the study and understanding of nature and human nature, you bring out his best. If I had my way, God would never be taught as a theological conception, but children would reach a conception of God, unconsciously and indirectly by being taught through the range of their experience the great social, ethical and spiritual ideals, which together, form the God idea, so that children would come to think of God in terms of this cosmic spirit of life which manifests itself in terms of the spiritual and ethical qualities regnant in the universe.

I would list these ideals and then grade them according to the psychological level of the different age grades in children. And I would bring to bear in terms of each of these ideals, what is best in the Bible and Midrash and in the great literature of all peoples, ancient and modern.

And as the child develops, he would come to feel more strongly the urge to progress which has been manifesting itself in the human race at its highest and in the lives of its best spirits. He would then come to think of God as that force in life which makes life purposeful, worthwhile, holy. When he gets along to the place where he can grasp the unity of all nature and see the inner power working through and in all of life, then he has gotten to the place where he can understand something of what we mean by God. And secondly, one of the outstanding needs is a revision of Biblical teachings that will include more of the known facts of Biblical science.

I find, as I move about among the classes of my religious school and hear the Bible taught, that there is hardly a word spoken of a factual nature concerning the real history about the Bible. Rather, I hear reiterated moralizations upon Biblical texts; the drawing of lessons for conduct and belief seems to combine with Bible study at the expense of fearless and clear-cut statements of Biblical criticism.

The reasons are twofold: firstly, that our teachers are unprepared, and secondly, that we fear to raise the problems for children. Then in preparing our teachers, let us beware not to make them amateur preachers and give them instead, the facts. For, why teach what is untrue?

Children will not be confused by scientific approach to the problem. The approach need not be critical. It can be a plain statement of the best we know, and if the Bible is not needed by very young children, then it is clearly the duty of liberals to postpone the teaching of it until it can be of service to them.

One thing we must not further succumb to, and that is presenting the Bible chronologically, and starting the youngest children of our religious school off with the most complicated chapters of the Bible just because the Book of Genesis happens to be the first book. Let us postpone the teaching of Genesis as long as possible, until it can be presented when the curiosity of the child leads it to ask concerning how the world came into being. Then we can tell him what we know from science about it, and enrich his imagination by telling him the poetic way the Jewish people answered this question. And by comparing our story of Genesis with parallel stories in the folklore of other peoples, bring out the ethical lessons which lie imbedded in Genesis and which indicates that from the very beginning, the Hebrew prophets, who wrote the Bible in the main, had an ethical conception of God based on human experience and social problems of their day very much like that with which we have to deal today.

And the third factor in improving the teaching about God is to revise the devotional literature now in common use. We must reconstruct our service of worship. The vocabulary is anthropomorphic. The belief that God sits upon a throne above the clouds was perhaps never intentionally taught by liberal teachers or text-book writers. Yet the fact that an astonishingly large percentage of children accept the idea as true indicates that their chief contact with it in Sunday School comes through the devotional literature, especially the hymns.

And fourthly, I would urge that in the liberal religious schools, we should permit freedom of thought and freedom of expression concerning God and the Bible. We must encourage children to ask what would have been embarrassing questions to our teachers if we had asked them. For above all, we want to keep the minds and the emotions of the children as free as possible from thwarting conditioning. We must not inculcate a conception of God which is admittedly inadequate for his maturity. By making use of the findings of Biblical research and by introducing into our religious teaching the facts of science as we know them, we will be leading the child to the acceptance of the standard of thought and knowledge which prevails in the scholastic and scientific world. Otherwise the child, because of his easy access to ideas that run contrary to that which he hears from a conservatively minded teacher, will be led to think of religion as something outside of the category of modern thought.

I cannot emphasize too strongly in closing this paper, firstly the need of reconstructing our God-conception and the theology that derives therefrom. Secondly, that the teaching of God must come through the presentation of manifestations of Godliness, rather than through definition, if we expect the God-idea to function for children and to make a difference in their lives. And thirdly, let us remember, above all, that children and young people are persons. Let us strive to help them as friendly guides who approach them in the spirit of respect and ethical love. Then we shall be working with them in the co-operative endeavor of seeking to develop those finer qualities in human nature that aid man in facing the emergencies of life with strength and courage, with faith and hope.

THE PSYCHOANALYTIC STUDY OF JUDAISM

by
ABRAHAM CRONBACH

THE PSYCHOANALYTIC STUDY OF JUDAISM

ABRAHAM CRONBACH, Hebrew Union College, Cincinnati, Ohio.

PART I

EXPOSITORY

THE application of psychoanalysis to the contents of Judaism is of interest not only to the student of the Jewish past but equally to the student of the Jewish life of to-day. Though most of the published material[1] deals with doctrines, stories and rituals of ancient inception, these are themselves of no little bearing on the problems and processes of our own time. Many of the old stories, Biblical and non-Biblical still have their appeal.[2] The cause of that appeal may well be that in the modern mind ancient trends still persist. Many of the hoary rituals are still in use. Altered though constructions and interpretations may have grown as the ages have passed, some of the early motives behind those rituals may still be operative. Add to this the fact that contemporary observations in the clinic furnish with regard to the past the clue to not a few novel insights. Who knows on what contemporary Jewish issues, psychoanalysis may yet contribute some novel illumination!

The present study is to fall into two parts—an expository part and a critical part. The expository part will attempt a systematic presentation of everything that has been published relative to the various aspects of Judaism in the way of psychoanalytic surmises. Not until the second part shall we undertake to appraise these surmises or any of their implications.

The divisions to be constructed in our expository part are:

I. Ambivalence.

II. The Heterosexual.

III. The Homosexual and the Narcissistic.

[1] Bibliography in Appendix I.

[2] A list of these in Appendix II.

IV. Incest.
V. Hostility between Father and Son.
VI. Conciliation between Father and Son.
VII. Amalgamations.
VIII. Totemism—Incest.
IX. Totemism—Hostility between Father and Son.
X. Totemism—Conciliation between Father and Son.
XI. Totemism—Amalgamations.

Sex is the theme of all of the divisions after division I. The Oedipus Complex is the theme of all of the divisions after division III. The totemistic manifestations of the Oedipus Complex occupy—as the names indicate—the last four of these divisions.

I. Ambivalence

That sex plays a conspicuous role in psychoanalysis is too well known to need recalling. Yet psychoanalysis is concerned not so much with sex as with the conflicts of sex. Throughout the present study sex is complicated by a factor known as *Ambivalence*. Ambivalence designates the circumstance that a person may like and at the same time dislike one and the same person or action. One may love and at the same time abhor one's father; one may crave and at the same time repudiate sexual promiscuity.[3] A deeper philosophy might relate ambivalence to the fundamental multiplicity and diversity of human purposes. The same person or action may be agreeable or disagreeable according to the purpose of ours that chances to be affected. Psychoanalysis, however, does not pursue philosophical imports that far. It treats ambivalence as something virtually ultimate.[4]

[3] Amazing examples of ambivalence are listed in Freud's *Totem und Tabu* (Leipzig, 1913), pp. 38–48, "Das Tabu der Herscher" where, basing himself on Frazer, Freud cites instances in which primitive rulers receive a treatment that is a combination of extreme adulation and extreme abuse. Can the inveterate abuses heaped upon the President of the United States be a persistence of this?

[4] Theodor Reik attempts to exhibit the biological underpinning of ambivalence. He suggests that the unity of the liked and the disliked which ambivalence implies is derived from the infantile unity of the I and the not-I or from the unity of the original urge out of which all divergent urges evolved or the unity of the original organism out of which the several variations

Let us first examine then the material which operates with the concept of ambivalence exclusively. To this belongs the story of David's Census.[5] The story has been explained as a cryptic intimation that David, unforgetful of his long outlawry, feels hatred as well as affection toward his people. That which the pestilence wrought was only that which David unconsciously wished.[6]

The other factor of the ambivalence appears in David's self reproach.[7] It is asserted that neurotic acts of self-punishment often simulate—*middah keneged middah*?—the doings that supposedly require the punishment. The pestilence by which David is penalized is analogously but an objectification of the pestilence invoked upon Israel by David's unconscious grudge.

Again the element of numbers and of counting is asserted to be related to notions about demons, demons being in turn the projections of the malevolence in the human mind.[8] The story of David's census involves indeed Satan, the chief of demons. Theodor Reik, the exponent of these views, cites the Gallas of West Africa who regard the counting of the herd as an ill omen and the Lapps who believe that census taking increases the death rate.[9] Reik supposes the underlying idea to be that enumeration being an extension of human control over the unknown is something sacrilegious.[10]

emerged. Cf. Reik, *Der Eigene und der Fremde Gott* (Leipzig, Wien, Zuerich, 1923), pp. 233, 239, 240, 243. The multiplicity and diversity of human purposes is discussed in "The Social Consequences of the One and the Many" *Hebrew Union College Monthly* (Dec. 1929, Jan. 1930).

[5] Theodor Reik, "Psychoanalytische Studien zur Bibelexegese," *Imago*, V, 353 "Die Suende der Volkszaehlung." The Biblical references are II Sam. 24, I Chron. 21.

[6] It is surprising that Reik makes no point of the fact that the pestilence was a matter of David's own choice.

[7] Reik refers to II Sam. 24.10; I Chron. 21.8.

[8] *Op. cit.*, p. 352, also, *Der Eigene und der Fremde Gott* p. 138, 141, and Freud, *Totem und Tabu* p. 123.

[9] "Die Suende der Volkszaehlung," *Imago*, V, 351.

[10] *Ibid.*, p. 352, footnote 21. Reik, p. 351, regards as untenable Frazer's interpretation that David's sin consisted in his doubt of the Divine purpose that Israel would become as the sands of the sea or in David's invasion of tribal autonomy. The latter, thinks Reik, would not be a "sin for all Israel"

Inasmuch as the Deity is in II Sam. 24 represented as counseling the census, the implication is that the Deity Himself is ambivalent toward His people, loving them and at the same time hating them.[11]

Reik sees further manifestations of ambivalence in various mourning customs.[12] He holds that mourning once consisted of self mutilations intended to appease the dead for previous unkindly attitudes toward them on the part of the living. Etymologically "mute"—the dead being mute—and "mutilate" are said to be connected, like "*stumm*" and "*verstuemmelt.*"[13] The primitive like the unconscious mind does little discriminating. A death due to murder differs little from any other kind of death. The mere unconscious urge to kill is by the *Allmacht der Gedanken* equivalent to killing. Plato is accordingly quoted to the effect that the ghost of the slain is angry at the slayer.[14] The Yasos of British Central Africa believe that, in the guise of sickness or insanity, Chirope (like the Eumenides of Orestes) will beset the murderer of a fellow tribesman.[15] The honors bestowed by certain primitives upon the skulls of their slain enemies are also instanced. Among the West African Negroes and the Brazilian Indians, according to a quotation from Frazer, the executioner yields some of his own blood and bears scars upon his body to show that the victim has received due satisfaction.[16]

In this light Reik understands the sign of Cain[17] as well as

(I Chron. 21.3). The theory of Nowack that the matter reprehended was plans for taxation and the strengthening of the monarchy is rejected by Reik on the grounds that such would not be a sin but a political blunder. Regardless of the validity of Reik's objections, it is not clear why Reik should be at all troubled by the views of Frazer and of Nowack. Those views relate to the conscious. Psychoanalysis is concerned with the unconscious. Unconscious trends can co-exist with conscious trends of a most divergent character. Reik himself speaks of the "overdetermination" of all mental phenomena (*Imago*, V, 347).

[11] Exod. 33.3 is instanced as another example of Divine ambivalence.

[12] "Das Kainzeichen," *Imago*, V, 31–42.

[13] *Ibid.*, p. 37.

[14] *Ibid.*, p. 34.

[15] *Ibid.*, p. 35.

[16] *Ibid.*, p. 35.

[17] *Ibid.*, p. 34. Reik rejects the theory that the sign of Cain was a tatoo which protected against blood revenge. This, he argues, would be precluded by the wide prevalence of tatoo. Ludwig Levy, by way of rejoinder to Reik

such Jewish mourning customs as the *Keri'ah*, the *Shib'ah* and *Sereṭ*.[18] *Tefillim* likewise gain significance here.[19] Agreeing with Stade, Reik views *Tefillim* as surrogates for tatoo. He recalls that Arabic women carry tatoos on those parts of the body where the *Tefillim* are placed by the Jews. Just as the tatoos of mourning assuage the demons, *Tefillim* according to a passage in Berakot have the power to ward off demons.[20]

Ambivalence is further invoked to account for various threshold customs and superstitions.[21] Reference is made to the Biblical passages Jer. 34.4; II Kings 12.10; Zeph. 1.9; I Sam. 5.1–5;[22] also to the Catholic custom of placing holy water at the church door and to the Jewish *Mezuzah*. Reik thinks that stepping on the threshold unconsciously implied a somewhat aggressive and non-deferential attitude toward the master of the house.[23] He mentions Freud's observation that neurotic patients divulge their attitude toward the physician by neglecting to close the door, that some neurotics fear to touch door knobs and that one neurotic woman dreaded stepping on the indentations of cement sidewalks.[24]

The parallels from anthropology are copious. According to a quotation from Captain Condor, stepping on the threshold is in Syria deemed unlucky.[25] In Fiji only persons of highest rank may

adduces elaborate arguments to the effect that the sign of Cain was a sign of membership in the clan, hence a guaranty of protection by the clan and the god of the clan ("Ist das Kainzeichen die Beschneidung?" *Imago*, V, 290–293). But are these several views mutually exclusive? We could apply here the same comment as that in note 10 discussing Reik's controversy with Frazer and Nowack concerning the census of David.

[18] Reik, *op. cit.*, p. 33. The Biblical references are Lev. 19.27, 28; Deut. 6.8; 11.18; 14.1.

[19] *Loc. cit.*

[20] Berakot 23ab, R. Joḥanan takes his *Tefillim* to the place of evacuation in order to be protected from the demons.

[21] "Die Tuerhueter," *Imago*, V, 344–350.

[22] Reik apparently overlooked Exod. 12.7 and Isa. 6.4.

[23] *Op. cit.*, p. 348. It was not possible to find this point in the reference given: Freud's *Vorlesungen zur Einfuehrung in die Psychoanalyse* (Vienna, 1917), p. 275. See infra p. 621.

[24] Reik might have instanced the superstition among American children that stepping on cement pavement indentations is an ill omen.

[25] *Ibid.*, p. 345.

step on thresholds. Marco Polo reports that tall doorkeepers would impose fines or beatings on persons who would step on the threshold when entering the palace of Kublai Khan in Peking. According to a thirteenth century monk, Rubriquis, a ruling of the chancellor of Mangu Khan barred from ever entering the palace an envoy who stumbled on the threshold quite accidentally. Frazer is quoted as reporting a similar custom among the Morwa of Northwest India. For stepping into the hut or tent of a Tartar prince, death was the penalty. In India, the bride entering her new home presses the threshold hurriedly and only with her right foot. In Altmark the groom carries the bride from the wagon to the hearth. Reik believes that the corresponding Roman custom is not, as Plutarch thinks, a survival of wife stealing but a measure to avoid putting the foot on the threshold. The Mongolians have a proverb. "Step not on the threshold; it is sin." Of one at whom he is angry, the German says, "Der kommt mir nicht ueber die Schwelle."[26] There is also the German proverb, "Mit Gott tritt ein, bring Glueck hinein."[27]

Frazer surmises that ancestral ghosts were supposed to inhabit the threshold as house guardians.[28] Reik agrees that such may have been one of the roots of the custom conjointly with the factor of ambivalence. By the psychoanalytic law of "overdetermination," the motives or strata of motives that operate in one and the same reaction may be many.

A further manifestation of ambivalence is seen in the differentiation between gods and demons. A number of writers contend that originally one deity combined in himself the divine traits and the diabolical ones. Later a separation occurred, the friendly traits becoming segregated into a god, the offensive ones being purged out into a devil.[29] Reik observes that Australian tribes draw little distinction between gods and demons.[30] Once the

[26] *Ibid.*, p. 349. [27] *Ibid.*, p. 350. [28] *Ibid.*, p. 347.

[29] E. D. Martin, *The Mystery of Religion* (London and New York, 1924), pp. 148, 149. Oscar Pfister, *The Psychoanalytic Method*, translated by C. R. Payne (New York, 1917), p. 138. Ernest Jones, *Der Alptraum*, Deutsch von E. G. Sachs (Leipzig and Vienna, 1912), Chap. VI. Theodor Reik, *Der Eigene und der Fremde Gott* (Leipzig, Vienna, Zurich, 1923), p. 140.

[30] Reik, *Der Eigene und der Fremde Gott*, p. 135.

Egyptian demon Set was worshiped as a deity,[31] similarly the Babylonian demon Tiamat. In Num. 22.22 the angel of the Lord is a "Satan"[32] while in Job, Satan is one of the servants of the Lord.[33] The tempter of David who is Satan in I Chron. 21.1 is the Lord in II Sam. 24.1. Leaping through the centuries, Reik sees a similar identification of God and the Devil in the words "*Deo solo gratia*" inscribed upon the sword of the inquisitor.[34] In Amos 5.8 and Isa. 45.7 God creates the darkness as well as the light.[35] Reik goes so far as to hold that whoso abandons the belief in the devil soon abandons belief in God, the two being that closely interrelated.[36] Ernest Jones connects the word "devil" etymologically with "two," "duo," "double" expressing a bifurcation of something which was one originally. The fear of the demon is asserted to be only the fear of the god displaced.[37] Of course the god-demon distinction is in turn derived from the ambivalent attitude of the child toward the loved and hated father.

Demons are sometimes the degraded gods of former religions.[38] Hence but a slight variant of the distinction between god and demon is that between one's own god and a strange god.[39] It is held that the feeling of uncanniness is always due to some subtle identification between the transcended and the attained.[40] The uncanniness of strange gods can therefore be accounted for only by some latent identification between the strange god and one's own.[41] This uncanniness is also related to the child's hostility toward the father and the resultant sense of guilt. Here again by the *Allmacht der Gedanken* a hostile thought amounts to a hostile act.[42] Reik calls attention to the fact that various prominent Hebrews were named after Baal which is reminiscent of the time when Baal was an object of worship little diversified from Jahweh.[43] He further holds that the prophetic denunciation

[31] *Ibid.*, p. 136.
[32] *Ibid.*, p. 138.
[33] *Ibid.*, p. 140.
[34] *Ibid.*, p. 149.
[35] *Ibid.*, p. 149.
[36] *Ibid.*, p. 147.
[37] *Ibid.*, p. 162.
[38] *Ibid.*, p. 138.
[39] *Ibid.*, pp. 176, 178.
[40] *Ibid.*, pp. 183, 185, 188.
[41] *Ibid.*, pp. 180–182.
[42] *Ibid.*, p. 188.
[43] *Ibid.*, p. 137.

of false gods betrays a popular hankering after them which intimates their original identification with the true God.[44] Explicable in the same terms is the uncanniness which Jesus and Mary possess for the Jews. Reik sees here "a reaction of something that surges up from the repressed unconscious."[45]

Of one stripe with the foregoing is the distinction between one's own earlier god and one's later god. The earlier god is akin to the strange god and, like the strange god, demonized readily.[46] As neurotics resist acknowledging their own infantilisms, the earlier god from whom one's contemporary god developed gets to look like a caricature.[47] Similarly is the hell of one age interpreted by Reik as being the emotionally distorted heaven of an earlier time.[48]

Another faint variant of the same distinction is that between the communal god and the private god. An old god can continue as the object of private worship long after the clan has changed gods.[49] Reik traces to this divergence the later distinction between the orthodoxy of the many and the heresy of the few.[50] What a strange reversal of our customary anticipations! We usually expect to find Orthodoxy linked with the old and innovation the program of heresy.

This theory concerning the nature of demons is essentially no different from that already broached in which demons were explained as projections of one's own hostile sentiments.[51] There is little gap between hostile sentiments in one's self and hostile actions in others. Hostile sentiments in one person lead to hostile actions in others and *vice versa.* Indeed when sentiments are hostile, the actions of the hated person appear hostile no matter what they may be. Hostility thus gives rise to the demon concept whether men locate the hostility in themselves or in another; while friendliness gives rise to the god concept whether the seat of the friendliness be the subject or the object.

Outside of the Jewish domain such illustrative ambivalences are treated by Reik as that of Jesus and Judas—splittings of the

[44] *Ibid.*, p. 148, note 1.
[45] *Ibid.*, p. 217.
[46] *Ibid.*, p. 142.
[47] *Ibid.*, p. 179.
[48] *Ibid.*, p. 152.
[49] *Ibid.*, p. 155.
[50] *Ibid.*, p. 157.
[51] Supra p. 607 and note 8.

same personality—and correspondingly that of Mary, mother of Jesus and Mary Magdalene.

A highly complicated form of ambivalence is exemplified by religious persecution. The atrocities with which persecutors charge their victims are, according to Reik, atrocities which the persecutors themselves desire to commit.[52] In punishing their victims they are by mental displacement inflicting self-punishment. Thus in the crucifixion charge (and cognate to it the blood accusation) the hostility toward the Christian god for which the Christian indicts the Jew is in reality a latent hostility harbored by the Christian himself.[53]

Not far from the ambivalent attitude toward one's own god is ambivalence toward one's own doctrines. That one can favor and at the same time oppose one's own dogmas is, according to Reik, evidenced by the fact that the greatest religious hostilities are those resulting from the smallest theological differences.[54] "There are only trivial differences" says Reik, "between that which people extol and that which they abhor." Apparently related to this in Reik's estimation is the circumstance that in moments of stress people pray though they are otherwise negative religiously.[55] We Jews are familiar with the type of Jew who, though totally unobservant in other matters, singles out for observance Yom Kippur or the mourning customs.

Further akin to this is the theological hairsplitting by which doctrines are fanatically defended in a manner which to the psychoanalyst only betrays an unconscious scepticism. Reik instances Talmudic casuistry as well as Christian dogmatics.[56] Unrelenting preoccupation with theological subtleties has striking parallels in certain neurotic conditions in which desire and aversion, belief and disbelief struggle together without surcease.

Reik also finds in some religious manifestations the ambivalence of people toward their own ambivalent selves, hatred of

[52] *Ibid.*, p. 198.
[53] *Ibid.*, p. 201.
[54] *Ibid.*, pp. 219, 249.
[55] *Ibid.*, p. 171.
[56] Reik, "Dogma und Zwangsidee" *Imago*, XIII, 292, 296–298. The Talmudic illustrations are Kid. 52b, Nazir 99b where R. Judah excludes the disciples of R. Meir for chicanery and B. M. 59b, the dispute between R. Eliezer and R. Joshua regarding the stove.

self wrangling with love of self. "Attacks upon others are attacks upon one's self because the self and the other were originally one[57] . . . Thus the I turns upon its hated *alter ego.*"[58]

Little surprising, in view of all this, is the ambivalence in the Christian's attitude toward the Jew, esteem for the Jew and contempt for the Jew alternating constantly.[59]

II. The Heterosexual

Having thus far considered data in which ambivalence is the dominant matter of illustration, we now proceed to that in which the outstanding factor is sex—sex of course in the usual psychoanalytic connection of sex conflict and the ambivalence attending it. Presently we shall take up the Oedipus Complex whose role in the psychoanalytic interpretation of Judaism is enormous. First however let us turn to sex material that lies outside of the Oedipus Complex. This we shall classify as:

a. The Heterosexual.
b. The Homosexual.
c. The Narcissistic.

Three significant treatments of Jewish matter from the standpoint of heterosexual desire are, "*Sexualsymbolik in der Paradiesgeschichte*" by Ludwig Levy,[60] "*Zur Funktion der Juedischen Tuerpfostenrolle*" by Georg Langer[61] and "*Die Ehe des Propheten Hossea in Psychoanalytischer Beleuchtung*" by Adolf Allwohn.[62]

A.

Levy makes out that, in the Paradise story, the forbidden fruit means *coitus*.

Was the originator of the story setting forth his views regarding cohabitation? If not consciously, was there such intent

[57] *Der Eigene und der Fremde Gott*, p. 251.
[58] *Ibid.*, p. 224.
[59] *Ibid.*, p. 213.
[60] *Imago*, V, 16–30.
[61] *Imago*, XIV, 457–468.
[62] *Beihefte zur Zeitschrift fuer die Alttestamentliche Wissenschaft* (44. Verlag von Alfred Toepelmann, Giessen 1926).

unconsciously? Or did that intent begin with some elaborator or editor or some reader or hearer? Just when the identification of forbidden fruit and sexual intercourse occurred, Levy fails to suggest.

And yet, facing the author's wealth of anthropological citation, one can hardly avoid admitting the prevalence of sex ideas in Genesis, chap. 3. The story abounds in phrases and images with which, at various times and places, sex has been associated. We summarize these as follows:

1. First, the word "know" which, in the Paradise story and in the Cain-Abel story that follows, occurs no fewer than nine times.[63]

That which the first parents come to know is the fact of their nudity, that is, of their sexual difference.[64]

This is related to the frequent use of *yada'* as a sex euphemism, a usage which the author reports to obtain in Arabic, Syriac, Assyrian, Greek (gignoscein) and Latin (noscere, agnoscere, notitiam habere).[65]

Allied to this is the view that the phallus is the seat of knowledge. The knowledge may be that of certain unusual emotions or the knowledge how human beings originate.[66] Unsupplied with knowledge are sexually unripe children[67] as well as the aged who have outlived their sexual potency.[68]

The equation of knowledge and cohabitation our author finds further validated by the conjunction of "tree of knowledge" and "tree of life."[69] He regards the *waw* in *"we'eẓ ha-da'at ṭob wara'"* (Gen. 2.9) as *waw explicativum* requiring the translation, "The tree of life in the midst of the garden, *that is*, the tree of all knowledge whatsoever." On the identity of the two trees

[63] Gen. 2.9, 17; 3.5a, 5b, 7, 22; 4.1, 17, 25.

[64] "Sexualsymbolik in der Paradiesgeschichte" *Imago*, V, 18. Ibn Ezra to Gen. 3.7; on the relation of nudity to sex.

[65] *Op. cit.*, p. 20.

[66] May not the word "know" for sexual intercourse also derive from the intimacy of the relation and the closeness of the personal acquaintance involved?

[67] Deut. 1.39; Isa. 7.14b, 15a.

[68] II Sam. 19.36.

[69] *Op. cit.*, pp. 21, 22. On Waw explicativum, Gesenius-Kautsch § 154, note b.

he cites the Midrash.[70] Gen. 3.22 which in all events the critics assign to a heterogeneous source he regards as an editorial insertion arising from the erroneous supposition that in Genesis 2.9, two trees are meant. If "tree of knowledge" and "tree of life" i.e. of procreation are indeed the same, the nexus of knowing and cohabitation is further confirmed.

2. The author adduces considerable anthropological material on the connection between *libido* and apples. He assumes, of course, that the identification of forbidden fruit with apples is ancient.

Apples, he holds, are replica of the female breast.[71] Haupt's "Liebeslieder" are quoted for the modern Palestinian song, "Her pomegranates are fresh, swelling, budding."[72] Goethe's "Faust" is quoted:

"Der Aepfelein begehrt ihr sehr
Und schon vom Paradiese her."[73]

and a Latin poet: "Libros non lego, poma lego."[74] The golden apples of the Hesperides are also regarded by our author as sexually symbolic.

He further recalls the quince eaten at Greek weddings as well as the pomegranate of Persephone and the pomegranate in the hand of Here at Argos and of Zeus at Pelusium.[75]

If the forbidden fruit be regarded not as an apple but, following the Midrash and the Talmud,[76] as a fig, the reminder becomes pertinent that the fig also is a phallic symbol.[77]

3. On the phallic symbolism of the fig, Levy quotes the Latin sources, Horace and Martial who speak of phallic images

[70] Midrash Agada, Ed. Buber on Gen. 2.17. It was not possible to locate this passage. The author does not state who the critics are that assign Gen. 3.22 to a heterogeneous source. Gunkel takes it as homogeneous with its J context.

[71] Levy, *op. cit.*, p. 24.

[72] The passage is given as on p. 86 of the "Liebeslieder."

[73] Levy, *op. cit.*, p. 19.

[74] The reference is to Priap. Carm. LXVIII, 1ff. for "*Libros non lego, poma lego.*"

[75] Levy, *op. cit.*, p. 20. It appears that the author has overlooked Cant. 2.3, 4.

[76] Gen. Rabba XV, 8, the opinion of R. José, also San. 70b top.

[77] Levy, *op. cit.*, p. 27.

carved from the wood of the fig tree.[78] In certain Greek orgies, a box containing the golden phallic snake was made of fig wood.[79] In the Dionysian rites, the snake itself was of fig wood.[80] Athenian girls would, on these occasions, carry figs in baskets. Dionysius is said to have planted a fig tree at the door of Hades. In French "*figue*" means "vulva."[81]

4. The act of eating has sexual implications. The striking passage is Prov. 30.20 which Levy supplements with passages from the Midrash and the Gemara.[82]

5. The death which is threatened as a consequence of the eating carries, according to Levy, pronounced sexual implications. The physical relaxation after coitus suggests death.[83] Celsus is quoted, "*Seminis emissio est partis animae jactura.*" Declining sex power is the sign of advancing age and approaching death.[84] Plants wither after they bear fruit. The old generation dies out after producing the new.[85] Death sometimes results from childbirth. Our author finally alleges that the wish for *coitus* is in dreams sometimes signified by death.[86]

6. Eden which means "delight" suggests sexual delight. Rashi is quoted on the resemblance between Eden and a man's wife.[87]

[78] *Ibid.* The Latin sources cited by Levy are Horace I Serm. 8, 1; Martial VII–LXX, 1. It should be VII–LXXI, 1.

[79] Levy, *op. cit.*, p. 25.

[80] *Ibid.*, p. 27.

[81] If the forbidden fruit be wine (Gen. Rab. XV, 8; San. 70a end), the connection with sex would be still easier to establish. Cf. "Baccho et Venere." Levy's reference to San. 29b appears to be an error.

[82] Ket. 65b on Prov. 30.20. I can not find the reference to Sab. 63b given in *Imago*, V, 19. The other references are: Gen. Rab. LXXXVI end, *leḥem asher hu okel.* Num. Rab. IX, 2, *mipitteka akalta umikoseka shatita.* Gen. Rab. XV, 8 and San. 70b top connect immature childhood with the inability to eat wheat.

[83] Levy, *op. cit.*, p. 22, refers to W. Stekel, *Die Sprache des Traumes,* p. 94.

[84] Levy, *op. cit.*, p. 24.

[85] *Ibid.*, p. 22.

[86] *Ibid.*, p. 23.

[87] *Ibid.* Levy might have cited the word *'edna* in Gen. 18.12 and the interpretation of *petigil* (Isa. 3.24) in Sab. 62b. Rashi in Ber. 57a on *mubtaḥ lo shehu ben 'olam haba* states that Eden resembles a man's wife.

7. The serpent is a phallic symbol:

a.) The snake issuing from holes appears to be a treasure guardian.[88] Treasure—such appears to be Levy's construction—suggests that which is highly desired and this in turn suggests *coitus*. Again treasure suggests temptation and thus again *coitus*.

b.) The snake is asserted to be an erotic symbol in dreams and in neurotic phantasies.[89]

c.) Figuring in Greek orgies is a golden snake in a box or a snake drinking water out of a bowl, where box and bowl symbolize the female sex anatomy.[90]

d.) A snake winds around the staff of Esculapius who, being a healer, is a conqueror of death. Procreation is likewise a conquest of death.

e.) In Roman folklore, the genii that guard the marriage bed are snake demons or beings that carry snakes.

f.) North Transvaal maidens have a ritual in which they dance around a lime snake, blow a fire and then carry on their backs the figure of a child.[91]

g.) In the Suaheli language, the word for "snake" is the same as the word for "penis."[92]

h.) A Jewish legend holds that the snake mediates the seduction of Eve by Satan.[93]

8. On the principle of *middah keneged middah* highly emphasized in Hebrew antiquity, the curses imposed for eating the forbidden fruit point clearly to sex dereliction.[94]

[88] Levy, *op. cit.*, p. 25 refers to "The Symbolism of the Serpent" in *International Journal of Psychoanalysis* (1926), VII, 2. It was not possible to find this article at the place indicated.

[89] Cf. also Major J. W. Povah, "*The New Psychology and the Hebrew Prophets*", p. 135. (London: Longmans Green & Co., 1925.)

[90] Levy, *op. cit.*, p. 25 refers to Barbara Renz "Schlange und Baum als Sexualsymbole in der Voelkerkunde," *Archiv fuer Sexualforschung* I, 2, 342.

[91] Levy, *op. cit.*, p. 26.

[92] *Loc. cit.*

[93] The author refers to Bousset, *Die Religion des Judenthums im Neutest. Zeitalter*, p. 490. Slavonic Enoch 29. 4 and 31. 3 represents Satan as the seducer of Eve. Gen. Rab. XVIII end reads: (*hanaḥash*) *mitok shera'ah otan misassekin bedabar aḥer nitaweh lah.* The correct passage is Slavonic Enoch 31. 6.

[94] Levy, *op. cit.*, p. 28.

The snake is to crawl on his belly.[95] Levy thinks of the French *courir sur le ventre* for the sex act. The snake's eating of earth suggests the sex symbolism of eating already noted in point 4, above. Earth, as we shall presently notice, symbolizes the female member in the sex relationship.

The birthpains of the woman have an obvious relation to sex.

By a few metaphorical removes, the penalty imposed on the man refers also to sex. Plowing the earth is an obvious symbol for *coitus* (see infra pp. 637, 638). Earth is something female as the invariable feminines *Adamah*, *Ereẓ*, *Terra*, *Erde* indicate. Offspring are spoken of as *Zera'*, seed and children as *Peri*, fruit. Of Esther the Talmud says, "*Karka' 'Olam hayeta*."[96] Adam's punishment, the toil of plowing, thus comports with the sexual plowing which was his misdeed.

Such are adduced by Levy to show the libidinous implication of the Paradise story. Levy holds that prophetic attempts to substitute an ethical religion for heathen fertility cults required a subordination of sex.[97] There resulted the ambivalence: the natural sex inclination on the one hand and, on the other, a deprecation of sex. This, according to Levy, is what the Paradise story conveys.

B.

Georg Langer argues for a primary sexual implication of the *Mezuzah*.[98] His thesis is that the *Mezuzah* is a modified phallus, the door to which it is affixed being a vagina symbol. He reasons as follows:

1. Throughout the primitive world posts, stakes or staves in front of houses, especially near the doors, possessed a phallic implication. Langer quotes Hastings to the effect that holy door

[95] Levy might have added a reference to Sotah I, 7 on the swelling of the thigh and the abdomen. On the entire doctrine of *middah keneged middah*, Sotah I, 7–9.

[96] Sanhedrin 74b.

[97] Levy, *op. cit.*, p. 30. It was not possible to obtain a copy of Levy's study of the sex symbolism of the Samson story mentioned *Imago*, V, 19 and of the stone casting (Eccles. 3.5) in his commentary on Ecclesiastes.

[98] "Zur Funktion der Juedischen Tuerpfostenrolle" *Imago*, XIV, 457–468.

posts among the Phoenicians had phallic attachments.[99] He quotes Otto Stoll that the Abyssinians affix to their door posts the amputated and stuffed genitals of their enemies,[100] Langer being reminded here of I Sam. 18.25 where David's men secure the Philistine foreskins and—*wayemalle'um* (stuffed them?). Langer further recalls that the Greeks and Romans had in front of their houses stone or wood posts called Hermes or Priapos posts, with phallic appendages. He thinks that something similar is implied by the word *yad* in Isa. 57.8 as well as by the *ammot* of Isa. 6.4; *ammah* being "phallus" as well as "cubit" and "column," somewhat like the English word "yard" which, according to Ernest Jones, is nautical slang for "phallus."[101] Langer also quotes F. Starr that certain American Indian tribes had a sacred staff stuck in the ground in front of their domiciles.[102] This staff would be wrapped up—like a *Sefer Torah*—when carried along on journeyings. From Benzinger, Langer gathers that among polyandric Arabic tribes a man visiting a woman places his staff in front of her tent.[103]

2. With these phallic posts or stakes or staves, the *Mezuzah* has in common not only its position near the door but also various other features:

a.) The inscription. Inscriptions stood on the Priapos posts of the Greeks and Romans.[104] Sometimes the post was discarded and the inscription marked on the side panel of the doorway, just as sometimes the head of Priapos would be attached near the door when the post representing the body had been abandoned. According to Jeremias, Babylonian boundary posts bore curse inscriptions.[105] Similarly inscribed posts, we are informed, are reported by A. Morel as existing in Egypt.[106]

[99] Hastings, *Encyclopedia of Religion and Ethics*, X, 96, article, "Poles and Posts." The article is by George A. Barton.

[100] *Geschlechstleben in der Voelkerpsychologie*, (Leipzig, 1908.)

[101] "Die Theorie der Symbolik," *Internationale Zeitschrift fuer Psychoanalyse*," Band V, S. 257. How about *yado* in Cant, 5.4?

[102] *American Indians*, p. 195ff.

[103] *Hebraeische Archaeologie*, III Auf., S. 113.

[104] Langer, *op. cit.*, p. 460.

[105] *Ibid.*, p. 463. Jeremias, *Handbuch* S. 118ff.

[106] Morel, *Mystéres Egyptiens* (Paris 1922), p. 16.

b.) The apotropaic character of the *Mezuzah* resembles that of the Hermes posts of the Greeks and similarly placed sticks among African Negroes, as reported by Frobenius[107] and among the Melanesians, as reported by R. H. Codrington.[108]

c.) The Talmud refers, albeit disparagingly, to the practice of attaching the *Mezuzah* to a staff.[109] The passages are Menaḥot 32b and Kelim XVII, 16. The practice mentioned in Kelim—a staff with a *Mezuzah* enclosed—resembles the present oriental practice of sinking the *Mezuzah* into the side panel of the doorway. Langer surmises that the Talmudic objection to a staff-Mezuzzah betrays its heathen character and its relation to the heathen notions mentioned above.[110]

d.) The truncated size of the *Mezuzah*, like the wrapping of the *Sefer Torah*,[111] has a castration significance.[112] Langer refers to the female attire and the female role of males castrated in the Cybele cult as well as among the Mujaredo Indians, Hindus etc. Back of this "castration," depriving the *Mezuzah* of everything but its apotropaic powers, Langer surmises a transition from a gynecratic to an androcratic form of social organisation.[113]

3. The door is a female sex symbol.[114] Langer quotes Ketubot 10a, "I found an open door" (i.e. "my bride is not a virgin") and "Thou hast torn out door and bolt" (i.e. "Thou hast been sexually too vehement").[115] Langer understands, in this light, the blood sprinkled on the door posts in Exod. 12.21–30. "Der

[107] Frobenius, *Allerlei aus Volks-und Menschenkunde.*

[108] Codrington, *The Melanesians* p. 174, also Hasting's, *Encyclopedia*, X, 96.

[109] Langer, *op. cit.*, pp. 461, 462.

[110] *Op. cit.*, p. 462.

[111] "Eine Analogie bietet schliesslich auch die juedische Gesetzrolle, deren phallische Stabgestalt in ein Frauenkleid (*mitpachat*) gehuellt wird." *Op. cit.*, p. 465.

[112] *Ibid.*, p. 464.

[113] *Ibid.*, p. 465.

[114] A similar idea is quoted from Dr. Hans Sachs in Reik's "Die Tuerhueter," *Imago*, V, 349, that "fuer das Unbewusste die Schwelle die Vagina ebenso wie das Haus den weiblichen Koerper bedeutet."

[115] Langer might have found additional examples in Levy's *Talmudisches Woerterbuch*, under the word "*petaḥ*."

Daemon empfindet vor dem 'Betreten' des mit Blut bestrichenen Hauses denselben Abscheu wie der Primitive vor dem Verkehr mit der Frau in der Menstruationzeit."[116] The blood on the threshold would thus have the same apotropaic character as the phallic posts or staves mentioned above.

Langer is impressed by the etymologic resemblance between *miftan*, "threshold" and *peten*, "viper," the viper being like any serpent a phallic symbol. Similarly in I Sam. 5.4,5, Dagon the fish is brought into connection with the threshold; and fish also is a phallic symbol.

The burial of children at the gates of a newly founded city (I Kings 16.34) suggests to Langer a uterus character in the gates. He further adduces from Bachofen "die etruskische Sitte an dem Tuerpfosten des Grabes das weibliche Spurium abzubilden."[117]

Finally Langer instances Indian and Russian folktales about talking door posts.[118] In the Russian tale, the door posts simulate the voice of a girl who, in order to cover her escape, left at the door posts some of her sputum. "Speichel ist aber wie aus der Psychoanalyse bekannt . . . ein Spermasymbol . . . das Haus und die Tuer . . . ein Symbol des weiblichen Genitales."[119]

4. The sexual is further intimated in the passage, Menahot 31b which, speaking of the distribution of the letters and words on the *Mezuzah*, says that the formation must not be that of a *kubbah* and must not be that of a tail. Langer observes that *kubbah* means "abdomen" and "*Freudenhaus*" as well as "tent."

5. The requirement that if there be a *Mezuzah* in a room in which sexual intercourse occurs, the *Mezuzah* be covered and

[116] Langer, *op. cit.*, p. 464. Considering the word "*ba*," Exod. 12.23, Langer notices its implication of "cohabit" as in Gen. 29.21b; 35.16b, 18b, etc. On the repulsiveness of menstruation, Lev. 15.19–33; 18.19; 20.18.

[117] The reference to Bachofen is Band I, S. 325.

[118] Langer, *op. cit.*, p. 463.

[119] *Ibid.* On the psychoanalytic point, Langer's reference is the works of Abraham and Ferenczi in *Internat. Zeitschrift fuer Psychoanalyse*, Band. IV, S. 71ff. Band IX, S. 67. Ferenczi tells of a woman whose mouth watered when the physician brought his head near to examine her heart. Abraham tells of a patient who spoke of mouth "pollutions" which he afterward associated with the erogenous.

rendered invisible[120] Langer explains as due to the fact that "Der drohende Vaterphallus mobiliziert die Kastrationsangst und verhindert dadurch die sexuelle Betaetigung."[121] He holds it to be the same father-penis character with its implied threats and penalties that ensures to the *Mezuzah* its apotropaic potency.[122] We shall later in this study treat this conception more in detail when, in connection with the Oedipus Complex, we consider the notion of paternal hostility.

Langer maintains that it is not the contents of the *Mezuzah* that provide its apotropaic potency, there being in the Biblical passages used naught of an apotropaic character.[123] Rather is it the *Mezuzah* that invests these passages with qualities apotropaic. Langer finally admits: "Allerdings ist es infolge des langen, intensiven, Verdraengungsprozesses nur recht wenig was vom urspreunglichen phallischen Charakter uebrig blieb; die apotropaeische Kraft, wie sie die roemischen Priaposinschriften, die babylonischen Kudurrugrenzsteine, die afrikanischen und indianischen Totemstaebe und Phalli am Eingang der Wohnstaetten hatten: und ihre laengliche Form."[124]

C.

We now come to Allwohn's study of the prophet Hosea.[125] Allwohn contends that the prophet was impelled by an unconscious urge toward sensuality and at the same time by a contrary urge toward sex restraint.

Evidences of the sensual are his subjection to the lure of whoredom[126] as shown by his marriage with a harlot and at the same time his furious denunciation of harlotry.[127] Allwohn points out that persons given to fierce censures of moral laxity may

[120] See Yoreh De'ah 286, 5, the Be'er Heṭeb to *nir'et.*

[121] Langer, *op. cit.*, p. 468.

[122] *Ibid.*, p. 465.

[123] *Ibid.*, pp. 466, 467.

[124] *Ibid.*, p. 467.

[125] *Die Ehe des Propheten Hosea in Psychoanalytischer Beleuchtung* (Giessen, 1926.)

[126] Allwohn, *op. cit.*, p. 62.

[127] *Ibid.*, pp. 64, 65. Allwohn agrees with the scholars who regard the marriage with a harlot as real and not merely rhetorical. *Op. cit.*, p. 66.

be themselves inclined toward moral laxity, their excoriations of others being at bottom a grapple with their own proclivities. Hosea betrays an unusual preoccupation with sex.[128] He is influenced not a little by concepts derived from Baal worship with its proverbial sensuousness—for instance the idea of a marriage between the deity and the land.[129] Allwohn thinks that the sensuous longings were awakened in Hosea by the sight of the Baal religion notwithstanding his aversion to that cult.[130] According to Allwohn the repressed tendencies become active when in ecstacy there is a "narrowing of consciousness" and a suspension of conscious control.[131]

The other member of the ambivalence is exhibited in the prophet's restlessness and in the ecstacy resultant from that restlessness.[132] Such restlessness, according to Allwohn, indicates that sex impulses have been repressed and are seeking "abreaction." Also to be noted is the prophet's zeal for Yahweh, the God of chastity,[133] the conversion of the inclination to marry a whore into a Divine command to marry a whore[134] and the subsequent application of it all to the relations of Yahweh and Israel.[135] The denunciations of harlotry, while divulging sensuous desires, also exhibit a struggle against and a substitution (Ersatzbildung) for those desires.[136] The censorious names given the children, by expressing disparagement of the mother, imply a revulsion

[128] *Ibid.*, pp. 56, 63. Allwohn lists the sex allusions of Hosea as follows:
2.4–15, especially 5, 7, 12.
4.2, 10–14, 15, 17. On *ḳalon* in vv. 7, 18 cf. Jer. 13. 26.
5.3, 7. As in Chap. 6, v. 7 *bagad* is the same as *na'af*.
6.7, 9 (*zimmah*).
7.14a. Do not emend to *mizbeḥotam*.
9.1, 9, 10 (*boshet* as in Chap. 10, v. 6), 11, 14.
10.6, 9.
12.15 (*ḥerpah*).

[129] Allwohn, *op. cit.*, pp. 56, 60.

[130] *Loc. cit.*

[131] *Ibid.*, pp. 60, 72.

[132] *Ibid.*, pp. 60, 61, 63.

[133] *Ibid.*, p. 56.

[134] *Ibid.*, p. 60.

[135] *Ibid.*, pp. 62, 63, 64, 66.

[136] *Ibid.*, p. 63.

toward the unchastity associated with the mother.[137] Gomer, the focus of the unchastity is, at length, definitely repudiated.[138]

This conflict of sensuousness and chastity is the starting point for Hosea. There gradually developed in him a diminution of the sensuous and an augmentation of chastity or rather of the Yahweh zeal identified with chastity.[139] This reduced the tension of the conflicting urges and thus prepared the way for the final step, that of sublimation i.e. the transmutation of sensuousness into love. Love is, as it were, the force resultant when, chastity dominating, chastity and sensuousness combine.

Allwohn thinks that the relaxation of the tension may have occurred during the few years that elapsed between Hos. 2.4 and 3.1.[140] He surmises that the absence of any reference to harlotry in the name "Jezreel" shows a temporary abatement of the sensuous inclination[141] and that the intensification of the Yahweh zeal—intensification in fact up to the point of expelling Gomer—appears in passages like Hos. 1.9 and 2.4.[142]

Our author then traces the unfolding of Hosea's purified love, step by step, from embryonic obscurity until, at the end of chapter 3 it is full blown. First there are the children and children commonly improve the relations between husband and wife.[143] Hosea was fond of children as Hos. 11.1 intimates. In the name "Lo Ruhamah" at least the expectation of love is expressed. In Hos. 2.4–15 the prophet's sensuousness toward Gomer metamorphizes into affection, his anger here being due to nothing so much as to the disillusionment which his affection encounters.[144] While in 2.9, 10 he is still egoistic, in 2.17ff. and 3.1 he is so far from egoism that he is willing to forego the reciprocation of his love.[145] He finally announces that the marital deprivations are to be but temporary and that in due time full marital satisfaction will prevail.[146]

[137] *Ibid.*, p. 33, 66.
[138] *Ibid.*, p. 70.
[139] *Ibid.*, pp. 66, 68.
[140] *Ibid.*, p. 71.
[141] *Ibid.*, p. 66.
[142] *Ibid.*, p. 71.
[143] *Ibid.*, p. 69.
[144] *Ibid.* Expressive of affection are vv. 2, 9b, 16, 17.
[145] *Ibid.*, p. 70.
[146] The temporary character of the marital deprivations is seen by Allwohn in the words *yamim rabbim* 3. 3; complete national satisfaction in chap. 3, vv. 4, 5.

Allwohn then shows that a reading of the same process is obtainable from the God conceptions whose unfolding parallels that of the relations between Hosea and his wife. At the outset Yahweh is the angry husband of whoring Israel.[147] But Hos. 2.4–15 exhibits a fluctuation between Divine wrath and tender yearning.[148] Gradually Yahweh's punishment gets to be something reformative and disciplinary,[149] arousing the conscience and eliciting affectionate return.[150] With the alteration of the children's names, God is conceived as forgiving, ameliorative and increasingly bounteous.[151] At length just as there is to be full marital satisfaction in the prophet's life so is there to be under Yahweh complete national satisfaction. While in Hos. 1.2 the prophet's desire and Yahweh's are in conflict, in Hos. 3.1 they are harmonized.

Hosea, according to Allwohn, effected a synthesis between a Yahweh religion of austerity and a Baal religion of fertility and geniality.[152] At first lust conflicts with abstemiousness, Baal with Yahweh. The solution lay in the conversion both of lust and of abstemiousness into love. Yahweh thus became the God of Love.

D.

A few minor observations of Biblical material remain to be mentioned. Ludwig Levy discerns a sex symbolism in the Biblical shoe rituals of Deut. 25.9 and Ruth 4.7; the shoe representing the female and the foot the male sex factor.[153]

Felix Kanter calls attention to an inadvertent betrayal of sex

[147] Allwohn, *op. cit.*, p. 70.

[148] The vacillation between verses 4 and 6, between 5 and 12, and between 7b, 8 and 10 is particularly noted.

[149] Allwohn, *op. cit.*, p. 70. The verses cited are 2, vv. 8, 9, 16, 17.

[150] The verses cited are 2, vv. 18, 19.

[151] The alteration of the children's names in 2 vv. 3, 24, 25. Amelioration in 2, vv. 1–13, 17, 25. Bounty in 2, vv. 20, 21, 23, 24

[152] Allwohn, *op. cit.*, p. 75. Allwohn holds that even in the idea of a severe God, some intimation of love is not altogether absent. At least through cults and rituals can the favor of such a deity be won (p. 72).

[153] "Die Schusymbolik im juedischen Ritus," *Monatschrift*, Jahrgang, 62 pp. 182–184.

desire on the part of Ruth in Ruth chapter 2.[154] Speaking to Naomi, Ruth reports (v. 21) that Boaz had directed her to keep near the young men. Naomi (v. 22) corrects this to "near the young women," which was indeed what Boaz (v. 8) did say. "Ruth" observes Kanter, "war . . . ein junges und wie es scheint begehrendes Weib das mit dem Leben durchaus nicht abgeschlossen hat."[155]

E.

We now leave the Biblical domain and come to other examples of conflict involving heterosexual desires. This brings us to Reik's discussion of the Jews and Jesus.[156] Reik finds much here that is symptomatic of sex repression. He recalls that in traditional Jewish conceptions of Jesus obnoxious aspects of sex figure extensively.

Thus Mary is in the "*Toledoth Jeshu*" represented as an adultress.[157] "*Parthenos*," virgin is distorted into "Pantheros," a Roman soldier, the supposed paramour of Mary.[158] Mary is also called a *niddah*, a woman who violated the law against menstruous cohabitation.[159] To this the pictorial red hair of Jesus is said to be related.[160] Again Mary is regarded as a harlot, the harlot Mary Magdalene being her "duplicate."[161] The Jewish circumlocutions for the name of Jesus resemble, in Reik's opinion, the forgetting to which the mind subjects the sexually revolting.

Reik offers as an illuminating parallel the case of a young woman who, on a certain occasion, was unable to recall the name of the book "Ben Hur." In a company of persons who were conversing about the origins of Christianity, this young woman stated that "she had found in a certain English novel a

[154] "Die Psychoanalyse in der Bibel" in Hickl's *Illustrierter juedischer Volkskalendar*" 5688, p. 115.

[155] Kanter, *op. cit.*, p. 115.

[156] *Der Eigene und der Fremde Gott* (Imago Buecher III, Leipzig, Wien, Zuerich, 1923), Chap. I.

[157] *Ibid.*, p. 19.

[158] *Ibid.*, p. 23.

[159] *Ibid.*, p. 21.

[160] *Ibid.*, p. 22.

[161] *Ibid.*, p. 25.

fascinating depiction of the many religious forces active in that day," a novel in which "the life of Christ is delineated from his birth to his death."[162] Yet neither the young woman nor anyone else in the company was able to recall the title. Reik who was present undertook to explain this forgetfulness psychoanalytically. In the young woman he unearthed the following associations:[163]

Ecce Homo. (Erroneous guess at the name of the book).
Homo is "Mensch" in German.
"Mensch" is vulgar Viennese for "prostitute."
Three kings who visited the Christ Child.
Three kings, "drei Koenige" is argot for menstruation.
Menstruation suggests virginity.
Ben Hur. (Correct name of the book).
"Hur" is German for prostitute.[164]
The mother of Jesus was a prostitute.

Reik claims that in the case of the young woman the wish suppressed[165] was her unconscious desire to identify herself with Mary i.e. to be a prostitute and likewise the desire to have children without male intermediation.[166] The analogous Jewish deprecations of Mary and Jesus are said by Reik to involve similar repressions.[167]

Dr. Felix Kanter calls psychoanalytic attention to name

[162] *Ibid.*, p. 2.

[163] The young woman was the only one in the group willing to be psychoanalyzed. A casual remark by the author (p. 18) vaguely intimates that the young woman was a Jewess.

[164] *Op. cit.*, p. 24. Reik compares the young woman's change of the word "Hur" from a father's name to a maternal appellative with the reverse process by which Jewish diatribes make of "Parthenos" (the maternal appellative) "Pantheros" the father's name. Reik compares the "*Ben Ish*" of the Talmud with the "Ecce Homo" of the girl's guess (p. 18). He also dwells upon the use of two languages in the young woman's "Ben Hur" and in the Rabbis' "Ben Pantheros" (p. 29).

[165] "Unbewusst setzt sie das Aussprechen von Ben Hur einem sexuellen Angebot gleich und ihr Vergessen entspricht demnach der Abwehr einer unbewussten Versuchung dieser Art" (p. 69).

[166] *Ibid.*, p. 8, footnote.

[167] *Ibid.*, p. 217. Speaking of the uncanniness of Jesus and Mary for the Jew, Reik sees "in diesen Gefuehlen die seelische Reaktion auf ein aus der Verdraengniss Wiederkehrendes."

repressions in the brothers with reference to Joseph and in Saul with reference to David.[168] Kanter points out that, excepting in two passages, the brothers of Joseph never say "Joseph." They say "dreamer," "brother," "the youth," "his son." Only after the reconciliation do the brothers say "Joseph."[169] Similarly Saul avoids mentioning David's name." Son of Jesse" is his usual appelative. Saul says "David" only before the quarrel and after the reconciliation.[170] While these observations posit no sex factors, they can best be mentioned here because of the name suppression upon which they bear. We may also add in this connection that Stekel comments on the psychoanalytic correctness of the interpretations that the brothers accord to the dreams of Joseph.[170]

Finally Georg Langer contends that in many folklores fire has been found to be a sex symbol.[171] He recalls that L. Levy in his "*Sexualsymbolik der Simsonsage*"[172] sees such in the firebrands of Samson's foxes as well as in the foxes themselves. Langer connects with this the promise in Sab. 24b that, for fidelity in kindling the Sabbath and Hannukah lights, learned sons will be the reward.

III. Homosexuality and Narcissism

A. Homosexuality

Only to a scant degree does the literature before us utilize the concept of homosexuality.

Dr. Ludwig Levy sees in the *Keleb* of Deut. 23.19 a sacred

[168] Dr. Felex Kanter in Zwittau Maehren, "Die Psychoanalyse in der Bibel" in Hickl's *Illustrierter Juedischer Volkskalender fuer das Jahr 5688—1927–1928*, 27 Jahrgang. Juedischer Buch-und Kunstverlag Bruenn Orli 9, pp. 112–115.

[169] Kanter refers to Gen. 45.26 and 50.15, 16 (perhaps 17 ?).

[170] Kanter refers for "Son of Jesse" to I Sam. 20.27, 30, 31; for "David" to I Sam. 16.22; 18.8; 24.17; 26.17, 21. We can not readily accept Kanter's application of 18.8 and of 24.17. In 18.8, Saul uses the name "David" although enraged at David. In 24.17, the name "David" is used not by Saul but by the narrator. The passage from Stekel is *Die Sprache des Traumes* (1922), p. 7. It has been said that Robert E. Lee never mentioned the name of Grant, his opponent, but always referred to him as "that man."

[171] Georg Langer, "Die juedische Gebetriemen" *Imago*, XVI, 1930, 475, 476.

[172] *Zeitschrift fuer Sexualwissenschaft* Bd. III H.6–7.

pederast.[173] He refers to Rev. 22.15 where "dogs" are listed with fornicators, murderers, idolators and "everyone that loveth and maketh a lie." He connects the name "dog" with the homosexual *coitus more canino*, recalling that the very verb *raba'* applied in the Talmud to homosexual relations is used for the sex act of animals ordinarily.[174] The dog moreover is with the Hebrews a despised animal and is deemed a shameless animal since it cohabits openly in the street.[175] Finally, with more specific reference to psychoanalysis, Levy quotes W. Stekel that the dog is regarded as a homosexually inclined animal.[176]

Related to homosexuality is masochism, the tendency feminine rather than masculine to obtain libidinous pleasure from undergoing certain kinds of pain. A touch of such masochistic self infliction is seen by Reik in circumcision.[177] Circumcision also has the implication of castration, emasculation and hence feminization.[178] Reik recalls in this connection children's theorizings about the possibility of changing the male into a female.[179]

Further illustrative of masochism Reik finds the endless Jewish references to the sufferings of the Jew and to the justifica-

[173] "Hundegeld," *Imago*, VI, 396, 397.

[174] Levy refers to Sanhedrin 9b. He might have added San. 70a. A slightly divergent view is that of Gen. Rab. XX, 5 which lists the dog with the animals." "*Shemeshammeshim aḥor keneged aḥor.*"

[175] Levy's references are II Sam. 9.8, II Kings 8.13, Matt. 15.26.

[176] *Die Sprache des Traumes*, p. 128. In the 1922 edition, pp. 106, 108.

[177] *Der Eigene und der Fremde Gott*, p. 71. Circumcision, aside from being painful in itself, exposes the Jew to derision and opposition (p. 213). Reik (p. 210, footnote 1) quotes Freud's *Sammlungen Kleiner Schriften zur Neurosenlehre* 3. Folge p. 26 as quoting Weininger to the effect that, reducing his sexual appendages by way of circumcision, the Jew suffers a deprecation in common with that of woman. Our author might have quoted the rhyme with which gentile boys in Germany jeer at Jewish boys,

"Jude Mosche
Katze dosche
Lange Finger
Kurze . . ."

[178] Reik, *op. cit.*, p. 72. Reik might have mentioned the mediaeval superstition that Jewish males menstruate.

[179] *Op. cit.*, pp. 209, 210.

tion of those sufferings as a punishment for sin.[180] Hostile nations and kings who are viewed as Divine instruments for the punishment of Israel become like Cyrus themselves almost divine.[181] Reik suspects that there has even been in Jewish conduct something that masochistically invites persecution.[182]

Then there is the conception of suffering as the evidence of Divine love and as being almost a blessed end in itself.[183]

The Jewish doctrine of Israel's election also has masochistic components according to Reik, among them the masochistic enjoyment of circumcision.[184] In the unconscious presumably, the masochistic thrill resultant from suffering is equated with the thrill of occupying a privileged position.[185] Reik also speaks of a Jewish self-disparagement which he connects with a "sadistic castration fear" and which he treats as a kind of alternate or derivative of the masochistic self-adulation.[186] Psychoanalysts affirm a close interconnection between sadism and masochism, the one being rarely absent where the other is present.[187]

[180] *Ibid.*, p. 73. A young American Jew, Albert Weinberg, anticipated Reik in these surmises in "The Enemy within Ourselves," *Menorah Journal* Vol. IV, June 1918, pp. 186–194.

[181] Reik, *op. cit.*, p. 209.

[182] *Ibid.*, pp. 71, 236.

[183] *Ibid.*, pp. 236, 237. Reik might have instanced Ps. 94.12; 119.75. Job 5.17; Judith 8.25; II Macc. 6.16; Heb. 12.6; Rev. 3.19 as well as "*semeḥim beyissurin*" (Yoma 23a, 36b, Sab. 88b) and the "*yissurin shel ahabah*" (Ber. 5a). "In der Auffassung der Strafe als Liebesbeweis erkennen wir den theologisierten Ausdruck von libidinoesen Regungen welche im individuellen Seelenleben entscheidende Beitraege zu typischen Schlagephantasien der Pubertaet liefern, welche die inzestuoese Liebesbeziehung zum Vater zur Ziel haben."

[184] *Ibid.*, pp. 205, 206, 208.

[185] "Wir stossen hier wieder auf die masochistische Form des Auserwaehltglaubens die gerade durch das Leiden bestaetigt wird" (p. 236).

[186] *Ibid.*, pp. 208, 215.

[187] As long as we can identify ourselves with others and others with ourselves, masochism and sadism are obviously interchangeable. The matter is discussed *op. cit.*, pp. 228, 229, 230, 236. Reik reports that neurotics often show a combination of the afflicter and the afflicted (p. 228). Reik uses in this connection the term "equivalence" which he defines as "die Thatsache, dass die psychische Auswirkung des einen Teiles eines Triebgegensatzpaares einer gleichzeitige Wirkung des anderen ergaenzenden Teiles voraussetzt" (p. 229). In a foot note on p. 228 he instances a similar equivalence of exhibitionism and voyayeurism. Both sadism and masochism, he thinks, have a common root in the baby's desire to gain power over its own body (p. 232).

According to Reik, there is likewise something masochistic about the rigidities of the Jewish law and consequently in the Jewish resistance to Christ who embodies the release from those rigidities and a negation of the masochistic feminine attitude.[188]

Reik finally indulges in surmises regarding the historical origin of these homosexual and masochistic strands. It is one of his conjectures that the suppression or the absence of a mother goddess in Judaism resulted in attaching to Jehovah homosexually the libido that a mother goddess would otherwise have attracted.[189] Again, while some persecution may have been masochistically invited by the Jew, much of his homosexuality may have been the result of persecution. Reik speaks of wounded Narcissism and the circumstance that libido repelled and diverted from the self attached to Jehovah.[190] Reik also appears to surmise in this masochism a kind of Jewish vindictiveness toward the God that sent or permitted the sufferings of the Jews. He says something to the effect that a love object which disappoints is "taken up into the I and penalized" one part of the I being maltreated by the other.[191] Moreover, masochism in the persecutor may also have been operative; persecutors sometimes enjoy the pain of their victims by placing themselves imaginatively in their victims' place.[192]

B. Narcissism

Narcissism is the name for sex feeling directed toward one's own person. Related to it according to Reik is the assumption of "the omnipotence of thought" (*Allmacht der Gedanken*). Reik holds that, in the life of the infant, the self and the not-self are originally one.[193] At a time when the self is not yet confronted by an

[188] *Ibid.*, p. 71. Reik maintains that when Christ had created the rigidities of the Catholic system, he was in turn overthrown by Luther.

[189] *Ibid.*, p. 63.

[190] *Ibid.*, p. 207. Oscar Pfister in *The Psychoanalytic Method* translated by C. R. Payne (New York 1917), is persuaded that Amos, Hosea, Isaiah, Micah and Jeremiah sought "a transformation of the libido into social activity."

[191] *Ibid.*, p. 208.

[192] *Ibid.*, p. 235.

[193] "Erst spaet sondert sich ein Teil des Ur-Ichs ab und stellt sich als Aussenwelt dem Ichrest (secundaeren Ich) gegenueber" (p. 234).

intractable not-self, a sense of the omnipotence of thought could easily develop.

He contends that the separation of the not-self from the self must have been resisted by the original unity.[194] Certain aspects of religious persecution, he thinks, show vestiges of that primordial resistance.[195]

He further believes that the original unity of the not-self and the self underlies the phenomenon that the pain inflicted on others can be masochistically enjoyed as though it were inflicted on one's self, the bearing of which phenomenon on religious persecution has just been noticed.[196]

Reik specifies a number of theological consequences that flow from the *Allmacht der Gedanken*. One is the belief in the efficacy of prayer. Between wishing and obtaining, *Allmacht der Gedanken* admits no gap.[197] Another is the belief in the sinister efficacy of the bad intentions attributed to the followers of the opposing religions; by *Allmacht der Gedanken* desiring ill is the same as inflicting ill.[198]

Closely bound up with *Allmacht der Gedanken* and its related Narcissism are various types of self-adulation. The belief in the omnipotence of God is, according to Reik, an eject of the belief in one's own omnipotence.[199] Another derivative of self-adulation is the doctrine of the election of Israel.[200] Further attributable to

[194] "Es ist als wollte die Materie ebenso wie der Organismus allen Inhalt behalten und setzte dem Teilungsstreben einen dumpfen Widerstand entgegen . . . Das Ewig-werdende ist ein Teil des Ewig-gleichen, das Vorwaertsdraengen eine retardierte Rueckkehr" (p. 243). Reik almost identifies the scission of self and not-self with the cellular fissions of Biology.

[195] *Ibid.*, pp. 238, 240, 249. For instance the fact that small differences occasion the greatest hostilities.

[196] "Wer sich an anderen vergreift, vergreift sich an sich selbst, denn der andere war urspruenglich ein Stueck Ich . . . Die gegen Angehoerige fremder Religionen geuebten Verfolgungen sind eigentlich unbewusste Selbstverfolgungen." To speak with perfect accuracy, some of these manifestations are not so much phases as correlates of narcissism. Equivalence, narcissism and *Allmacht der Gedanken* would all be survivals of the original unity. Until there is a not-self there can be for the libido none but a narcissistic direction.

[197] *Ibid.*, p. 173.

[198] *Ibid.*, p. 189.

[199] *Ibid.*, pp. 175, 181, 255.

[200] *Ibid.*, p. 71.

self-adulation is the propensity for stressing differences between religious groups,[201] overlooking or, in the manner of clinical *anagnorisis*, forgetting their original identities.[202] Hostility is felt toward gods that were at one time, as we have already seen (supra p. 611), the same as one's own. The Hebrew opposition to the stone and tree cults, the calf totem, Baal worship etc. are cited as examples. Narcissistic self-adulation is to be blamed for the unwillingness to admit the kinship of opposing cults.

Religious doubt also, according to Reik, "presupposes in the long run a Narcissistic overappraisal of one's own mental processes."[203]

Types of inverted or negative self adulation are the belief in the importance of humility and the belief in a devil. The might of God implies humility because it implies the feebleness of man;[204] while concommitant with the exaltation of self which precipitates a god there arises a disparagement of self of which the devil is the projection.[205]

The Jewish assumption that whoso suffers great distresses deserves great privileges and exemptions—an assumption strongly re-enforcing the Jewish doctrine of election[206]—also has a Narcissistic root.[207] Reik's idea is apparently that self-adulation demands compensation for the repressions and humiliations endured by the self.[208] This applies even to masochistically enjoyed sufferings and to self inflicted sufferings such as circumcision.[209]

If the Jew is at times beset with a sense of unworthiness and

[201] "Was sich als Differenz zwischen den einzelnen Menschengruppen bruestet, ist narzistischer Stolz, der die gemeinsamen Wurzeln ignorieren moechte, ist das Straeuben gegen die unbewusste Erinnerung an jene Zeit da alle eine homogene Masse waren" (p. 255).

[202] *Ibid.*, p. 180. The connection with religious persecution is obvious (p. 73).

[203] *Ibid.*, p. 172.

[204] *Ibid.*, p. 173 foot note.

[205] *Ibid.*, p. 255.

[206] *Ibid.*, pp. 69, 70.

[207] *Ibid.*, p. 207.

[208] *Ibid.*, pp. 72, 207. One is reminded of the Inferiority Complex enunciated by Alfred Adler.

[209] Reik, *op. cit.*, p. 208.

if circumcision is at times occasion not for elation but for embarrassment and apology, we have once again the Narcissistic trend functioning negatively or invertedly.[210]

Jacob Becker discerns Narcissism in R. Nachman of Bratislaw (1772–1811).[211] In line with Freudian theories, Becker adduces as evidence R. Nachman's extra-ordinary self-adulation. R. Nachman regards himself as "the glory, the beauty, the grace of the entire universe."[212] How, at one point, R. Nachman ranks himself higher even than the Deity is shown by a prayer which he composed for his followers.[213]

Becker also perceives in his subject signs of oral and anal erotism. Quoting Freud, he suspects oral erotism in R. Nachman's inordinate proclivity for eating at one period in his life and his abhorrence of food at a subsequent period.[214] Anal erotism appears in R. Nachman's likening the accumulation of money to wallowing in filth.[215] Becker cites here of course the Freudian notion of the unconscious copric significance of money. In R. Nachman's construction of the words in Isa. 48.19 "*Ze'eza'e me'eka kema'otaw*" to mean "Thine excrements are like someone's money," Freudian suppositions about "filthy lucre" receive amazing illustration.

Becker further applies to his subject some of the conceptions of Jung's "*Wandlungen und Symbole der Libido.*" In the daring and luxuriant imagery of R. Nachman's "*Ma'asiyot,*" he sees conclusive evidence of what Jung calls "introversion."[216] R. Nachman's metaphor of arrow shooting to denote ejaculation is of sexual import undisguised.[217]

[210] *Ibid.*, p. 206.

[211] ר' נחמן מברצלב מחקר פסיכואנליטי: מאת יעקב בקר הוצאת ,דעה' ירושלים תרפ"ח.

[212] *Ibid.*, p. 17: ליקוטי הר"ן סימן צדיק הצדיק האמיתי הוא הפאר והיופי והחן של כל העולם כולו. והוא הבעל הבית של כל העולם והוא בבחינת הבעל הבית של בית המקדש כי הוא מאיר לבית המקדש ולכל העולם כולו.

[213] *Ibid.*, p. 18: יהי רצון מלפניך או"א שכל הודויים והבקשות שהתודיתי ובקשתי מלפני הצדיק מלפניך יהיו רצויים ומקובלים לפניך כאלו התודיתי ובקשתי רחמנות.

[214] *Ibid.*, pp. 13, 14.

[215] *Ibid.*, p. 16. It was not possible to locate this in Freud's *Ges. Schr.*. V, p. 286, referred to by Becker.

[216] *Ibid.*, p. 26.

[217] *Ibid.*, pp. 29, 30.

IV. Incest

We now take up the vast subject of the Oedipus Complex. The theory is that the male infant, as a result of physical contact with its mother, acquires libidinous desires toward its mother and that those desires persist more or less covertly into later years. The literature of psychoanalysis deals with this condition extensively. Resolving the Oedipus Complex and its consequences into their leading components, we disengage from the data before us the following elements:

1. Incest wishes of the son toward the mother.
2. Hostility of the father toward the son.
3. Hostility of the son toward the father.
4. Conciliation of father and son involving:
   a.) The father's friendliness toward the son.
   b.) The son's friendliness toward the father.

Incest motives are discerned in the following features of Judaism:

a.) The Sabbath.
b.) The Fifth Commandment.
c.) The Conception of a Promised Land.
d.) The Wanderings of the Jews.
e.) The Story of Cain.
f.) The Story of Jacob.
g.) Jewish Opposition to the Jesus and Mary cults.
h.) Paradise, New Jerusalem, Ark of Covenant etc.
i.) Sabbath Joy.
j.) The Expectation of the Messiah.
k.) Repentance.
l.) The Quest of Elijah at Horeb.
m.) Sheol.
n.) *Ḥaliẓah.*
o.) *Sukkah.*
p.) *Ḳiddush ha-Ḥodesh.*

It is pointed out by Ehrich Fromm that when work on the Sabbath is forbidden, the work referred to is primarily agriculture.[218] The verb is *'abad* which means "to plow." We have

[218] "Der Sabbath," *Imago*, 1927, XIII, 223–234.

already encountered the theory that the plowing of the earth can be a symbol of sexual intercourse[219] (supra p. 619). "That which was primarily to be averted on the Sabbath" says Ehrich Fromm, "was the incestuous appropriation of Mother Earth."[220] "The Sabbath was originally a reminiscence of winning the mother."[221]

Also Reik has much to say about the incestuous implications of agriculture. He calls to mind the Semitic agricultural ceremonies described by W. Robertson Smith and the belief reported by Doughty that, at plowing, the *ginns* have to be propitiated by the sprinkling of blood.[222] "Plowing" says Reik, "was illicit and perilous because it amounted to a gratification of incest wishes."[223] "Mother Earth" represents a man's literal mother,[224] his first love object. Reik further links with this the supposed Jewish dislike for agriculture[225] and the rebuke in store for one who interrupts his studies to admire the beauties of nature.[226]

Similar incest implications by identification with earth (*adamah*) reside, according to S. Radó, in the Fifth Commandment.[227] Radó interprets: "Honor thy father (by avoiding intercourse with) thy mother in order that (*middah keneged middah*) thy days may be long on *adamah* (Mother Earth).[228]

Reik holds that the Promised Land is, generally speaking, a "mother substitute."[229] Fulfilment of the promise depends on

[219] Neither Levy, Fromm, nor Reik appears to have noticed the expression for *coitus interruptus* in Yeb. 34b and Tos. Yeb. II, 6, "*dash mibifnim wezoreh mibbaḥuẓ.*"

[220] Fromm, *op. cit.*, p. 226.

[221] *Ibid.*, p. 234.

[222] Reik, "Das Kainzeichen" *Imago*, V, 39. His reference is to W. Robertson Smith, *The Religion of the Semites.*

[223] Reik, *op. cit.*, p. 40, refers to a paper on "Plowing" by Hans Sachs before the 1913 Psychoanalytic Congress in Vienna.

[224] Reik refers to Dietrich "Mutter Erde" in *Archiv fuer Religionswissenschaft* VIII, 1 and to Storfer, *Marias Jungfraeuliche Mutterschaft*, p. 112.

[225] Long before Reik, Sombart alluded to this in *Die Juden und das Wirtschaftsleben*, p. 363.

[226] The author refers no doubt to Abot 3, 9.

[227] "Das Fuenfte Gebot," *Imago* 1923, IX, Heft 1.

[228] *Ibid.*, p. 129.

[229] "Ja'akobs Kampf," *Imago*, V, 334.

Israel's obedience, that is to say on the repression of incestuous longings for the mother that entail hostility toward God, the Father.

Also related to this, according to Reik, are the wanderings of the Jews in search of their original home.[230] "All wanderings of nations" he says, "are a search for an original home just as all sex desire in the individual is a search for the mother, the never abandoned object of one's first love."[231]

Cain's connection with *adamah,* the soil suggests that incest was also his dereliction.[232] This comports with a tradition about the rivalry of Cain and Abel for an older sister. In psychoanalysis it is a commonplace that a sister can figure as a mother substitute and a brother as a father substitute.[233] Reik accordingly regards the story as "eine Doublette der Suendenfallerzaehlung." Modern poetry likewise ascribes libidinous desires to Cain.[234] Psychoanalysis finds moreover that a city can be the unconscious equivalent of the female body; and Cain was the first city builder.[235]

The Jacob story is likewise held to reflect incest motifs.[236] Reik notices Rebecca's fondness for Jacob with the intimation of a reciprocally incestuous attitude on Jacob's part. There is also the partial merging of Rebecca, the mother, and Rachel, the bride. Rachel is the niece of Rebecca and niece like daughter can be a mother substitute. Again Rachel like Rebecca makes her first appearance at a well. The seven years of waiting for Rachel as well as the sterility which Jacob blames on Rachel are, according to Reik, hints of something illicit. Reik regards the incest committed by Reuben, the son of Jacob, with Bilhah, concubine of Jacob as but a variant of the same theme.

[230] *Der Eigene und der Fremde Gott,* p. 60.

[231] *Ibid.,* p. 54.

[232] "Das Kainzeichen," *Imago,* V, 39. Referring to Gunkel's remark (*Genesis,* p. 5) about the play on the word "*adamah,*" Reik observes "dass dergleichen Hauefung von Ausdruecken einzutreten pflegt wenn affektive Vorgaenge wirksam sind."

[233] Charles Baudouin, *Psychanalyse de l'Art,* (Paris 1929), pp. 60, 61.

[234] Reik, "Das Kainzeichen," *Imago,* V, 41.

[235] Reik refers to Storfer, *Marias Jungfraeuliche Mutterschaft,* p. 119 and to Rank, *Der Mythus von der Geburt des Helden.*

[236] "Ja'akobs Kampf," *Imago,* V, 339.

Reik also detects a struggle with incest longings in the Rabbinic antipathy to the Jesus and Mary cults. He asserts that the annointing of Jesus by a Mary represents a sexual union of the god with his mother.[237] He contends that Mary is "a younger sister of the great love goddess."[238] "Her relations with Jesus have their prototype in the relations of West Asiatic mother goddesses and their son-consorts, such as that of Ishtar and Tammuz, of Astarte and Adonis, of Isis and Osiris etc." The bride of Christ in Rev. 21.9 appears to Reik to be the same personage as his mother in 12.5.

Reik thinks that the contempt of the Rabbis for Jesus and Mary is explicable only as a reaction against incest wishes of their own. "Unconsciously the Rabbis identify themselves with the revolutionary son-god and lover of the mother goddess."[239]

In the opposition to Jesus and Mary, earlier Hebrew history was in a sense repeating itself. Reik argues that an Israelitish mother goddess was worshiped in early times. He cites the adoration of the Queen of Heaven against which Jeremiah inveighs.[240] He instances the Hebrew predilection for Ishtar, Astarte etc.[241] and observes that a sexual longing for a mother goddess finds in Hosea, Jeremiah etc. recurrent censure.[242] He even surmises a connection of Miriam of Exodus with Mary Magdalene and Mary, mother of Jesus.[243] The *argumentum e silentio*, he holds, loses force in view of the familiar psychoanalytic mechanisms of repression and displacement.[244] The abandonment of the mother goddess Reik attributes to the hardships of the arid country and to the oppressions of stronger peoples.[245]

[237] *Der Eigene und der Fremde Gott*, p. 129. Reik refers to John 11.2; 12.3; Mark 14.3.

[238] Reik, *op. cit.*, p. 17.

[239] *Ibid.*, p. 29. Regarding the sexual though not specifically incestuous import of the Rabbinic attitude toward Jesus, something has already been said supra p. 627.

[240] Reik, *op. cit.*, p. 54. The references to Jeremiah are 7.17, 18; 44.9, 15.

[241] Reik, *op. cit.*, p. 58.

[242] *Ibid.*, p. 63 foot note.

[243] *Ibid.*, p. 57.

[244] *Ibid.*, p. 34.

[245] *Ibid.*, p. 58. Reik does not mention the feminine implication of *wate-ḥollel* in Ps. 90.2 or of *yelidtika* in Ps. 2.7 or of *ruaḥ elohim meraḥefet* in Gen. 1.2. Reik claims that Luther repeated the suppression of Mary. She was repressed

In connection with incest longings, the psychoanalytic writers have much to say about the unconscious desire for a return to the womb. Projections of that desire have been found in various religious fancies such as the New Jerusalem, Paradise, the ark of the covenant, the grave of Christ etc.[246] Ehrich Fromm in his psychoanalytic study of the Sabbath traces the desire for the intra-uterine state in at least three Jewish concepts.

One is that of Sabbath joy. This he calls "die Wiederherstellung der Harmonie der Mutterleibsituation."[247] Sabbath joy, implying a regression to the intra-uterine state of perfect rest, becomes a glad substitute for the Oedipus gratification which has been renounced.[248] "Verzichtscharakter" becomes "Erfuellungscharakter."

Another projection of the wish for intra-uterine security is the Messianic Age. The Messianic Age means Paradise regained when, as in the mother's womb, the bitter need for work will no longer exist.[249] In the Talmud, Fromm finds a synthesis of the first and the second of these projections. He refers to a Talmudic assertion that the Messiah will come when Israel keeps the Sabbath perfectly.[250]

In the Jewish idea of Repentance, i.e. of *Teshubah*, a returning, Fromm discerns a cognate import. Analytically speaking, chastise-

as "Abgoettin und mit ihr der Bilderdienst, der Mythos und die Sinnenfreudigkeit die zugleich mit ihr immer wieder ihren triumphierenden Einzug in die Religion hatten" (p. 67). This reminds us of Allwohn's comments on the joyousness of the Baal cult which Hosea resisted but by which he was nevertheless influenced (supra pp. 624, 626).

[246] Berguer, G., *Some Aspects of the Life of Jesus* (New York, 1923), p. 118. Jung, C. G., *The Psychology of the Unconscious* (translated by Beatrice M. Hinkle, New York, 1916), p. 380. Martin, E. D., *The Mystery of Religion* (New York and London, 1924), pp. 97, 237.

[247] "Der Sabbath" *Imago* 1927, XIII, 228.

[248] *Ibid.*, p. 229.

[249] *Ibid.*, p. 233. He refers to Isa. 11.6; 30.26.

[250] *Ibid.*, p. 233. The author is probably thinking of Sab. 118b. The reference to the Messiah is somewhat inaccurate both here and in the Jewish Encyclopedia article "Sabbath" referring also to Sab. 118b. The text says that were Israel to keep perfectly two Sabbaths in succession they would be immediately redeemed ("*miyyad nigalin*"). The author might also have mentioned Ber. 66b that the Sabbath is one sixtieth of the world to come.

ment for the primordial incest is supplanted by a return to the womb. "An illicit and punishable satisfaction thus gives way psychically to the lawful satisfaction of being unborn."[251]

Major Povah thinks that in the story of Elijah at Horeb the cave is the womb and that Elijah's entrance and emergence are a symbol of rebirth.[252] He also regards as related to the wish for intra-uterine Nirvana, the idea of She'ol. In this connection he quotes Job 1.21; 3.10–26 and Jer. 20.14–18.[253]

Among the many ways in which, according to Jacob Becker, R. Nachman of Bratislaw betrays his Oedipus Complex is his interpretation of the *Ḥaliẓah* shoe as a symbol of woman and of the *Sukkah* as a mother symbol in truly Freudian style.[254] While Gezá Roheim, the Freudian, divines mother longings in moon myths and rituals, R. Nachman connects *ḳiddush ha-ḥodesh* with *ḳiddushin* in the sense of marriage.[255] R. Nachman regards the moon as undergoing a consecration like that of a bride to her husband. Jacob Becker suspects the Oedipus Complex in all of this.[256]

V. Hostility between Father and Son

A. Hostility of the Father toward the Son

The son's approaches to the mother provoke the rivalry and hostility of the father.

The impress of this hostility is alleged to persist in various

[251] *Op. cit.*, p. 232.

[252] *The New Psychology and the Hebrew Prophets* by Major J. W. Povah B. D. (London, 1925), p. 131.

[253] *Ibid.*, p. 89. Reik (*Der Eigene und der Fremde Gott*, p. 152) makes a similar point of the story that Orpheus got his beloved from the underworld. Underworld is the womb of Mother Earth. Descent into Hell means incestuous union with the mother. Reik recalls that "Hell" comes from "Hela," the name of a goddess. He quotes Grimm (*Deutches Woerterbuch*, S. 1747ff.) as suggesting that, like the womb where the embryo resides, Hell is a narrow and hot place. He recalls that Boccaccio makes the vagina mean hell and the penis the devil.

[254] Not unlike the modern views of Ludwig Levy, supra p. 626.

[255] "Mondmythologie und Mondreligion," *Imago*, 1927, XIII, 530.

[256] *R. Naḥman mi-Braẓlaw*, p. 29. It was not possible to locate this in Freud's, *Ges. Schr.* X, p. 210 referred to by Becker.

religious fears.One of these is the fear of demons.[257] Another is the fear already noticed as connected with plowing when "sexual" advances are made to "mother" earth.[258] Reik traces the same apprehension in various fears associated with the *Kol Nidre*. The phrase *ha-ba 'alenu leṭobah* in the *Kol Nidre* displays according to Reik the apprehension that good may *not* attend the coming year.[259] A similar uneasiness is seen by him in the *sheheḥeyanu* formula shortly following the *Kol Nidre*. A vestige of an "*Unheilserwartung*" he calls this. Such "*Unheilserwartung*" Reik finds pervading the entire Amoraic epoch of Jewish history during which, he supposes, the *Kol Nidre* to have originated.[260]

Just as the insurgent sons would, if they could, devour the obstructive father, the resentful father—again *middah keneged middah*—would like Chronos in Greek mythology devour his aggressive offspring. Reik mentions in this connection children's fears of being eaten by giants or ogres.[261] The charge that the Jews eat *mazzot* containing Christian blood is asserted to belong to this same complex.[262]

The God that keeps Moses out of the Promised Land is also a punitive father. The Promised Land, as we have seen, represents the mother. Something in the relation of Moses to his mother is thus the occasion of God's killing him.[263]

Various initiation rituals carry the same import. The manhandling of the candidate goes back to the rude treatment which the irate father would visit upon his youthful rivals. Reik discusses in detail the initiation rites of the Australian Negroes in which the Balum monster terrifies and pretends to destroy the young initiates.[264] Among some primitives, the candidates are beset by the ancestral ghosts by whom they are intimidated,

[257] *Der Eigene und der Fremde Gott*, p. 161.

[258] "Das Kainzeichen," *Imago*, V, 40.

[259] *Probleme der Religionspsychologie*, (Leipzig und Wien), 1919, p. 168.

[260] *Ibid.*, p. 174.

[261] *Der Eigene und der Fremde Gott*, p. 199.

[262] *Ibid.*, p. 215.

[263] Reik, "Der Moses des Michaelangelo und die Sinaivorgaenge," in *Probleme der Religionspsychologie*, p. 287.

[264] Reik, "Die Pubertaetsriten der Wilden," Chap. III in *Probleme der Religionspsychologie*.

alarmed, bitten and supposedly killed.[265] Reik construes these rituals as variants of one central theme—the killing of the sons by the father upon whose sexual prerogatives with the mother the sons would trespass.

Reik does not cite the modern Boy Scout ritual in which a personage somewhat resembling the Balum monster accosts and confuses the young initiate who is, for that purpose, required to remain alone in a forest. The elements of cruelty often undisguised in various lodge initiations and student hazings are familiar. Our own Confirmation service exacts of the children not a little arduous study, burdensome discipline and embarrassing public appearance. Over every initiation apparently the shadow of paternal vindictiveness rests.

Also in the projected sacrifice of Isaac, Reik sees a resemblance to the simulated sacrifice of youth demanded by the Balum monster. The god commands what unconscious paternal hostility desires.[266]

When we considered Langer's discussion of the Mezuzah we noted his surmise that in its menacing character as a suggestion of paternal sex prerogatives lay its apotropaic power.

The rite of circumcision is, according to Reik, of identical import. Originally the father would slay the son.[267] Later, castration—very logically the maiming of the offensive function—would be substituted[268] and still later circumcision, an attenuated form of castration.[269] Among some primitives the substitute is

[265] Reik, "Ja'akobs Kampf," *Imago,* V, 333.

[266] Reik, *Probleme der Religionspsychologie,* p. 236.

[267] "Es ist warscheinlich, dass urspruenglich die wirkliche Toetung des Erstgeborenen wie sie manche primitive Voelker noch jetzt ausueben durchgefuehrt und erst spaeter durch die Kastration ersetzt wurde. Die Kastration (Beschneidung) ist bereits die mildere Taktik welche allerdings die sexuelle Motive der Rivalitaet zwischen Vaetern und Soehnen klar erkennen laesst" (*Der Eigene und der Fremde Gott,* p. 214). "Eine zewite spaetere Sage hielt die Erinnerung daran fest dass einmal Vaeter aus Motiven der Vergeltungsfurcht die Soehne kastrierten oder noch spaeter am Penis verstuemmelten" ("Ja'akobs Kampf" *Imago* V, 331).

[268] Reik, "Ja'akobs Kampf," *Imago* V, 334.

[269] The author cites Freud "Analyse der Phobie eines fuenfjaehringen Knaben" in *Sammlung Kleiner Schriften zur Neurosenlehre* III, p. 26; also *Totem und Tabu,* p. 141 footnote. Reik tells us that among the Arundas the

not circumcision but the pulling out of the hair, knocking out of teeth and the like.[270]

Lorenz takes the confusion of tongues at the Tower of Babel to mean castration just as the building of the tower is to him the anti-paternal aggression of the son (infra p. 648). Again, coupling with the interruption in Gen. 35.21 the words of Gen. 49.4b Dr. Ludwig Levy reads not *ḥillalta* (second person *pi'el*) but *ḥalalti* (first person *kal*) and renders "I have bored through" i.e. "I have castrated." Recalling how Oedipus lost his eyes and how in the Indra myth the curse that Indra's body become covered with sex organs is changed to the curse that eyes cover his body, Ludwig Levy sees castration in the blinding of Samson and in the blinding of the Sodomites.[271]

Reik holds that in some of its aspects anti-Semitism is connected with castration-circumcision.[272] "The contempt for the castrated i.e. the circumcised" he says, "is bound up with the dark fear of undergoing a similar fate." The Christian, in other words, is haunted unconsciously by the dread of castration at the hands of a jealous father.[273] This fear becomes transformed into detestation of the circumcised (i.e. the castrated) Jew. Sometimes the Jew is abhorred as an inflicter of castration.[274] Reik makes out that the figure of Shylock is a disguise for that of a castrator.[275]

As an account of such a paternal castration or initiation,

prolonged seclusion of the youth while recovering from the circumcision wounds is allowed to foster the supposition that the monster Twanyirika has abducted them.

[270] Sigmund Freud, *Totem und Tabu*, (Leipzig und Wien), 1913, p. 141.

[271] Ludwig Levy "Die Kastration in der Bibel," *Imago*, VI, 394.

[272] Reik, *Der Eigene und der Fremde Gott*, p. 214.

[273] "Der Kastrationscomplex ist die tiefste Ursache des Antisemitismus aber auch der Unheimlichkeit welche die Juden fuer eine lange Zeit des Mittelalters und fuer viele Leute noch unserer Zeit umgibt" (*ibid.*, p. 209).

[274] *Ibid.*, pp. 210, 211.

[275] There is a *Verschiebung nach oben* in the demand for the pound of flesh. The play does not at first specify the part of the body from which the flesh is to be taken (*ibid.*, p. 211). Antonio is, according to Reik, a "son figure" also an *Abspaltung* from Shylock (p. 212). Isador H. Coriat in *Internat. Journal of Psychoanalysis* 1921, pp. 354-360, has an article on anal-erotic character traits in Shylock.

Reik treats the story of Jacob. If beneath numerous alterations and disguises that purport is unrecognizable we have, thinks Reik, only another instance of the displacements and distortions familiar in neuro-pathology.[276]

On page 638 we noticed the evidences of incest or incest longings in the life of Jacob. With these Reik connects the following indications of a punitive castration:

1. The Peniel incident, he claims, belongs not to the manhood of Jacob but to his youth.[277] It belongs, in fact, to the time and place of the Beth-El incidents of Chapter 28.[278] The awfulness of the place in Gen. 28.17 comports not with a fair promise but with a dark conflict.[279] The Jacob who conquers God is hardly the same as the Jacob who dreads Esau. Reik also accords weight to the apparent discrepancy that puts Jacob South of the Jabbok in Gen. 32.23, 24 and North of the Jabbok in v. 25.[280] He further cites Gunkel's contention that the Peniel story is alien to its present context.[281] He seems however to overlook the confirmation that his theory might receive from Hos. 12.4b, 5b[282] and from the poetic intuitions of Beer-Hofman who fuses the Peniel and the Beth-El incidents into one.[283]

2. That Jacob has been in conflict with his father, Reik finds implied in Gen. 32.29, "Thou hast striven . . . with men and hast prevailed."[284] In the deceiving of Isaac he also sees a struggle between father and son, espcially since "What is thy name?" of Gen. 32.28 sounds so much like, "Who art thou, my son?" of Gen. 27.18.[285] Esau, angry at Jacob[286] and dreaded by Jacob, also Laban, cheating[287] and afterward pursuing Jacob,

[276] Reik, "Ja'akobs Kampf," *Imago*, V, 337.

[277] *Ibid.*, p. 336. [278] *Ibid.*, p. 337.

[279] *Ibid.*, p. 338.

[280] Reik does not mention the conflict between Gen. 32.23, 24 in which Jacob's retinue is on one side of the Jabbok with vv. 8,11 which puts them on both sides.

[281] Gunkel "*Genesis*" Goettingen 1902, p. 323 (not p. 365 as Reik gives it, *op. cit.*, p. 336).

[282] "By his strength he strove with God . . . at Beth-El he found him."

[283] Richard Beer-Hofmann, *Jaakobs Traum.*

[284] Reik, "Ja'akobs Kampf," *Imago*, V. 338.

[285] *Ibid.*, p. 340. [286] *Ibid.*, p. 339. [287] *Ibid.*, p. 340.

look to Reik like "father substitutes." They embody the father hostility.[288] The assailant deity of Gen. 32 is obviously hostile.

3. The solitariness of Jacob at Beth-El and at Peniel suggests the seclusion to which, in various primitive rites, the young initiates are subject.[289]

4. In view of the connection between limping and castration among various peoples, Reik takes the limping of Jacob to mean castration:[290]

a.) The sudden vanishing of the deity at day-break suggests a dream. Reik is not reminded of the Beth-El dream but he does cite the clinical observation that in nightmares in which the dreamer is beset by some unknown being, fears of castration because of illicit sexual acts or fancies attain expression.[291]

b.) Reik further recalls that the Rabbis and the Zohar identify the *gid ha-nasheh* with the sex organ.[292]

c.) The fact that in the subsequent biography of Jacob there is no further reference to the maiming shows, according to Reik, that the maiming was circumcision; circumcision, a common practice taken as matter of course, necessitating no further mention.[293]

Reik defends this bizarre recasting of the story by calling

[288] *Ibid.*, p. 339.

[289] *Ibid.*, p. 337.

[290] *Ibid.*, pp. 332, 333. Reik recalls how Hercules sustains a hip injury in one of his wrestlings. Reik probably did not know the Indian tale of Hiawatha's wrestling with Mondamin (Longfellow, *Song of Hiawatha*). On the identification of limping with castration Reik refers to his "Pubertaetsriten der Wilden" which is chap. II in his *Probleme der Religionspsychologie.*

[291] Reik, "Jaa'kobs Kampf," *Imago*, V, 332. Reik thinks in this connection of the ghost in Hamlet which vanishes at daybreak. In a letter dated Berlin Jan. 13, 1931, Reik writes: "The ladder is a symbol of sex-intercourse and as such used in many dreams. That means that the climbing up a ladder is unconsciously compared with the rythm of the act."

[292] Does he simply mean that in Rabbinic Hebrew *gid* also means sex organ as in San. 68b and Ḳid. 25a? Reik's Zohar reference is *Parashah Wayishlaḥ* 170, where it says חמן הוא יצר הרע רביע.

[293] Reik *op. cit.*, p. 334 refers to Stade on *Gib'at Arelim Z.A.W.* VI, p. 132. It is surprising that Reik does not find castration symbolized, by several displacements, in the blindness of Isaac. On the connection between blindness and castration, supra p. 644, infra 688. On the connection between circumcision and castration, supra p. 643.

attention to identical dislocations in the mental occurrences treated by the psychiatrist.[294]

Covering his assertions by references to Chadwick's "*Die Gott-Phantasie bei Kindern*"[295] and to Freud's "*Totem und Tabu*," Becker instances the early *timor mortis* of R. Nachman of Bratislaw as one of many evidences of the Oedipus Complex in that noted mystic; similarly his early sense of fear of the Deity. Displacements for terrors inspired by the offended father are what these are taken to be psychoanalytically.[296]

B. The Hostility of the Son toward the Father

Concurrent with the father's opposition to the son because of rivalry for the mother is that reciprocal phase of the Oedipus complication, the hatred of the son for the father. Psychoanalysts claim to have encountered in their psychiatric practice copious evidence of this hostility. Patricidal impulses with incestuous correlates are said to be clinical commonplaces. There have been children who have fancied themselves in the act of sexually mutilating their father;[297] while, as we have already noted

[294] "Wie ist diese unorganische Verbindung zu erklaeren? Keinesfalls dann, wenn wir die Erzaehlungen nebeneinander laufen lassen, sie flechenhaft auffassen. Aber sie liegen auf verschiedene Ebenen, nur eine historische und genetische Betrachtung kann sie aus ihrem jetztigen Ineinander sondern" (p. 340). "Betrachten wir, wie sehr die Bearbeitung der Sagengeschichten der seelischen Arbeit der Zwangsneurotiker gleicht, wie sie in einem Symptom alles laengst Entschwundene und Neues zusammenschweisst, neue wahrhafte Motivierungen und Rationalisierungen schafft, Auslassungen, Ellipsen und falsche Verbindungsglieder herstellt, um den urspruenglichen unbewusst gewordenen Sinn ihrer Zwangsgedanken zu verwischen" (p. 343). Speaking of the taboo of the thigh sinew, "Wir werden gewiss die falsche Motivierung des Verbotes der wahrhaften Umdeutung der Neurotiker vergleichen, die Unwahrscheinlichkeit, ja Unsinnigkeit der Motivierung hat uns ja den Weg zum Verstaendniss der wahren unbewussten Gruende des Verbotes gefuehrt" (p. 341).

[295] *Imago*, 1927, p. 383. However there happens to be nothing in this reference to substantiate Becker's assertion.

[296] Becker "*R. Naḥman mi-Braẓlaw*," p. 9.

[297] Reik ("Jaa'kobs Kampf" *Imago*, V, 342) gives two illustrations from clinical experience. Ludwig Levy ("Die Kastration in der Bibel" *Imago*, VI, 393) calls attention to the Talmudic belief, San. 70a, that Ham castrated his father Noah.

(supra p. 00), the juvenile fear of being eaten by a beast or an ogre has been traced psychoanalytically to the dread of being deservedly penalized for a murdering and devouring of the male parent at least in phantasy.[298]

Basing himself not only on clinical data but also on reports of Darwin and of Atkinson that in the combat for the females wild horses have been known to kill their sires, Freud posits an *Urmord*, a slaying of some primitive father or fathers by the sexually assertive sons.[299] That certain sacrificial rites are a "commemoration of a mythical tragedy" is an opinion in which Freud eagerly concurs with W. Robertson Smith.[300]

In all events writers treating the psychoanalytic roots of Jewish belief, observance and vicissitude find the patricide hypothesis extensively serviceable.[301]

Ehrich Fromm thinks that just as in the dreams of children, sleeping represents death, the story of God's resting on the Sabbath exposes a wish for the father's death.[302] This is further borne out by the connection of the Sabbath with the phases of the moon, in which the waning moon signifies the dying of the moon or the moon god.[303]

An uprising against the father has also been descried by Lorenz in the Tower of Babel story.[304]

[298] Reik, *Der Eigene und der Fremde Gott*, p. 199.

[299] Freud, *Totem und Tabu*, p. 131.

[300] *Ibid.*, p. 140. The reference to W. Robertson Smith is "*The Religion of the Semites*," p. 412, 413. Highly interesting are the accounts ("Totem und Tabu," p. 139) which Freud quotes from Frazer, *Golden Bough* regarding the annual slaughter of Latin kings. These kings were, according to Freud, father representatives.

[301] Reik holds that the aboriginal patricide became a model on which many a subsequent phantasy was constructed. "Die Ueberwaeltigung des Vaters der Urhorde war das Vorbild aller spaeteren Sohnesrevolutionen" (*Probleme der Religionspsychologie*, p. 269).

[302] Fromm, "Der Sabbath," *Imago*, XIII, 226.

[303] *Ibid.*, p. 227. He refers to Nielsen, *Die altarabische Mondreligion und die mosaeische Ueberlieferung*, (1904), p. 10. He mentions (p. 226) a Babylonian myth of Berosus in which Bel commanded a god to decapitate him and to make men and beasts of the blood mixed with earth. The reference is Schrader, *Keilinschriften*, p. 489. We dwelt upon the sex and the incest implications of the Sabbath supra, pp. 636, 637, 640.

[304] *Imago*, XIII, 139, in review of an article by Fluegel.

Boudouin in his "*Psychanalyse de l'Art*" classes the Cain and Abel story with an entire group of myths in which a brother is, psychoanalytically speaking, a father substitute and a fratricide a disguised patricide.[305] We have already noticed (supra p. 638) how Reik calls this story "eine Doublette der Suendenfall-erzaehlung.[306]

Abraham's intention to sacrifice Isaac has also been construed as an intimation of an anti-paternal uprising.[307] Reik claims that the son may be the "revenant" of his own grandfather. Abraham would thus not be a father sacrificing a son but a son sacrificing a father. Similarly Reik thinks that the ambiguity of the Hebrew antecedent in Gen. 32.26 can admit the meaning that Jacob wounded the deity i.e. that a son castrated his father. Basing himself on Sanhedrin 70a, "*Ḥad amar sirreso*" Ludwig Levy makes out likewise that Ham castrated his father.

Jacob's deception of Isaac as well as his collisions with Laban, his father substitute, are deemed by Reik further glimpses of a son's insurrection.[308] The taboo of the thigh vein, Reik thinks, goes back to an occasion on which a son for sexual reasons killed and devoured his parent with the result that such killing and devouring was afterward expressly prohibited.[309]

Reik hears further echoes of the son's insubordination in the repeated characterizations of the Israelites as a "stiff-necked people";[310] while Korah[311] and the builders of the Tower of Babel[312] are only types of the Hebrew rebel against the father, Yahweh.

In another passage, Reik suggests that circumcision can signify a punishing of the father by means of self punishment.[313]

305 Paris 1929, pp. 60, 61.

306 Reik, "Das Kainzeichen," *Imago*, V, 40.

307 Reik, *Probleme der Religionspsychologie*, p. 237.

308 Reik, "Ja'akobs Kampf," *Imago*, V, 340.

309 *Ibid.*, p. 341. Other features of the Jacob story are considered supra pp. 638, 645 and infra p. 658.

310 Reik, *Der Eigene und der Fremde Gott*, p. 68. 311 *Loc. cit.*

312 Reik, *Probleme der Religionspsychologie*, p. 303. Absalom's insurrection against David (II Sam. 15–19) and the attendant access to David's concubines (II Sam. 16.22) probably await treatment from this standpoint.

313 Reik, *Der Eigene und der Fremde Gott*, p. 208.

Various writers have seen opposition to the father in the resistance of children to religious instruction[314] as well as in Atheism[315] and other types of religious dissent.

Blasphemy and kindred phenomena have likewise been attributed to anti-paternal tendencies.[316] Ehrich Fromm suspects a touch of blasphemy in the idea in Gen. 1 and Exod. 20 that God so much as needs a rest.[317] That deeply conscientious persons are particularly subject to outbursts of rebelliousness has been noticed repeatedly.[318] Monks have confessed themselves as disposed to blaspheme during prayer.[319] Freud reports an analogous tendency in one of his patients.[320] With this, Reik connects the jest about the two Jews whose hostility toward one another comically reasserts itself in the very act of becoming reconciled.[321] Reik further alludes to the child who said, "I want

[314] *Ibid.*, p. 221. The author refers to Freud's "Aus der Geschichte einer Infantilen Neurose" in *Sammlung Kleiner Schriften zur Neurosenlehre*, II. Folge, S. 650f. An attempt to find the article at the place mentioned was not successful.

[315] Oscar Pfister, *The Psychoanalytic Method*, translated by C. R. Payne, New York, 1917), p. 411; also "Anwendung der Psychoanalyse in der Paedagogik und Seelsorge," *Imago*, 1912, p. 76.

[316] Reik, *Der Eigene und der Fremde Gott*, p. 52. Reik says that blasphemy is one of the esteemed purposes of religion. "Es kann schwer geleugnet werden, dass die Religion eine soziale Institution ist, zu deren vornehmsten Zielen auch die Sanktionierung von Gotteslaesterungen gehoert." He instances the recurrence of the Jewish Pantheros in the guise of a Panther and a Barpanther in an accepted genealogy of the Virgin Mary; also the juxtaposition of the Virgin and a thief in the *Dies Irae*:

"Qui latronem exaudisti
Et Mariam absolvisti."

He refers for further elucidation to Freud's *Zwangshandlungen und Religionsuebungen* and *Totem und Tabu*. "Ohne Gotteslaesterung wuerde es kein Gottesdienst geben" (Reik *op. cit.*, p. 224).

[317] Ehrich Fromm, "Der Sabbath," *Imago*, XIII, 225. The reader thinks by contrast of Isa. 40.28, "The creator of the ends of the earth is not weary."

[318] Reik, *Probleme der Religionspsychologie*, p. 157. A pertinent example not mentioned by Reik is the mind wandering of the praying saint cited by James Harvey Robinson, *The Mind in the Making* (New York, 1921), p. 39, foot note.

[319] Reik, *op. cit.*, p. 166.

[320] The case is said to be described in Freud's *Bemerkungen ueber einen Fall von Zwangneurosen.*

[321] Reik, *op. cit.*, p. 158.

to be good but can not." He might also have quoted Rom. 7.15 "Not what I would, that do I practice; but what I hate, that I do"; or Horace:

"Meliora video proboque
Deteriora sequor."

Whether or not Oedipus trends will, as Reik assumes, account for the discrepancy between ideals and practice, the problem so far as religion is concerned is one of paramount importance.

A most amazing application of the Oedipus idea occurs in Reik's treatment of the *Kol Nidre,* a topic to which he devotes forty-five pages.[322] Apparently as much at home in the *Wissenschaft des Judenthums* as in psychoanalysis, Reik appears fully conversant with the literature and all of the theories regarding the *Kol Nidre,* its history and its import. His views are not those of a tyro astounding though they may be.[323] The conclusion he reaches is that the *Kol Nidre* is symbolically an act of sexually motivated patricide.

Underlying this staggering hypothesis is a unique theory with reference to vows. Reik contends that all vows are but derivatives of a certain original primordial vow which related to one thing only and that was the *Urmord.* The sons in the *Urhorde* having slain the father and having subsequently been stricken with remorse resolved never to repeat the deed:[324] at least a mental repetition was always possible. Vestiges of patricide lurk, according to Reik, in the phrases "as God liveth," "by the life of the god," etc. commonly attached to vows.[325] The use of empty skins, the proximity of the dead, etc. when taking oaths also betray, he thinks, a homicidal origin of vows, oaths being but vows to tell the truth.[326]

If vows signify in last analysis respect for the life of the father or of the deity (who is but an apotheosized father), the breaking of vows means a disrespect for that life which, by the

[322] *Probleme der Religionspsychologie,* pp. 432–477.

[323] Greatly to be regretted is the mistranslation *Stimme des Geluebdes* standing parenthetically under the title, *Kol Nidre.* Fortunately the blunder does not recur anywhere in the discussion itself.

[324] *Op. cit.,* p. 155, p. 163.

[325] *Ibid.,* pp. 163, 164.

[326] Reik's word *Eid* applies both to oaths and to vows.

Allmacht der Gedanken, is the patricide or deicide over again. Reik argues that the innumerable prescriptions in Judaism touching the matter of vows indicate a powerful inner tendency to violate vows, with all that such violation implies.[327]

Kol Nidre declaring the abrogation of vows is therefore a reassertion of the patricidal tendency.[328] With this view, according to Reik, the fact comports that the elders of the congregation must formally confer upon the precentor the authority to chant the *Kol Nidre* and that the precentor does not in this as in other instances begin with the invoking of Divine aid. Curiously Reik fails to mention the introductory reference to the *abaryanim*.

There are several reasons why the Atonement service is prefaced by a resurgence of the patricidal urge.

One is the advantage of displaying concretely the sinfulness that requires atonement. God is called upon to notice how desperately forgiveness is needed. "Die Unmoeglichkeit voellig auf Triebefriedigung zu verzichten wird ihm *ad oculos* demonstriert."[329]

Then there is the necessity of providing an outlet for vicious tendencies before the service begins, that there be no sinister eruption of those tendencies during the service itself.[330] The carnival preceding Lent is a parallel.

Beneath it all Reik sees the familiar patterns of neurosis mechanisms[331] in which repressed inclinations break out, are with much remorse and many a fresh resolve "to lead a better life" again repressed, only to break out later and thus in a continuous cycle.[332] Reik is reminded of a neurotic woman who would assiduously clean out a drawer and then dump the dirt back again; "the suppression of the opposing tendency was insufferable."[333]

[327] Reik, *op. cit.*, p. 161.

[328] Karl Abraham, "Der Versoehnungstag," *Imago*, VI, 83, 84. Reik, *op. cit.*, pp. 165, 166.

[329] Reik, *op. cit.*, p. 167.

[330] *Ibid.*, p. 172. Reik sees (p. 177) an analogy to the Catholic *Confiteor* which is also an advance purgation of evil thoughts that may arise during the service.

[331] *Ibid.*, p. 165.

[332] Karl Abraham, "Der Versoehnungstag," *Imago*, VI, 89.

[333] *Ibid.*, pp. 84, 85. The dances of the girls in Ta'anit IV, 8 indicate that the *Kol Nidre* is not the only reassertion of repressed tendencies elicited by the austerities of Yom Kippur.

The use of the indicative instead of the optative in the *Kol Nidre* Reik finds analogous to the wish fulfilments common in dreams and in neurotic fancies.[334]

All of the displacements alleged in his interpretation of the *Kol Nidre* Reik holds to be paralleled in dreams and in jests as well as in neuroses.[335]

In an article "Zur Psychologie der Bundesriten" Gezá Roheim adduces additional anthropological material in support of Reik.[336] Roheim's treatment of vows, oaths, compacts etc. invokes all of the Oedipus factors of our present discussion, namely, incest, the father's antipathy toward the son, the son's antipathy toward the father and—rounding out the ambivalence—the reconciliation between them.

Roheim instances the Bohemian oath form which consists in placing earth on the head and saying, "Mother Earth cover me if I do not tell the truth." He also cites the Wadschagga intertribal compacts at which a youth and a maiden are either buried alive in "Mother Earth" or buried after being cut in two. A regression to the intra-uterine situation is what Roheim thinks these express. Rebirth is symbolized according to Roheim in the covenant ritual of the *ben ha-gezarim* type (Gen. 15.17); by reason of their rebirth from the same mother, the participants become brothers. The miraculous passage of the Hebrews through the Red Sea is, in Roheim's opinion, analogous. He then quotes Jellinek that the beverages drunk at primitive compact makings represent mother's milk. All of these are mother reminiscences, hence incest vestiges.

The factor of paternal hostility toward the son is seen by Roheim in the aforementioned Wadschagga custom of signifying inter-tribal agreements by the slaying of a youth and a maiden.

[334] Reik, *op. cit.*, p. 167.

[335] *Ibid.*, p. 168. Reik cites the case of Freud's patient who said "If I marry that woman, misfortune will befall my father." What the patient really meant was: "If I marry that woman, my father will get angry and I shall wish his death." "Wieder haben wir hier Gelegenheit die grossartige Verschiebenheit unbewusster Tendenzen in der Abloesung von der Urspruenglichen Situation und in der weitgehendsten Verallgemeinerung zu bewundern" (p. 169).

[336] *Imago*, VI, 397.

The father's retaliatory slaughter of his offspring is thereby depicted.

The son's hostility toward the father is displayed in the Samoan custom of dissecting, at oath taking, the image of one of the gods. The slaying of the sacrificial animals on votive occasions is also a simulation of patricide.

Since the passing between the animal pieces typifies rebirth while the animal itself stands for the father, the ritual thus means, among other things, rebirth through the father. This implies, on the part of the son, renunciation of incest and, on the part of the father, the gracious annulment of the son's death and bringing him to life again. In the fact that, among the Wadschagga, it is the weaker party to intertribal compacts that supplies the youthful human victims, lies the thought of a self slaughter of the son or a vicarious slaughter for the son with a self-punitive and therefore conciliatory intent. A mitigated form of youth slaughter is that of circumcising the young persons and—suggestive presumably of vicariousness—drinking the blood mixed with water.

Another manifestation of the anti-paternal attitude is seen in the hostilities and rivalries among religious sects. Reik asserts that hostility toward other religions is but a cover for hostility toward one's own father-god.[337] The rebellion of others against our god is essentially the same as our own rebelliousness. We persecute others as a substitute for persecuting our own recalcitrant selves.[338] Reik claims that hatred and enmity are inseparable from all religions,[339] that religions are tolerant only when they are weak[340] and that the predilection of churches for military talk and imagery is as inevitable as it is notorious.[341]

The controversies between Judaism and Christianity are, in Reik's estimation, especially illustrative of the patricidal trend. Reik surmises two reasons for the animus with which Jesus is

337 Reik, *Der Eigene und der Fremde Gott*, p. 220.

338 *Ibid.*, p. 224.

339 *Ibid.*, p. 223.

340 *Ibid.*, p. 228. The persecuted turn persecutors, and there is "a return of the repressed."

341 *Ibid.*, p. 224, p. 225 foot note.

viewed in Jewish circles. Jesus being in some ways identical with Yahweh, the Jewish hostility toward Jesus is a disguised hostility toward Yahweh.[342] This identity of Yahweh and Jesus is particularly established by the contrast figure of Judas. The relation of Judas to Jesus, Reik thinks, is that of an insurgent son toward an assaulted parent.[343]

In other respects Jesus is himself the insurrectionary son and thus for the Rabbis the embodiment of their own latent rebelliousness.[344] "Unconsciously the Rabbis identify themselves with Jesus, the revolutionary son-god and lover of the mother goddess . . . Their condemnation and contempt can be understood only as a reaction against their own wishes."[345]

There is even a sense in which fidelity to Yahweh can express opposition to the father. Reik holds that Yahweh was himself once a revolutionary son-god.[346] As a "revenant" he can, in relation to Jesus, continue with his insurrectionary role. Reik alleges that in this very aptitude for rebelling against his successor lies one of the reasons why a superceded god tends to become a demon.[347]

Largely similar are the dynamics of Christian hostility toward the Jew. The Jew is hated as the father representative, being the inflicter of circumcision or castration.[348] Reik, as we saw (supra p. 644), pronounces Shylock a castrator; the pound of flesh from a part of the body not mentioned at first but afterward mentioned as the breast exhibits a "*Verschiebung nach oben*."[349]

Again, the Christ whom the Jew opposes, being identical with Yahweh, the father, the Jew in killing Christ is but doing what the Christian unconsciously craves to do. As the Jew punishes himself by assailing the Christian in whom his own

[342] *Ibid.*, pp. 123, 128.

[343] *Ibid.*, p. 129. We might add that in the film "King of Kings," the defection of Judas is represented as being due to Jesus' alienation of Mary Magdalene's affections from Judas.

[344] *Ibid.*, pp. 118, 119, 142.

[345] *Ibid.*, p. 27, p. 119.

[346] *Ibid.*, p. 129, p. 130 foot note.

[347] *Ibid.*, p. 147.

[348] *Ibid.*, p. 210.

[349] *Ibid.*, p. 211.

longings are manifest, the Christian achieves self-punishment for his own deicidal proclivities conversely by harrowing the Jew.[350]

With a curious extreme of subtlety, Reik then works out through many removes of association, the following additional connection between the Christian persecution of the Jew and the Christian patricidal urge:

The Christian in persecuting the Jew voices the charge that the Jew is responsible for the evils of the world. The Jew, being responsible, the Christian is not responsible. The Christian therefore needs no atonement. Christ's atonement is consequently superfluous. In this way is Christ, the father-substitute, disparaged and the dignity, which by a slight remove means the life of the father, assailed.[351]

The charge of ritual murder and of host desecration are only expansions of the crucifixion charge.[352] It all signifies the killing and devouring of the father, a universal craving which either sect punishes in itself by attacking the other sect upon which its own self has been mentally projected.[353]

The precocious piety of R. Nachman of Bratislaw is explained by Jacob Becker also as a symptom of opposition toward the father[354] another indication of such opposition being a remark made by R. Nachman when, in a fit of depression, he observed that he was "leaving for a wilderness to chop down the trees growing there." Trees, we are apprised, are psychoanalytic imagery for the father. Chopping down the trees would thus signify overcoming the father.[355]

An amusing application of the Oedipus concept developes in the observation which Reik makes, no longer in the domain of sectarian fanaticism but in the antipodal domain of Biblical criticism. Reik thinks that the penchant of some scholars for

[350] *Ibid.*, p. 123.

[351] *Ibid.*, p. 202.

[352] *Ibid.*, pp. 128, 129. "Die Anklange des Ritualmordes stellt eine vom unbewussten Schuldbewusstsein diktierte Projektion der Feindseligkeit gegen den eigenen Gott auf einen fremden Stamm vor" (p. 201).

[353] *Ibid.*, p. 201.

[354] *R. Naḥman mi-Braẓlaw*, p. 9.

[355] *Ibid.*, p. 23.

emending *immo* to *abiw* in Gen. 24.67—"And Isaac was comforted for his mother"—arises from an unconscious wish in the academic mind to have the father out of the way and to possess the charming Rebecca.[356]

VI. Conciliation between Father and Son[357]

A. The Father's Friendliness toward the Son

At this juncture we must call to mind again the phenomenon of ambivalence which occupied our attention at the outset. If rivalry for the mother provokes hatred between father and son, other interests conduce to the opposite attitude. The complimentary member of the ambivalence is friendliness, cordiality, affection between father and son.

Not without demonstration of this are the primitive initiation rites studied by Reik. After his ordeal the novice is welcomed into the *Maennerbund*.[358] He is free to marry. Illicit sex desires having been punished and suppressed, legitimate sex gratification is now in place. Between father and son there is now conciliation.[359]

Where circumcision is practiced, the circumcised youth are, as it were, emasculated, feminized[360] and hence the beloved of the fathers.[361] When we considered homosexuality (supra p. 629) we noticed the consequences of this.

Jacob whose incestuous leanings elicited such bitter antagonism from the father or the father-god now receives the paternal or divine blessing. According to one account, the blessing consists

[356] Reik, "Unbewusste Faktoren der Wissenschaftlichen Bibelarbeit," *Imago*, V, 361–363.

[357] Reik might have dwelt upon the etymological resemblance between *Sohn* and *Versoehnung*.

[358] Reik, *Der Eigene und der Fremde Gott*, p. 205.

[359] *Ibid.*, "Nach dieser Schaedigung, durch die dem inzestuoesen Begehren der Juenglinge gewissermassen Einhalt geboten wird, wird der jungen Generation der legale Weg zum Weibe freigegeben." A similar idea in "Jaákobs Kampf," *Imago*, V, 331, 334.

[360] Ernest Jones, *Essays in Applied Psychoanalysis* (London, 1923), p. 430, sees such emasculation in the celibacy, robes and tonsure of the Christian clergy. This applies particularly to the sects that worship Mary in relation to whom incestuous attitudes are a possibility.

[361] Reik, "*Der Eigene und der Fremde Gott*," p. 205.

in change of name, like the new name which, in primitive initiations, the novices receive.[362] The young initiates have presumably been killed and resurrected or reborn. At Beth-El the blessing for Jacob is the promise of fruitfulness[363] as Jacob proceeds to his marriage.[364] With the waning of the hatred that prompted the circumcision, the circumcision is according to Reik taken to be a condition of heightened fertility. Jacob presently becomes reconciled both with Esau and with Laban, his father substitutes.[365] The promised land is conferred upon Jacob because incest suspicions involving "Mother Earth" have now been allayed.[366]

It will be recalled that a similar access to "Mother Earth,"—a legitimate not an illicit one,—is seen by S. Radó in the Fifth Commandment, "in order that thy days may be long on the *adamah* which the Lord, thy God giveth thee" (supra p. 637).[367]

Reik holds that, "I and not an angel, I and not a seraph, I and not a messenger" hagadically interpreting Exod. 12.12 also expresses paternal kindliness particularly in view of those other passages—Exod. 23.20; Num. 26.16—in which the angel substitute does function.[368]

Further explicable from this standpoint are certain features of *Yom Kippur* and certain aspects of the Sabbath:

Yom Kippur which begins with the *Kol Nidre*, the unconscious symbol of patricide, has as its object and sequel forgiveness and reconciliation.[369] Immediately upon the *Kol Nidre* follow the phrases of forgiveness from the Book of Numbers.[370] Finally vocative of the great reconciliation, the *Ne'ilah* at the end of the day brings the declaration that God is one.[371] "The covenant has been restored;" says Karl Abraham, "the slain father-God is acknowledged anew by His sons and He in turn resumes His obligations toward His children."[372]

[362] Reik, "Jaákobs Kampf," *Imago*, V, 333, 334. [363] *Ibid.*, pp. 338, 343.

[364] *Ibid.*, p. 337. In his "Kainzeichen," *Imago*, V, 31–42, Reik overlooks the possibility of a similar interpretation of Cain's marriage.

[365] *Ibid.*, p. 339. [366] *Ibid.*, p. 334.

[367] Rado, "Das feunfte Gebot," *Imago*, IX, 129.

[368] Reik, *Der Eigene und der Fremde Gott*, p. 146.

[369] Reik, *Probleme der Religionspsychologie*, p. 167.

[370] Num. 15.26; 14.19, 20. [371] Reik, *op. cit.*, p. 89.

[372] Karl Abraham, "Der Versoehnungstag," *Imago*, VI, 89.

As regards the Sabbath, the note of paternal cordiality appears in the transformation of the Sabbath from a *dies nefas* to a day of joy.[373] Ehrich Fromm thinks that this occurred at a time when the omission of a day's work was no longer economically perilous.[374] A Sabbath of Puritan gloom then gives way to a Sabbath of Hassidic gaiety.[375] We have already observed how Paradise and the Messianic Age become associated with the Sabbath and how these stood for re-established harmony between man and nature.[376] They also stood for immunity from work—that work which originally penalized a dereliction connected with sex[377] (supra p. 637).

B. THE SON'S FRIENDLINESS TOWARD THE FATHER

Far more extensive is the variety of religious manifestations derived from the genial factors in the son's feelings toward the father. The theory is that after the primordial patricide the kindlier filial sentiments reasserted themselves.[378] In the very act of eating the slain father some notion of appropriating his admired powers is alleged to have been operative.[379] For the hideous deed there supervenes a sense of guilt and a process of self-punishment that has left its imprint upon religion in many ways.[380]

[373] Ehrich Fromm, "Der Sabbath," *Imago*, XIII, 227. This author quotes Isa. 58.15 and *Oraḥ Ḥayyim* 260, 262, 280, 287, 288, 290, 328, 329. He might have noted in addition the sex implications of 262 and 280.

[374] Fromm, *op. cit.*, p. 229.

[375] *Ibid.*, p. 234.

[376] *Ibid.*, p. 225.

[377] *Ibid.*, p. 233. According to Lorenz, just as the confusion of tongues for the attempt to build the Tower of Babel represents castration, so does the glossalalia of the Christian Pentecost and of other glossalalia myths stand for the remedying of the castration. Cf. supra pp. 644, 648.

[378] Reik, *Probleme der Religionspsychologie*, p. 155. Freud "*Totem und Tabu*, p. 132.

[379] Reik, *Der Eigene und der Fremde Gott*, p. 202. There is some parallel here to the supposition that eating the forbidden fruit of Paradise would make the eater resemble the gods. Cf. Ehrich Fromm, "Der Sabbath," *Imago*, XIII, 226.

[380] Abraham, "Der Versoehnungstag," *Imago*, VI, 84. Reik, *Probleme der Religionspsychologie*, pp. 163, 174, 176. *Der Eigene und der Fremde Gott*, p. 201.

Various religious acts of silence for instance—would Reik have included our own silent devotions?—are said to have implied originally an emulative imitation of the dead father and at the same time a punitive self-slaying. Reik dilates upon this in his interpretation of the passage, "All the earth keep silent before Him."[381] Reik instances a clinical case of aphasia in which a patient whose voice became fainter and fainter and finally extinct was found upon analysis to be symbolically putting herself to death in self-punishment for certain mentally committed derelictions.

Fasting as a religious act is similarly viewed. Fasting is a negation of the eating of the father.[382] The taboo of the thigh tendon is also traced by Reik to that hypothetical patrophagy, especially in view of the sexual implications of the thigh tendon and the sexual occasion of the murder.[383]

Indeed asceticism in all of its forms is said to belong here.[384]

Another species of self-punishment is circumcision (castration), a doing to one's self what one's father, goaded by jealousy, would do to one.[385] Variations and derivatives of circumcision are not only the pulling out of hair and the knocking out of teeth but also, according to Reik, rituals as modern as baptism, communion and the *Seder*.[386]

Reik further understands the mark of Cain to have been such a punitive circumcision.[387] He is sustained by Biblical evidence of circumcision among the Kenites[388] as well as by the psychoanalytic doctrine, illustrated by the Cain-Abel story, that a brother can be a father-substitute (supra pp. 638, 649).

The self-execrations conditionally expressed in vows and

[381] Reik, "Die Bedeutung des Schweigens," *Imago*, V, 357. The Biblical passages are Hab. 2.20; Zeph. 1.7; Zech. 2.17.

[382] Ehrich Fromm, "Der Sabbath," *Imago*, XIII, 232.

[383] Reik, "Jaákobs Kampf," *Imago*, V, 341.

[384] Reik, *Der Eigene und der Fremde Gott*, p. 224 foot note.

[385] Freud, *Totem und Tabu*, p. 141.

[386] Reik, *op. cit.*, p. 218.

[387] Reik, "Das Kainzeichen," *Imago*, V, 41.

[388] Reik refers to the Biblical passages, Judg. 1.16; Exod. 4.24, 28. He surmises that Saul may for this reason have spared the Kenites (I Sam. 15.6). Reik refers to H. Zeydner, *Kainzeichen, Keniter und Beschneidung*, p. 120.

oaths are also, according to Reik, vestiges of the identical self-punishments. Reik reports analogous manifestations in the neuroses.[389]

A large element of self-punishment for patricide or for patricidal wishes is discerned by Ehrich Fromm in the various Jewish Sabbath stringencies. The Sabbath, Fromm recalls, is not unrelated to the Babylonian *dies nefas* and to Atonement Day. The very act of abstention from work involves a risk of privation. Fromm instances the prohibition of cooking, baking, leaving the house, kindling fire,[390] fighting, plucking grain, healing of slight ailments, cutting,[391] the use of cosmetics,[392] touching of implements etc. as well as the prohibition of cohabitation[393] with all that this implies relative to incest; and the identity of these restrictions with mourning limitations.[394] The death penalty for violations brings the Sabbath signally within the range of "measure for measure."[395]

On Atonement Day not only is eating foregone in expiation of having eaten the father; cohabitation also is forbidden in reminiscence presumably of the incest longings in which the conflict originated.[396] Karl Abraham regards as particularly relevant the reading of the incest passages from Leviticus at the services of Atonement morning.[397] On the Sabbath, as we saw, the work chiefly avoided was that of *'abodah*, plowing (supra p. 637), the incest symbolism of which we duly noted.[398] Circumcision, the substitute for castration is obviously related to incest.

389 Reik, *Probleme der Religionspsychologie*, pp. 154, 156.

390 Ehrich Fromm, "Der Sabbath," *Imago*, XIII, 226. The references are Exod. 16.23, 29; 35.3.

391 His reference is I Macc. 2.32; II Macc. 5.25; 6.11.

392 Sabbath X, 6.

393 Jubilees 50. 8, also the Karaitic view attacked by Ibn Ezra on Exod. 34.21 "*beḥarish ubakaẓir tishbot.*"

394 Fromm., *op. cit.*, p. 223.

395 His reference is Exod. 35.2.

396 Fromm., *op. cit.*, p. 232. See *Rabbi Burns* by Aben Kandel (New York 1931): "I'm afraid I'll have to look up a wench later on," continued Adam. "You know—there's something erotic about Yom Kippur. I first became conscious of passion on that day. I guess the Day of Atonement is an aphrodisiac."

397 Karl Abraham, "Der Versoehnungstag," *Imago*, VI, 86.

398 Fromm., *op. cit.*, pp. 225, 226, 234.

When we read in Reik's "Das Kainzeichen" that "the mutilation of the sex organ is a punishment for those incestuous wishes that precipitated the fratricide"[399] we must keep in view the legend about the rivalry of Cain and Abel over their sister and, once again, the psychoanalytic theory that sister can be a mother-substitute as brother can be a father-substitute.

We must also consider what Jacob Becker says about the son-toward-father cordiality of R. Nachman of Bratislaw. Becker relates to the Oedipus symptoms previously discussed[400] (supra pp. 641, 647, 656) the ascetic practices of R. Nachman. R. Nachman's distress at and disparagement of sex relations[401] are, in Freudian theory, signs of incestuous fixation and self-punishment for the fixation.[402]

We have been apprised that our persecution of others can be a disguised persecution of our own rebellious selves[403] and that Christian persecution of the Jews amounts to a Christian self-punishment just as Jewish antagonism to Christians can be a Jewish self-punishment.[404] Unconsciously identifying himself with his victims Torquemada, says Reik, was the chief heretic sought by Torquemada.[405] Internecine contentions among the Jews or among the Christians themselves have often the same import.[406] We have already heard (supra p. 631) that the Jews were even so masochistic as to desire persecution[407] and that their conduct did much to invite persecution;[408] all by way of self-punishment for patricidal or deicidal memories or impulses.[409] The last word

[399] Reik, "Das Kainzeichen," *Imago*, V, 41. Reference is made here to Rank and Sachs, *Die Bedeutung der Psychoanalyse fuer die Geisteswissenschaft*, p. 44.

[400] Becker, *R. Naḥman mi-Braẓlaw*, p. 23.

[401] *Ibid.*, p. 12.

[402] *Ibid.*, p. 13. It was not possible to find this point in Freud's *Ges. Schr.* VII, p. 27, referred to by Becker.

[403] Reik, *Der Eigene und der Fremde Gott*, pp. 123, 128, 224, 256. Elsewhere (p. 201), Reik explains that one's own hate for the god is projected upon others and then those others punished because of one's love for the god.

[404] *Ibid.*, pp. 124, 125.

[405] *Ibid.*, p. 226. [406] *Ibid.*, p. 120.

[407] *Probleme der Religionspsychologie*, p. 303.

[408] Reik, *Der Eigene und der Fremde Gott*, p. 236.

[409] *Ibid.*, p. 227.

concerning religious persecution may thus be self-punishment for the primordial patricide or for the never uprooted patricidal desire.[410]

The vicarious atonement doctrine everywhere bears intimations of a restitution for the all overshadowing "*Vatermord*."[411] In old Mexican initiation rituals a youth would be killed.[412] Elsewhere child sacrifice or its attenuation in the form of circumcision prevailed; all of which represents vicarious compensation for the patricide which youth committed primordially or psychically.[413] Reik sees the same notion in the death of the mother lovers, Attis, Adonis and Tammuz.[414] The Christian Christ is of course the best known instance,[415] although Moses in Exodus likewise offers himself vicariously.[416] Freud ascribes an identical sense to the suffering hero in Greek tragedy[417] as Reik does to Shakespeare's Antonio who is in relation to his friends like a son-god assuming the guilt of his brothers.[418] The ritual murder phantasy, Reik thinks, belongs also to this pattern.[419] A child, substituting for the son-god, is slain and its blood supposedly eaten in *mazzot*.[420] The *mazzot* themselves can, like the eucharist, be the equivalent of a son-deity in whose consumption the devouring of the father-god obtains vicarious retribution.[421]

Further manifestations of the son's cordiality lie in the various attempts at averting patricidal outbreaks. We have seen how, according to Reik (supra p. 651) all vows are derivatives of a prototype vow never to repeat the patricide.[422] A repudiation

[410] It must at no time be overlooked that by the "*Allmacht der Gedanken*," the desire to kill is, in psychoanalysis, the same as actual killing.

[411] Reik, *Der Eigene und der Fremde Gott*, p. 200.

[412] *Ibid.*, p. 202.

[413] *Ibid.*, p. 218.

[414] *Ibid.*, p. 141.

[415] *Ibid.*, p. 120.

[416] Reik, *Probleme der Religionspsychologie*, p. 285. The reference is to Exod. 32.32.

[417] Freud, *Totem und Tabu*, p. 144.

[418] Reik, *Der Eigene und der Fremde Gott*, pp. 210–213.

[419] *Ibid.*, p. 203.

[420] *Loc. cit.*

[421] *Ibid.*, p. 202.

[422] Reik, *Probleme der Religionspsychologie*, pp. 155, 163.

of patricide is therefore the sense of the strong Jewish compunctions about vow fulfilment as also of the extensive casuistry by which the impulse to violate vows is combatted or circumvented.[423] Special precautions against vows seem to have been needed during the Jewish penitential season. In the sixteenth century the taking of vows and oaths during the ten days of penitence was specifically forbidden.[424] Times of repression are precisely the times when the danger of outbreak is greatest.[425]

In the *Kol Nidre*, as we saw, the outbreak actually occurs.[426] The *Kol Nidre* verbs in the past tense are understood by Reik to signify an eagerness to terminate the period of peril and suspense.[427] Both Reik and Abraham[428] view the insertion which throws the discourse into future time as a "*Vorbeugungsmassregel*"—an act of averting outbreaks yet to come.[429] In neuropathology, we are informed, such time transpositions are familiar.

Another way of making amends to the father is that of rejecting the son.[430] Reik claims that the Jews would tolerate a Messiah only so long as he remained a phantasy,[431] exactly as individuals toy with fancies whose realization they would find abhorrent. The Messiah, Christ, received the hostile trends of the ambivalence toward the father while Yahweh received the affectionate ones.[432] Corresponding to Yahweh, the adored and

[423] *Ibid.*, p. 311, p. 165. We may recall that Quakers decline altogether to take oaths.

[424] *Ibid.*, p. 170.

[425] Reik instances the case of the reservations that would be attached to her vows by a neurotic woman who was in the habit of vowing by the life of her husband and then of becoming seized with an obsession to violate her vows.

[426] "Der Kol Nidre ist der periodisch wiederholte Versuch sich von der Last dieses Zwanges durch einen einzigen gewaltsamen Akt zu befreien. Auf den Exzess musste dann die Busse und die Neuerrichtung des Bundes folgen" (Karl Abraham, "Der Versoehnugstag," *Imago*, VI, 85).

[427] "Die Verschiebung auf das vergangene Jahr liegt durchaus im Sinne der zwangneurotischen Symptome und ist durch die Ausdehnung der Erwartungsangst motiviert" (Reik, "*Probleme der Religionspsychologie*," p. 170).

[428] Abraham, "Der Versoehnungstag," *Imago*, VI, 86.

[429] The word is Karl Abraham's.

[430] Reik, *Probleme der Religionspsychologie*, p. 283. "*Der Eigene und der Fremde Gott*, pp. 32, 33.

[431] *Der Eigene und der Fremde Gott*, p. 120.

[432] *Ibid.*, p. 121.

Jesus, the hated among the Jews was Jesus, the adored and Judas, the hated among the Christians; Judas, as we have already heard, being a kind of son-substitute in relation to Jesus (supra p. 655).

Reik thinks he glimpses indications that in prehistoric times the Hebrews faced an alternative between loyalty to a hated father-god or to a revolutionary son-god. By an "*Affektumkehr*" the choice was eventually in favor of the father-god.[433] The result was an elimination and rejection of son-gods from Judaism, precisely as in the life of the individual amnesia is the fate of that which is repudiated with vigor.[434]

To friendliness toward the father is also attributed the regulation forbidding the use of iron at altar building[435] and the custom of pouring blood upon the altar.[436] It was believed that the deity resided in the altar and that iron would wound the deity. The blood on the altar was nourishment for the deity.

Reik reads an overcompensation for the injury done the father in the New Testament charge that the Jews adorned the graves of the prophets whom they had slain.[437]

Eventually there is the resurrection of Christ, the substitute for the slain father who thus in phantasy comes to life again,[438] while the homage accorded Christ, the father-substitute, is homage to the father.[439] Similarly at the *Ne'ilah*, as Karl Abraham has told us (supra p. 658), "the slain father-god is acknowledged anew by his children" in the declaration that God is one.[440]

433 *Ibid.*, p. 32.

434 Reik gives an example of such amnesia in the case of the young woman mentioned supra p. 628 who in her revulsion toward her own sexual desires, came to forget the name "Ben Hur." Reik says: "Das Herausdraengen des Sohnesgottes aus dem Judenthum entspricht indessen ebenso wie das Vergessen des Romantitels seitens der jungen Dame der Abweisung der staerksten eigenen Wuensche" (p. 28).

435 Exod. 20.25.

436 *Probleme der Religionspsychologie*, p. 308.

437 *Der Eigene und der Fremde Gott*, p. 124. The reference is to Matt. 23.29–31.

438 Ehrich Fromm, "Der Sabbath," *Imago*, XIII, 233.

439 Reik, *op. cit.*, p. 201.

440 Karl Abraham, "Der Versoehnungstag," *Imago*, VI, 89.

VII. Amalgamations

Before leaving this phase of our subject it may be well to stop and admit that our dissecting of the Oedipus Complex into the trends discussed above was, though necessary, not without precariousness. Often a number of opposing trends amalgamate in the production of one and the same act.

The primitive eating of the father, we saw, combined in one act the hatred that annihilates and the admiration that would incarnate and emulate. Reik mentions specifically the Jewish Paschal meal and the Christian Eucharist as rites in which, by original implication, the honoring of the father is merged with the eating of the father.[441] Persecution can be at one and the same time a persecuting of one's self and a persecuting of one's opponents. The persecutor abuses his own god even while he abuses the enemies of his god.[442]

Theological and ritual casuistries are, according to Reik, specimens of the same tendency. In them, belief and disbelief, hostility and devotion are inextricably tangled and relentlessly in conflict.[443] Similarly with "a return of the repressed out of the repressing" do patricidal and anti-patricidal urges mingle in oaths[444] (supra pp. 651, 652).

The defiant words of the *Kol Nidre* are wedded to a melody which, with ineffable grace, expresses submission and repentance.[445] This conflict of tendencies is, in Reik's opinion, at the bottom of the sobbing and other demonstrations of emotion by which the Orthodox singing of the *Kol Nidre* is customarily attended.[446]

The crucifixion, Reik holds, represents not only the expiation

[441] Reik, *op. cit.*, pp. 202, 203.

[442] *Ibid.*, p. 222.

[443] Reik, "Dogma und Zwangsidee," *Imago*, XIII, 292, 296, 297, 378.

[444] Reik, *Probleme der Religionspsychologie*, p. 162. Reik thinks in this connection of a picture by Rops in which there appears to a praying monk in the place of a crucifix the vision of a voluptuous woman.

[445] Karl Abraham, "Der Versoehnungstag," *Imago*, VI, 81.

[446] "Im individuellen Seelenleben vollziehen sich dieselben aufwuehlenden und nachhaltigen Kaempfe die in der Geschichte des Volkes den Anstoss zu grossen, religioesen, sittlichen und sozialen Einrichtungen lieferten (*Probleme der Religionspsychologie*, p. 169).

of the patricide but also a repetition thereof;[447] while angels, he surmises, embody a comprise between a god that reigns and a god that is dethroned and demonized.[448]

Into this discussion also we can best place a number of observations offered concerning R. Nachman of Bratislaw. R. Nachman's visual[449] and auditory[450] hallucinations are asserted by Becker to have been such as Freud finds symptomatic of repression connected with longings that are adultrous and incestuous. Such particularly is believed by Becker to have been the nature of R. Nachman's "great and fearful trials"[451] attending his struggles against certain sex propensities. Other symptoms were such events in R. Nachman's career as his sudden and inexplicable wanderings to Medzibocz, to Kaminitz and to Palestine,[452] his frivolous deportment at Stamboul en route to Palestine,[453] his epileptic fit at the grave of R. Naphtali[454] and his revulsion of feeling toward Palestine the moment he arrived there. All of this is interpreted by Becker as indicative of the unconscious promptings connected with Oedipus trends and their concommitant repression.

Rank and Sachs contend that religion is such a body of compromises exclusively.[455]

VIII. Totemism—Incest

All that has thus far been said is supplemented and complicated by a set of striking totemistic phenomena,—that is phenomena involving the identification of men and of gods with animals.

[447] Reik, *Der Eigene und der Fremde Gott*, p. 128. [448] *Ibid.*, p. 147.

[449] Jacob Becker, *R. Naḥman mi-Braẓlaw*, p. 11. It was not possible to locate this in Freud's *Ges. Schr.* V, p. 463, referred to by Becker.

[450] *Ibid.*, p. 12. [451] *Ibid.*, p. 11. [452] *Ibid.*, p. 21.

[453] The reader is reminded of the frivolous conduct of Friar Juniper in "The Little Flowers of St. Francis."

[454] Becker, *op. cit.*, p. 21.

[455] "All the religious practices as compromise products have a double face; their effect consists in the facilitation of the renunciation of the gratification of socially hostile instincts; their essence lies in their allowing partly merely in the myth creating phantasy, partly by cultistic and ritualistic practice, the forbidden acts represented in the phantasy." (Rank and Sachs, *The Significance of Psychoanalysis for the Mental Sciences* [New York, 1916], p. 70.)

We are told that, like our own children, primitive people regard animals as the equals and the kindred of men, readily conceiving themselves as descended from animals and of animals as incarnating the souls of the human departed.[456] Much in Judaism has been interpreted totemistically.[457] Attention is called to such names as Caleb, Rachel, Leah, Deborah, Jonah, Hamor, Tola, Zippor—in all, fifty-three names of animals which are used in the Bible as personal or as clan names.[458]

An example to which we shall have frequent occasion to refer is the *shofar*. The horn of an animal, Reik tells us, can represent the father or the god into which the father evolved; because originally the re-incarnated father or the god was an animal possessing horns and the horn is the part for the whole.[459] Reik recalls that horned figures of the gods have been unearthed in Babylonian excavations.[460] The moon was in antiquity conceived of as a horned being and as a god; and the phases exhibited by the moon were the original determinants of the Jewish Sabbath.[461] Resembling the cases of Triton, Heimdall, Brahma, the sound of the horn is in certain Biblical passages treated not as a representation of the deity's voice but as that voice itself.[462] Reik dwells extensively upon the curious wording in Exod. 19.13, "*bimeshok ha-yobel hemmah ya'alu bahar.*"[463] It is the *yobel*, the ram that makes the sound when Yahweh makes the sound. The sound of the animal's horn and the sound of its voice are of course

[456] Freud, "*Totem und Tabu,*" 1913, pp. 117–122.

[457] Freud (*op. cit.*, p. 126) quotes Robertson Smith, *Religion of the Semites* (1907), p. 412, that the Semites had totem sacrifices which consisted in killing and eating the totem animal. That point however does not stand on p. 412 of the 1907 edition of Smith's work.

[458] Reik, *Probleme der Religionspsychologie*, p. 232.

[459] *Ibid.*, p. 215. Reik calls the horn "eine Resterscheinung des urspruenglichen goettlichen Totems."

[460] Frieda Fromm-Reichmann, "Das juedische Speiseritual," *Imago*, XIII, 240.

[461] Ehrich Fromm, "Der Sabbath," *Imago*, XIII, 227.

[462] Reik, *op. cit.*, pp. 205, 206. The Biblical references are Zech. 9.14; Isa. 27.13; Rev. 1.10. This already shows an elevation over the Yahweh who does not blow the horn but who bellows like a beast.

[463] Reik, *op. cit.*, p. 202. Reik notices that Baentsch ascribes the passage to E1 and the context to E2 and (we may add) to J.

easily equated. When people hear the horn they hear Yahweh.[464] The signal given by the horn is the signal given by Yahweh. The sound of the horn is not that alongside of which but that *in* which Yahweh speaks. Nor is this the only Biblical passage in which the deity is identified with a horned animal, especially the ram.[465] In the ritual—such is Karl Abraham's probably erroneous statement—one may not look upon the blower of the horn just as one may not, without risking death, look upon Yahweh.[466]

We shall now follow our former scheme of arraying the several factors of the Oedipus situation in the order: Incest Longings, Father's Hostility toward the Son, Son's Hostility toward the Father, Father's Friendliness toward the Son, Son's Friendliness toward the Father.

Totemistic incest implications have been attributed to the following: The *Shofar*, the halo, the law regarding unclean animals, the law against seething the calf in its mother's milk, the law about letting the mother bird go free.

The *Shofar* is connected with sex and with incest in a number of ways:

1. The horn is an instrument of sound and psychoanalysts have long observed a unique connection between sex and sound. Neurotics sometimes whisper and become afflicted with aphasia because unconsciously they associate, with speaking, sexual license.[467] The mouth zones whence sounds issue are inseparable from the sexual demonstrations of kissing and of breast sucking.[468]

464 Reik, *op. cit.*, pp. 205–207.

465 Reference is made to Amos 1.2; Num. 23.22. Yahweh is called "*Abir Ja'akob*" in Gen. 49.24; Isa. 1.24; 49.26; 60.16; Ps. 132.2, 5. "Wenn der Gott, der urspruenglich von den Juden verehrt wurde, der Stier oder der Widder war, verstehen wir warum seine Stimme aus dem Horne eines Widders toent" (Reik, *op. cit.*, pp. 207, 208). Reference is also made to Scheftelowitz, *Das Hoernermotiv in den Religionen*, p. 450.

466 "Bezeichnend ist der von Strenggläubigen eingehaltene Gebrauch den Blick vom Schofarblaeser abzuwenden" (Karl Abraham "Der Versoehnungstag," *Imago*, VI, 87. Cf. also pp. 88–89). It has not been possible to verify this assertion.

467 Reik, *Probleme der Religionspsychologie*, p. 217. Supra p. 660 concerning the neurotic woman whose voice grew progressively fainter.

468 Abraham in *Internationale Zeitschrift fuer Aertzliche Psychoanalyse* IV, 1916, 2. The article is on page 74.

To the technique of love making, singing and serenading belong.[469] Reik recalls the German phrase, "*einer Dame ansprechen*."[470] He might have added the Hebrew phrase "*dabber el leb*."[471] Before Reik, Storfer had observed that words *spoken* to Mary at the annunciation resulted in her pregnancy.[472]

2. The horn is further related to sex by reason of its resemblance to the male organ of sex.[473]

3. The horn is also unconsciously regarded as an instrument of castration, the presumed punishment for derelictions of sex. Thus neurotic children have a fear of being butted by some animal.[474] The child interprets sexual intercourse as a castration of the mother by the sex organ of the father.

4. The horn also stands for strength, then specifically for sexual strength and ultimately for the strength to impregnate the mother.[475] Blowing the horn thus signifies, through many removes of association, the committing of incest.[476]

Halos, aureoles etc. are refinements of horns evolving out of the resemblance of horns to the sun's rays both in appearance and as embodiments of power—ultimately, of course, of sex power.[477] Mediaeval art displays the transition from horns to rays when, with two rays emanating from his head, God, the father is pictured.

[469] Reik, *op. cit.*, p. 211.

[470] *Ibid.*, p. 217.

[471] Cf. George Adam Smith *Commentary on Isa.* 40.2. A similar use of *dabber el leb* in Gen. 34.3; Ruth 2.13. The use is non-sexual in Gen. 50.21 and in II Chron. 32.6.

[472] Storfer, *Marias jungfraueliche Mutterschaft*, p. 84.

[473] "Es ist als Sexualsymbol stellvertretend fuer das maennliche Genitale" (Reik, *Probleme der Religionspsychologie*, p. 215).

[474] *Ibid.*, p. 216. "Butt," we may add, is an American pornophemy.

[475] *Ibid.*, p. 209 and Scheftelowitz, *op. cit.*, p. 456.

[476] "Wenn nun die Glaeubigen . . . sich des Hornes des Totemtieres bemaechtigen, so entspricht dies der Durchsetzung jenes unbewussten Wunsches, sich in Besitz des grossen Penis des Vaters zu setzen, sich seine sexuelle Kraefte anzueignen" (Reik, *op. cit.*, p. 217). "Wir glauben dass dies in erster Linie auf die symbolische Penisbedeutung des Hornes zurueckzufuehren ist, die ja auch das horntragende Tier urspruenglich zur Vater-Imago im Sinne des Totemismus besonders geeignet gemacht hat" (p. 239).

[477] *Ibid.*, p. 264.

According to Frieda Fromm-Reichmann, incest motives figure likewise in the Biblical distinction between clean and unclean. She argues that the clean species are those that have horns or horn-like substances such as fins or scales or are capable of having such.[478] The circumstance that this is not stated in the text but is rather circumlocuted and concealed is to her additional evidence of a sex import, inasmuch as sex invites concealment.

Frieda Fromm-Reichmann brings as evidence some striking clinical observations. She tells of a young man reared in an Orthodox Jewish home who confessed that the sight of forbidden meat aroused in him sexual reactions.[479] There would be erection, palpitation, swift breathing etc. and then subsequent to the eating of the forbidden food a relaxation like that following *coitus*. A woman patient twenty years of age similarly experienced sexual excitement when eating food of the kind spurned by her Orthodox Jewish parents, although violation of other ritual requirements left her unaffected. "These examples" says Frieda Fromm-Reichmann, "show that the unconscious intent of the dietary code was to prevent incest."

Frieda Fromm-Reichmann's theories would carry more plausibility if the horned animals were not the permitted ones but the forbidden ones. We could then interpret: The horn represents the sex power of the father. We are forbidden to appropriate that power.

However, the logic of the unconscious is erratic. Perhaps we should understand that the limiting of the dietary to certain species signifies a limit imposed upon incestuous tendencies, while the factor of horns designates that incest is the thing subject to the limitation.

Frieda Fromm-Reichmann herself believes that the dietary laws must be viewed in connection with the prohibition of blood eating.[480] Since blood is omitted from the dietary the essential, the "life," is omitted. The eating of the horned animal thus

[478] Frieda Fromm-Reichmann, "Das juedische Speiseritual," *Imago*, XIII, 239.

[479] *Ibid.*, p. 240.

[480] *Ibid.*, p. 241. The Bible passages are Lev. 3.17; 7.26, 27; 17.10ff.; Deut. 14.21.

becomes innocuous. Since the eating of horned creatures is innocuous, the eating of all others must be sexually obnoxious.

"Thou shalt not seethe the calf in its mother's milk" is also declared to be a prohibition of incest.[481] It is construed to mean: "thou, the son, i.e. the calf, shalt not cohabit with thy mother." "So begeht man das Urverbrechen des Inzests."

Finally laden with the same implication is the law in Deuteronomy, "Thou shalt not take the dam with the young."[482] "To take" in Hebrew means to wed, hence to cohabit. The verse thus connotes, according to Frieda Fromm-Reichmann, "Thou shalt not cohabit with thy mother."[483] The promise of prosperity and long life is a point of resemblance between this command and the Fifth Commandment.[484] That the unconscious sense of the Fifth Commandment was incest prohibition, we have already been told by Radó (supra pp. 637, 638.

IX. Totemism—Hostility between Father and Son

A. HOSTILITY OF THE FATHER TOWARD THE SON

Extremely rich in totemistic implications of the father's hostility toward the son is the *Shofar*.

First there is the copious association of the *Shofar* with death. The *Shofar* is blown on Rosh Ha-Shanah when the heavenly decision is rendered for life or for death.[485] There was a time when the *Shofar* would be blown to announce the death of eminent Rabbis. Like the Roman *tuba* it would be blown at funerals.[486] Suggestions of death lurk also, Reik thinks, in the Maimonidean homily that the *Shofar* awakens the sleeping; sleep is a familiar equivalent of death.[487]

[481] *Ibid.*, pp. 241, 242. The passages are Exod. 23.19; 34.26; Deut. 14.21. Frieda Fromm-Reichmann thus ventures an answer where Karl Abraham (*Imago*, VI, 88) declares himself unable to answer.

[482] Deut. 22.6, 7.

[483] Frieda Fromm-Reichmann, *op. cit.*, pp. 242, 243.

[484] The author might have made some use of the story in Kid. 39b involving both of these passages.

[485] Reik, *Probleme der Religionspsychologie*, pp. 220, 241.

[486] *Ibid.*, p. 189. Moed Katon 27b speaks of the use of the Shofar to announce a death in the community.

[487] *Ibid.*, p. 242.

Again the *Shofar* is associated with danger and terror. It would be sounded to give alarm upon the approach of the enemy.[488] Excommunication would be proclaimed by its blast. Awe-inspiring it resounds at the Sinaic theophany.[489]

Reik sees numerous resemblances between the *Shofar* and the bull roarer of certain primitive tribes. Like the bull roarer the *Shofar*, by the paucity of its tones, shows its primitiveness.[490] As the bull roarer is preserved in the tribal *Maennerhaus*, the *Shofar* is preserved in the synagogue or Temple. The bull-roarer is used among aborigines to frighten the young novitiates at their initiation.[491] It simulates the thunderous voice of the Balum monster or of some dead ancestor.[492] At Sinai the Hebrews, frightened by the *Shofar* were in the position of initiates who are being inducted into the *Maennerbund*.[493] As the *Shofar* has been associated with death and resurrection, the initiatory rites of aborigines are, in Frazer's words, "the ritual of the death and the resurrection."[494] Reik surmises back of all of this a warning against incestuous and patricidal impulses just as to the child

[488] *Ibid.*, p. 186. We may supply the note that all of the shofar passages are assembled in the Michael Sachs Machsor for Rosh Ha-Shanah, Berlin 1860, pp. 180–182.

[489] Reik, *op. cit.*, p. 188. The correct Talmudic references are Moed Katon 16a, San. 7b and Raschi to the latter passage.

[490] Reik, *op. cit.*, p. 184. To-day's shofar, being unornamented is, according to Cyrus Adler, more primitive than the shofar of the Mishnah.

[491] Reik, *op. cit.*, p. 240.

[492] *Ibid.*, p. 239.

[493] "Ein gutes Pendant dieses Vorganges bietet die Maennerweihe der Wilden, in der die Vertreter der Vatergenerationen in der Vermummung als Totemtiere die Juenglinge erschrecken und sich durch diese Gestalt den Gehorsam der Juenglinge erzwingen" (*ibid.*, p. 268). Reik reports (p. 242) how "bei den Minankabos von Sumatra wie oft bei den anderen Staemmen das Schwirholz aus dem Stirnbein eines Mannes, der wegen seiner Tapferkeit beruehmt war, angefertigt wird. Vom Stirnbein eines Mannes zu einem Widderhorn ist kein groesserer Abstand als von einem Anthropomorphen Gott zu dem alten Totemgott." From the totem sounds connected with the bull roarer various other ritual sounds employed at initiations were derived such as banging, flute tones (p. 243), roaring (p. 244), drumming and, as in Thrace, rattling. The Dionysian rhombus was a bull roarer. The bull roarer is an extensively used ritual object as well as toy (p. 238).

[494] *Ibid.*, pp. 241, 242.

the voice of the father is a threat of punishment for its misdeeds.[495]

Bad luck is said to result from the faulty blowing of the *Shofar*. Reik thinks that the inhibition to which faulty blowing is due has some relation to the patricidal tendency which provokes the father's retaliation.[496]

The mask worn by Moses is construed by Reik as a variation of the horn. The mask represents the skin of the totem. Meanwhile it is closely related to the horns attributed to Moses by the Vulgate and by Michaelangelo and to the dazzling rays derivative from horns. The wearing of the mask, we shall presently learn, is one of the several ways in which Moses identifies himself with Yahweh. Now the function of the mask is not to accommodate the onlookers as the text in Exodus says but to frighten. Children are alarmed at masks even though they know who is behind. The mask of Moses is thus also an instance of *pater* or *deus terrificans*.[497]

We have noticed the equation of the earth or the land and the mother (supra pp. 619, 637, 638). The circumstance that Moses is kept from entering the land of promise shows how he has been guilty of incestuous longings or approaches and how a vindictive father slays him in retaliation.[498]

Finally, the fish that swallows Jonah is suspected of being a variant of a totem god that eats his own offspring.[499] Modern psychiatry is conversant with the animal phobias of children and with children's fears of being bitten, gored or eaten.[500] We are

[495] *Ibid.*, p. 220.

[496] *Ibid.*, p. 222. May we not add that the ancient Hebrew teachers may have known something about unconscious inhibitions? A remarkable instance is the praying of R. Ḥanina ben Dosa (Ber. V, 5).

[497] Reik, *op. cit.*, p. 266. I once observed two boys competing with one another in an endurance test that was to determine which could keep silent for the longest period at a stretch. In the course of the ordeal the boys donned masks. There also appeared to be involved some masochistic self-infliction. This combination of silence (death ?), mask (intimidation ?) and masochism (sex ?) strangely suggests the usual Freudian synthesis.

[498] Reik, *op. cit.*, p. 287.

[499] Karl Abraham, "Der Versoehnungstag," *Imago*, VI, 86.

[500] Reik, *Der Eigene und der Fremde Gott*, p. 204. Freud, "*Totem und Tabu*," pp. 117–122.

told that "an unconscious fear of castration is at the root of these infantile apprehensions,"[501] the animal being a substitute for the exasperated parent to the child as to the savage.[502]

B. HOSTILITY OF THE SON TOWARD THE FATHER

It is claimed that a totemistic vestige of the primeval patricide was, in ancient times, the slaying of the sacrificial animal. The patricide is thereby totemistically repeated.[503] Karl Abraham offers a similar surmise regarding the *Kappara* of Yom Kippur eve.[504] As fowl are often enumerated in the sacrificial code alongside of cattle and sheep, fowl can function totemistically in the place of cattle and sheep.[505] The *Kappara*, according to Abraham has a purpose identical with that which Reik ascribes to the *Kol Nidre*;[506] it is the symbolic repetition of the prehistoric or psychic patricide as a preface to atonement for the patricide.

Again, the blowing of the *Shofar* is declared by Reik to be an imitation of and therefore an identification with the father and to symbolize unconsciously a revolt against the father, an appropriation of his sexual organ and powers and a usurpation of his prerogatives.[507] Reik deems the Cabbalistic *Shofar* prayer, "O destroy Satan" to be decidedly in place because in the very act of blowing, Satan—that is, the anti-paternal and anti-divine trend—breaks forth.[508]

According to the minute analysis of Reik, Moses in some aboriginal conception was a vanquisher of Yahweh, the totem-father. Reik advances the following points:

[501] Reik, *Probleme der Religionspsychologie*, pp. 213, 216.

[502] *Ibid.*, p. 213. The pretended tearing up of the initiates in certain primitive initiations is analogous.

[503] *Ibid.*, p. 252.

[504] Karl Abraham, "Der Versoehnungstag, "*Imago*," VI, 82.

[505] *Ibid.*, p. 83. The author probably had in mind Leviticus, chapters 1. 5, 14.

[506] *Ibid.*, pp. 84, 89.

[507] Reik, *Probleme der Religionspsychologie*, pp. 214, 216.

[508] *Ibid.*, p. 223. This really applies not to a prayer but to the initials ק׳ר׳ע שׂ׳ט׳ן in the series of Psalm verses that precede the shofar blowing.

1. The Vulgate, Aquila and Michaelangelo take "*karan or panaw*" in Exod. 34.29 to mean that Moses had acquired horns.[509] The mask he wears is an abbreviated totem skin just as the horns are totem horns. The mask makes a deity of Moses.[510] By means of the mask he terrifies others in order to deter them from practicing on him who has now become a god the patricide or deicide which he himself has committed. Reik calls attention to something vaguely resembling an animal in the Michaelangelo statue.[511] This he takes as a subtle indication of an unconscious feeling that Moses is the son and the vanquisher of a father-god possessing animal form.[512]

2. The rage that Moses expends in shattering the calf at the foot of the mountain is a displacement for the rage with which he has shattered Yahweh higher up in the mountain.[513] The tablets of stone were demolished somewhere up on the mountain side and the tablets, we shall presently see, are but variants of the calf. Killing *for* the god may have been originally a killing *of* the god. The guilt imputed to the people is but a "displacement" for the guilt that originally attached to Moses.[514] The drinking of the ash-water by the people (Exod. 32.20) can be, thinks Reik, a variant of the ceremonial eating on the lower slope of Sinai in Chap. 24 and, as such, an occurrence in which the father-totem is eaten.

[509] *Ibid.*, p. 262. The incest intimation concerning Moses we noticed supra p. 674 in connection with his exclusion from the promised land.

[510] *Ibid.*, p. 265. Reik quotes Gressman, *Mose und seine Zeit*, pp. 151, 247 (it should be 247, 250). It is difficult to understand what Reik means when he says (p. 267), "Moses braucht dann im Verkehr mit diesem Gotte keine Maske, kein Tierfell, denn er entreisst es ihm ja und wurde selbst Gott." Does one lay aside one's trophies in the presence of the vanquished from whom they have been wrested? Reik would have been easier to understand had he said that Moses without the mask is a "displacement" for Yahweh deprived of the mask; the mask being the totem skin, the insignium of power. Reik is more intelligible when he says, "Moses der im Zelte zu Yahweh spricht ist eine spaetere Figur, da Moses selbst zu Yahweh geworden ist und so die Anwesenheit Yahwehs als eine doppelte erscheint" (p. 267).

[511] *Ibid.*, p. 260. The "Moses" is really half beast, half god (p. 263).

[512] *Ibid.*, p. 269.

[513] *Ibid.*, pp. 273, 274.

[514] *Ibid.*, p. 276.

It is true the calf mentioned in the text is a golden calf but the primitive mind does not discriminate between an original and a replica.[515]

The calf was originally not one animal but two animals as indicated by the plural *eleh* in verse 4b and also as suggested by the two bulls of Jeroboam in I Kings 12.[516]

Of the two animals at Sinai, one was a bull representing Yahweh the father and one a calf representing Moses the son.[517] Reik recalls Hosea's contemptuous application of the word "calf" to the bulls of Jeroboam.[518] Moses can be a calf as Christ can be a lamb.[519] Yahweh can be a bull even though elsewhere the ram appears to have been the Hebrew totem. One totem can supercede another as one tribe comes to dominate another or as, under changed conditions, new types of animals come to be bred.[520]

In Moses, the bull slayer, we have an analogy to the monster slayers, Siegfried, Hercules, Theseus, Dionysius, Orpheus, Attis, Mithra.[521]

3. The tablets of stone which Moses shatters are variants of the two animals or of the two statues of animals.[522]

[515] *Ibid.*, p. 273.

[516] *Ibid.*, p. 280.

[517] *Ibid.*, pp. 278, 280. He might also have quoted Ps. 106.20 where the animal worshipped is called a *shor*. Reik holds that Moses as calf and Moses as man is a splitting of personality with which psychoanalysis is highly familiar (p. 286).

[518] *Ibid.*, p. 271. The passages in Hosea are 8.5, 6; 10.5; 13.2.

[519] *Ibid.*, p. 284.

[520] *Ibid.*, p. 218, "Ob in diesem Stierkult der Einfluss eines sesshaften Volkes wie der Babylonier sichtbar wird oder eine selbststaendige Verzweigung einer ursemitischen Vorstellung vorliegt, welche letztere Hypothese mir warscheinlicher scheint, muss dahingestellt werden." Due to scarcity of water in Palestine, the Habiri, according to Stade and to Benziger, pastured only small cattle. Arabs do not breed large cattle. "Wahrscheinlich dass der Widder in der Domestikation des Kleinviehs vorangegangene Epoche die totemistische Gottheit der Juden war." Would not this make the ram totem earlier than the bull totem?

[521] *Ibid.*, p. 269.

[522] *Ibid.*, p. 293, p. 301. Reik might have cited the Talmudic statement that Moses, like various other notable characters, ***hittiaḥ debarim kelappe*** *Ma'alah* (Ber. 32a).

As the statues subject to destruction are sacred objects the fashioning of which was the duty of Aaron the priest, so are the two tablets sacred objects.[523]

The preservation of the tablets in the ark does not comport with the conception of them as vehicles of a law for public use.[524] The need of the hour was a journey god. Moses ascended Mt. Sinai presumably to secure such a god. The tablets which he obtained must therefore have represented such a god.[525] In the altar with its stones and its horns we have, Reik thinks, a composite of stone deity and animal deity.[526]

Reik maintains that the preparation of a second pair of tablets intimates a double sense for the tablets—as the psychoanalysts say of dreams, a "manifest" content and a "latent" one.[527] Reik believes that this duality of content is further evidenced by "the many contradictions and uncertainties of the text."[528] The repeated shatterings of the father-god, first in the tablets and then in the calf, suggest to Reik the idea of the repeated killings of the many headed Hydra or of the Egyptian demon Apepi.[529]

Archaeologically speaking, there may once have been a Yahweh father cult superceded by a Moses son cult.[530] "When sometimes Moses and sometimes Yahweh seems to be the writer of the tablets, the vacillation between a father god and a son god is still perceptible."[531] The very word "Moses," Reik informs us, comes from the Egyptian, "*Mesu*," a child—a word appearing in such familiar names as "Thutmosis" and "Ramses."[532]

The distortions and reconstructions of the narratives that Reik has to assume will, he thinks, lose their appearance of enormity if one reflects upon the corresponding dislocations in the childhood memories of individuals.[533]

[523] Reik, *op. cit.*, pp. 276, 294, 295.

[524] *Ibid.*, p. 298. Reik is supported by Gressmann, *op. cit.*, p. 189.

[525] Reik, p. 298. Reik (p. 297) also quotes the view of Gressman ("*Mose und Seine Zeit*," p. 186) that the tablets in the Exodus story are an anachronism.

[526] Reik, *op. cit.*, p. 310.

[527] *Ibid.*, p. 297.

[528] *Ibid.*, p. 305.

[529] *Ibid.*, pp. 290, 292.

[530] *Ibid.*, p. 282.

[531] *Ibid.*, p. 305.

[532] *Ibid.*, p. 278.

[533] *Ibid.*, p. 299.

Another patricidal insurrectionary unearthed by Reik is Jubal in Gen. 4.21, "the father of such as handle the harp and the pipe." Reik conjectures the substratum of this notice to have been an account of a son's overthrow of his father totemized as a ram.[534] The name "Jubal" resembling the *yobel* of Exod. 19.13 means "ram."[535] Jubal, being an inventor, must have been like those other inventors, Midas who was an ass, Marsyas who was a goat, Orpheus who was a fox and Dionysius who was a bull.[536] Again, as an inventor Jubal is an insurrectionary. In primitive myths inventors are commonly sons that rebel.[537] Australian myths in particular associate the invention of musical instruments with some father's overthrow by his son.[538]

Underlying it all, according to Reik, is the origin of music in the imitation of a totem animal or by imitating the voice of the envied father afterward incarnated in the totem animal or by imitating the groans of the assaulted and dying father, imitation being of course accession to the coveted powers. As Moses identifies himself with the father by acquiring the father's horns, Jubal identifies himself with the father by simulating the father's sounds.[539] Borrowing some support from an oriental legend that Jubal was a Kenite, Reik surmises a connection between the Jubal-Jabal brother relation and that of Cain and Abel whose significance as an example of the Oedipus conflict has already been brought to our attention[540] (supra pp. 638, 649).

Langer alleges that in some Jewish localities meat is on Shabu'ot eaten soon after cheese. This he regards as an analogue to those totem feasts in which taboos of totem eating are deliberately violated.[541]

[534] *Ibid.*, p. 245.

[535] Reik does not overlook the *yabla* of Rosh Ha-Shanah III, 2.

[536] *Ibid.*, p. 234.

[537] Examples are Orpheus, Osiris, Attis. Reik might have added Prometheus, inventor of the use of fire.

[538] *Ibid.*, p. 247.

[539] *Ibid.*, p. 288. The very fact that the Bible does not ascribe the origin of music to a deity indicates, according to Reik, that there once was a deity whose totemic character had to be concealed when higher conceptions developed (p. 230).

[540] *Ibid.*, pp. 179, 180.

[541] "Die juedische Gebetriemen," *Imago*, XVI, 472.

Finally Reik holds that the ram of Gen. 22 was a totem father-god and that Isaac was understood to deserve immolation for the slaying of this god.[542]

X. Totemism—Conciliation between Father and Son

A. The Father's Friendliness toward the Son

Only a few of the Jewish stories and observances animated by the sense of the father's friendliness toward the son fall within the totemistic group.

Frieda Fromm-Reichmann sees in the prohibition of seething the calf in its mother's milk a restraint upon paternal truculence.[543] Her psychoanalytic amplification of the law is approximately: "Do not, suspecting thy son of incestuous relations with his mother on whose milk he has been nourished, visit upon him the punishment of devouring him as thou wouldst something cooked."

Although the blowing of the *Shofar* inspires speechless awe, there is subsequent to the blowing a sense of relief[544] not unlike the joys following the Adonis festival in ancient Antioch when the suspense would be over and the forgiveness of sins assured.[545] So Reik affirms. Allied to this are the bounties of the Rosh Ha-Shanah dinner enjoined already in Nehemiah.[546] Reik speaks of the red apples eaten in mediaeval France, of the grapes eaten in Provence, of the Rosh Ha-Shanah figs and the calf's head and, as reported by Rabbi Jacob Moeln in the fourteenth century, the apples, honey and venison head.[547]

At the close of Atonement Day the deity now conciliated imparts his benign blessing to his children. We shall soon hear that the *talethim* in which the Aaronides wrap themselves when pronouncing the benediction are but modifications of the totem skin by wrapping in which priests of primitive cults would become

542 *Ibid.*, p. 237.

543 Frieda Fromm-Reichmann, "Das Juedische Speiseritual," *Imago*, XIII, 243.

544 Reik, *Probleme der Religionspsychologie*, pp. 221, 225.

545 *Ibid.*, p. 226.

546 Neh. 8.10.

547 Reik, *op. cit.*, p. 226.

like their totem;[548] while the spread fingers of the Aaronides' hands, so Karl Abraham would have us understand, simulate the totem's split paws or claws.[549]

The mask of Moses whose primary function was to terrify as a father or a deity terrifies becomes in the text of Exodus a device for human accommodation and protection.[550] Like the bull roarer the *Shofar* which sometimes means fear and death, at other times, means protection,[551] succor and finally resurrection,[552] whence its depiction on catacombs and tombs.[553]

B. THE SON'S FRIENDLINESS TOWARD THE FATHER

Numerous are the properties of religion displaying totemistically the genial factors in the son's attitude toward the father.

The totem, that is the re-incarnated ancestor is extensively an object of worship. Reik enumerates Apis, Ptoh, Chum, Anubis, Marduk, Adad, Elul, the moon god Sinu, Dionysius, Poseidon, Zeus, Ammon, Pan, Bacchus, Baal and the golden bulls of Jeroboam.[554] While the account in Exodus represents the calf worship as sinful, the original story is surmised to have placed the sin not in the worship but in the demolition.[555] The tablets of the Decalogue characterized by Reik as a stone god and as a doublet of the calf are to this day an object of reverence and adoration.[556]

In the act of pouring blood upon the altar, Reik sees a feeding of the totem deity just as we have found the shielding of the altar from the impacts of iron to constitute a protecting of the

548 Karl Abraham, "Der Versoehnungstag," *Imago*, VI, 87, also Frieda-Fromm-Reichmann, "Das Juedische Speiseritual," *Imago*, XIII, 238.

549 Karl Abraham, *op. cit.*, p. 88.

550 Reik, *Probleme der Religionspsychologie*, p. 266.

551 *Ibid.*, p. 242. Something similar, he says, is true of the bull roarer of the Unmatgans.

552 *Ibid.*, p. 225, just as the offending sons, Orpheus, Marsyas, and Dionysius are, after being torn to pieces, mourned and then resurrected and worshipped (p. 246).

553 *Ibid.*, p. 224.

554 *Ibid.*, p. 207. The bulls of Jeroboam in I Kings 12.28.

555 *Ibid.*, p. 303.

556 *Ibid.*, pp. 300, 301.

deity (supra p. 665). The altar having horns is equated with the totem having horns, in the manner of a child who, putting on a soldier hat, poses as a soldier.[557]

Again, the totem deity is honored in the requirement that the sacrifice be without blemish. The *Shofar* must similarly be without blemish.[558] The deity must not be caricatured. Reik is reminded of the Minangkabos of Sumatra and other tribes among whom the bull roarer is made from the skull of a man distinguished for bravery.[559]

Related to this is the entire Biblical recasting of the ancient patricide stories in order to give a more exalted conception both of God and of man.[560] The hostility is thus diverted from the god to the golden calf, his "split-off."[561] The despised idol becomes in this way the ambivalent of the thunder God majestic and exalted. The abhorrence which Moses feels for the calf worship can also mean his abhorrence for the Moses worship which he desires unconsciously.[562] Reik calls attention to Bible passages like Isa. 34.6; Jer. 46.10; Zeph. 1.7,[563] as Freud does to myths in which the deity himself is the sacrificiant—the worshiper being that loathe to commit the patricide even histrionically.[564]

Various sacrificial rituals involve demonstrations of mourning over the slain animal.[565] The antics of the Baal priests in I Kings 18 are melancholy. We are informed that sacrificial slaughters would be attended by various types of apology and expiation.[566]

Further tokens of filial regard are the prohibitions of the symbolic incest already noted—that of "taking" the mother bird (supra p. 672) and that of seething the calf in its mother's milk[567] (supra pp. 672, 680). The latter has been expanded into the Jewish

[557] *Ibid.*, p. 310. [558] *Ibid.*, p. 215. [559] *Ibid.*, p. 241.
[560] *Ibid.*, pp. 281, 305. [561] *Ibid.*, p. 290. [562] *Ibid.*, p. 304.
[563] "Die Bedeutung des Schweigens," *Imago*, V, 355.
[564] *Totem und Tabu*, p. 139.
[565] Reik, *Probleme der Religionspsychologie*, pp. 253, 25v.
[566] Frieda Fromm-Reichmann, "Das Juedische Speiseritual," *Imago*, XIII, 237. Her reference is to "*Totem und Tabu*," p. 161 (in Vol. X of the *Gesammelte Schriften*).
[567] Langer in "Die juedische Gebetriemen," *Imago*, XVI, 441, agrees with Frieda Fromm-Reichmann that the prohibition of seething the calf in its mother's milk is a restraint upon Oedipus tendencies.

law forbidding the combination of milk and meat in the diet. The interval required between them rests upon the supposition that one's identification with the calf lasts only so long as the meat is in one's body.[568] The punctiliousness attaching to the separation of meat and milk—the different dishes, pans, table cloths etc.—is viewed by Frieda Fromm-Reichmann as a familiar neurotic symptom.[569]

Another demonstration of regard for the father is, according to Reik, the prohibition of image making. Damage to a person's simulacrum was believed to entail damage to the person himself.[570] Yahweh was thus shielded against any patricidal outbursts such as were inflicted on the Egyptian Apepi statue.[571] Christianity which discarded this prohibition substituted for the hegemony of the father-god that of the rival son-god.

The prohibition of blood eating carries, according to Frieda Fromm-Reichmann, the same intent.[572] The blood is the life. To spare the blood is to spare the life. She suggests, as we saw, that this prohibition among the Hebrews accounts for the practice of eating animals of the totem type only, while among other peoples the totem was precisely the animal tabooed[573]. Frieda Fromm-Reichmann would add to this the practice of refraining from the use of food prepared by non-Jews. The hostile alien might cause the Jew to revert to certain degrees of totem eating that the Jew has abandoned.[574] Reik thinks that abstinence from eating nuts on the day the *Shofar* is blown also goes back to a resolve to desist from eating the father. He instances the *gematria* by which "*egoz*," "nut" is equated with "*ḥeṭ*," "sin" and the theory that the flow of saliva stimulated by nuts diverts the worshiper's attention from his prayers. At the root of it all, it is patricidal urges undergoing repression.[575]

568 Frieda Fromm-Reichmann, *op. cit.*, p. 242. 569 *Ibid.*, p. 241.

570 Reik, *Probleme der Religionspsychologie*, p. 290.

571 *Ibid.*, pp. 289, 291. 572 Frieda Fromm-Reichmann, *ibid.*

573 *Ibid.*, p. 238 and supra p. 671.

574 *Ibid.*, p. 244. The passage is difficult to understand but this is what it seems to mean.

575 Reik, *op. cit.*, p. 266. Reik is reminded (p. 247) of the abolition of cannabalism attributed to Orpheus. On page 622 supra saliva is mentioned as a sperm symbol.

We have noticed how the quelling of the desire to slay and devour the father and to cohabit with the mother is signified on Atonement Day by abstinence from food and from sexual intercourse (supra p. 661). Ehrich Fromm alines with this the prohibition of sandal wearing on Atonement Day. Sandals, being made of leather, can constitute an identification with the father-totem—that identification so ominously associated with patricide and usurpation.[576]

Inasmuch as blowing the *Shofar* involves such wicked identification, the use of the *Shofar* has been restricted to the month of Ellul and to specific ritual occasions.[577] Once upon a time the occasions for its use—alarms, announcements, festivals—were numerous.[578] Reik sees here an analogy with certain neurotic symptoms in which a given reaction which is aroused in the patient by persons and objects more and more removed from the prime cause of the reaction becomes, in the process of cure, gradually detached from the secondary persons and objects and tends to revert to its original limits.[579] A point is made about the exclusion of the bull from the group of animals whose horns can be used for *Shofars*.[580] The bull rather than the ram may have been the original Hebrew totem.[581] The real totem is thus spared the patricidal aggression.

[576] Ehrich Fromm, "Der Sabbath," *Imago*, XIII, 232. Ludwig Levy (*Monatschrift*, Vol. 62, p. 181) interprets differently the removal of the shoes on Atonement Day and on occasions of mourning. The shoe being a symbol of power and possession, its removal expresses subjection and surrender. This however need not exclude the interpretation of Fromm given in the text. Psychoanalysis is ever positing "over-determination." An object or an act which can signify one thing in a given connection can, in another connection, have additional signification. This point was broached supra note 10

[577] Reik, *Probleme der Religionspsychologie*, pp. 186, 188, 219.

[578] Supra pp. 672, 673. The references are II Sam. 6.15; 15.10; Isa. 8.1; Jer. 4.19–21; Ezek. 33.1–6; Amos 3.6; Job 39.24. Ta'anit 16b, Mo'ed Katon 16b, 27b, Sanhedrin 7b, Oraḥ Ḥayyim 576, 1.

[579] Reik, *op. cit.*, p. 220.

[580] *Ibid.*, p. 184. The reference is to Rosh Ha-Shanah III, 2 and to Oraḥ Ḥayyim 596. However the texts say *parah* not *par*.

[581] Reik, *op. cit.*, p. 231. This reason might conceivably obtain alongside of the other reason (p. 219) that when bull worship became offensive, the bull-horn *shofar* was tabooed. Still the bull was an earlier totem that the ram could not entirely efface (supra pp. 668, 669, 679, 680.

The *Shofar* bellowing like an animal undergoing slaughter[582] acquired the function of bringing the primeval patricide to consciousness and thus awakening remorse for one's sins.[583] Thirty times over it warns against the anti-paternal impulses and admonishes their subjugation[584] (supra p. 673). The resurrection which the *Shofar* announces is in store only for those in whom the patricidal craving has been stilled.[585] The blowing of the *Shofar* throughout the month of Ellul has been explained as a reminder of the Holy Days approaching. The implication is that there is a possibility of forgetting and in psychoanalysis, forgetting and repressing go together.[586] As we have already observed, periods of solemnity and restraint are not periods in which the likelihood of outbreaks is necessarily diminished (supra p. 652).

The Satan who is repudiated in connection with the *Shofar* blowing is the worshiper's own unfilial proclivity.[587] The *Shofar* whose use was primarily a triumph of Satan, that is, of the son's hatred of the father is thus turned against Satan. "O destroy Satan," as we have recalled (supra p. 675), is one of the accessory prayers.[588] A mediaeval version of the reason for blowing the *Shofar* throughout the month of Ellul is that Satan has to be deceived regarding the date of Rosh Ha-Shanah.[589] And Satan is the chief of demons. They who trespass upon the father's

582 *Ibid.*, p. 213. Reik also observes (p. 186) how Isa. 58.1ff. connects the *shofar* with sin.

583 Reik says (pp. 217, 218) that the ram's horn does not give the sound of the ram's voice but that of an ox bellowing with anxiety.

584 *Ibid.*, p. 221. "Das Zeremoniel hat wie die Symptome der Zwangneurose den Charakter des Schutzes gegen eine endopsychisch wahrgenommene Versuchung" (p. 220).

585 *Ibid.*, p. 224.

586 *Ibid.*, p. 228.

587 *Ibid.*, p. 223. Reik (p. 209) refers to the Hindu invocation that Brahmanaspati use his horns against the demon Aryi. The war god Indra is pictured as butting nations with his horns. My colleague, Dr. Lauterbach, calls attention to the fact that according to the interpretations of the Luryanic School the rooster of the Kappara as well as the scapegoat of Lev. 16 is a representative of demons or of Satan. The slaughtering is understood to effect a weakening of the demoniacal or Satanic power.

588 Reik, *op. cit.*, and infra p. 697.

589 *Ibid.*, p. 228.

prerogatives and appropriate his horns are not unlike those horned creatures, the demons whose worship is so emphatically forbidden.[590]

To the notable expiations already considered (supra p. 663), we may now add those involving totemism. Moses, the totem-vanquisher not only offers himself in expiation;[591] if we can agree with Reik that the calf which Moses shatters is not only Yahweh the father but also Moses the son, Moses actually performs the expiation,[592] Moses the expiatory calf being thus on a level with Christ the expiatory lamb. The hand grasping the beard in the Michaelangelo statue betokens, according to Reik, a masochistic rage directed against the self.[593]

By various tokens, the entire Jewish nation accepted the guilt of Moses as its own guilt.[594] Particularly is a symbolic identification of the people with the vicarious victim perceived by Reik in the Atonement ritual where the blood of the people's sin offering is mingled with the blood of the priest's sin offering.[595] Reik also predicates an identification of the worshiper with the scape-goat.[596] In the *Kappara* ritual, the fowl that is slain is expressly asserted to be the equivalent of the person by whom and for whom it is utilized.[597]

Isaac is similarly in peril of immolation because of the slain totem, the ram. Such is, in Reik's opinion, the "latent" sense beneath the innumerable "displacements" in Gen. Chap. 22.[598]

[590] *Ibid.*, p. 209. On demon worship, Lev. 17.7; Isa. 13.4 (?), II Chron. 11.10 (?); Deut. 12.31, 32.17; Ps. 106.37; II Chron. 11.15.

[591] Exod. 32.32.

[592] Reik, *op. cit.*, p. 285 and supra p. 677.

[593] Reik, *op. cit.*, p. 305.

[594] *Ibid.*, p. 202.

[595] *Ibid.*, p. 227. The passage is Lev. 16.18. Reik likens this to an Australian initiation rite in which there is a letting of the blood of the participants old and young or in which the youth, just circumcised, touches the head of an elder with a twig dipped in the circumcision blood.

[596] Reik, *Der Eigene und der Fremde Gott*, p. 125 and supra pp. 633, 634 regarding Narcissism and regarding identification.

[597] Karl Abraham, "Der Versoehnungstag," *Imago*, VI, 83.

[598] Reik, *Probleme der Religionspsychologie*, p. 237. "Wie Isaac wuerden alle Mitglieder der Gemeinde verdienen, wegen ihrer feindseligen, unbewussten Gesinnung gegen den Vater getoetet zu werden, da sie selbst ihn ja kraft der

As a final act of friendliness toward the father, Reik instances the restoration of the Decalogue stones. Thus is the slain father symbolically resurrected.[599]

Finally, of bearing on the son's friendliness toward the father is Langer's psychoanalytic interpretation of the phylacteries.[600] Langer sees in the act of winding the phylacteries about arm and head a symbolic self-castration, restrictive of incestuous aggressions upon paternal sex prerogatives. Langer reaches this conclusion by discovering in the phylactery usage male sex symbols, female sex symbols, cohabitation symbols, attitudes of rebellion and attitudes of self constriction.

A. Male Sex Symbols

The following are the masculine sex implications noted by Langer.

1. The leather of which the straps are made has a sexual implication. Its smell is sexually stimulating; hence the eagerness of the boy at puberty to put on the *Tefillim*.[601] Langer furnishes examples from Chinese, Greeks and other peoples in which leather carries a sexual import.[602]

2. Straps resemble snakes. Langer devotes a number of pages to the phallic significance of snakes in various parts of the world.[603] He recalls, among other things, how in ancient Rome, the straps of the *luperci* were supposed to induce pregnancy in the women whom they would strike.[604] He quotes Ludwig Blau as saying in "*Studien zum althebraeischen Buchwesen*" that there have been Torah rolls made of snake skin.

3. A passage in Sab. 108a debates whether *Tefillim* parchments may be made of fish skins. In Ket. 5a, the fish is a sex symbol. It is also a sex symbol among Babylonians, Arabs and others. It resembles the well known phallic snake. The Talmud itself says that a certain uncleanness attaches to the fish because of the snake which seduced Eve.

Allmacht der Gedanken getoetet haben." The totemistic slaying is presumably a supplementation of the "revenant" slaying which was mentioned supra p. 649.

599 *Ibid.*, p. 305.

600 "Die juedische Gebetriemen," *Imago*, XVI, 1930, 435–485.

601 *Ibid.*, p. 439.

602 *Ibid.*, p. 440.

603 *Ibid.*, pp. 483–485.

604 *Ibid.*, pp. 440, 441.

4. Various scrotum resemblances characterize the phylacteries. "Die von drei Seiten um den breiten Rand der Kapselbasis umgewickelten Riemen erinnern an das Skrotum, die beiden ueberragenden Enden der oben zusammengefalteten Schlinge stellen die Testikel dar. Das hohe, vordringende Haeuschen in der Mitte waere dementsprechend der Penis in statu erectionis."[605] Langer holds that the bag in which the phylacteries are kept also resembles the scrotum.[606] He recalls that in certain regions "scrotum" is a vulgarism for a *Tefillim* bag and that certain Jews in Prague had the custom of folding the *Tefillim* into the bag in a manner resembling the position of the sex organ in the scrotum.

5. Together with the eyes, the head piece of the *Tefillim* forms a triangle and the triangle is an erotic symbol.[607] The eyes themselves, as in the Indra myth (supra p. 644) have a phallic significance.[608] Clinically, eyes have meant testicles.[609] A progressive pushing up placed the head piece higher than the eyes.[610]

6. A legend in Sab. 49a tells how, in a certain emergency, head *Tefillim* changed into dove's wings.[611] Langer further recalls that for *Tefillim*, *Mezuzah* and Torah rolls bird skin is preferred[612] and that there is resemblance to a bird in the folded *Tefillim*.[613] But birds also have phallic associations. They have such in India, Arabia and elsewhere. In Greece, doves particularly are something phallic. Referring to the word *Kenafayim* in the *Sefer Emet* of Menahem Azariah of Fano, Langer asserts that in the Kabbala, the phallic principle (*Yesod*) is called the "winged."[614]

605 *Ibid.*, p. 453.

606 *Ibid.*, p. 454.

607 *Ibid.*, p. 450. He refers to L. Levy "*Simsonsage*," p. 13 and to R. Kleinpauls, *Sprueche ohne Worte*, p. 376.

608 Langer, *op. cit.*, p. 449.

609 *Ibid.*, p. 459. He refers to Stephen Helles in *Int. Zeitsch. f. Psychan.* IX, p. 72.

610 Langer, *op. cit.*, p. 448.

611 *Ibid.*, p. 452.

612 *Ibid.*, p. 455.

613 *Ibid.*, p. 453.

614 *Ibid.*, p. 455.

7. The finger has a phallic bearing. The Hebrew word *Ammah* can mean both finger and sex organ. Langer adduces, for the phallic significance of the finger, myths from Egyptians, Romans and South American Indians.[615] A phallic significance likewise attaches to the hand.[616]

8. The three windings of the strap around the third finger give the phallic number "three." Langer surmises that certain oaths expressed by lifting three fingers are allied to oaths voiced by touching the sex organ as in Gen. 24.2–4 and 47.29. He claims that there are vestiges of phallic oaths in the Kabala and even in the folk custom of touching the noses of children to ascertain whether they are telling the truth.[616] He further recalls that the three blowings of the *Shofar* have been liturgically equated with hips and sex organ.[616]

9. Phallic implications reside in various analogues of the head *Tefillim* such as the *Ḳorḥah* of Deut. 14.1 and the African *Totafot.*[617] The Talmud in fact (Meg. 34b) imputes an African origin to the word "*Totafot.*"

10. Certain oriental and ancient hand pieces of the phylacteries are cylindrical, that is, phallus shaped.

11. The hand piece has to be covered modestly—like the genitals.

12. Touching *Tefillim* "defiles" (Yadayim III, 3 and Zabim V, 12) like touching sexual parts.

13. Ber. 23a tells how a harlot once claimed to have received a pair of *Tefillim* as her compensation—like the staff of Judah in Gen. 38.18.[618]

B. Female Sex Symbols

These appear as follows:

1. Meg. 24b asserts that round or nut shaped head pieces are dangerous.[619] The nut, according to Langer, is the symbol of the mother's body. In Cant. 6.11, the nut is connected with such a female genital symbol as the pomegranate. In Midrash

[615] *Ibid.*, p. 462.

[616] *Ibid.*, p. 463.

[617] *Ibid.*, pp. 444, 445.

[618] *Ibid.*, p. 458.

[619] *Ibid.*, p. 446.

Rabba Shir 6, the nut is the symbol of the evil inclination. In Niddah 31a the foetus is compared to a nut. Nuts may not be eaten between Rosh Ha-Shanah and Sukkot allegedly because of the *gematria* of *Egoz* which, being 17, gives by the addition of the unity symbol 1, the number 18 and 18 is also the *gematria* of *Ḥeṭ*, sin.[620]

2. The cubic box is a female sex symbol.[621] It is a house and house we have seen (supra note 114) means woman. Langer refers to the familiar passage in Yoma 2a on Lev. 16.11 and to Meg. 13b on Esther 2.7.

3. We have already noticed the construction of a triangle in the wearing of the head *Tefillim*. Langer informs us that the triangle stands for the female genitals among Greeks, Hindus and Sumerians.[622]

C. Combined Male and Female Factors

Various features of the *Tefillim* represent the male and female sex factors in combination i.e. in a symbolized cohabitation:

1. As already noted, the cubic box figures both as a male and as a female sex symbol. Langer cites Chinese and Melanesean parallels.[623]

2. The eye which we have already found to be a male sex symbol is also a vulva symbol.[624] In Ber. 66b, a dream of eyes meeting is interpreted as signifying cohabitation with one's sister.

3. The triangle also has a bi-sexual meaning. The ecclesiastical symbol of an eye within a triangle is said by Langer to mean *coitus*.[625] The triangle stands for the male and also for the female sex organ among Greeks, Hindus and Sumerians. The triangle represents the union of male and female among Babylonians, Etruscans and South American Indians. Langer attributes a similar implication to the shield of David and to those triangular arrangements, mentioned in Men. 31b, of the letters on the *Mezuzah*, arrangements called respectively *Kubbah* (something feminine) and *Zanab* (something masculine).[626]

[620] *Ibid.*, p. 448. [621] *Ibid.*, p. 449. [622] *Ibid.*, p. 459.

[623] *Ibid.*, p. 451. [624] He refers to Levy, ***Simsonsage*** p. 11.

[625] Langer, *op. cit.*, p. 460.

[626] His "Tuerpfostenrolle," *Imago*, XIV, p. 467. Supra p. 622.

4. A bi-sexual significance adheres likewise to the number three.[627] The three windings of the *Tefillim* strap around the finger suggest the wedding ring[628] or the three-fold circling of the bridegroom by the bride.[629] The passage from Hosea recited while donning the *Tefillim* speaks of betrothal—*erastik li le'olam*. In this passage also occurs the word *yada'at* whose sexual implication has already been treated by L. Levy (supra p. 615). Kid. 30b says that in any individual's procreation three are involved—the father, the mother, the Deity. Langer quotes a Hindu proverb to similar effect. He then quotes F. Alexander[630] and S. H. Graber[631] as holding that the number three schematizes the attachment to the I, to the mother (or wife) and to the father (or super-ego). Karl Abraham conjectures that it represents the oral, the anal and the uro-genital zones.[632] Langer goes so far as to relate to this the tri-literal structure of Hebrew roots.

5. Langer also holds that there is a death and hence sex meaning in the number seven of the seven fold winding of the *Tefillim* around the arm.[633]

6. Finally Langer provides numerous examples from the Kabbala and from liturgic pieces influenced by the Kabbala where again *Tefillim* are invested with the erotic.[634]

D. Anti-Paternal Attitudes

Langer's contention that attitudes of agression upon the father underlie the wearing of *Tefillim* is based on the following considerations:

1. With Frieda Fromm-Reichmann (infra p. 695) he agrees that putting on the *Tefillim* signifies identification with the totem. This is additionally intimated in the Talmudic idea that God Himself wears *Tefillim*.[635]

627 Langer, "Die juedische Gebetriemen," *Imago*, XVI, p. 460.

628 *Ibid.*, p. 461.

629 *Ibid.*, p. 462.

630 *Ibid.*, p. 461. The reference is to "Der biologischer Sinn psychischer Vorgaenge" *Imago*, IX, 35.

631 "Ueber Regression und Dreizahl," *Imago*, IX, 476.

632 *Imago*, IX, 122.

633 Langer *op. cit.*, p. 462.

634 *Ibid.*, pp. 464–466.

635 *Ibid.*, p. 441.

2. When assuming the *Tefillim* the boy becomes ritually the equal of his father.

3. A paternal protest is concealed in the compunction about wearing the *Tefillim* in moments of flatulence. Flatulence is said in psychoanalysis to voice a protest against the physician or against the father.[636]

4. While the *Tefillim* may be removed in the presence of the father, they may not be removed in the presence of the teacher. The person to be respected, says Langer, is the father's extended *imago*, the *Urvater*, the King.

E. Self-Mutilation

The self-castration or self-mutilation factors in phylactery wearing reside in the following aspects:

1. Speaking of the double significance of the *Tefillim* cubes, Langer refers to his article on the "*Tuerpfostenrolle*" where he tells of the feminization or castration of masculine objects[637] (supra p. 621). He brings additional examples from Egypto-Jewish, African, Indian and other usages.[638]

2. Leather in mythology has an underworld significance and this in turn suggests death. Death in its turn suggests desexualization.

3. Through binding, masochistic tendencies are gratified. Algolagniacs have been known to fetter themselves with gloves and with head bands.[639] Binding of the "weaker" is thus symbolic of self-castration.[640] The binding of the hand or of the finger—phallic tokens—means obviously the reduction of the phallic power.[641]

4. Langer quotes Marie Bonaparte[642] to the effect that the horn—as we saw, the head piece of the phylacteries represents a horn (infra p. 696)—signifies a genital that has been detached.

[636] *Ibid.*, p. 467. Reference is made to Ferenczi in *Int. Zeitschrift fuer Psychan.* Bd. I, S. 38ff.

[637] *Imago*, XIV, 457–468.

[638] "Die juedische Gebetriemen" *Imago*, XVI, 550.

[639] *Ibid.*, p. 441.

[640] *Ibid.*, p. 439.

[641] *Ibid.*, p. 463.

[642] "Kopftrophaeen" *Imago*, XIV, 1928.

XI. Totemism—Amalgamations

There now remain to be considered those totemistic manifestations in which one act combines two or more of the tendencies which we have been considering separately. The act of ritual eating, for instance, whether it be that of the totem,[643] the *Kappara*[644] or the *Eucharist*,[645] can amalgamate the hostile act of devouring the father with four distinct acts of friendliness toward the father, namely:

1. That of admiring identification.[646]
2. That of a punitive devouring of an expiatory victim.
3. That of a penitential self-identification with the expiatory victim.
4. And finally, that of obedience to the father's commands.

The conception of eating as identification is said to be substantiated by myths, dreams and neuroses.[647] Reik instances an Abyssinian legend of a king who, by swallowing a worm, acquired an education in reading, writing, music and statesmanship.[648]

The drinking of the water containing the ashes of the golden calf signifies, according to Reik, not only the devouring of the father but also the self-identification of the people with their expiatory victim, Moses the calf, son of Yahweh the bull; just as the eating of the eucharist constitutes for the Christians a self-identification with their vicariate, Christ.[649]

Again, the eating of the sacrificial animal is not merely the symbolic eating of the father. The act, being represented as one divinely commanded, becomes also an expression of submission to the father.[650] Reik sees a condensation of this in the Gospel of John where Jesus, representing the father, hands a morsel of bread to Judas (the murderous son) and commands him to eat.[651]

[643] *Ibid.*, p. 252.
[644] Karl Abraham, "Der Versoehnungstag," *Imago*, VI, 82.
[645] Reik, *Der Eigene und der Fremde* Gott, p. 127.
[646] Reik, *Probleme der Religionspsychologie* p. 212.
[647] Frieda Fromm-Reichmann, "Das Speiseritual," *Imago*, XIII, 241.
[648] Reik, *op. cit.*, p. 248.
[649] *Ibid.*, p. 275.
[650] Reik, *Der Eigene und der Fremde Gott* p. 127.
[651] *Ibid.* The reference is to John 13.26.

Slightly different among the amalgamations which involve eating is that which, according to Frieda Fromm-Reichmann, appears in the command about seething the calf in its mother's milk. At one place we found this command to signify an admonition to the son to spare the father (supra pp. 672, 682) and, at another, an admonition to the father to spare the son (supra p. 680).

What is true of identification by eating is also true of the other identifications,—identification by imitating and identification by means of objects worn. Imitation of the father's sounds, movements or body parts can express at one and the same time a usurping of the father's prerogatives, an act of admiration and an act of loyalty. From the imitation of the father's or the totem's sounds, music both vocal and instrumental, is asserted to have taken its rise.[652] Usurpation becomes in this way hymnology and laudation.

Reik instances Freud's patient, a child who identified itself with its father by mimicking a horse and Ferenczi's patient, a child of three years and a half who, with similar purport, mimicked the crowing and cackling of fowl.[653] Various ritual acts of hopping, prostrating, crouching, swaying, handclapping, dancing (as among the Mohammedan dervishes and our own Ḥassidim),[654] jumping, marching and kneeling are, in Reik's opinion, traceable to similar father and father-totem mimickries.[655] Freud's little

[652] Reik, *Probleme der Religionspsychologie* pp. 247, 248, 250, 252. "Wie mit fortschreitender Kultur das Tierfell durch die Maske ersetzt wurde, so das Bruellen welches urspruenglich die Laute des Totemtieres nachahmen sollte, durch die Verwendung eines Instrumentes" (p. 211).

[653] *Ibid.*, pp. 213, 214.

[654] *Ibid.*, p. 255.

[655] *Ibid.*, pp. 250, 252, 256. Tragedy was the goat dance in honor of Dionysius (p. 251). First there were the Dionysian cult screams (p. 211), then hymns imitating the screams as the dances imitated the goat jumping. Opera, Reik thinks, originated in dithyrambic hymns. Reik instances the various dancing cults such as those of the Greek Hercules and Dionysius (p. 249), the bear imitations of the Carrian Indians (p. 210), the Buffalo dances of the Mandan Indians (p. 250), also the various dog, sheep, ox and frog dances. The Bible of course mentions the dances of the Baal priests. There is also a view which connects the name *Pesaḥ* with a hopping or skipping of lambs which would be imitated by the nomad worshipers at the time of their Spring festival

patient imitated the movements as well as the sounds of a horse. We should recall, in this connection, the Biblical dances of David, Miriam and the Psalms.[656]

Considering the connection of the various acts mentioned with various expiatory rites, the act of imitation merges also with acts of atonement.[657] Thus again are the aggressive and the submissive fused.

We have noticed the use of the horn as something ritually sounded. The horn is also something ritually worn.[658] In various cults, the priests wear horns. Frieda Fromm-Reichmann believes the *Tefillim* to have been horns originally, one of which becomes displaced to the arm.[659]

Another part of the totem's body made to serve for identification with the father is the skin, like the fish skin worn by Dagon worshipers or the sheep skin worn by the devotees of a Cyprian sheep goddess.[660] Derivatives of wrapping in skin are said to be the *Talith*[661] and the phylactery straps[662] as well as the masks used in certain cults.[663] These masks sometimes represent animal

(*Jewish Encyclopedia*, IX, 553 Article, "Passover" with reference to Toy in *Journal of Biblical Literature* 1897). "Die kultische Taenze" says Reik, "sind zuerst Nachahmungen der Bewegungen des Gottes, der sich auf einer bestimmten Stufe der religioesen Entwicklung als Totemtier darstellt."

656 *Ibid.*, p. 249. Dances are mentioned in Ps. 114.150, etc.

657 *Ibid.*, pp. 256, 257.

658 *Ibid.*, pp. 209, 211. Reik instances the horns of the Sumerian and Babylonian priests and of the Saliens, the priests of Mars, the horned caps of the Schamans of Siberia and of the American Musquakie Indians. Also Scheftelowitz. *op. cit.*, p. 472.

659 "Das juedische Speiseritual," *Imago*, XIII, 240. To similar effect Reik (*op. cit.*, p. 209). Reik relates to this the ram's head that figured among the culinary delicacies of Rosh Ha-Shanah. He refers to Kirchner, *Juediches Zeremoniel*, p. 112 (Reik *op. cit.*, p. 226). Reik in his "Gebetmantel und Gebetriemen der Juden," *Imago* XVI (1930), p. 433, disagrees with Frieda Fromm-Reichmann that the hand piece is the horn pushed down. He prefers to regard the head piece as signifying a hoof pushed up.

660 Reik, *Probleme der Religionspsychologie* p. 209 and W. Robertson Smith *Religion of the Semites* (1889), p. 416.

661 Karl Abraham "Der Versoehnungstag," *Imago*, VI, 87.

662 Frieda Fromm-Reichmann, *op. cit.*, p. 240. Reik, *op. cit.*, p. 268 and supra 691 and infra p. 696.

663 Reik, *op. cit.*, pp. 210, 211.

faces and are worn during dances simulating animals.[664] W. Robertson Smith is quoted as suggesting that, in this sense, the dress of the high priest was Yahweh's dress.[665]

In Reik's "Gebetmantel und Gebetriemen der Juden,"[666] *Talith* and *Tefillim* are treated in greater detail. It is there maintained that the handpiece of the phylacteries represents the hoof of the animal and the straps the skin,[667] The *Talith*, made as it is of wool, can represent the animal's hide, the fringes, the animal's legs and the knots in the fringes the joints of the legs. Reik adduces corroboration for this view from the traditional idea that by the windings of the phylacteries the Divine name is formed;[668] also from the Talmudic fancy that God Himself wears phylacteries, from the notion that whoso looks at the fringes looks at God,[669] and from the proximity of the phylactery passage in the Bible to the law of the Paschal offering which is of course the deity totemized. Reik further alludes to the custom of having *Tefillim* with two head pieces just as animals have two horns.[670] He lays chief stress however upon a book by Johannes Lund, "*Die alten juedischen Heiligtuemer*" (1701) which contains information to the effect that pious Jews have worn head *Tefillim* from which a few animal hairs would project and that these were interpreted as reminiscent of the red heifer or of the golden calf. Reik feels that this leaves no doubt that identification with the totem father or deity was the original significance of *Talith*, *Tefillim* and *Ẓiẓit*.

The spreading of the Aaronides' fingers at the pronouncing of the benediction is surmised by Karl Abraham to have been a simulation of animal paws or claws, supplementing the animal

[664] *Ibid.*, p. 255.

[665] Reik quotes W. Robertson Smith, *Religion of the Semites* p. 334 but it was not possible to find this point on p. 334 in the 1907 or any other edition.

[666] Reik, "Gebetmantel und Gebetriemen der Juden" *Imago*, XVI, (1930) 389–434.

[667] *Ibid.*, p. 422.

[668] *Ibid.*, p. 428.

[669] *Ibid.*, pp. 402, 429. He refers to Sifre 115 and to Sab. 118b on Num. 15. 38.

[670] *Ibid.*, p. 433 foot note.

skin which the *Talith* represents.[671] The Aaronide, wrapped in the *Talith* and spreading his fingers, is so far identical with the Deity that looking at him is perilous.[672] Abraham attaches significance to the fact that, whatever the Jewish objections to sculpture, it has been permissible to carve, on the tombs of the Aaronides, representations of the finger-spread.[673]

Again, the turban of Aaron, like the mask of Moses an insignium of usurpation, is at the same time a token of obedience to the father-God who is understood to have commanded the wearing of the turban. A similar point is made by Reik with regard to the *Tefillim*—trophies of rebellion and at the same time gestures of reverence.[674] As in a neurotic compromise, so also in ritual, the forbidden becomes permissible.[675]

We are further apprised of ritual acts combining grief over the father's death with joy over his defeat. Mention is made of sacrificial rites in which the participants force themselves to weep, like children forcing themselves to cry over a parental death which may be to them gratifying as well as saddening.[676] The etymological connection between *yalal*, howl and *hallel*, praise is held to embody this ambivalence.[677] Joy as well as awe is known to enter also into the *shofar* blowing. In the unconscious mind, "*ashre yod'e teru'ah*" can, among other things, mean, "Happy are those who were present at the patricide."[678] Reik discerns in the proximity of the Divine name to the *shofar* prayer, "O destroy Satan," a dual sense, making the phrase denote, at the same time, unconsciously, "O destroy God."[679] The change in the time of the *shofar* blowing from the morning service, where the context does not so thoroughly conceal its

671 Reik, *op. cit.*, p. 223, p. 246.

672 Karl Abraham, "Der Versoehnungstag," *Imago*, VI, 89.

673 Abraham *op. cit.*, p. 88.

674 Reik, *Probleme der Religionspsychologie* p. 268. For *tefillim* the reference is Exod. 13.16; for turban, Exod. 28.36–38.

675 *Ibid.*, p. 268.

676 *Ibid.*, p. 254.

677 *Ibid.*, pp. 253, 254, 255.

678 *Ibid.*, pp. 222, 255.

679 *Ibid.*, p. 224. Reik should have said that the words "Destroy Satan," "*kera' Satan*," are to be found in the initial letters of the succession of Psalm verses that are read just prior to the blowing. Supra p. 685.

purport, to the *musaf* is asserted by Reik to be a device for hiding its true significance. Parallels in the neuroses, he tells us, are well known.[680]

Certain ritual dances are said to convey moods of sorrow and of pleasure alternating.[681] It is reported that neurotics display the identical ambivalences. "Tendencies of liking and of aversion can combine in one and the same obsessive act."

We have dwelt on Reik's theory that back of the golden calf story is a fancy involving two animals or statues of animals, one of which was a calf and one a bull. Upon this Reik bases his surmise that there may have been a time when a bull father and a calf son were worshiped simultaneously.[682] In that event there would be amalgamated, in the homage to the golden calf, rebellion against the father with loyalty toward the father.[683]

Our attention has also been called to the ambivalence involved in Moses' shattering of the calf; a killing of the father and, at the same time, a punitive self-killing. The same double killing may be signified by the demolition of the two tablets.[684] To the *kappara* ritual, Karl Abraham imputes a similar duality.[685] It is a killing of the symbolized father-god and, at the same time, a killing of the killer, fowl and user being, as already stated, ritually identified. A corresponding ambivalence is ascribed to fasting. Fasting can symbolize a slaying of the totem and can, at the same time, be a self-punishment for the slaying, "just as in certain neuroses an act of self-affliction can be substituted for a repressed sadism."[686] Somewhat analogous are the passages already noted in which the deity is pictured as the sacrificiant. By the deity as slaughterer, the identity of the deity and the animal slaughtered is veiled.[687] A further signification may be the father's

680 *Ibid.*, p. 225. 681 *Ibid.*, p. 255. 682 *Ibid.*, p. 281.

683 "Die Darstellung der Tradition ermoeglicht es wie die des Traumes, zwei einander kontraer entgegenstehende Handlungen in eine zusammenzuziehen" (*ibid.*, p. 287).

684 *Ibid.*, p. 304.

685 Karl Abraham, "Der Versoehnungstag "*Imago*, VI, 82.

686 *Ibid.*, p. 83. The author might have recalled the fast day prayer of R. Sheshet in Ber. 17a "*Yehi ḥelbi we-dami shenitma'aṭ ke'ilu hikrabti lefaneka 'al gabbe ha-mizbeaḥ.*"

687 Freud, *Totem und Tabu* p. 139 and supra p. 682.

killing of the son together with the father's punitive self-killing compacted into one act.

Finally there is the exaltation of the God concept by means of which the Biblical accounts efface the primitive crudities. The primitive bull god is exalted into a supermundane law giver. Yet, in being thus exalted, the bull is abolished;[688] his elevation is his undoing.[689] Reik predicates an analogy here to the hero myths studied by Otto Rank.[690] A hero usually has two fathers, a real father of regal station and then a foster father who is likely to be a humble peasant or fisherman. Neurotics and adolescents have similar phantasies of exalted family connections. The thesis is that, in this way, the real father is, at one and the same time, extolled and effaced. Kindred may have been the process by which an assaulted stone god is transmuted into the adored tablets of stone. A single act unites the antithetic tendencies.

PART II

CRITICAL

The first part of this study was, on the whole, expository. Our second part is to be critical, that is critical of the contents of the first part.

The present writer must admit the limitation arising from the fact that his acquaintance with psychoanalysis is purely

[688] Reik, *Probleme der Religionspsychologie* pp. 272, 301. Reik thinks that the abhorrence of the bull worship alongside of the reverence for the stones in Exod. chaps. 32–34 would indicate that bull worship was suppressed earlier than stone worship.

[689] "In der Kompromisart neurotischer Symptome, schaltet sie naemlich nicht nur das Bild Jahweh sondern ihn selbst zugleich damit aus dem Kulte aus, was freilich durch die erhoehte Stellung des Weltgesetzgebers ueberkompensiert wird. Die durch die relative verstaerkte Liebe bedingte Erhoehung Jahwehs zum ewigen Gott darf uns nicht darueber taeuschen, dass damit zugleich eine durch den unbewussten Hass erklaerte Vernichtung desselben Gottes stattfand—genau so wie im Familienroman der Pubertaetsjahre mit dem sozialen Hinaufruecken des Vaters ein phantastasiertes Wegraeumen seiner realen Persoehnlichkeit verbunden ist" (*ibid.*, p. 281).

[690] Otto Rank, "*Der Mythus von der Geburt des Helden*" in "*Schriften zur angewandten Seelenkunde*" 5, (Heft, Wien und Leipzig) 1909, p. 64ff.

bibliographical. He has had no special training in psychoanalysis and no clinical or laboratory experience. The evaluations to be expressed however claim validity only as literary evaluations. The attempt is to assess the quality of the published material so far as this may be done without recourse to any further procedure. A layman's impression of psychoanalytic literature is the main purport of what follows.

In the course of this investigation, a statement setting forth the theory of psychoanalysis as apparently contained in the works studied was submitted by the writer to a number of expert psychoanalysts for criticism and correction. To the following psychoanalysts who have rendered this valuable service, obligation is hereby gratefully acknowledged:

Dr. Isador H. Coriat, Boston, Mass.; Dr. G. V. Hamilton, Santa Barbara, Cal.; Dr. Smith Ely Jelliffe, New York, N. Y.; Dr. Ernest Jones, London, England; Dr. Horace M. Kallen, New York, N. Y.; Dr. Edward Liss, New York, N. Y.; Dr. Cavendish Moxon, San Francisco, Cal.; Dr. Ralph Reed, Cincinnati, O.; Dr. Wilhelm Stekel, Vienna, Austria; Dr. Fritz Wittels, New York, N. Y. formerly of Vienna; Rev. Walter Samuel Swisher, Wellesley Hills, Mass.; Mr. Arnold Kamiat, Brooklyn, N. Y.

This second part of our study will accordingly comprise the following divisions:

I. Our statement regarding the import of psychoanalysis which was submitted to the experts.

II. A review of the comments and objections voiced by the experts who read and criticized the statement.

III. A defense of the proposition that the conclusions quoted in the first part of this article are not necessarily invalidated by their indelicacies, by the absurdities they contemplate or by their anthropological or philological inaccuracies but that they are nonetheless weakened by lack of statistical support.

IV. A plea for the subventioning of accurate psychoanalytic research into religious and specifically into Jewish problems.

I. The Statement Submitted to the Experts

The following, with a few minor corrections and supplementations, is the text of our statement on the theory of psychoanalysis. The reader will bear in mind that objections to this statement will receive attention later:

Having completed the exposition of the psychoanalytic interpretations that have been accorded various elements of Judaism, it now remains for us to appraise the several claims and to inquire how much if any of them is true. At once we find ourselves confronted with the formidable question: "When is any psychoanalytic proposition true?" What conditions must any psychoanalytic assertion fulfil in order to be correct? What are the assurances of validity in psychoanalysis and what the earmarks of non-validity? Despite the voluminousness of psychoanalytic literature, this question seems to be nowhere clearly treated. Psychoanalysts are mostly psychiatrists and clinicians whose interests are centered in curing the sick. Like scientists in other fields, they rarely stop to reflect upon the presuppositions underlying their own procedure. We ourselves, before we advance one step farther, must reckon with these persuppositions as best we can.

Our first move will have to be a fresh survey of certain backgrounds. These we can summarize in the following eight propositions:

1. Any person or group of persons consists of numerous purposes. "Wishes," "wants," "desires," "cravings," "urges," "yearnings," "plans," "motives," "goals," "objectives"—all are synonyms of "purpose."[691]

2. Purposes, whatever else they may be, are continuous with the automatic actions and re-actions of the organism and with those prenatal and postnatal conditionings, correctly or incorrectly called "instincts."

3. Sometimes purposes are realized, sometimes thwarted and sometimes abandoned.

[691] This view is elaborated in the article, "The Social Consequences of the One and the Many," *Hebrew Union College Monthly*, (December 1929, January 1930.)

4. Sometimes the divergent purposes of an individual or a group harmonize and sometimes they conflict.

5. Some purposes possess the character of master purposes in relation to which other purposes are subsidiary or auxiliary. A man may buy, sell, rent, borrow, lend, advertise, peddle, higgle, swindle, accommodate, serve in scores of ways and in myriads of instances. In each separate act or sequence of acts, he pursues a separate purpose. Yet all of these diverse pursuits are but accessory to one cardinal pursuit, that of making money. Money acquisition may be itself subsidiary to some more inclusive purpose such as the achievement of security, prestige or power. A man may pack his traveling case, telephone for a cab, drive to the railroad station, proceed from the cab to the ticket window, purchase a ticket, board a train, remain twenty-four hours on the train, leave the train etc.—all of which separate acts are fulfilments of separate purposes that coalesce into the major purpose of going to New York. This purpose may be itself subsidiary to the purpose of singing in the Metropolitan opera, a purpose which may in turn be subordinate to the purpose of acquiring fame as an opera singer etc.[692]

6. Purposes derive their names from the situations which constitute their fulfilment.[693] There is no other way of designating human purposes. This fact fully accords with the general function of all naming. We name in order to control. Every name stands for a certain mode of handling. Our control of human conduct is enhanced when we know (i.e. when we can name) what it is that a given individual likes or dislikes; in other words what it is that fulfils or thwarts his purposes.

7. It commonly happens that people are actuated by unnamed purposes. All of an infant's purposes are of this character. The infant, unable to state that food is what it desires, simply clamors when it is hungry. It frets when it is fatigued. "I am tired, put me to sleep" is more than it can say. This condition obtains also in adult life. We can want something without knowing just

[692] The ancient hierarchization of species and genera can perhaps be shown to be but an aspect of this purpose hierarchization.

[693] There is some analogy here to our practice of discovering the meanings of words from their contexts.

what we want. Eventually we may discover that what we want is a breath of fresh air or a glass of some stimulant or someone's companionship or love embraces or a new religion or higher ideals or the hearing of a symphony concert. Yet it is possible to have, at least temporarily, unarticulated wants.

8. As factors of purpose fulfilment or frustration, mental presentations such as images, thoughts, memories, phantasies, can function precisely as extra-mental situations. There would be no need of mentioning this were it not for the habitual dualism which fails to see that the distinction between mental and extra-mental is something entirely provisional. Mental experiences are experiences and extra-mental experiences are experiences in exactly the same sense. The extra-mental are simply those which, involving among other things, some social necessity, have the peculiar fixity that leads us to speak of space. So far as purpose expression is concerned, the "inner" and the "outer" are alike in every detail:

a. Diverse mental presentations follow one another or co-exist in time, just like extra-mental situations.

b. Exactly like "outer" situations, mental presentations can be pleasing or displeasing.

c. Just as one outward situation can lead to another, so can one mental presentation lead to another. Just as one outward act can be the means to another, so can one mental state be the means to another. The relation, when it obtains among mental states, is called that of suggestion or association of ideas.

d. Just as outward situations have a history, so do mental states have a history. To the historical aspect of mental states, we apply the term "memory" or "recollection." Their detachment from the space fixity enables mental states, as it were, to carry their history with them to a degree impossible with the non-mental.[694]

e. Master purposes assert themselves in mental states precisely as they do in "outward" acts. The master purpose of a man's overt conduct is named after some unitary result to which a considerable variety of different acts leads. Similarly is a master

[694] Rev. Walter S. Swisher calls my attention to an exposition of this doctrine in Bergson's *Creative Evolution* pp. 4 and 5.

purpose named after some unitary result to which a considerable variety of mental association trains leads. That is how we come, as a result of knowing an individual's thoughts and fancies, to characterize his temperament as one of self-aggrandizement or of "escape from reality" or of voluptuousness. Cato's "Delenda est Carthago" is only a celebrated example of how any diversity of mental association trains can draw up to the same converging point. When we adopt a name for the master purpose, the name is likely to be that of this converging point. The suitability of the name, like the suitability of any name, lies in the efficacy of that name as a means of control.

In these eight propositions and five subdivisions of one of them, psychoanalysis has not once been mentioned. The attempt was merely to sketch a background by listing a few familiar and presumably unchallenged observations the bearing of which upon psychoanalysis is now to be shown.

Familiar psychoanalytic themes are already brought into the picture by our reference to wishes, wants, desires, urges, "instincts," etc., as well as by our mention of conflicts, association of ideas, recollections and memories.

The unconscious desires of psychoanalysis are unnamed purposes. The only peculiar thing about them is that their names can be arrived at, if at all, only by means of the psychoanalytic technique. Some of them are master purposes to be discovered by following to their converging point numerous trains of mental association. Until he reaches such converging point, the psychoanalyst is baffled. Like other master purposes, the unconscious desires of psychoanalysis can be subsidiary to some master purposes still more dominant. Not readily is the psychoanalyst satisfied with the meaning that he reaches. He seeks ever more recondite meanings of the subject's dreams, phantasies or movements, more inclusive purposes, profounder converging points, such converging points being the strategic points for wielding influence. Above all, the *ultima ratio* of psychoanalysis is results—as it happens, therapeutic results—which completely fits our contention that the suitability of a name lies in its usefulness as a handle of control.[695]

[695] One might proffer reasons for asking the psychoanalysts to abandon

We might put it also this way: There is an association not only of ideas but also of emotions and volitions. Emotions or volitions attaching to one idea can, by the familiar phenomenon of conditioning, become attached to the associated ideas and can recur with the associated ideas even when the original idea does not recur. One may shudder at the fragrance of a tube rose without observing that the smell, being like that of funeral flowers, is a death suggestion. One may experience an inexplicable thrill in beholding an old sewing machine; one need not recall one's childhood delight in a toy found once in an attic where remnants of an old sewing machine were lying about. These original presentations behind emotional and volitional responses are apparently the salient psychoanalytic quest. The original presentation and, in our present usage, the master purpose appear, according to psychoanalysis, to be one and the same.[695a]

In the language of our background, every psychoanalytic term can, without difficulty, be redefined. Let us illustrate:

Repression. A purpose which lacks designation because it is frustrated by some conflicting purpose. Since purposes are named after that which fulfils them, a persistently unfulfiled purpose will undergo delay in securing a name.

Anamnesis. The resumption of the mental activities connected with the assertion of some previously repressed purpose. Recollection, as we noticed above, is the historical aspect of mental states. Since every mental state has its history, a resuscitated set of mental states would have a resuscitated set of histories. Anamnesis is primarily not so much a recovery of lost memories as it is a revival of certain detained purpose assertions.

their term "unconscious" and to substitute "unnamed" or to say instead of "the unconscious" "the unarticulated." One is unconscious only of that by which one's consciousness is totally unaffected, just as Isaiah was unconscious of the American continent, Homer unconscious of the radio, a sleeper unconscious of the bed on which he lies, a layman unconscious of Einstein's mathematical intricacies, an inspired orator unconscious of the handkerchief in his pocket or a healthy individual unconscious of the automatic functionings of his own organism. No one is in this sense unconscious of any of the desires that may be called his. The psychoanalysts admit that their "unconscious" desires do affect consciousness. Would not "unnamed" or "unarticulated" be the more accurate term?

695a This paragraph is a later addition and was not seen by the experts.

Compromise. This occurs when a mental state or an extra-mental situation serves two opposing purposes by the partial fulfilment of both and the complete fulfilment of neither.

Displacement. A species of compromise which consists in retaining certain presentation elements satisfactory to a given purpose while surrendering, in the interests of some conflicting purpose, the arrangement or distribution of those elements.

Rationalization. A species of compromise which consists in using little more than the name of a socially approved purpose while retaining all except the name of a socially unpresentable purpose.

Sublimation. The abandonment of a purpose fraught with troublesome repression and frustration.[696]

Defense Mechanism. A set of actions, mental or non-mental, that partly fulfils an unnamed purpose in such manner as to thwart some social purpose with which the observer is identified.

The I, the Id, the Super-Ego. The I is the aggregate of purposes constituting a given individual. The Id is the aggregate of unnamed purposes belonging to the I. The Super-Ego is the aggregate of socially endorsed purposes belonging to the I.

Psychoanalysis can thus be translated into terms of ordinary psychology. We must not however overlook its essential and notable uniqueness. Psychoanalysis is unique by reason of its technique.[697] Psychoanalysis may be defined as a technique for holding in check an individual's socially shared purposes long enough for his socially unpresentable and therefore repressed purposes to acquire names and become amenable to control. *The abeyance or relaxation of social pressure is the gist of the psychoanalytic method.* The "free" associations sought are primarily such as are free from social trammels. They represent conduct under relatively desocialized conditions—mental conduct of course; overt conduct of that kind would be disastrous. The

[696] Sublimation is identical with what behaviorists call "reconditioning" and religionists call renunciation.

[697] Dr. Coriat, one of the experts listed on page 700 supra takes issue on this. He says: "Psychoanalysis is unique not by reason of its technique alone but by its insistence on unconscious mental processes." There seems however to be nothing in the acceptance of this that need deflect our line of argument.

analyst can do nothing for his patient until he prevails upon his patient to eschew, at least so far as mental processes are concerned, the habitual social deference. The analyst is the vehicle of ethical neutrality. He succeeds only if he can suspend his patient's sense of shame.[698] Perhaps that is one of the reasons why the analyst is likely to be a physician, the individual before whom our sense of shame is expected to subside. He is the antithesis of the "Censor" whose presence or absence psychoanalysts claim to be able to trace in dreams. The suppressed anti-social purposes come, in this way, sufficiently near realization to secure names. Indeed it is doubtful whether psychoanalysis could at all have arisen in an age and place in which *mores* were not rapidly disintegrating. By all odds, the chief grievance still felt against psychoanalysis concerns its moral nonchalance.

The claims of psychoanalysis as thus far set forth will, of course, provoke little scepticism. Even though we may doubt whether any considerable suspension of social constraint is possible, we may recognize that psychoanalysis, despite its novel phraseology, is not far removed from ordinary experience.[699] *Psychoanalysis is little besides a specially intensive way of gauging an individual's purposes by observing his behavior.* What it practically amounts to is the observation of people under specially devised conditions analogous to those of the experimental sciences or of certain forms of medical diagnosis. But over and above what we have just synopsized, psychoanalysis vouches for certain specific empirical conclusions. These conclusions relate to the recurrence, the frequency and the extensiveness of certain mental happenings. We may summarize these conclusions in two statements:

[698] Dr. Moxon would qualify this statement by adding "to a limited extent." Dr. Coriat would change "sense of shame" to "feeling of guilt."

[699] One of the respondents listed on page 700 supra challenges the phrase "ordinary experience." He says: "That an infant desires to eat his father's penis and expel it *per rectum* is a good way from ordinary experience." To this we reply that it is *psychoanalysis* which is, according to our claim, not far from ordinary experience. This is remote from saying that the experiences reported by psychoanalysis are ordinary. The ordinary thing (approximately) is what the psychoanalyst does, not what the infant does.

1. Certain uniform master purposes of the unsocial type are evinced by all people or by large groups of people. This is the import of such stock terms as "Oedipus Complex," "Narcissism," "Infantilism," "Need for Punishment."[700]

2. There is a high positive correlation between certain recurrent images or groups of images and certain master purposes. Hence the psychoanalytic doctrine of symbols.

Keeping in mind the propensity of master purposes to function as subsidiary to larger master purposes, let us on our own initiative borrow from linguistics and apply the term "ultimate" to a person's most inclusive purposes, the term "antepenultimate" to the least inclusive and "penultimate" to those that lie between. Whether the recurrent purposes alleged by psychoanalysis are of the ultimate, penultimate or antepenultimate rank, the reader of psychoanalytic writings is usually left to make out for himself. With reference to these distinctions,

[700] In his *Zukunft einer Illusion, Gesammelte Schriften*, XI, 437, Vienna 1928, Freud disposes with cavalier terseness of Vaihinger's "*Philosophie des Als Ob*." Freud being, in matters epistemological, a layman it would not be arrogant of us to suggest that in the domain of psychoanalysis more perhaps than anywhere else is the doctrine of the *als ob* needed. The case of the Oedipus Complex would be immeasurably strengthened if we might say not that the subject has desires for his mother but that the subject acts in some respects *as if* he had desires for his mother. What the subject displays is not all but only some of the activities implied by "mother attachment." Since it is always easier to think concretely than abstractly, we supplement the abstractions in which we happen to be interested with something that will concretize them. In such manner we speak of electric currents although no liquid of any kind runs through the wires. We speak of planetary attraction although planets have neither arms nor sex appeal and we say that water "seeks" the lowest level although water possesses neither eyes nor brains wherewith to seek. All metaphorical usage is an extension of this concretizing process. The Oedipus Complex, as well as many other of the psychoanalytic entities, are ultimately perhaps instances of the *als ob*. At least regarded as such their demands upon our credulity are greatly reduced. When psychoanalysts speak of the libido as though it were a kind of fluid quantities of which can be directed from one channel into another, what is there to be found anywhere more typical of the *als ob*? One of our respondents is on the verge of the *als ob* conception when, speaking of the Oedipus Complex he remarks: "It is solely a formulation for dynamic measuring—a pressure 'gage'—manometer, barometer, thermometer, and a lot more—to be applied to any act and get a reading in terms of 'developmental adaptation.' "

the published literature is hazy. Freud and Reik seem to regard the Oedipus Complex as something ultimate and something universal.[701]

A more serious shortcoming of psychoanalysis resides in its lack of statistical validation for either of the two conclusions just cited. Nowhere in its ocean of literature do we find figures informing us how many people have been analyzed in a given study and what was the recurrence of the master purposes unearthed, whether ultimate, penultimate or antepenultimate as shown by the converging points of association trains and by the practical efficacy of the designations adopted. How many were the persons of the one sex or the other, one state of health or another, one vocation or another, one cultural opportunity or another, one age or another, one past or another who evinced this or that recurrent purpose, ultimate, penultimate or antepenultimate? How often in a given study has the same image cluster recurred, how often has each image or image cluster figured in association trains leading to this, that or the other master purpose? A penchant for that mathematical tabulation which many deem the *sine qua non* of scientific method is not among the proclivities of the psychoanalysts.[702] Perhaps the clinic has needed the psychoanalysts so urgently that, for the laboratory, they have had little leisure.

The psychoanalytic doctrine of infantilism involves the additional need of statistical reports on observations of infants. Before a given act or phantasy can be classified as a mother fixation or an infantile response, more should be known statistically concerning what infants actually do.[703] Also desirable, from a

[701] One of our respondents advises us to distinguish between the Oedipus Complex in its normal and the same complex in its neurotic manifestations. Naturally the statement about universality is not applicable to the neurotic manifestations.

[702] Sometimes the conclusions offered in the name of psychoanalysis—such as the hypersexuality of prudes, the doctrinal uncertainties of fanatics or the sexual strains in religious excitement—are surmises that can be supported by ordinary observation or introspection without recourse to psychoanalysis. (One of the respondents claims that psychoanalysis in any event deserves credit for drawing our attention to much that, without psychoanalysis, we would never have surmised.)

[703] Of course such obviously infantile acts as snuggling, breast sucking, lothes soiling may, without compunction, be designated as infantile.
c

scientific point of view, would be a more accurate listing of the reactions called sexual, that is, reactions peculiarly associated with the stimulation of the organs of procreation.

For the lack of statistical confirmation,[704] however, a striking consensus of opinion compensates in a way.[705] The scope of agreement among psychoanalysts is surprising. Nearly all of them accept the doctrine of the Oedipus Complex. Practically all of them grant the existence and the signification of certain symbols such as a door for the female organ of sex, a tree for the male organ, and speaking or singing for the sexual act; if not these images themselves, at least these images in certain allegedly frequent combinations with other images. The presumption is that such fancies as door, tree, voice, have in the course of numerous psychoanalyses, appeared again and again in conjunction with certain reactions familiarly identified with procreative occurrences. The well nigh monotonous unanimity with which psychoanalysts of a number of schools and in various parts of the world have subscribed to many of these interpretations is as impressive as the lack of statistics is bewildering.

When psychoanalytic inductions are collated with the findings of anthropology as in the discussions occupying the first part of this essay, the results are affected both by the weakness of contemporary psychoanalysis and by its strength. These anthropological conjectures are a choice example of inference; they are a procedure from the known to the unknown on the basis of resemblances. Their logic is that the association trains revealed in anthropology are so closely akin to those found in psychoanalysis that the predication of identical master purposes in both

[704] One of the respondents calls attention to the statistics in the *Psychoanalytic Review*, IV, 209–216 and *The International Journal of Psychoanalysis*, IV, Nos. 1 and 2, 1923, 254–269. These however are not statistics of association clusters. They are statistics of clinical visits, diagnostic results and finances. It has not been possible to consult *Zeitschrift f.d.g. Neurologie* 130 Heft 4–5 mentioned as a possible source of statistics by the respondent quoted on page 712 infra as opposed to statistics.

[705] Rev. Swisher writes: "It is amazing how even a little psychoanalytic practice tends to confirm Freud's basic ideas. I began by being very sceptical myself, setting down the basic concepts first as 'highly improbable,' then 'unverified,' and finally 'verified.' "

of them were not a rash conclusion. Nor is it a rash conclusion. The rashness lies in dispensing with statistical exposition of those clinical events upon which the inferences are founded.

II. The Comments of the Experts

We shall now synopsize the comments of the experts named on page 700 in so far as they take issue with the foregoing statements. Expressions of approval will be quoted only when, in relation to some expression of disapproval, they voice a contrary opinion. We shall also leave aside comments which challenge not the views advocated in our statement but the views quoted in our statement;[706] we do not enter into controversies which the psychoanalysts have among themselves. Comments calling for mere linguistic changes have already been met by alterations in the text while certain minor differences of opinion have received acknowledgment in the supplementary notes.

Above all it is our intention to disregard comments touching the non-psychoanalytic portions of our statement. While the authority of psychoanalysts is to be recognized in psychoanalytic matters, there is no occasion to defer to them in extra-psychoanalytic matters. On questions of sociology,[707] metaphysics and

[706] Examples are comments on the infantilism mentioned on pages 708, 709 and on the fixed symbolism of pages 708, 710. The respondent observes: "There is no psychoanalytic doctrine of infantilism" and "fixed symbolism is nonsense." The first part of this essay abounds in examples to the contrary. Similarly his statement: "Psychoanalysis does not 'observe people under specially devised circumstances' nor does it 'vouch for specific empirical conclusions.' " This surely does not accord with the positions of other writers.

[707] One of the respondents writes *a propos* the moral nonchalance pp. 706, 707: "The whole conception of the activity of the Super-Ego negatives this idea of moral nonchalance." Another writes: "The conception of the super-ego which is highly moral completely disposes of the misstatement that the chief grievance still felt against psychoanalysis concerns its moral nonchalance." We thoroughly agree that it *ought* to dispose of the grievance. In fact we see no reason why there should have been any grievance in the first place. Yet almost every day we encounter people who do look askance at psychoanalysis on moralistic grounds. Another respondent calls our reference to disintegrating mores on page 707 "abusive." It might as well be commendatory; mores often deserve to disintegrate. The point, in all events, has nothing to do with psychoanalysis as such. It is an observation of purely sociological import.

epistemology, the opinion of a psychoanalyst is no more compelling than that of any other interested layman. It will be noticed that psychoanalysis as such does not enter our presentation until page 704. Three of the respondents have taken issue on various points in these opening pages; but since the issue is metaphysical rather than psychoanalytic, we content ourselves with acknowledging that such objection has been voiced. The same applies to a number of subsequent points.

Whether the objection raised is psychoanalytic or non-psychoanalytic was occasionally difficult to decide. An example is the remark of one of the respondents touching the matter of statistics called for on page 709. His words are:

"Insofar as, in my opinion, none of the master, ultimate or penultimate purposes have anything to do with psychoanalysis as here stated, to try to get statistics indicates a total lack of comprehension of the situation. As well try to get statistics on the pressure of the sap in all of the trees at any or all times of the year in the forest. 'Tis nonsense to state the proposition. A biometrician may count a million shells of Pecten irradiens to try to determine a single master pattern. When anyone is willing to count millions and millions of millions of patterns in human behavior then the so-called 'delusion of statistics' can be demonstrated."

It is not easy to judge whether this shall be viewed as a pronouncement of a psychoanalyst on psychoanalysis or as the pronouncement of a psychoanalyst on epistemology. The fact that the respondent cites botanical and ornithological phenomena as well as his explicit admission that the points involved are extra-psychoanalytic would seem to indicate that the matter he treats does lie outside of his specialty.[708]

To the criticism of two of the respondents that our statement deals exclusively with Freudian psychoanalysis and ignores rival schools such as those of Rank, Jung and Adler, our reply is that the standpoint of the writers quoted in the first part of this

[708] This same respondent who will be frequently quoted in these pages states in a later communication: "My remarks were hastily scribbled down between patients and may be incompletely expressed." Elsewhere in his first letter this respondent observes "One brain, structurally requires 20–30 years to study by statistics. One individual studied 'functionally' would require at least a couple of light years." (Is not a light year a measure of distance?) Perhaps the writer did not mean these remarks to be taken seriously.

article happens to be Freudian. Followers of the other schools have not applied their findings to Jewish data. The aspects of mental life stressed by the Freudians are broached in the writing which we have surveyed while those stressed by the others are not broached. So far as these schools themselves may conflict with one another, any attempt to decide between their opposing claims falls, of course, outside our present scope.

Not a little rejoinder was evoked by our note 695 on the substitution of "unnamed" for "unconscious." One respondent writes:

"This is not correct. The unconscious is repressed material, which may or may not be capable of being brought to the conscious perceptive system—i.e. verbalized—or as you state it, 'named.' Whether capable or not capable of verbalization is a purely dynamic situation; comparable to solid, liquid, gas, in dynamic statement."

"The meaning of 'unconscious' as given is not clear in the psychoanalytical sense. In the strictly psychoanalytical sense, the unconscious consists of dynamic mental processes, not merely latent thoughts in general. These dynamic mental processes do not reach consciousness in spite of their effectiveness and intensity and cannot be brought into consciousness by any effort or will or act of memory. The unconscious is a special function of a particular system of mental apparatus.

Yet another respondent, slightly diverging from the other two, has this to say:

"Unconscious is not the same as 'ignorant of' even in everyday speech. The unconscious (in general) was once the conscious and is capable of becoming again conscious. Certain primitive neural response patterns perhaps may be said to belong to the unconscious in the sense of having constituted a part of the experience of the organism. The unconscious in its practical therapeutic aspect has to be regarded not merely as a static store-house of memories but as having a dynamic quality."

The question arises: Would these three respondents have raised this objection had they kept in mind the dynamic conception of all knowledge subscribed to in our earlier paragraphs[709] or had they even noticed our sentence on page 704," their names may be arrived at, if at all, etc."? Again is the likelihood entirely absent that we are confronting once more one of those meta-

[709] Speaking of our presentation as a whole, the first of the respondents here quoted observes: "If the statements were formulated from the dynamic angle, the whole situation would receive a different mode of treatment "

physical questions expertness in which is not necessarily guaranteed by psychoanalytic expertness? Surely that which has already been said regarding psychoanalysis and the *als ob* is not without bearing on this point.[710]

Two of the respondents are less sweeping in their dissent. One of them holds:

> "This dictum is true only if you asseverate that there is to be only one meaning of the word 'unconscious.' Actually there are several meanings in the field."

while another claims analogously that the word "'unnamed' while suitable to certain types of thinking is not suitable to the feelings involved."

Meanwhile, Dr. Wilhelm Stekel, commenting on the same note declares: "Auch ich bin Ihrer Ansicht und finde dass 'Namenlose' oder das noch nicht 'Verwoerterte' besser waere."

Issue was further taken with the words "observing" and "observation" on page 707. The sentence: "Psychoanalysis is little besides a specially intensive way of gauging an individual's purposes by observing his behavior" ought perhaps to be emended: "Psychoanalysis is *among other things* a specially intensive way of gauging an individual's purposes by observing his behavior." The sentence in its original form referred, like all the rest of our statement, to pronouncements contained in the first part of this article where obviously nothing but observation is involved. The respondents, being psychiatric practitioners, are promptly aware that their work entails much more than observation. One of them writes:

> "It may be this and more. Psychoanalysis is not observation of the patient by someone but a mode of bringing the patient to see himself—an 'Alice in the looking glass' procedure."

Another asserts:

"This betokens great ignorance . . . what about interpretation?" May not this distinction between observation and interpretation also be one of our metaphysical excursuses? Likewise not entirely free of metaphysics is a comment of a drift somewhat contrary to the preceding, a comment on our remark (page 704)

[710] Note 700 supra.

that the *ultima ratio* of psychoanalysis is results. Here the respondent protests:

"The *ultima ratio* is not results, for psychoanalysis is not all therapeutic, but is the science of unconscious mental processes and in its broadest sense is the province of knowledge opened up through the utilization of this science of the unconscious."

There was also divergence of opinion touching our description of the psychoanalytic technique as a relaxation of social pressure (supra pp. 706, 707). One of the respondents comments:

"No psychoanalyst would say so . . . on the contrary [the process of analyzing] is [something] intensified and concentrated."

Another respondent prefers to construe it as a new socialized situation, a living over of the child relation to the parent, the psychoanalyst representing a parent possessed of an enhanced capacity to understand. Another respondent however who on other points assails our statement most vehemently regards our surmise about the relaxation of social pressure as "a very interesting thought." It should be noticed, of course, that were we to alter our statement to comply with the objections, there need still be no alteration of that for which the statement attempts to account. The fact still remains that attitudes which often come to light under analysis are said to be lascivious, incestuous and homicidal.

By far the greatest number of objections seem to converge on the series of illustrative definitions given on pages 705, 706. One of the respondents asserts:

"None of these definitions has anything to do with the economic dynamic ideas of psychoanalysis. They represent a series of illy defined notions chiefly taken from amateur analysis or in some cases from the earlier cruder stages of psychoanalytic emergence and evolution."

Dr. Coriat offers the following series of rectifications:

" 'Repression' is better defined as the mental process by which perception and ideas which would be painful to consciousness are rejected from consciousness and forced back into the unconscious system, but still remaining dynamic."

" 'Displacement' is better defined as a transference or attachment of an emotion from one group of ideas which may harmonize with unconscious thinking to other and quite opposite ideas as they exist in consciousness."

" 'Rationalization' is better defined as the inventing of a reason for an attitude or action, the real motive of which attitude or action is not recognized by consciousness."

" 'Sublimation' is not identical or synonymous with what the behaviorists call 'reconditioning.' Sublimation is a psychological tendency whereas reconditioning is essentially a physiological reaction (see Pavlov's 'Conditioned Reflexes'). Therefore, sublimation had better be defined as the process of deflecting the energy of the sexual impulses to any objects or aims of a non-sexual or socially useful goal. Sublimation is really a desexualized sexual impulse."

"*Ego*, in the psychoanalytical sense is the superficial part of the id which has been modified by the direct influences of the external world through the senses, has become imbued with consciousness and whose chief function is the testing of reality."

"*Id.* Define as the impersonality of the mind apart from the ego; the true unconscious or deepest part of the mind and as such, the reservoir of instinctive impulses. It is the dynamic equivalent of the descriptive unconscious.

Super-ego. Define as that part of the mental apparatus which criticizes the ego and causes pain to it whenever it tends to accept impulses emanating from the id.

In his criticism of our definition of repression, Dr. Coriat is joined by three of the other respondents. Dr. Reed also says:

"Repression is a form of activity, more than merely a purpose—it is a *fait accompli* . . . The memory of an experience is repressed not so much because it conflicts with some purpose or other goal but because it conflicts with one's cultural acquisitions and super-ego ideals, i.e. it is a part of one's self unacceptable to the remainder."

Dr. Jelliffe regards our definition as incorrect from the dynamic economic point of view. Rev. Swisher similarly dissents. He would define repression as "the involuntary exclusion from consciousness of painful ideas and desires."

While Dr. Reed's redefinition of displacement comports with that of Dr. Coriat, Dr. Coriat's treatment of rationalization is paralleled by the comment of Dr. Hamilton that "the unwitting ('unconscious') nature of rationalization ought to be included in a definition of the term."

Five of the respondents in addition to Dr. Coriat take issue on our definition of sublimation. Note 696 relating sublimation to certain behavioristic concepts proved particularly objectionable. Rev. Swisher, quoting the dictionary, offers the correction that sublimation "is redirection of energy belonging to a primitive tendency into new, non-inherited channels." He quotes Jones that sublimation is "the deflection of the energy of a sexual impulse to a non-sexual and socially useful goal." Swisher's own definition is "the diversion of the libido from sexual to non-sexual creative ends." Dr. Hamilton's and Dr. Reed's criticisms are similar.

Four of the respondents in addition to Dr. Coriat call for a revision of the definitions of Ego, Id and Super-Ego. Dr. Jelliffe corrects as follows:

"I or Ego—Reiaity testing mechanism—conscious perceptive system. The Super-Ego is a dynamic censorship process—partly ontogenetic, partly phylogenetic, to aid the repressing mechanism of the Ego. The Id is the totality of the mental systems and divisible into the conscious-perceptive Ego, the intermediary (conscience of theology in part, Super-Ego or Idea Ego) and the deeper unconscious."

It would appear that interchaning our definitions of the Ego and the Id would go a considerable way toward embodying these corrections. Dr. Moxon asks: "Could not the super-ego embody a purpose of the individual not endorsed by the social will?"

A propos all of these criticisms we shall not repeat what has already been said about metaphysical intrusions and about the overlooked role of the *als ob* in psychoanalysis (pages 711, 730 and note 700). Nor dare we, a layman, faced by experts, claim much validity for our feeling that some of our definitions provide, although with different wording, for much or all that the corrections affirm. It can not be denied of course that our definitions contain much that is erroneous and that their need of revision is great. The important question however is: Will such revision alter the status of the point that the definitions attempt to illustrate? That point was that psychoanalysis is a mode of defining and controlling certain human purposes which are inaccessible to ordinary observation and that success in such control is the final standard of distinction between the psychoanalytically correct and the psychoanalytically incorrect.

A number of the respondents flatly deny that the processes of psychoanalysis can at all be translated into more general terms. Dr. Jones writes:

"When you say that psycho-analysis can thus be translated into terms of ordinary psychology one should be sure that one can substantiate this remarkable claim. In the list of definitions you give on the preceding page there is no evidence that you can substantiate the claim, because many of them are simply re-definitions of your own psychoanalytic terms rather than a translation into ordinary psychological terms of what psycholanalysts actually mean by their terms. The case of sublimation is perhaps the best example," etc.

Dr. Liss writes similarly:

"I find your psychoanalytic conceptions are based upon fallacious interpretation of the literature. It is the old trouble of trying to convey in different language a similar thought. It is rarely accomplished. At best a compromise is arrived at with the feeling 'If only the other person spoke as we do!' "

Dr. Jelliffe says:

"Psychoanalysis can never be translated over into older psychologies. It is an emergent, a novelty and therefore is not definable any more than any other novelty."

Dr. Reed is of the opinion:

"Psychoanalysis has to do mostly with a different order of activity, the unconscious. That is why it is not quite so easy to translate it into every day language."

while Dr. Wittels probably has this same matter in mind when, referring to our statement as a whole, he says: "I find I cannot agree with your views on psychoanalysis."

On the other hand, Dr. Moxon writes:

"I found the attempt to translate the theory very valuable and clear."

Dr. Hamilton writes:

"I think your pages (on the translation of the theory) are a real contribution, and your purpose on the whole a most fruitful one."

Rev. Swisher expresses the view:

"It is a good thing to translate psychoanalytic terms into everyday, comprehensible terms, and I think that with the exceptions I have cited, you have done it admirably."

Mr. Arnold Kamiat says:

"You do well to relate psychoanalytic concepts to fundamental psychological notions, for it is one of the tests of the truth of a proposition that it can come into relations of unity with other propositions accepted as true."

Prof. Kallen writes:

"I like the reinterpretation of the psychoanalytic concepts into more familiar forms: that is sound and scientific."

Finally, counterbalancing the blanket dissent of Dr. Wittels is the blanket approval of his compatriot Dr. Wilhelm Stekel:

"Ich finde Ihre Auseinandersetzung sehr interessant und moechte gar keine Stelle geaendert haben. Es ist gleichgueltig ob ich in Allem uebereinstimme."

As we bring this section to a close, the only question of moment before us is: Granting the validity of all the psychoanalytic and not merely metaphysical strictures raised, how would our final position be effected? We have presented all of the objections. Crushing indeed were some of them. Yet do not our essential conclusions emerge unscathed? Those conclusions were that there does exist in psychoanalysis a distinction between "correct" and "incorrect," that the distinction rests here as everywhere on certain practical concerns and that lack of statistical validation is as weakening in psychoanalytic generalizations as it is in generalizations of any other kind. May not one of the respondents whose criticisms were of the severest have had this in mind when, in a subsequent letter he wrote:

"Thus I have no dissent but only a pleading for a deeper penetration of the mysteries of the unconscious."

III. Valid and Invalid Objections to the Contents of Part One of this Article

One purpose of the foregoing was that of fending off certain antagonisms. The grotesqueness, the absurdity, often the indelicacy of some of the deliverances quoted in the first part of this article will probably stir vehement opposition. But the grotesque, the absurd and the indelicate are precisely the stamping ground of psychoanalysis. The uncontrolled mentation which is the subject matter of psychoanalysis can not very well be anything except absurd. The grotesque, the absurd and the indelicate are such because of their variance from social standards and the realm of the unsocialized is the realm of psychoanalysis.

Surely no one will insist that the grotesque the absurd and the indelicate are absent from human life. What can be more absurd than the reveries, the day dreams and the night dreams of anyone? Many of the absurdities exhibited in our Part One are only such as are commonplace in anthropology and inseparable from primitive mind processes. There need be nothing absurd in reporting the absurd.

Objection will also be raised because of anthropological, philological, liturgic, exegetic or historical misstatements some of which we have already noted and many more of which can doubtless be detected. Yet the extent to which blunders of this kind can enfeeble the conclusions reached is not overwhelming. For brevity, let us use the term "anthropological" to cover the anthropological, the philological, exegetic etc. or whatever other areas outside of psychology our writers may have invaded. Let us use the word "complex" for any of those "unconscious" wishes or combinations of wishes which our writers claim to have ferreted out. We shall then find the framework of their reasoning to be a syllogism somewhat thus:

> Certain image or action types are peculiar to such and such complexes.
>
> The facts in the given anthropological case indicate those image or action types.
>
> Therefore, the facts in the given anthropological case indicate such and such complexes.

The major premise of this syllogism is entirely a matter of psychoanalytic, clinical or laboratory observation. It is not strengthened by anthropological accuracy nor weakened by anthropological error. The minor premise does involve the anthropological, the facts in question being in a very large number of instances anthropologically ascertained. Yet even here anthropological misstatement need not invalidate. The facts that remain after the misstatement has been discounted may still indicate the alleged image or action type. Nay more, the facts that emerge from a correction of the misstatement may also indicate that image or action type.

One circumstance however complicates the problem. On pages 614, 615, discussing Levy's interpretation of the Paradise story, we observed that the author had neglected to state in whose mind those associations had occurred. Was it in that of one or more of the original narrators or of one of the first writers or of one of the editors or of subsequent readers or of several or of all of these? With the exception of the Allwohn analysis of Hosea, the Becker analysis of R. Nachman, Reik's analysis of the young woman who forgot the name, Ben Hur, and of the exegetes who emended *immo* to *abiw*—likewise some of Kantor's and Reik's comments on David, Ruth, Joseph etc. assuming these to have been actual personalities—the same questions concerning whose mind entertained the associations apply to virtually all of our material.

From this diffuseness and non-individuation of the complexes considered, another syllogism takes shape:

> Certain complexes are as prevalent or almost as prevalent as human nature.[711]
>
> Certain types of acts and of images are peculiar to those complexes.
>
> Therefore, certain types of acts and of images indicate complexes as prevalent or almost as prevalent as human nature.

Here it is the minor premise that is purely psychological, unaffected by anthropological considerations while it is the major premise that comes under anthropological influence. To establish universality or extensiveness, laboratory data must be supplemented by the anthropological. Still the same applies here as in our previous syllogism. Anthropological error need not undermine. The premise may remain secured by anthropological points that are correctly stated and even by points arising from the rectification of the error.

It follows that the weight of the argument rests not on anthropology but on psychology. Error in the latter domain rather than in the former is that which weakens. The question is therefore in place: "How much error in the latter domain have our writers committed?" But the psychoanalytic expertness required for a reply to this question is beyond the reach of the present study. Psychoanalytic competence is something that the writer of these words does not possess. All that it is possible to do is to take cognizance of what, at least to a layman, are certain inadequacies.

We can notice that the writings surveyed in the first part of this article exhibit, so far as their use of modern psychological research is concerned, four distinct features:

[711] Freud actually insists, "Ohne die Annahme einer Massenpsychose einer Kontinuitaet im Gefuehlsleben der Menschen, welche gestattet sich ueber die Unterbrechungen der seelischen Akte durch das Vergehen der Individuen hinwegzusetzen, kann die Voelkerpsychologie ueberhaupt nicht

1. References to individual cases.
2. References to types or classes of cases.

Within each of these divisions we have to distinguish between:

3. Initial facts.
4. Alleged subsequent findings interpretative of those facts.

1.

Specific cases covered were:

The Jewish man who reacted erotically to forbidden food (p. 671).

The Jewish woman who reacted erotically to forbidden food (p. 671).

The young woman who forgot the name of the book, Ben Hur, (p. 628).

The child who spoke of desexualizing his father (p. 647).

The child, Freud's patient, who mimicked a horse (pp.694, 695).

The child, Arpad, Ferenczi's patient who mimicked fowls (p. 694).

The neurotic woman who would clean out a drawer and then dump the dirt back again (p. 652).

The patient whose voice grew progressively fainter (p. 660).

The woman who dreaded stepping on the indentations of cement sidewalks (p. 609).

The woman given to swearing by the life of her husband (note 425).

The man who feared that his marriage to a certain woman would prove fatal to his father (note 335).

Freud's patient who was beset with an inclination to blaspheme (p. 650).

These instances are reports of observed facts. They involve no interpretation and entail no psychoanalysis. Their credibility depends upon nothing except the veracity of those reporting. One may believe these reports or disbelieve them whether one's attitude toward psychoanalysis is friendly or hostile.

bestehen . . . keine Generation ist im Stande bedeutsamere seelische Vorgaenge von der naechsten zu verbergen" (*Totem und Tabu* p. 146).

2.

The same applies to certain types or classes of cases the following examples of which have been furnished by our writers:

Married couples whose relations improve when there are children (p. 625).

Hostile sentiments that lead to hostile actions (p. 612).

Patients who neglect to close the physician's door (p. 609).

Children who theorize about the possibility of changing male into female (p. 630).

Children who fear being eaten by giants or ogres or being butted or eaten by animals (pp. 642, 648, 670, 674, 675), or who are alarmed at masks (p. 674).

Distortions in people's memories of childhood events (p. 678).

Displacements and distortions familiar in neuropathology (pp. 645, 664).

Neurotics who fear to touch door knobs (p. 609).

Neurotics in whom there is a pronounced struggle between belief and disbelief, desire and aversion (p. 613).

The concommitance of masochism and sadism (p. 631 and note 187).

People who dream of death (pp. 617, 648), of snakes (p. 618), or of being assailed by some unknown person (p. 646).

Persons given to fierce censure of moral laxity who are themselves morally lax (pp. 623, 624).

Algolagniacs who fetter themselves with gloves, head bands etc. (p. 692), neurotics with mouth "pollutions" (note 119).

Scrupulous persons with a proclivity for rebelliousness (p. 650).

People, especially adolescents, with whipping phantasies (note 183).

Persecutors who enjoy seeing the torments of their victims (p. 632).

Neurotics who speak in whispers (p. 669).

Phantasies of exalted family connections (p. 699).

"Split" or multiple personalities (p. 613).

Neurotics who confuse the dates and the sequences of occurrences (note 294 and pp. 646, 647, 664).

The self execrations involved in vows and oaths (p. 660).

Clinical anagnorisis (p. 634).

Ambivalences (pp. 607–614 etc.).

Here also we are still in the domain of the commonly observable. Credence rests upon our own personal observation or upon our confidence in the honesty or sanity of the person reporting.

3.

But this is not yet psychoanalysis. Cases of the kind enumerated are only the starting point of psychoanalysis. Psychoanalysis occurs when, for the sake of interpreting the readily observed, "free association" unearths something more recondite. Psychoanalysis introduces something more debatable than the observed facts. It purports to reveal hidden and unsuspected mental contents. As a consequence credibility calls for more than the veracity of the persons reporting. It depends also upon their skill and upon the technical correctness of their procedure. With regard to our individual cases, examples of the more recondite findings are:

That the young woman forgot the name Ben Hur because she desired to be a prostitute (p. 628).

That the eroticisms of the forbidden food cases were something incestuous (p. 671).

That patricidal impulses underlay the horse and fowl mimickries (p. 694).

That the woman whose voice grew fainter and fainter was condemning herself to death for mentally committed sexual derelictions (p. 660).

That the man who feared fatal consequences for his father was potentially a murderer of his father (note 335).

4.

The following are instances of such alleged findings applicable to the types or classes of cases:

That restlessness indicates that sex impulses have been repressed and are seeking abreaction (p. 624).

That repressed tendencies become active when, in ecstacy, there is a narrowing of consciousness and a suspension of conscious control (p. 624).

That patients' unconscious attitudes toward the physician are divulged by the forgetting to close the door (p. 609) or by flatulence (p. 692).

That snake dreams or phantasies or death dreams mean coitus (pp. 617, 618).

That dreams of being attacked by an unknown person signify castration (p. 646).

That children's dreams about sleeping persons signify death (p. 648).

That people's execrations of others are a rebuke of their own propensities (p. 624).

That neurotic acts of self punishment simulate the dereliction unconsciously taken to require the punishment (p. 607).

That an act of self affliction can be substituted for a repressed sadism (p. 698).

That in dreams or phantasies, sister or niece can be a "mother substitute" and brother or uncle a "father substitute" (pp. 638, 649, 660).

That cities or houses can symbolize the female body, doors the vagina, trees the father; sounds, eating and ladders, sexual intercourse; tombs or countries the maternal womb; and money the feces (pp. 638, 621, 670, 617, 640, 642, 635, notes 114, 291).

That there are neurotic symptoms in which the reaction is aroused by persons and objects more and more removed from the original stimulus to the reaction (p. 684).

That the hypothesis that eating signifies identification is substantiated by dreams (p. 693).

That in neurotic compromises, the forbidden becomes permissible (p. 697).

That we persecute ourselves in our persecutions of others (p. 613).

That neuroses seek to conceal something (pp. 697, 698).

That neurotics resist acknowledging their own infantilisms (p. 612).

That the feeling of uncanniness is due to a subtle identification of the transcended and the attained (p. 611).

That when Narcissism is wounded or when a mother goddess is lacking, the libido may be diverted from the self to other objects (p. 632).

That narcissism can function invertedly (p. 634).

That phantasies of whipping have an incestuous significance or at least a sexual one (note 183).

That humility is inverted self adulation (p. 634).

That neuroses are the breaking out of repressed inclinations (pp. 652, 699).

That the unconscious mind does little discriminating (p. 608).

That dreams, jests and neuroses are wish fulfilments (p. 653).

That among these wishes is the wish for a return to the womb (p. 640).

That the self execrations involved in oaths and vows are a covert form of self punishment (pp. 660, 661).

That whatsoever is strongly repudiated falls subject to amnesia (pp. 627, 665, 685).

That there are such phenomena as overdetermination (note 10). *Allmacht der Gedanken* (pp. 608, 611, 632), *Verschiebung nach oben* (note 275 and p. 688), repressions and displacements (pp. 645, 646), mental disguises (pp. 644, 645), neurotic reinterpretations (pp. 607, 646, 678) and compromises (note 689).

Here we are no longer in the domain of something that anyone can observe for himself. Credibility here will depend upon the details of the evidence that is offered. Especially great will be the need of such details in connection with the types or classes of cases because here as everywhere much more evidence is needed to establish a general conclusion than a particular one.

It is in this matter of evidence that our writers default. Nowhere in the writings that we have utilized are we provided with anything but conclusions. The only exception is the very scant and abridged account of the analysis conducted by Reik upon the young woman who forgot the name Ben Hur.

The works we have quoted abound in references to other

works which other works are in turn loaded with references to still other works. So far as it has been possible to scan these remoter writings, the status of the matter remains unchanged. Everywhere we find conclusions, never a delineation of processes. Beyond the *ipse dixit* of the writer[712] and, it must be confessed, the impressively concordant *ipse dixits* of numerous writers, we are not permitted to go. As laymen we would probably be incompetent to pass judgment upon the details even if they were presented. At the same time there is nothing to prevent our noticing when detailed evidence is furnished and when it is not. As laymen we can also notice that when it comes to anthropological applications, only the types or classes of phenomena are of any value. The basis of inference offered by individual cases is surely too slight to count.

Of course it does not by any means follow that the conclusions quoted in our Part One are necessarily incorrect.[713] All that follows is that so far as the accessible literature takes us, the conclusions are "not proven." We are justified in expecting that some day there may come within our ken writings already in existence or in the future to be brought into existence wherein will be provided the proofs which as yet are lacking. Meanwhile the layman must stand particularly on guard against supposing that where conclusions are psychoanalytically erroneous, the alternative conclusion that may chance to be psychoanalytically

[712] Not by any means to be underestimated is the circumstance that in the psychoanalytic writer's own mind the alleged train of mental associations has indubitably occurred. Of this much his *ipse dixit* is incontestable evidence. In these mental association trains of the psychoanalytic writer himself, there is nothing perceptibly different from the familiar rangings of our own day dreams and subtler emotions. A strengthening of the writer's conclusions would accordingly ensue if it could be shown that the association train operative in his own study of any given clinical or anthropological problem is not something peculiar to the writer but something generally human.

[713] Take for example Reik's discussions (supra pp. 627, 632, 639, 655, 664) of the Jewish attitude toward Jesus. The traditional Jewish abhorrence of Jesus is hardly to be explained as solicitude about academic correctness on some point of historical or theological information. The passion for theoretical accuracy is something far milder than this. The Jewish attitude toward Jesus involves too many similarities with emotional conflict to permit of any glib dismissal of Reik's hypothesis.

correct will be any the less absurd, grotesque and indelicate. We must repeat: The absurd, the grotesque and the indelicate are the territory of psychoanalysis *par excellence.*

IV. The Need of Subventioned Research

The one persuasion to which we are inevitably impelled is that there should be generous financial provision for psychoanalytic research. While the economics of psychoanalysis are themselves in need of research, the impression may not be altogether unwarranted that the average analysis costs three thousand dollars in money and requires from six months to two years of time.[714] Liberal subventions are needed enabling gifted analysts to devote themselves entirely to investigations along rigidly scientific lines. Large numbers of persons should be analyzed. Records should be kept of their purposes ultimate, penultimate and antepenultimate. The ratio of the respective occurrences of these purposes among people of different sexes, varying ages, vocations, degrees of health, racial heritage etc. should be computed. Recurrences of uniform image clusters and their relations to the respective master purposes should be measured. Such study must also not ignore those less disreputable purposes whose determination, like those of the money maker and the opera singer in our illustrations (supra p. 702), require no psychoanalysis.

Special endowments should support the psychoanalytic investigation of religious phenomena, whether it be religious phenomena in general or Jewish religious phenomena in particular. Urgent practical interests as well as theoretical ones are at stake. Virtually the entire story of religion is the disposal, either by sublimation or by compromise, of man's socially unpresentable purposes. Sublimation seems to obtain in such experiences as repentance, self-sacrifice, earnest prayer, personal purity, social service, religious art. Compromise is exemplified in the various religious ceremonies, creeds and persecutions—at any rate according to some writers. Who knows but, aided by psychoanalysis, we

[714] Respondents who expressed themselves on this point thought that the monetary sum stated was excessive.

might reckon more successfully with such problems as Temple attendance, satisfactory devotions and sermons, inspiring religious instruction, Jewish loyalty, social mindedness or whatever else may be the conundrum that the religious worker is expected to solve!

To illustrate the possibilities of psychoanalytic theory, let us take purity as an example. The spiritually minded man of to-day must heed the sex *mores* if he would be at peace with his conscience. Observe how the Freudian anthropology provides a pattern or paradigm of this. The Freudian psycho-anthropology posits a primitive father owning all the women of the tribe and a son inhibited from these women until, having endured the rigors of initiation, he receives with the father's blessing a wife from the father's hands. This tribal father, according to the Freudians, evolves into the Cosmic Father, the God of the modern worshiper, a God Who is in turn identified with the conscience of the worshiper. Like the primitive son, the spiritually minded man of to-day can not be at peace with his God unless he abstain from all women except "the woman that Thou gavest me," acquired only after his hard initiation into economic competence and conferred only in the marriage ceremony presided over by the minister, the priest or the Rabbi—the representatives of God. To the spiritually minded man, the sex urge having become sublimated, the beauty of girlhood is the beauty of the Divine, its presence the reverently if not adoringly felt presence of the Divine. Pure and lovely it can readily be conceived as belonging to the Divine, transfused with the radiance of the Divine, anchored eternally in the Life Divine! It must therefore be left to the Divine.[715] Its dishonoring would be the irreparable outrag-

[715] It is hard to forego quoting at least two stanzas from a well known love song illustrating the religious sublimation of sex. The stanzas are from "All Through the Night" a Welsh song translated by Walter Maynard:

"Sleep, my love, and peace attend thee,
All through the night;
Guardian angels God will lend thee
All through the night.
Soft the drowsy hours are creeping,
Hill and vale in slumber steeping;

ing of conscience, the voice of the Divine. The Freudian anthropology may be entirely erroneous. The Freudian psychology as a description of concealed, unnamed, anti-social purposes generally prevalent may be mostly erroneous. Yet that psychology as patterning the religious import of sex scruples need not be erroneous. Since, according to the Freudians, every woman who attracts a man is his "mother surrogate," the Oedipus Complex may be true as a religio-psychological paradigm, though untrue as anything else. It may be an invaluable *als ob*.

Again who knows how much resistance to various social reforms may be but a displaced resistance to some unnamed mental obstacle! Bringing that obstacle into designation and control, as psychoanalysis claims to do, might be the correction of the displacement. That much of the barrier to social betterment might thus be removed.

It was discouraging to miss among the contents of our Part One any mention of the bearing on modern religious and synagogal phenomena of such familiar factors as the animosities that lie outside of the Oedipus scheme, such as personal grievances, racial, national and class antipathies. One would also wish to know about the ritual and ecclesiastical consequences of self seeking and self aggrandizement whether of narcissistic or other derivation. One would further desire more light on the connection between sex and reverence, a connection intimated already by Riggal.[716] Such features as those of silence and of submissiveness are striking points of resemblance between them.

Love alone his watch is keeping
All through the night.

"Hark! a solemn bell is ringing,
Clear through the night;
Thou, my love, art heavenward winging
Home through the night.
Earthly dust from off thee shaken,
Soul immortal, thou shalt waken,
With thy last dim journey taken,
Home through the night."

[716] R. M. Riggal, *Religion and Psychoanalysis* (London, 1920), p. 19.

There is also the phenomenon of doctrinal and ritual selection —Jews who follow the dietary laws at home yet flout them outside of the home or who violently object to holding a religious service on any day except the traditional Sabbath although themselves spending the traditional Sabbath at their customary occupations; or Jews who are punctiliously orthodox in their observance of Atonement Day or of the mourning customs although totally unobservant in other particulars. These and doubtless many others are among the problems that are yet to be handled.

Not only must the socially inadmissible purposes of the laity be diagnosed. The motives of the leaders are in equal need of control. Nothing but genuinely scientific inquiry can uncover the extent, the nature and the injuriousness of our "suppressed desires." There dawns upon us the promise of something better than the lot of the New Testament writer who complained, "Our wrestling is not against flesh and blood but against the principalities, against the powers . . . against spiritual hosts of wickedness in heavenly places" (Eph. 6.12). Once the struggle is brought into the open, flesh will have to cope with nothing worse than flesh. The person who will contribute money for religio-psychoanalytic inquiry will have entered upon the way of all ways in which religion can be furthered by money. As Jews we covet for our religion the privilege of being the pioneering domain and for our own people the honor of being the first to devote to this captivating enterprise the resources of their material prosperity.

APPENDIX I

Bibliography of Specifically Jewish Interest

Abraham, Karl, Der Versoehnungstag. Bemerkungen zu Reik's *Probleme der Religionspsychologie. Imago*, VI, 1920, Heft 1, 80–90.

Allwohn, Adolf, *Die Ehe des Propheten Hosea in Psychoanalytischer Beleuchtung.* Beihefte zur *Zeitschrift fuer die Alttestamentliche Wissenschaft* (44. Giessen, 1926).

Becker, Jacob, *R. Naḥman mi-Braẓlaw Meḥkar Psychoanalyti.* Ḥelek Rishon Yerushalayim tarpaḥ (1928).

Freud, Sigmund, *Totem und Tabu* (Leipzig, Wien), 1913.

Fromm, Ehrich, Der Sabbath. *Imago*, XIII, 1927, 223–234.

Fromm-Reichmann, Frieda, Das juedische Speiseritual. *Imago*, XIII, 1927, 235–248.

Kanter, Felix, Die Psychoanalyse in der Bibel. *Hickl's Illustrierter Juedischer Volkskalender fuer das Jahr 5688—1927–28. Juedischer Volkskalender* fuer das Jahr 5688—1927–28. Juedischer Buch und Kunstverlag, Bruenn Orli 9. (For this reference I am indebted to my colleague, Dr. Jacob R. Marcus).

Koenig, Ed., *Die Sexualitaet im Hohenlied und Ihre Grenze. Sexuelle und Psychoanalytische Deutungen des Althebraeischen Schriftthums.*

Langer, Georg, Zur Funktion der juedischen Tuerpfostenrolle, *Imago*, XIV, 1928, 457–468.

Die juedischen Gebetriemen. *Imago*, XVI, 1930, 435–485.

Levy, Ludwig, Sexualsymbolik in der Paradiesgeschichte. *Imago*, V, 1917–1919, 16–30.

Sexualsymbolik der Simsonsage. *Zeitschrift fuer Sexualwissenschaft.* Bd. III H. 6–7.

Die Kastration in der Bibel. Hundegeld. *Imago*, VI, 1920, 393–397.

Die Schuhsymbolik im juedischen Ritus. *Monatschrift*, Jahrgang 62 pp. 178–185.

Lewkowitz, Albert, Psychoanalyse und Kulturphilosophie. *Monatschrift*, Jahrgang 74 (1930) Heft 7–8, pp. 241–254.

Lorenz, *Tower of Babel* (See book review by F. C. Fluegel, *Imago*, XIII, 1927, 139).

Oppenheim, James, *A Psycho-Analysis of the Jews* (Haldeman-Julius Co., Girard, Kansas), No. 1112.

Povah, Major J. W., *The New Psychology and the Hebrew Prophets* (London 1928).

The Old Testament and Modern Problems in Psychology (London 1926).

Radó, S., Das fuenfte Gebot. *Imago*, IX, 1923, 129, 130.

Reik, Theodor, Psychoanalytische Studien zur Bibelexegese. *Imago*, V, 1917–1919, 325–363.

Probleme der Religionspsychologie. Leipzig, Wien, 1919.

Der Eigene und der Fremde Gott. Leipzig, Wien, Zuerich, 1923.

Dogma und Zwangsidee. *Imago*, XIII, 1927, 247–382.

Zur Psychoanalyse des Juedischen Witzes. *Imago*, XV, 1929, 63–88.

Gebetmantel und Gebetriemen. *Imago*, XVI, 1930, 389–434.

Róheim, Geza, Zur Psychologie der Bundesriten. *Imago*, VI, 1920, 397–398.

Weinberg, Albert K. The Enemy Within Ourselves. *Menorah Journal*, Vol. IV, June 1918, pp. 186–194.

Wiener, M., Juedische Froemmigkeit und psychoanalytische Religionsbetrachtung. *Ethik* (Leopold Klotz Verlag, Gotha) Jahrgang 5, Heft 7, Juli 1929, pp. 462–467.

APPENDIX II

A. List of Topics

B. List of Passages

(Explanatory Note:—Roman figures indicate page numbers; italic figures indicate notes.)

BAB. ḲIDDUSHIN

BAB. BABA MEZIA'

BAB. SANHEDRIN

BAB. MENAḤOT

BAB. NIDDAH

YOREH DE'AH

ORAḤ ḤAYYIM

ZOHAR

THE SIGNIFICANCE OF JUDAISM
for
THE PRESENT AND THE FUTURE

by
H. Graetz

THE SIGNIFICANCE OF JUDAISM FOR THE PRESENT AND THE FUTURE.

It is, perhaps, not inopportune to discuss the question as to the significance of Judaism at the present time. Certainly it is a problem which must engage the attention of Jewish thinkers, who cannot live spiritually from hand to mouth, but must desire to account to themselves why they are Jews, and why they remain within the pale of Judaism. Merely regarding it as one of the religious beliefs which are significantly enough called the ruling creeds—quite apart from its rights of primogeniture—the question as to its right to further existence is not a superfluous one. We live in an age of criticism, a fact which some deplore, others praise, and thus every branch of knowledge which claims any rank in the hierarchy of science must justify itself by showing whether it takes a part in general culture, or is an indispensable factor in the intellectual and moral development of humanity, or contributes somewhat to the totality of human effort; or, on the other hand, whether it forms only an isolated, and perhaps moribund, member in the social organism, with an existence only permitted as a matter of custom. Theology itself is required to prove its right to live. Divinity, which in earlier times stood at the summit of all the sciences, held them under control, and defined their place, holds that lofty position no longer; and even if it still takes the first rank in some academic circles, it owes that apparent advantage only to the past, and to a regard for seniority. It must itself recognise that it has no longer any right to the title of queen of sciences. Even philosophy, that claimed the precedence in the last century, must now lay aside royal privilege in favour of the exact sciences. The more cultivated classes who have tasted of the tree of knowledge live no longer in a state of *naïve* faith, ready to accept all that theology teaches as truth, that requires no proof and brings certain salvation. Criticism, which once only whispered its doubts, or was forced to keep silent if it spoke too loud, has nowadays become bold and arrogant. It has usurped the throne, and summoned all the sciences to its court; it tests all means of ascertaining truth, and allows nothing to pass approved which cannot be rigorously tried or ascertained by facts, or numbers, or undoubted records.

It is true that the ruling religion is not much affected by the attacks of criticism. Although some cultured persons stand in a critical or sceptical attitude towards it, and turn their back on it, it does not find its position very precarious so long as a numerous following, above and below, remain true. Among the upper classes religion is carefully preserved as a means of power even more than ever, at least among the empires of the Continent. Religion has become the close ally of the state, and therefore finds in the state an unassailable support. Among the lower classes, whose powers of thought are poorly developed, and entirely directed to the satisfaction of their present needs, it has still the majority on its side. The ruling religion, whether Catholic or Protestant, United or Orthodox Greek, does not trouble itself about its continued existence, and does not find it necessary to establish scientifically its right to live. This is not even necessary in America, where Rationalism or Atheism has founded a kind of opposition Church of incredulity. The ruling religion has an overwhelming majority, and can rest satisfied with that. Possession gives it nine points of the law.

But how about Judaism? It has no outward means of maintaining itself. It has no hold on the political powers. No minority is so weak as one whose members are scattered through all parts of the world, and live disconnected from one another. Besides this, Judaism has numerous enemies both within and without its ranks. The external opponents who contest its right to existence are by no means its most dangerous enemies.

In consequence of the tragic fate that befell its adherents, who had for centuries to wander here and there in degrading slavery, Judaism has itself adopted a garb which is by no means especially attractive, but which, as a whole, unlike some of its entirely emancipated followers, it has scarcely the power or wish to remove. And yet, notwithstanding this in nowise brilliant exterior, it demands from its adherents more earnest and serious sacrifices than any other religion, though these duties appear to many as externalities—obsolete survivals of a sad past which should be rather laid aside than preserved. The modern finery which the Reforming party in Judaism has introduced into the synagogue and public life has had no influence on that side of Jewish life which has not a synagogal or a ritual character, viz.: on married life, on the family, and on the home; these because they are matters of conscience, and find their strength in the affections, cannot be so easily transformed. Rigid conservatives say of ritual matters: "*Sint ut sunt aut non sint.*" And it is just on this side of Judaism, in its ritual, that scepticism, not to say scorn, makes its appearance among those who have lost their respect for the past, for criticism is much more sharp and incisive among Jews than elsewhere. Now criticism in Judaism is confined to the cultured, and makes them indifferent to the heritage of many thousand years, if it does not make them despise it. These inner enemies of Judaism are, so far, more dangerous than the others, because the latter, except the rabid anti-semitic *Judenfresser*, who cast scorn on Moses and the Prophets, at any rate show their respect for Jewish antiquities. The opponents of Judaism among its own sons banish all reverence for the long roll of their ancestral heroes of intellect and martyrs of faith. How can Judaism maintain itself if its most distinguished sons, the cultured classes, turn their back on it? Or shall the word of the prophet find fulfilment: "A poor and lowly people shall be left in the midst of thee?" And the fidelity of these lowly ones is not quite assured. They as a rule urge their children to adopt the culture of the time, and these in their turn strive to obtain equality and social position by means of scientific ability. This is the case where Jews exist in large numbers, as in Germany, Austria, Russia and its dependencies, Roumania and the Balkan principalities; this striving after European forms of culture, in its way so praiseworthy, has spread even to the Turkish Orient, and has crossed over into Africa. It is encouraged by the *Alliance Israélite Universelle* and by the Anglo-Jewish Association. In two generations there must be a relative increase in the numbers, if not of Apostates, at least of Indifferents. How shall the existence of Judaism continue?

Or will it have no further existence? Has it already fulfilled its mission, and is it no longer anything but a ghost longing for the rest of the grave? Must it withdraw from the scene of practical influence because the civilizing element in it has passed over into the general atmosphere of culture, and its principles have become an integral part of public law and justice? Has it done its duty, and may it now retire from the stage?

The question of the function of Judaism in the present and the future has become a burning and vital question for cultivated Jews. Is the ancestral heritage so valuable that for its sake one should put up with a despised position in life, and for ever submit to the ban which the intolerance of Central and Eastern Europe has imposed on the adherents of

Judaism? Is it worth while taking up a martyrdom not alone for oneself but for one's children? It is true the Jews in the most civilised lands, in which the principles of liberty have been carried out to their full consequences—*i.e.*, in England, France, and also in Italy—are more fortunate; they do not suffer any loss through their religion, whether political or social. But Judaism requires even from them sacrifices, if not of a material nature, still sacrifices of blissful sentiments and yearnings.

Readiness of sacrifice for an ideal can only be inspired by the most strenuous conviction of its truth and excellence. But how shall the present generation become possessed of such a conviction? It has grown sceptical under the influence of the exact sciences, and only lays weight on figures and facts.

Perhaps it may be possible to gain such a conviction of the importance of Judaism even at the present day without forsaking the firm ground of actuality. It may be possible to produce proofs that Judaism has pre-eminent value, just because it rests on the solid basis of actual phenomena, and can therefore look forward to the future with equanimity, and needs no material power. It may perhaps be demonstrated that its ideal mission, its capacity of fruitfulness, which is even more or less allowed by its external opponents, and its power of transformation, still continue and must continue. This necessity is easy to recognise if one clearly understands, on the one hand, the essence of Judaism and its characteristic qualities, by which it is distinguished from other forms of religion; and if, on the other hand, one compares with these the prevailing ethical and religious tone, as manifested in society and in the life of the individual.

In order not to mistake the essential characteristics of Judaism, one must not regard it as a *faith*, or speak of it as "the Jewish faith." The application of a word is by no means unimportant. The word often becomes a net in which thought gets tangled unawares. From an ecclesiastical standpoint, the word "faith" implies the acceptance of an inconceivable miraculous fact, insufficiently established by historical evidence, and with the audacious addition, *Credo quia absurdum.* Judaism has never required such a belief from its adherents. When it is said that religion stands in fierce conflict with science or with reason, that only applies to forms of religion whose dogmas and the foundation of whose institutions rest on unprovable facts, which faith alone has raised to certainty. Such a faith must naturally be engaged in an internecine struggle with science.

But Judaism is not a mere doctrine of faith. What is it

then? The celebrated and original French historian Renan, who often gives expression to striking *aperçus*, though he has never entirely freed himself from the memories of priest-craft, has said of Judaism that it is "a minimum of religion." This *aperçu* sounds rather curiously when one thinks of the huge folios which contain the Jewish religious codices, the Talmud and its addenda, Maimonides' *Mishne Thorah* or Caro's *Shulchan Aruch*, with their commentaries and super-commentaries, which offer a boundless extent of religious duties. And yet Renan's utterance is true, as true in reality as it is concisely expressed. It hits the mark not only in the sense that Judaism demands few, or no articles of faith, but also in the sense that its centre of gravity is not to be found in the religious sphere. What then is its essence? It has been characterised often enough, and yet misconceived by friend and foe, as much misconceived as if it were an esoteric mystery or a coarse superstition. When the king of Judah and his people were carried away by such a misconception that they even brought human sacrifices in imitation of foreigners, the prophet Micah said: "Thou askest what the Lord requireth of thee? Only to do justly, and to love mercy, and to walk humbly with thy God." That is a minimum of religion, is it not? Similarly, 700 years later, the great Hillel characterised it to a heathen who had asked him what was the quintessence of Judaism: "'Love thy neighbour as thyself.' That is the whole of the law; all the rest is but commentary on this text." So too, 150 years later, an authoritative council also reduced the fundamental duties of Judaism to a minimum. The Emperor Hadrian, who in his own lifetime ordered his worship as a God, had decreed a terrible religious persecution on all the Jews of the Roman Empire, as a punishment for the way in which the Jews of Palestine had fought for liberty and still higher possessions against the Roman legions. The least display of a religious symbol or the slightest sign of religion was to be met by corporal punishment, or even by death. By this means, Judaism was to be driven from the hearts of its adherents, and uprooted from the memory of men. Under these sad circumstances, the Rabbis of the time came together in council in order to provide the people with a rule of conduct. Though they were themselves prepared to undergo a martyr's death for every single precept, yet they did not require the same degree of self-sacrifice from the whole of Israel. In this mournful condition of affairs, the Council of Lydda made a well-weighed distinction between the fundamental provisions of Judaism and those that merely applied to the ritual. The latter might, under certain circumstances, be transgressed, in order to avoid punishment; but the former, on the other hand, must not be denied even for fear of death in its most horrible shape. The council reduced the fundamental principles of Judaism to three: avoidance of idolatry, avoidance of unchastity, and, finally, avoidance of an attack on human life.

It is easy enough to perceive from all this that Prophets and Talmudists did not regard sacrifice or ritual as the fundamental and determining thing in Judaism, but another and higher element, or, more rightly speaking, two elements which apparently do not belong to one another, but are in reality radically interdependent. We must, to a certain extent, analyse these elements, in order to recognise and to formulate their fundamental constituents. Both elements have a positive and a negative side; the one element is ethical, the higher ethics, including in its positive aspects, love of mankind, benevolence, humility, justice, and in its negative aspects, respect for human life, care against unchastity, subdual of selfishness and the beast in man, holiness in deed and thought. The second element is religious, and in it the negative side is predominant, to worship no transient being as God, whether belonging to the animal kingdom, the race of men, or the heavenly world, and in general to consider all idolatry as vain and to reject it entirely. The positive side is to regard the highest Being as one and unique, and as the essence of all ethical perfections, and to worship it as the Godhead—in a single word, Monotheism in the widest acceptation of the term. The ethical is so far intimately connected with the religious element, because the divine perfection gives the ideal for the moral life. "Be ye holy even as I am holy," is the perpetually recurring refrain in the oldest records of Judaism. On the other hand, idolatry leads to debased acts and feelings, as the history of the world has conclusively proved in the coarsest fashion. The worship of paganism was for the most part orgiastic. If Zeus is a god, licentiousness is no sin. If Aphrodite is a goddess, chastity cannot be a virtue.

To biblical critics it would be superfluous to prove that these two elements, the ethical in its richness and the religious in its purity, are the fundamental principles of Judaism. The Law, the Prophets, and the other books of the Canon, are full of them. They force themselves on the notice of every reader of the Bible, and the verses which speak of them require no interpretation. The Prophets directed their burning eloquence essentially against transgression of either element, against vice and against idolatrous worship. They rarely touch on ritual problems. Even in the Decalogue, the foundation of Judaism, the commandments apply to the two elements, and only a single one, the sanctification of the Sabbath, has a ritual character. In Deuteronomy even the Sabbath is based on an ethical principle, viz., that the man-servant and maid-servant may also enjoy rest. The prophet Jeremiah positively depreciated sacrifice, for he makes God say: "I did not enjoin sacrifice at the Exodus from Egypt." The prophets Amos and Hosea establish the same principle, that sacrifice—the chief element in the culture of ancient peoples—and, therefore, that ritual, was of subordinate importance.

The foundation of Judaism has accordingly rested on these two elements since its first revelation. This truth cannot be too often repeated or made known too widely, for it has often been misunderstood and is still misunderstood at the present day. It is the characteristic of Judaism and is its essential difference from all other forms of religion. A profound French thinker and historian, Eugène Burnouf, has demonstrated that no religion, not even Christianity, in its initial stages lays stress on ethics or the theory of morals as being involved in religion. Only gradually does religion become humanised, so to speak, *i.e.*, bring morality within its fold. Classic paganism at first failed to recognise the ethical element and when Marcus Aurelius and Julian the Apostate realised its worth and desired to introduce it into the Roman religious world, it was too late. Christianity was originally only faith and only made ethics its aim after a long development, and then simply because it was a child of Judaism. To the sharp eye of criticism the ethical element, which was added later, is easily to be distinguished from the original dogmatism. The mechanical mixture of the two elements shows its artificial nature. What has the belief that Jesus is the Christ to do with "Christian Charity"? They belong to different orders of thought.

It is not so in Judaism. In it the ethical element and the pure worship of God are clearly the earliest data. Abraham is selected by God as the father of many nations so that he might teach his house and his descendants to keep God's way, to exercise kindness and justice. Thus it is written in the very first book of Holy Writ. The "way of God," or "knowledge of God," is nothing more nor less than what we term "humanity," or morality in the widest extent of the word. That is the essence of Judaism, and does not stand in any conflict with reason or with science. It does not affect this foundation in the slightest whether criticism explains the stories and miracles of the Scriptures as legends and poetic ornaments or not.

Can this doctrine—Judaism describes itself by this name rather than as faith or as religion, *i.e.*, cultus composed of sacrifice and ritual—can this doctrine, which has worked as an elevating, sanctifying, and enfranchising element for thousands of years, have lost its influence? The religions which have been born in its bosom have only taken a part of the blessings with which this original teaching is gifted. I will only refer to one. The inequality of property threatens to subvert the very foundations of society, and the difficulties cannot be removed from the world by means of force. Judaism suggests a means of avoiding this precipice, a means deduced from its ethical principles. It does not despise mammon, and does not imagine that the rich man cannot enter the kingdom of heaven. It recognises that individual possession is justified, but it sanctifies it by demanding that it should be used and applied in a moral way, and thus overcomes the egoism of possession. It is true that the statutes of the law relating to the sabbatical and jubilee years, in which debts were released in a fixed cycle, and the ordinance that the products of the earth should be accessible to all, even to the penniless—these enactments are not applicable to the economic circumstances of the present day in the same form. But if the ethical principle underlying these laws were always borne in mind and were properly carried out, so that, *e.g.*, the soil of the United Kingdom should not be monopolised by 200,000 owners, but the remaining 35,000,000 inhabitants should also have some small rights in it, this recognition would, at any rate, do something to soften the ever-increasing bitterness of the indigent against the accumulation of riches. On this principle institutions might be established which might avert the chaos with which the European states are threatened. The tender care for the poor which the laws of the Thorah, that is, of Judaism, display in regard to the harvests and the tithes, which were only to the narrowest extent adopted by Christianity, might also be applied to modern circumstances. If Judaism disappeared, the ethical postulates which it includes, and on which the continuance of society and civilisation depend, would disappear also.

More urgently necessary still is the continued existence of Judaism at present and in the future for the preservation of the religious principle. In the strictest sense, absolute monotheism, as Judaism has revealed it, is rationalism; it is the negation of all the absurdities by which the religious views and the cultus of the ancient nations were dominated.

But it required a high stage of cultivated intelligence to arrive at the conviction that the gross fetiches, the deities of wood and stone, that Baal and even Zeus, who stood under the power of Atè, that Jupiter, whose grave was shown in Crete, that Thor with his hammer, that all these gods, and even the luminaries of day and night, were not divine beings, that the goddess of love, under the names Astaroth, Mylitta, Beltis, Aphrodite, Venus, and the worship of Priapus were abominations (תועבה), as Judaism called them. Idolatry, which sanctified immorality, only appears absurd and abominable to the present generation because Jewish rationalism has for centuries arrayed itself against it; because the prophets, with their burning language, struggled against it, because the Jewish Sibyl and the Book of Wisdom, Philo and Josephus and other Jewish thinkers made this offspring of mad fancy food for laughter. The worship of the emperors lasted on even into Christian times, *i.e.*, the emperors, even the most vicious of them, were *divi*, and had to have sacrifices brought to them. The ruling creed is likewise anthropolatry; cathedrals, cloisters, and pilgrims' shrines are dedicated to it. The only defenders of true monotheism, in other words, of rationalism in religion are still the adherents of Judaism. From Zion went forth this rationalistic teaching.

How stands the matter at the present time? Rationalism, which seeks to distinguish the ethical from the mystical in religion, which was all powerful in the last century, and in Germany had no less patrons than the philosophical King Frederick and the king of poets, Lessing, this rationalism has altogether lost its potency in that country, and has become powerless there. The leading spirits in religion scorn rational thought with such audacity that any opposition is despised as heresy. In France the upper classes are either intensely bigoted, or they become atheists in order to avoid becoming clericalists. In England there has arisen a tendency towards Ritualism with a Roman Catholic tinge, because no place is allowed to rationalism in the sphere of religion.

Thus Judaism, which is throughout rationalistic, is the sole stronghold of free thought in the religious sphere. Its mission, to overcome erroneous belief, is far from being fulfilled. There are still enough phantoms in the temples of the nations and in the hearts of men which are by no means innocuous. Millions of men still recognise a representative vicar of God on earth, whose words they credulously accept as an infallible oracle. Such phantoms, to which even the most civilised peoples on earth continue to pray, can only be banished by Judaism, as it destroyed the altars of Baal and Astarti, of Zeus and Aphrodite, and hewed down the trees of Woden and Friga

—for the inspiration came from Judaism, though the agents were Christian iconoclasts. The visionary images which becloud thousands of minds and produce the maddest enthusiasms can only be dispersed by that pure idea of God formulated by Judaism. Rationalism has no other representative but Judaism.

Regarded from this point of view, Judaism has still the same importance for the present and for the future, as it had in the past. Its mission is on this side by no means superfluous. We Jews are the representatives of Judaism and its mission; its ideas and principles pulsate in our veins. If the apostles of the pure monotheistic idea had been destroyed in their conflicts with Assyrians, Chaldæans, Greeks and Romans, the madness of idolatry, with its orgiastic forms of worship, would still exist to-day, and the civilisation of Europe would not have developed itself.

But even on the ethical side Judaism still gives example and impulse. There has been a certain phrase formulated about carrying out practical Christianity. If this phrase is to have any sense, it can only mean that morality should penetrate the institutions of the State; Judaism preached this doctrine thousands of years ago. The ethical principles which it lays to heart were not alone to be carried out by individuals, but were to become the leading principles of government. They had not only to be written on the doors of houses, but at the gates of cities. The King was always to carry with him the Book of the Law, which put the essence of Judaism in the short sentences, "Thou shalt love one God with all thy heart," and "There shall be no poor in thy cities." Methods were also indicated in this Book which might realise the ethico-religious ideals.

Thus Judaism is the source alike of humanity, of monotheism, and of religious rationalism. It has still its function to play, its mission to fulfil, in bringing these ideals to reality. If it vanished from the world, if its adherents, one and all, deserted it, there would be wanting a mighty factor for the progress of ethical and religious civilisation; it would be wanting now, just as much as it would have been wanting of old, if Judaism had disappeared before the rise of Christianity.

Of course, Judaism contains an elaborate ritual besides these ideal principles, which, unfortunately, owing to the tragic course of history, has developed into a fungoid growth which overlays the ideals. But originally the ritual in its pure form had its justification, and was intended to surround and protect ideal sin themselves of an ethereal nature. It must be reserved for a later article to explain the manner in which the ritual was adapted to the ideal.

H. GRAETZ.

THE SIGNIFICANCE OF JUDAISM FOR THE PRESENT AND THE FUTURE.

II.

THE inquiry whether fixed articles of faith form the essential kernel of Judaism, learnedly discussed in this Review by Mr. Schechter, and the accuracy of the classification of the differences in religious opinion among English Jews, so cleverly elaborated by Mr. Israel Zangwill, are both internal questions which have only a very incidental relation to the real subject-matter of my former article.

I had not then, nor have I now, to deal with what may be considered as orthodox or heterodox in Judaism, whether touching the importance of the ritual or even the apparently fundamental dogma of Revelation, of which the denial in Rabbinic language is expressed by האומר אין תורה מן השמים or in modern phraseology, by doubt in the supernatural. According to Mr. Zangwill's classification, there is among English Jews a group of persons "professing natural Judaism." This might, indeed, occasion a practical question within the Jewish community itself. For the question might arise whether holding such heterodox opinions would unfit a man for giving evidence in a matter of ritual, as *e.g.*, in a marriage or a divorce "*more Judaico.*" In such a case, a rabbi would be not a little puzzled to decide whether the marriage or the divorce would be ritually valid. For the code-book he would have to consult would not enlighten him on matters of dogma. It would, for instance, give him no information how to act in the case of a witness who had never violated the sabbath in his actions, but who was not thoroughly imbued with a belief in the supernatural command to obey it. Moses Mendelssohn's dictum that Judaism only judges actions and not religious opinions remains unshaken. Whether an intelligent Jew finds more happiness, assurance, and solace from his convinced belief in the ideal principle of Judaism and its ethical consequences than a Russian or Polish Chasid from the mechanical performance of some ritual ceremony, and from a vague messianic hope is purely a matter of sentiment. It could only become practically important if the externalities of the synagogue were undergoing transformation. We might then have to determine whether more consideration was to be shown to Moses Mendelssohn, who rejoiced in the thought that the essentials of Judaism were in perfect harmony with deistic philosophy, or to Steinheim, who was filled with joy at the conviction that the truths of revealed Judaism were at variance with the dogmas of philosophy. Translating these differences of theory into practice, we might then have to decide whether the repulsive abuses commonly regarded as Jewish and religious should be abandoned, or whether the feelings of a naïve believer should rather be spared who finds his spiritual bliss in the noisy shaking of the willow branches upon the Feast of Tabernacles.

But, as aforesaid, these reflections are foreign to my subject. I only desire to consider whether Judaism has still a real significance and value in the critically-minded present, and in that future which may be yet more estranged from all religious forms, only to show that those who are deeply convinced of its fundamental principle and historic influence, may joyfully make it their vocation to hold by Judaism steadfastly, and so transmit it to posterity. Taking as my guides the Bible, the Talmud, and the intelligent rabbis, I have endeavoured to prove that this fundamental principle must be sought for in ethical idealism (humanity in the highest sense of the word), and in pure rational monotheism, adverse to all mysticism and disfigurement. I have also attempted to show that for the future of mankind these qualities have not yet become superfluous for the education and regeneration of society.

The immense influence, which these two most closely connected sides of the law of Moses, "the heritage of the congregation of Israel," have exercised on the development of human civilization, has indeed been freely admitted even by Christian thinkers. No matter how much Mr. Zangwill may doubt the validity of this statement and oppose to it the argument that Confucius and Sophocles, and Aryan celebrities in general, were equally impressed with the categorical imperative of the moral law, he cannot maintain that these individuals caused a world-wide and historic change in the thoughts and actions of the whole civilized portion of mankind, or that they looked upon their own convictions as material for what we may call an ethical circulation of the blood. Socrates may have had a more accurate conception of the Deity than his countrymen and the Sophists, but only a paradoxical disputatiousness could assert that he was fully penetrated with the conviction that this conception of the Deity postulated the sanctity of life and the purest morality. Plato and Aristotle might indeed have learnt "practical reason" from the Jews, for their ethical doctrine compares most disadvantageously with that of Judaism, as was already known to Philo.

Christianity was perfectly justified in priding itself on having vanquished the essential corruption of paganism, but it ought not to have ignored the fact that it was only the organ and interpreter of an original inspiration behind it, and that it had not itself remained free from some heathen contamination. As long as Judaism was gagged and silent, Bossuet could attribute the whole progress of civilization to Christianity, a view in which Ranke, undisturbed by Buckle's conclusions, has partly followed him. But at the present day, the ban which suffered no dispute to the assertion that salvation came forth from Golgotha and not from Zion is gradually being broken through. For it is now admitted as an undeniable historical fact by many earnest Christian thinkers, such as Kuenen and Renan, and even half-and-half by German historians despite a touch of anti-Semitism, that the ethical consciousness is the property of the people of Israel, that it was called into the world by the three great prophets, Amos, Hosea, and Isaiah, and that they may be said to have been evangelists eight hundred years before the rise of Christianity, although without the mystic bye-taste of a kingdom of heaven. To this admission we must cling fast, without at present examining closely whether this ethical revelation was first proclaimed from Mount Sinai, or from the wilderness of Tekoa. A part, I might say the flower, of this pure ethical system, has become the common property of the world, through the medium of Christianity—justice, charity even towards the stranger, care for the poor, the sanctity of life, conscientiousness. But the world has not yet fully appreciated the root of this rich development, that pure monotheism which teaches that God is the father of the fatherless and the protector of the widow, and that, as holiness is the essence of his nature, all unholiness, unchastity, and self-pollution,[1] are an abomination to him. Neither has

[1] The Talmudists very keenly realised this element in the Jewish conception of God אלהיהם של אלו שונא זמה. "The God of Israel hates unchastity, bestiality."

the world always adequately realized that this lofty conception of Deity is the true teaching of Judaism.

What relation then exists between the ceremonial system and this fundamental principle or essence of Judaism? It cannot be denied that in its constitutive document, the Pentateuch, in which ethical laws fill a considerable space, we find also prescribed a whole series of ritual enactments, though the prophets treat these ordinances almost with contempt. Through Talmudism and Rabbinism they have been so improperly exaggerated, and received so enormous an extension in the various codes, that the ethical element seems to have been almost entirely crowded out, and Judaism has consequently appeared to consist of nothing but outward ceremonies, and to place the highest value in the mechanical performance of an infinite series of ritual acts. Let us now inquire whether this ritualism in *its original form* was related to the ethical element, or whether it is to be considered as something foreign to its purpose, an interpolation from without. From the earliest times, both Jewish and non-Jewish circles have been in the habit of considering Judaism as composed of two distinct parts—articles of faith and moral laws on the one side, ceremonies and ritual observances on the other. It was reckoned as one of the merits of the founder of Christianity, that he aided the progress of religious consciousness by eliminating the ceremonial law. On this view he becomes in a sense the founder of a reformed Judaism. The reform party of modern times sought to justify the transformation of Judaism by means of another line of argument. They held that the national character, which the Jewish law has always retained, was unessential as compared with its religious and ethical features, and as much of the former had necessarily been given up with the destruction of the national independence, all that had any tinge of nationality might now also be eradicated. Judaism was thus to adopt a universal or cosmopolitan character, and be able, as it were, to compete with Christianity, at any rate with Unitarianism. This is the point of view of a large number of Jews in America.

The value or worthlessness of the ceremonial element in Judaism, and its original signification, are well worth considering. That it has some deeper meaning is sufficiently proved by the testimony of the book of Deuteronomy, which was found in the temple by the high priest Hilkiah. Although it places the ethical laws in the foreground, it also enforces ritual observances, though on a far less extensive scale than in the other books of the Pentateuch.

The ceremonies must therefore possess at least a certain value and some definite relation to the ethical elements. It is worth while to investigate what this relation is.

When the prophets gave frequent utterance to the prediction, "The earth shall be full of the knowledge of the Lord, as the waters cover the seas"—full, that is, according to our interpretation, of ethical idealism and submission to God—they did not delude themselves with the belief that this "kingdom of heaven" was near at hand. They relegated the realization of the ideal to "the end of days." The two prophets, Isaiah and Micah, who predicted eternal peace on earth in connection with Israel's mission, that "nation shall not draw the sword against nation, and that they shall not learn war again," preface this statement with the words, "and it shall come to pass in the last days." They were gifted with the prevision that the teaching which goes forth from Zion would have power to effect a great moral transformation over the whole world—in some distant age.

But how is this teaching to endure to the end of days? How is it to be taught and to spread its influence abroad? A doctrine must possess its teachers. It must therefore have created for itself an organ, an interpreter, who should proclaim it and preserve it, and lead it to victory. Not an association, pledged by contract to carry on the work, not an order which has to be constantly recruited lest it should die out, was chosen to be the bearer of this teaching, but a *tribe* which, united in itself, even after apparent extermination is ever again renewed. The oldest record, the Scriptures, tells of the selection of a race of guardians for the regenerating doctrine. Abraham was chosen, so that he might command his sons and their descendants after them to keep the way of the Lord and to practise justice and righteousness. The promise to Abraham was that he would thus become the father of many nations, because his tribe, the people of Israel, was entrusted with the mission and the task of guarding the teaching of salvation until the end of days. Such is the language of Scripture. Or did this tribe become the guardian and preserver of the teaching because in it the ethical consciousness, though but in feeble outline, had been awakened and developed very early, and it was therefore more fitted than other nations for this ethical office?

In whichever way the fact be expressed, Israel, the descendant of Abraham, has played its part in the history of the world as guardian and propagator of a peculiar regenerative teaching. The Hebrew language has created a special name for the ideal import of this tribe. It is called Jeshurun

(ישורון), of which word the etymological meaning is, "The perfection of uprightness, or integrity." In this one term is comprehended what is elsewhere described as, "Thy people shall be all righteous, the work of my hands that I may be glorified"; or again: "a kingdom of priests and a holy people." As such an ideal, Israel, the servant of God, is destined to be a light to the nations and to bring unto them righteousness or salvation. If Israel possesses this lofty destiny and historic mission "for the latter days," its existence has an *exceptional* significance. Its beginnings are therefore represented in a peculiar light, and certainly were of an extraordinary character. It is an undoubted fact that the Israelites were slaves in Egypt, an undoubted fact that they left the land of their captivity, and equally certain that in order to reach the land in which they undeniably lived for seven hundred years, they had to pass through a terrible wilderness. These events, together with the passage of the Red Sea and the revelation of the Decalogue, which the older poetry glorified, and in so doing confirmed, were looked upon as the gracious proofs of a special Divine guidance. The prophet Jeremiah calls those days the bridal state of Israel. These first chapters of Israel's national history were to be all the more zealously remembered, inasmuch as they were to serve as an encouragement to remain steadfast through thousands of years of inward and outward trials and temptations. Israel's servitude and misfortunes at the beginning of its history, and its subsequent deliverance through a wonderful providence, were therefore immortalised by special ritual observances. The law itself does not enforce these observances as ends in themselves, but designates them as *means* for a higher end, "so that thou mayest remember all the days of thy life." In these words the connection between the spiritual essence of Judaism and a considerable part of its ritual observances is clearly designated: they are the means to an end, and that end is the memory of the past. National memories are dear to every nation; they urge it on to activity, to the maintenance of what it has already achieved, and to the increase of its fame. But the people of Israel was to pride itself not on the great deeds of its ancestors, but on the Divine guidance, which had shaped its destiny; and its national memories were intended to keep alive and unforgotten its own exceptional position and significance.

Another consideration is the following. This tribe was to be the bearer and guardian of what, in modern language, we should call moral and religious truth. But it lived among nations who despised these truths, or rather it lived among a polytheistic and orgiastic world. Contagion from this world was inevitable and did not fail to come. Polytheistic error had so entirely undermined morality, that the law had to threaten with severe punishment fathers who sacrificed their children to Moloch, or who sacrificed their daughters' purity to other shameful divinities. It had to forbid the price of prostitution being brought into the temple. Sins which we now regard as impossible, and cannot reflect on without a shudder, must therefore have become domiciled amongst the Israelites just as they were in Babylon, Tyre, Corinth, and throughout the ancient world. Hence the continual relapse of the people to the abominations of polytheism and apostasy, which recurred even after the reigns of Hezekiah and Josiah, until at the return from the Babylonian captivity the apparently inexhaustible tendency to idolatry was finally overcome.[1]

The law, the "Torah," had therefore to take measures by which to wean the people from its polytheistic aberrations. Just as the Great Synagogue in the post-exilian period introduced "hedges" forbidding certain things that had been hitherto permitted, in order to prevent some essential law from being transgressed, so the Torah prescribed a series of ritual observances, which were intended to counteract polytheism and its worship. We may call them anti-polytheistic observances. Separatism followed as necessarily as B follows upon A. In the Pentateuch, stress is even laid upon separatism. The preservation of national memories and the necessity of exclusiveness made ceremonialism indispensable. The observances have thus either a mnemonic or a prophylactic character. Those which were to remind the people of their early history have necessarily a national character. First comes the institution of the festivals. The rationalists at the end of the last and beginning of the present century thought they were attaching an ineradicable stigma to

---

[1] The views of modern criticism, that represent both David and Solomon as polytheists, and fix the date when Yahvism developed into monotheism at as late a period as possible, are contradicted by the fact that in Solomon's Temple the Holy of Holies (דביר) lay towards the west, just as in the description of the Tabernacle, the entrance to it was in the east, and the Holy of Holies in the west. As Helios was worshipped by almost all nations, the centre of the temple, the *Adyton*, was turned towards the east. The contrast between the Israelitish and the polytheistic temple arrangements is strikingly given in Ezekiel viii. 17. He saw twenty-five Israelites, worshippers of idols, standing at the entrance of the inner temple, towards which they turned their backs, while they looked towards the east, and prayed to the sun in the east, והמה משתחויתם קדמה לשמש. If Solomon had been still a polytheist, he must have placed the Holy of Holies in his temple in the east.

Judaism by proving that the two great festivals of Passover and Tabernacles were originally nature festivals, commemorating the beginning and end of the harvest. No doubt they were so originally, but they were converted into national festivals. In this assimilation or metamorphosis, is shown the spiritual energy which stamped its mark on all it found. The new ethical and religious conceptions had no *tabula rasa* before them; it was a people already accustomed to certain habits and institutions, which had to receive, preserve, and develop them. Thus the festival of the spring was converted into a national festival, to remind the people of their deliverance from slavery; and the harvest festival, the grape and fig harvest, which was spent in the open air and in booths, became a reminder of the many years spent in the wilderness. The exodus from Egypt was further to be called to mind by the redemption and sanctification of the first-born, by the removal of leavened bread, by the wearing of certain visible signs (phylacteries and tefillin) on forehead and hands, and possibly also by the blue fringes on the edges of the garment. If it should be proved that the nobles of Egypt wore fringes either for ornament or in compliance with some religious custom, we should here again have an example of the transformation of an old custom into a symbol of a loftier conception of life. It has not yet been made quite clear in what the so-called phylacteries (טוטפות, זכרון) and tefillin (אות) originally consisted. As they are enforced in Deuteronomy, they must have been of considerable importance, inasmuch as the fifth book of Moses frequently modifies the injunctions of the central three.

As the book of Deuteronomy accentuates more sharply than the others the fundamental monotheistic doctrine, it uses the law of Tefillin and Phylacteries, as well as that of the Mezuzot, to impress and to sharpen the monotheistic idea. The special significance of this commandment lay, no doubt, in the words, "Hear, O Israel, the Lord our God, the Lord is one," which were to be fastened to every door-post, so that everybody at every moment of the day might be exhorted to conceive the God of Israel as a perfect Unity.

As I have already explained in my first article, this confession, or more accurately, this consciousness of monotheism, was not intended to be an article of faith, but an antithetical protest against polytheism; and polytheism was abhorred, not so much on account of its logical error, but first and foremost because of its incitement to ethical corruption. Hence the prophylactic ceremonials. Paganism laid special stress upon sacrifices to the dead, which originated in hero-worship. The departed kings, national leaders and heroes, were represented as continuing to exist in Hades or elsewhere, transfigured into divinities (*manes divi*). This was the foundation of the superstition respecting evil spirits and demons. In Egypt especially, the deceased kings entombed in their pyramids, were made the objects of an elaborate system of worship. The mummies were considered sacred. The Israelite conception of God had to protest energetically against adoration of the dead, and it consequently pronounced the state of death to be unclean and a source of pollution. To touch a corpse, even that of a parent or a king, made a man unclean. Whoever had come in contact with a corpse, a skeleton, or a funeral feast, was not permitted to enter the sanctuary of the holy God until he had submitted himself to a seven days' purification, which purification had also a symbolical meaning. This is the probable origin of the Levitical laws of purification, against which so many objections have been raised. Perhaps it is only a natural sequence that dead animals were also pronounced unclean, with reference to the Egyptian custom of holding sacred the dead bodies of animals that were worshipped as divine.

It is possible that the command not to eat the flesh of certain quadrupeds, birds, fishes, and reptiles also had its origin in the reaction against the Egyptian worship of animals, which even included reptiles (רמש). This explanation is further suggested by the warning to avoid uncleanness by touching the carcases of such animals, and also by the motive given for the institution of these laws: "Ye shall sanctify yourselves and be holy, for I, the Lord your God, am holy, therefore you shall not defile yourselves."

Two of the sacrificial rites were certainly introduced as a counterblast against the Egyptian animal worship. The laws respecting the *red heifer* are extremely remarkable. A red heifer, that had never borne a yoke, was to be taken outside the camp and burnt to ashes. The person who accomplished the process was thereby rendered unclean, and yet the ashes were to be used for purification in cases of Levitical pollution. Even to the Talmudists, who were not apt to be taken aback by irrationalities, this ceremony appeared exceedingly strange. But when we remember that the bull (Mnevis) worshipped in certain districts by the Egyptians had always to be red in colour and never to have borne the yoke, the Pentateuchal ritual of the *red heifer* becomes intelligible. The god-ox or god-heifer was to be destroyed, and the "Parah adumah" represents the climax of pollution. The ceremony of mixing the ashes with water and sprinkling it with a bunch of hyssop, as a means of purification had, no doubt, also a symbolical meaning.

The rite of the scape-goat, which has so often served in the past as well as in the present for the slandering of Judaism, finds a complete explanation by reference to the Egyptian worship. In that country the goat was worshipped on account of its lasciviousness, as is related by two eye-witnesses, Herodotus and Diodorus Siculus. One could not possibly repeat in a living language the horrible details given by the latter historian concerning this worship. A Latin translation may be quoted here.[1] Women used openly to practise bestiality with goats; this was part of the religious ceremonial. The Israelites were wont to imitate even this abominable goat worship; therefore the Law (Lev. xvii. 7) admonishes them "to sacrifice no more unto *goats*, after whom they have gone a whoring." For this reason the scape-goat, *i.e.*, the symbol or essence of unchastity, was to be sent away into the wilderness, to "a land cut off" (ארץ גזרה), which was called Azaz-El, and there, according to the traditional interpretation of the passage, it was to be flung over a precipice. But before this conclusion of the ceremony, the high priest was to lay his hands upon the scape-goat and confess and renounce all the sins and transgressions of the people of Israel, that is to say all idolatrous and obscene worship. With all this the celebration of the Day of Atonement is also closely connected, and certainly the Israelites could not do sufficient penance for having yielded to the debasing and disgusting worship of Astarte and the goats.

It is thus evident that the ceremonial system in its origin stood in near relation to the fundamental idea or essence of Judaism; that its office was to promote and combine with that essence, and that it was not by any means invested with a magical character (as was the case with the cult of ancient religion generally), in order to check the interference of demoniacal powers (ἀποτροπιασμός) or to conciliate the gods and appease their anger. Now the sacrificial ritual in the Pentateuch accords so little with the essence of Judaism that some prophets openly proclaimed its inappropriateness. The combination of these heterogeneous elements into one

---

[1] *Diodorus Siculus*, I., 88. Hircum ob genitale membrum inter Deos retulere, quomodo apud Græcos etiam Priapum honorari perhibent. Animal enim hoc in Venerem eximie propensum; et membrum illud corporis, generationis instrumentum, honore dignum esse, quod abeo natura animantium ortum suum derivet. Denique pudenda, ajunt, non apud Aegyptios tantum, sed apud alios quoque non paucos in mysteriorum ritibus religiose habentur, ut a quibus generatio animalium promanat.

uniform teaching positively invites criticism. The explanation given by Maimonides was that the sacrificial ritual was a concession to the customs of the Israelites, who were used to heathen ideas, and that the commands concerning it were only a pedagogical means for setting bounds to the craving after sacrifice (*Morch Nebuchim,* 3, 32). But this explanation leaves the contradiction unsolved. If it was really a pedagogic means, it failed to attain its end, for the multitude considered the sacrificial worship so essentially important, and the ethical laws of so little value in comparison to it, that the prophet Isaiah was compelled to declare: "To what purpose is the multitude of your sacrifices unto me? saith the Lord. . . . Bring no more vain oblations; incense is an abomination unto me. . . . Make you clean, put away the evil of your doings" (chapter i.).

This part of Leviticus, however, shows itself externally as well as internally to be a foreign element. A fortunate chance led, in the reign of Josiah, to the discovery of the beautiful book of Deuteronomy, which has an obvious tendency to modify the sacrificial worship, and reduce it to a minimum. One of its most noticeable injunctions is: "If thou shalt forbear to vow, it shall be no sin in thee" (Deut. xxiii. 22). Next, there is not a word about sin offerings or guilt offerings, but only about peace and thank offerings, which were to be sacrificed, and eaten in the family circle. The ethical side of the ceremony is, moreover, strongly insisted on. The Levites, who had "no part or possession" of their own, the poor, the widow, the orphan, and the stranger, were to be invited to share the feast. Unlike the older code, the book of Deuteronomy attaches no sacred character to the firstlings of the cattle; and, instead of assigning them to the priesthood, ordains that they are to be eaten (like the festive offerings) in the family circle, while the poor must be allowed to have their share. Only on one ceremonial point does Deuteronomy lay special stress, and that is that no sacrifices were to be offered except in the one central and chosen locality.

Deuteronomy sought to deprive the priesthood of the greater portion of the tribute assigned to it in Leviticus; only a small part of the sacrifices, together with the first-fruits of corn, wine, oil and wool were to be allotted for its support. The tithes were to be the property of the owners of the cattle and the ground, on condition that they shared them with the poor.

The book of Deuteronomy breathes another atmosphere than Leviticus. Ceremonialism occupies only a small portion of it, while the ethical precepts are treated at length and enforced with heart-moving earnestness. It is one of the fatalities that have hindered the development of Judaism that the line laid down by Deuteronomy was not followed up. On the contrary, one excess has caused another. Because the Torah was known and valued but little and by few during the centuries of the first temple, while the tendency to polytheism remained persistent till the time of the Babylonian captivity, and because during that period the conviction became vivid and strong that the chastisements threatened by the prophets had come to pass in consequence of obstinate transgression of the Law, the general post-exilic view was, that all its commands and precepts must be minutely and conscientiously obeyed or else a new judgment would overtake the guilty community. As there was then more opportunity for carrying out the ceremonial than the moral laws, these came to the front, and post-exilian Judaism received a ceremonial character. In addition to this there came the advice of the Great Synagogue to make a fence round the law, without considering the injunction not to set the fence above the plantation.[1] Thus in order to prevent some remotely possible infringement of a law, the erewhile permitted became now forbidden. The rigorousness of the Talmudists was grafted on the hedge of the Soferim, and on that of the Talmudists the scrupulousness of Rabbinism and the superstitions of the Kabbala. During the long years of persecution and suffering, the few voices that were raised in warning against this excess of ceremonialism passed unheard; Judaism gradually assumed a repellent aspect. As a consequence there followed (and there follows still) apostasy. The pure well-spring of Judaism, the Bible, was so buried under all this accumulation that it almost seemed to have disappeared altogether. The system of instruction was as erroneous as the habitual method of thought. The natural consequence was that as soon as the first ray of enlightenment penetrated the Ghetto, throwing upon the outward aspect of Judaism a sudden and glaring light, indifference and apostasy followed close upon each other. Nothing but the strong sense of family union, deepened and fortified by centuries of suffering, offered resistance. Now that at the present day the outward appearance of Judaism has assumed a more attractive form, and the uncultivated Polish customs have been nearly banished from the public ceremonial (while Christianity, on the other hand, has lost something of its ancient halo), the apostates from Judaism are less numerous than those who are merely

[1] *Aboth di R. Nathan*, ed. Schechter, Version II., page 2.

indifferent; indifference is chiefly caused by ignorance. For Judaism, which does not rest upon the broad basis of State institutions, indifference is far more deadly than apostasy. If this indifference is to be shaken into life, Judaism must more lavishly display and make use of its civilising riches; it must seek to engrain the conviction that its apostolic mission is not yet ended. Long ago it lifted the ancient world out of the slough of moral corruption into which it had sunk, and although its right of original priority is ignored or denied, a part of its moral principles has been crystallised in State institutions, and has passed into the consciousness of all civilized humanity. Whereas the Latin race is more permeated with the spirit of Hellenism, the Anglo-Saxon race is penetrated with the Biblico-Judaic spirit; because its mind is more directed to truth than to beauty. Now what has not been crushed by the mailed footsteps of history must be indestructible and of lasting value. Not in vain has the Jewish people continued to exist for more than three thousand years; not in vain has it survived all catastrophes, caused by a succession of hostile forces, and even the immense disadvantage through the past eighteen hundred years of struggling as a small and a feeble minority against a powerful and hostile majority. Its continued existence—in itself a wonderful fact—is an irrefutable proof of its historical necessity, and what would the Jews be without Judaism, the body without the soul, the Levitical bearers without the ark of the covenant?

H. GRAETZ.

THE MODERNISTS REVOLT AGAINST GOD

by

BERNARD J. HELLER

THE MODERNISTS REVOLT AGAINST GOD

BERNARD J. HELLER

I

If one examines the long and checkered story of human thoughts, one would not be able to point to a period where the exponents of atheism were as bold and blatant as they are today. In studying the dissenters of the past, we must avoid the pitfalls of the modern outliners who are so facile in identifying outstanding heretics of yesterday with positive atheism. The simplification and extension of knowledge is commendable. It must, however, not be done at the expense of exactness and truth. Anaxagoras, Sophocles, Socrates, Aristophanes, Voltaire and Ingersoll have ridiculed the popular notions of God and Religion. That, however, does not indicate that they definitely subscribed to the credo of atheism. On the contrary, we have definite evidence that many of these critics did affirm their belief in the existence of an inconceivable and unprovable Being or Beings. One is as much justified in considering Anaxagoras an atheist because of his ridicule of the popular conception of God as one would be in including Maimonides in that category because of his insistence that the attributes applicable to God must be only negative.

The atheists of today are not only more numerous and more dogmatic, but more active. They seem to be possessed with the zeal of missionaries. They are not of the academic type of a La Metrie, a Holbach, or a Haeckel. Their writings are more akin to pamphleteers or propagandists. They are engaged now not in a defensive, but in an offensive campaign.

H. L. Mencken's recent book may be cited as an excellent illustration. I feel that I must stop and examine at some length the arguments and the attitude of the modern apostle of atheism before we can consider the methods of teaching the God-idea in our schools. Should his estimate of God and Religion be valid, then we would be guilty of fostering not a blessing, but a blight upon future generations. Secondly, the literary standing which Mr. Mencken possesses and his wide influence, especially among the so-called Jewish intelligentsia, makes it imperative that we do not ignore him.

In estimating the opinions of Mr. Mencken we must bear in mind the rôle to which he has elected himself. Mr. Mencken is a professional iconoclast. Refusing to align himself with any party or set of convictions, be they social, philosophic, as well as religious or irreligious, he flits about, casting stones in places where the crowds are thickest, and against modes of beliefs and behavior which are most widely recognized and revered. He advocates libertarianism, but as he beholds the slow but gradual discarding of the Puritan attitude on the part of increasing numbers, he stages a plea for monogamy. When men are impelled to bear arms, he is inclined to pacifism; but when men dream and strive for peace, he blurts out with a defense of militarism. He admits he spends his time in sardonic laughter at the homo sapiens. He has utter contempt for the human species, the exception, of course, being himself. When he speaks, he speaks with a pontifical assurance. He is skeptical of everything except his own skepticism. Mr. Mencken subscribes to no tenet, but he adheres to a particular technique. He entertains no philosophy, but he has definite prejudices.

In this—his latest effusion—Mr. Mencken is more than free in his bestowal of low motives to all those with whom he professionally differs and dislikes. That he should brand teachers of Religion as "half-wits," "most immoral of men," "hangmen, rather than deliverers," etc., etc., is to be expected. Consider, for example, the explanation which he gives to the establishment of the Rockefeller Institute:

> "No one will deny, I take it," he says, "that we owe the Rockefeller Institute, at least in part, to certain purely theological tremors in the donor. As a good citizen, no doubt, he desired simply to do something for the human race, but as a good Baptist he must have also given some thought to his own probable fate post mortem. Thus the Institute may be viewed as a magnificent sacrifice to the divine author of the Ten Commandments, in propitiatory atonement for some of the ways in which the money that paid for it was amassed."[1]

[1] p. 316.

In discussing the relationship of Science, Philosophy and Religion, he accounts for the belief in their compatibility on the part of some of the greatest thinkers of the ages on the ground that they were either insincere or hypocritical, as he deems was the case with Plato and Aristotle; [2] or on the basis of cowardice or superstitious atavisms, which he attributes to such men as Eddington, Whitehead and Millikan.

> "Ostensibly," he says, "that effort is based upon a modest sense of the limitations of the human mind—upon an humble and hence highly laudable readiness to admit that many of the great problems of being and becoming remain unsolved, and must probably go unsolved forever. But actually there is something else. In part, I suspect, it is simply cowardice —a disinclination to provoke formidable and unscrupulous antagonists too far—a craven yearning for the cheaper sort of popularity. But in part it is also due to inner turmoils, congenital doubts." [3]

Yet Mr. Mencken considers himself and his kind as the paragons of honesty, honor and gallantry.[4]

If I were inclined to do unto Mencken as he does unto others, I feel I would be perfectly justified in calling him an intellectual charlatan. In the first place, his title is a misrepresentation of the contents of the book. He should call it "A Diatribe against the Gods" instead of a "Treatise on the Gods." In the Preface, which many people not infrequently turn to before they purchase a book, Mr. Mencken considers it to be the product of his "amiable skepticism."

---

[2] pp. 101–2.

[3] "The only real way to reconcile science and religion is to set up something that is not science, and something that is not religion. This is done with great earnestness by Robert A. Millikan, A. S. Eddington, and other such hopeful men—all of them bred so deeply in the faith that they have been unable to shake it off in their later years, despite their training in scientific method and their professional use of it." (P. 306.)

"They must be endured patiently, and with them the damage that they do to the intellectual decencies. It is too much, indeed, to ask a man bred in a country parsonage and educated at a backwoods denominational college to get rid of his infantile dreads and superstitions altogether, even after a year at Göttingen and a long and useful career in the laboratory. But to be polite to such unhappy amphibians is one thing, and to take their incurable piety seriously is quite another." (p. 302.)

[4] p. 317.

"I am quite devoid of the religious impulse, and have no belief in any of the current theologies. But neither have I any active antipathy to them save, of course, in so far as they ordain the harassing of persons who do not believe in them."[5]

In that very same preface, he states:

"Religion can be very swinish, but that swinishness is surely not of its essence. What brought it into the world was man's eternal wonder and his eternal hope. It represents one of his bold efforts—and perhaps not the least of them—to penetrate the unknowable, to put down the intolerable, to refashion the universe nearer to his heart's desire."[6]

How flagrantly irreconcilable the title and the prefatory statements are to the tenor and the tenet of his whole book, I leave any reader to decide. However tempting and justified I may be, I shall not accuse Mr. Mencken of putting out a bait for the sale of the book. I shall merely attribute it to his inconsistency, which characterizes the Menckenian creed or lack of creed.[7]

Let us now examine some of the views of Mr. Mencken, and see whether they stand the test of research and reason. Mr. Mencken builds up his argument on three major premises, which he, of course, considers to be absolute facts.

First, Religion, he avers, has not only its root in fear, but advanced and refined as it may become it still is nourished by fear.[8]

---

[5] p vii.

[6] p. ix.

[7] Since the delivery of this paper an announcement has come forth that Mr. Mencken is engaged to be married and that the ceremony will be performed by a pastor in a conventional manner. This goes to show that many of our modern professional moral iconoclasts, like some ministers of religion, do not always practice what they preach.

[8] "When men cease to fear the gods they cease to be religious in any rational sense. They may continue to mouth pious formulae, but they are no longer true believers." (P. 112.)

"Under all, and more important than anything else, is the primary motive of fear. Theology has sought to refine it away, but it remains today, as it was in the beginning, the be-all and end-all of religion." (P. 330.)

"It sends fears to haunt him—fears which stalk upon him out of the shadows of the Ages of Faith, the Apostolic Age, the Age of the Great Migrations, the Stone Age. Its time-binding afflicts him with moral ideas born of the needs of primitive and long-forgotten peoples—ideas violently out of harmony with the new conditions of life that his own immense curiosity and

Secondly, he maintains that it was cultivated and developed, if it was not invented and imposed on the masses by shrewd and clever priests, who were hungering for power.

> "It is highly probable, indeed, that the first priest appeared in the world simultaneously with the first religion; nay, that he actually invented it."[9]

Lastly, the scientific method of explanation makes the continuation of religion totally unnecessary and even baneful to social, as well as intellectual progress.[10]

---

ingenuity have set up. It is, in its very nature, a machine for scaring; it must needs fail and break down as man gains more and more knowledge, for knowledge is not only power; it is also courage." (P. 350.)

How careless Mr. Mencken is in his characterization of works as well as imputation of motives may be seen in his statement that William James' *Varieties of Religious Experience,* which were the product of long and deep study, seldom have any scientific merits.

[9] p. 10.

[10] "Today every such man knows that the laws which prevail in the universe, whatever their origin in conscious purpose, manifest themselves in complete impersonality, and that no representation to any super-human Power, however imagined, can change their operation in the slightest. He knows that when they seem arbitrary and irrational, it is not because omnipotent and inscrutable Presences are playing with them, as a child might play with building blocks; but because the human race is yet too ignorant to penetrate to their true workings. The whole history of progress, as the modern mind sees it, is a history of such penetrations. They have come slowly, and, as time appears to transient and ardent man, at weary intervals, but nevertheless one has followed another pretty regularly, and since the beginning of the Seventeenth Century they have been coming ever faster and faster. Each in its turn has narrowed the dominion and prerogative of the gods." (Pp. 298–99.)

"Christian theology is not only opposed to the scientific spirit; it is opposed to every other form of rational thinking. Not by accident, you may be sure, do the Christian Scriptures make the father of knowledge a serpent—slimy, sneaking and abominable. Since the earliest days the church as an organization has thrown itself violently against every effort to liberate the body and mind of man. It has been, at all times, and everywhere, the steady defender of bad governments, bad laws, bad social theories, bad institutions." (Pp. 305–6.)

"The fact that they (some laws of nature) are unknown, in itself, is of no evidential value; it simply tells us what every enlightened person already knows, to wit, that man's knowledge of the universe is still incomplete. But it is certainly more nearly complete than it was fifty years ago, or a century ago, or a millennium ago, and so there is every reason to believe that it will become still more complete hereafter—that all the natural processes, in the course of time, will be brought into harmony with invariable laws."

"It is the custom of the craven 'scientists' I have mentioned, confronted by theological dudgeon, to seek a miserable peace by putting an arbitrary

It becomes evident at once that Mr. Mencken is guilty of over-simplification of a very complex subject, a sin which is quite common to modern popularizers of human knowledge. He has selected and overstressed a pet judgment and made it the dominating motif in his account. The facts that conflict with his pet point of view he either ignores, minimizes, or casuistically transmutes into a contrary implication in a manner which would make the medieval scholastics seem amateurish.

Mr. Mencken attributes the origin and prevalence of religion to the fear of the yet unknown forces. It was fear that made the primitive man clutch at the reeds of faith. It was fear that made him hug the deities and drove, and still drives, him into the churches and temples. The sacrifices and libations, the prayers and hymns of the moderns, are all aimed to propitiate the dread-inspiring deity.

Latest researches into this field present a rather different, if not antagonistic view. They reveal to us that primitive man felt more a kinship with, than a fear of, his gods. Mr. Robertson Smith expresses this view in the following paragraph.

> "It is not true that the attempt to appease these powers is the foundation of religion. From the earliest times, religion, as distinct from magic or sorcery, addresses itself to kindred and friendly beings, who may indeed be angry with their people for a time but are always placable, except to the enemies of their worshippers or to renegade members of the community. It is not with a vague fear of unknown powers, but with a loving reverence for known gods who are knit to their worshippers by strong bonds of kinship, that religion in the only true sense of the word begins. Religion in this sense is not the child of terror; and the difference between it and the savage dread of unseen foes is as absolute and fundamental in the earliest as in the latest stages of development."[11]

Mr. Mencken not only overrates this impulse that to a certain degree beat at the heart of primitive man, but he fails also to per-

---

limit upon this increase in human knowledge. Eager to pass as virtuous, they give assurances that science will stop before it gets into really close quarters with divinity." (Pp. 309–10.)

[11] *Religion of Semites*, pp. 54–5.

ceive and analyze the diverse strains that made up the impulse. For example, in that feeling which he terms fear, there are present the rudimentary beginnings of that sense of awe and reverence for the mysterious and inexplicable phenomena of nature, a craving for completeness which is satisfied through an association with higher powers of God. These motives are present in fear.[12]

To say, therefore, that religion is the product of mainly fear is a half truth, which is equivalent to a distortion of the truth.

Furthermore, there are facts that contradict this theory. For the objects which the primitive man worshiped were not all objects which were capable of injuring him. Some things and objects were those that aided and benefited him, the brooks, and the trees, etc. He worshiped these not only because he felt himself dependent on them, but because he detected in them also marvelous powers that transcended comprehension.

That a man of the wide reading and critical acumen of Mr. Mencken should seriously and sincerely entertain the view that religious acts and attitudes were devised by cunning priests which they shoved down the throats of men everywhere from the beginning of time unto this very day, is amazing—aye, even incredible. I can excuse a Roman philosopher for such a fanciful conception. The science of psychology was then only a babe in swaddling clothes. But Mr. Mencken lives in the twentieth century. The nature of man has been probed and explored, even unto the subconscious. He may deem God an illusion, religious rites and ceremonies senseless hocus-pocus, but how can an intelligent man fail to see that the tendency is ingrained in the soul of man. Let him call it "instinct" or "behavior pattern" or whatever he will. He need not consider its universality as a proof of its objective reality. It should, however, disclose to him the fact that it springs from within and is not imposed from without.

If religion is only a yoke which was foisted upon him by priests,

---

[12] Some writers see in the primitive religious expressions the beginnings of ethics and philosophy, etc. That is why all the primitive religions made their gods the Judge and Source of social behavior. That is why all the early religions occupied themselves with accounts of the origin of the world and man. That they are but myths is beyond the point. To them they were sufficient explanations of the whence, the how and the whither of things.

how account for the submissiveness and willingness to bear it. For despite his assertions that it is waning and men are increasingly emancipating themselves from its thraldom, the latest statistics tell us that memberships in churches are mounting—in urban even more than in rural sections.

That the apostles of religion were not always on the side of social progress and free inquiry is indisputable. They have compromised and capitulated to Caesar and Mammon, it is true. On the whole, however, they do not deserve the censure and odium which Mencken heaps upon them. If the religious influence in such cultural and social advancement could be precisely determined, it would be found to be not insignificant.

Mr. Mencken seems to be totally unaware of the prophets of Judea and their fearless denunciations of the social and the economic evils. It is true that their utterances do not constitute a program of social justice sufficient to guide men in civilizations that are more complex. Their cries, however, in behalf of the weak and the poor kept ringing in the ears of those who unfurled and carried the banners of right and justice, and the multitudes that followed and fought to make those ideals real. Religion may not have always supplied the spokesmen and generals of these revolutionary movements. It has, however, supplied it with inspiration and impulse. At least that is true of Judaism, whose motto was "Justice, justice, shalt thou pursue," and "The seal of the Holy One, blessed be He, is Truth."

Whether wittingly or unwittingly, Mr. Mencken ignores all this, even when he deals with Judaism, which he, by the way, identifies with the earliest portions of the Pentateuch. Its code of ethics he sees in the law of "eye for an eye and tooth for a tooth," and Yahweh to him is not the God of Holiness and Righteousness, but a depraved, vindictive deity dripping with blood.

I must confess that in reading the reviews of this book, which emanated mostly from the synagogs, I was very much depressed and disheartened. These rabbis seemed to be hot with anger because Mr. Mencken made some uncomplimentary racial characterizations of the Jew, which I thought and still think, were rather mild, and to a certain degree not baseless. They stigmatized him as an Anti-Semite and what not. The mud which he slung on Judaism and the perversions of its God-idea and ideal seemed not to have touched them at all. Would that the Jews, and especially the rabbis of today, had more of the attitude of that psalmist who cried out: "Not unto us, O Lord, not unto us, but unto Thy Name give glory, because of Thy Loving Kindness and Thy Truth."

The third and the last assumption of Mencken is as gratuitous and as vulnerable as the other. Here I must confess that I am a little hard-pressed for contradiction. For I cannot invoke the testimony of philosophers and scientists to show the legitimacy and the compatibility of religious as well as scientific methods of explanation.

Mr. Mencken, as I said above, discredits their testimony by saying that their beliefs are prompted by cowardice and superstitious atavisms or their craven desire for popular approval. I shall therefore quote the opinions of one who "was brought up far from Sunday School atmosphere of conventional religiosity." This individual is not merely a mild liberal, he is a modernist who has placed a halo of glory and goodness over current anti-Puritan tendencies. He is not only an erudite scholar, and a profound metaphysician, but one who explored and explained to us the secrets of human nature and art. I have in mind Mr. Havelock Ellis. In a chapter on the Art of Religion, in his book *The Dance of Life*, Mr. Ellis has the following to say:

> "It has become a commonplace among the unthinking, or those who think badly, to assume an opposition or hostility between mysticism and science. If 'science' is, as we have some reason to believe, an art, if 'mysticism' also is an art, the opposition can scarcely be radical since they must both spring from the same root in natural human activity." [13]
>
> "The very fact that science, in the strict sense, seems often to begin with the stars might itself have suggested that the basis of science is mystical contemplation. Not only is there usually no opposition between the 'scientific' and the 'mystical' attitude among peoples we may fairly call primitive, but the two attitudes may be combined in the same person. The 'medicine man' is not more an embryonic man of science

[13] pp. 182-83.

than he is an embryonic mystic; he is both equally. He cultivates not only magic but holiness, he achieves the conquest of his own soul, he enters into harmony with the universe; and in doing this, and partly indeed through doing this, his knowledge is increased, his sensations and power of observation are rendered acute, and he is enabled so to gain organized knowledge of natural processes that he can to some extent foresee or even control those processes. He is the ancestor alike of the hermit following after sanctity and of the inventor crystallizing discoveries into profitable patents. Such is the medicine man wherever we may find him—in his typical shape—which he cannot always adequately achieve—all over the world, around Torres Straits just as much as around Behring's Straits. Yet we have failed to grasp the significance of this fact." [14]

"But this harmony with the essence of the universe, this control of Nature through oneness with Nature, is not only at the heart of Religion; it is also at the heart of science. *It is only by the possesssion of an acquired or inborn temperament attuned to the temperament of Nature that a Faraday can achieve his results.* And the primitive medicine man, who on the religious side has attained harmony of the self with the Not-self, and by obeying learnt to command, cannot fail on the scientific side, also, under the special conditions of his isolated life, to acquire an insight into natural methods, a practical power over human activities and over the treatment of disease, such as on the imaginative and emotional side he already possesses. If we are able to see this essential and double attitude of the Shaman—medicine man—if we are able to eliminate all the extraneous absurdities and the extravagances which conceal the real nature of his function in the primitive world, the problem of science and mysticism, and their relationship to each other, ceases to have difficulties for us." [15]

"The course of human evolution involves a division of labour, a specialization of science and of mysticism along special lines and in separate individuals. But a fundamental antagonism of the two, it becomes evident, is not to be thought of; it is unthinkable, even absurd. If at some period in the course of civilization we seriously find that our science and our religion are antagonistic, then there must be something wrong either with our science or with our religion.

---

[14] pp. 183-84.
[15] pp. 184-85.

Perhaps not seldom there may be something wrong with both. For if the natural impulses which normally work best together are separated and specialized in different persons, we may expect to find a concomitant state of atrophy and hypertrophy, both alike morbid. The scientific person will become atrophied on the mystical side, the mystical person will become atrophied on the scientific side. Each will become morbidly hypertrophied on his own side." [16]

That has become the case with Mr. Mencken, no less than with the Pope who banned scientific research and independent philosophic speculations.[17]

The outburst of atheism at this time, which has become crystallized in the utterances of Harry Elmer Barnes and the writings of H. L. Mencken cannot be thoroughly understood unless we psycho-

---

[16] pp. 187–88.

[17] "We have not only to realize how our own prepossessions and the metaphysical figments of our own creation have obscured the simple realities of religion and science alike; we have also to see that our timid dread lest religion should kill our science, or science kill our religion, is equally fatal here. He who would gain his life must be willing to lose it, and it is by being honest to one's self and to the facts by applying courageously the measuring rod of Truth that in the end salvation is found." Havelock Ellis, *Dance of Life,* p. 219.

"When all deduction has been made of the mental and emotional confusions which have obscured men's vision, we cannot fail to conclude, it seems to me, that science and mysticism are nearer to each other than some would have us believe. At the beginning of human cultures, far from being opposed, they may even be said to be identical. From time to time, in later ages, brilliant examples have appeared of men who have possessed both instincts in a high degree and have even fused the two together, while among the humble in spirit, and the lowly in intellect, it is probable that in all ages innumerable men have by instinct harmonized their religion with their intelligence. But as the accumulated experiences of civilization have been preserved and handed on from generation to generation, this free and vital play of the instincts has been largely paralyzed. On each side fossilized traditions have accumulated so thickly, the garments of dead metaphysics have been wrapped so closely around every manifestation alike of the religious instinct and the scientific instinct—for even what we call 'common sense' is really a hardened mass of dead metaphysics—that not many persons can succeed in revealing one of these instincts in its naked beauty, and very few can succeed in so revealing both instincts. Hence a perpetual antagonism. It may be, however, we are beginning to realize that there are no metaphysical formulas to suit all men, but that every man must be the artist of his own philosophy. As we realize that, it becomes easier than it was before to liberate ourselves from a dead metaphysics, and so to give free play alike to the religious instinct and the scientific instinct. A man must not swallow more beliefs than he can digest; no man can absorb all the traditions of the past; what he fills himself with will only be a poison to work to his own auto-intoxication." Havelock Ellis, *Dance of Life,* pp. 224–25.

analyze the apostles and the devotees of modernism. Atheism usually comes on the heels of a new discovery or of a startling revolutionary movement. Despite the technological achievements of science, no such radical change has taken place in the realm of human knowledge. Our progress, it seems to me, constitutes but an extension and translation of ideas, which were already propounded. The seeds of Einsteinian relativity may be found in the philosophy of Heraclitus and the Eleatics. Even the creed of our behaviorists represents to me nothing more than a development of the views of Cabanis, who said that "thought stands in the same relation to the brain as bile to the liver and urine to the kidneys," or that of Moleschott, who averred that "without phosphorus there is no thought." It was Ludwig Büchner, who, in his *Force and Matter*, defined psychical activity as "nothing but a radiation through the cells of the grey substance of the brain of a motion set up by external stimuli." As far as the theories of scientists are concerned, they have become less rather than more materialistic than those that prevailed in the nineteenth century. With all due respect to the marvelous achievements of this age, I contend that no Copernicus or Wellhausen has appeared on the scene, which should justify the vigorous and the virulent activity of modern atheism.

Mr. Mencken's outburst cannot be considered the product of a war disillusionment. In the first place, he never expected anything from the homo sapiens. Secondly, war is not to him a serious offense. Being a Nietzschean, he hails it as a salutary opportunity for humankind to get rid of those weaklings which have impeded the progress of the superman. As for the folly and fanaticism of the sectarians, that affords him an opportunity to laugh, without which he would become dethroned from the office of High Priest of the cult of Mercurianity, as one rabbi called it.

I can only explain the dogmatism and denunciation of contemporaneous atheists by linking them up with the desires and forces that agitate their subconscious selves. The wide currency of Menckenism is due not only to his brilliant style, but also to the fact that human beings love to see a fight. They will endure discomfort, rub shoulders with men whom they ordinarily would not want to look upon, and pay a fabulous price in order to see a pugilistic exhibition. A debate of Barnes, a vituperative article by Mencken against things that are universally accepted and respected, vicariously satisfies that desire, which is a sublimation of the pugnacity that is still within them, refined as they may be. Mencken to them is a little David who dared to go out and slay Goliath. They are thrilled by what seems to them to be courage. If they would only realize that this little David, instead of slinging stones, ejects but soft and cooked peas, which make no impression on the giant, their interest and admiration, I think, would wane.

Secondly, humility is certainly not a virtue of the modernist. He has been fed on arrogance and pride to the point that it has filled up all the nooks and crevices of not only his conscious, but even his subconscious self. The belief in a God—a being more powerful and perfect than the modern—disturbs and challenges his pet belief in his superability and nobility. The modern man wants to occupy a throne and look, not above him, but below him. In order to succeed, he must dispense with the stars and the heavens. His denial of God and his debunking of heroes of the past are the result, to no little extent, of his subconscious desire to reign supreme over the things that are above as well as below.

Lastly, the modernist exalts the animalistic instincts under the guise of self-expression. He has flung to the winds all the "don'ts" of the past. He, however, still remains human. He is higher than a beast, despite Mr. Mencken's beliefs to the contrary. He may have reasoned away his conscience, but moral scruples still haunt him and his religious yearnings still remain undowned. If he could but slay God and put him out of sight, that ghost would cease to tantalize him. Just as rabid asceticism is a transubstantiation of one's suppressed passion and craving for worldliness, and just as Jesuitical chastity is an illegitimate child of imprisoned but raging impulses, just so is the atheistic zeal of the modernist to be attributed to that voice of conscience which, though in feeble tones, still continues to upbraid him. If he could only choke it, he would be able, he instinctively feels, to go about his business of self-gratification unmolested. Mr. Mencken and his kin therefore ought to be considered as inverted Stratons.

Atheism as a profession, and not as a protest, even when it expresses itself soberly and without vituperation, is subject to the following weaknesses. It is no less dogmatic than is theism, and I believe with less justification. Atheism blinks its eye at snags which are not imaginary. To account for spiritual phenomena by dogmatically and arbitrarily stating that they are the product of material things, atoms, electrons, force, energy, etc., is pedantic bosh. Psychical phenomena and events cannot be translated adequately by a quantitative reduction into physical terms. The atheists who make such affirmations, subscribe metaphysically at least to a belief in a *"creatio ex nihilo."* Even the cocksure theist to whom God is more than a "Great Perhaps," even if he possesses a theodicy which enables him to know exactly the meaning and purpose of every object and occurrence, does not do as much violence to the facts of experience as does the absolute mechanist or behaviorist. A materialistic or mechanistic explanation is, as David Hume pointed out, no explanation at all, though it aids us a great deal in harnessing the forces and predicting the occurrences of nature. What scientific accounts do is to describe to us the succession of events, and even in doing this the scientist erects a structure on foundations which are purely fictitious.

> "Matter is a fiction," writes not the blind theologian, or the timid scientist, but Mr. Havelock Ellis, "just as the ideas with which sciences generally operate are mostly fictions, and the scientific materialisation of the world has proved a necessary and useful fiction, only harmful when we regard it as a hypothesis and therefore possibly true. The representative world is a system of fictions. It is a symbol by the help of which we orient ourselves. The business of science is to make the symbol ever more adequate, but it remains a symbol, a means of action, for action is the last end of thinking." [18]

Absolute space, force, atom, electrons are just such symbols and fictions. They are true so long as they work and increase man's knowledge. The same criteria ought to be applied to religion. A purely materialistic and mechanistic account of nature and man utterly fails to explain to us the facts of growth and development,

---

[18] *Dance of Life*, p. 92.

facts which the theory of evolution especially emphasizes. It fails to adequately account for the presence of thought or the sense of value, and the consciousness of human freedom, which we feel are as real as any of the material objects which exist or which we imagine to exist outside of us. Once the atheist will cease to invalidate such experiential facts, he is bound to slide into the camp of the humanists, and if he does not stop thinking, he is sure to land among the enlightened theists.

II

The proverbial prayer, "God protect me from my friends, I'll take care of my enemies," could well describe the attitude of the Jewish religionists to the so-called modern Jewish humanists of the lay and more so of the rabbinical variety. We need not fear the atheist and skeptic. He has adopted a philosophy and has taken a definite position. He tells people unequivocally what he believes or disbelieves and where he stands. He calls a spade a spade. This makes it easy for us to comprehend his views and appraise them and point out what seems to us their inadequacies. It is, however, not so with the Jewish humanists. They vacillate and equivocate. They negate the cardinal affirmations and attitudes which religion demands or implies, and yet they persist in using the term God. They propound the tenets of secular ethicism, but yet they insist on doing it from the pulpits of synagogs. When this dichotomy is called to their attention, they retort that they are reinterpreting old concepts by pouring new wine in old bottles. They forget that such procedure is legitimate when the essence and nature of the new and the old are more alike than they are different. It is *all right to pour new wine into old wine bottles, but it is certainly improper to pour vinegar into receptacles that were wont to contain champagne.*

Judaism is a system of thought and life which is grounded in the belief of an Infinite, Eternal, but Personal God, who is the Supreme Source and Sanction of the ever expanding ethical and social ideals. He is beyond our reach and yet we intuitively feel that He is near us and with us wherever and whenever we wish to turn to Him in sincerity and truth. He is inconceivable and deemed unprovable to the human mind, and yet to the heart and soul He is the most primal fact. He is not only the omega, but the alpha of our thought. He is the root as well as the fruit of all knowledge, whether it laboriously cometh by way of the test-tubes of the laboratory or whether it cometh in a flash of lightning at an unseen and unheralded moment. Inhabiting the celestial realms, yet He permeates this world of nature, even the lowliest blade of grass. He is impersonal and above human whims and wants, and yet He is vitally concerned with the ethical actions and aspirations of the most insignificant of men, through whom and by whom He reveals supremely and superbly His glory and goodness.

This, in a general way, is the basic creed, or rather conviction, of Jewish and all enlightened forms of Theism. Mythological excrescences, superstitious fungi have sprung up on the bark of the oak, but they must not, however, be identified with the tree itself. *In eliminating the overgrowths we dare not cut down the tree itself.*

If we closely examine the doctrines of the *Jewish humanists,* we will find that they are *neither true to Judaism nor to Humanism.* They give us not a version but a perversion of both Humanism and Judaism. I shall now try to prove this point.

Jewish Humanism as propounded by its clerical apostles (Professor Mordecai Kaplan and Rabbis Solomon Goldman and Herman Lissauer) commences with eliminating the vital God idea from their purview and program. If they use the term, they sublimate it into vague principles or into a poetic symbol. The God of Theism and Judaism, they aver, is incompatible with scientific facts and forms of explanation. Theism and Judaism, say they, imply supernatural implications, which of course do not and cannot remain under the same roof with science. The complete and uncompromising denial of the possibility of any and all forms of supernormal, or, as they term it, "supernatural," reading of events, impels them to discard all notions of revelation and miracles from their system. That constitutes a corollary to their first proposition.

They affirm also that the ethical and social strivings of man need not and must not be linked up with any theistic creed or God-idea. The basis and sanction of any ethical act, say they, must be its utility to the individual or to the group The theistic ethics which persists in linking itself up with God they brand as a form of blind authoritarianism. When these men are questioned as to the meaning and justification of their Jewish attachments, they say that Judaism primarily is and was a culture or a civilization. God and religion played a part in it, but were not synonymous with the whole of it. Significant as it may have been to the Jewish scheme in the past, it is not essential to it in the present. They translate their Jewish devotions as being loyal to the Jewish group and its ethos, whose preservation they exalt into a cardinal creed or a categorical imperative.

Professor Kaplan defines Judaism as follows:

> "Judaism is the funded cultural activity which the Jewish people has transmitted from generation to generation. It is the living, dynamic process of intellectual, social, and spiritual give and take of Jews in the course of their relationship to one another as individuals and as members of various groups."[19]

This definition, though true, is misleading. It fails to tell us where Jewish civilization was unique, except in the fact that it was professed and practiced by a particular group. Jewish civilization was not something that could be broken up or departmentalized into discrete (intellectual, social and spiritual) elements. It was a civilization that was knitted together by a divine idea and ideal, which gave motive and meaning to each of its parts. It was like a beautiful mosaic. One cannot break up a mosaic and jumble the pieces together and still believe that he has the whole and essence of it. What precedes and follows that definition clearly illustrates its inadequacy.

The inexactness of Professor Kaplan becomes an aberration at the hands of his pupils. "It is difficult to maintain," writes Rabbi Solomon Goldman, "as some would have it, that it is religion or the God idea that holds Jewry together." It is only its cultural *milieu*, he contends. "God is absorbed in the nationalism or more correctly in the nationality of Israel. He serves as the symbol for Israel's

---

[19] *Reconstruction of Judaism*, p. 21.

noblest aspirations and loftiest ideals. He is the national God. He is the soul of the nation."[20]

Rabbi Goldman in his reasoning is guilty of the following fallacies, because of his failure to discriminate between the necessity of a belief in the reality of God (however he may arrive at it, whether by the way of tradition, logical deduction, or pure intuition) and a detailed picturization or conception of God. *Judaism permitted the widest latitude to the latter, but as to the necessity of the former, it remains firm and adamant.* To say that God to the Jew was nothing more than a symbol of national aspiration and ideals, noble and lofty as they may be, is nothing less than a falsification of truths and facts.

The Prophets centered their faith in and love around Israel because it served or gave promise of serving God, *who was not a mere symbol, but a living Being, who possessed attributes of Supreme and Infinite Personality.* The long line of generations of Jews who joyously resigned themselves to untold insults and indescribable persecutions, did it not for the sake of a "Kultur," but for the Torah. The martyrs that braved death with a smile, did it not for an ethos, but for "Kiddush Hashem" (the sanctification of His Name). The flagrant fallacy of this nationalistic creed is seen by their very refusal to allow those Hebrews who have accepted belief in the divinity of Jesus, but who still desire to remain racially and nationally affiliated with Jews, to collaborate with them in the rebuilding of Palestine. Where is their consistency?

The latest convert to Jewish Humanism is Rabbi Herman Lissauer. He frankly says:

> "I am not sure whether we may properly use the term God since our meaning of the term is so different from our fathers'. We do not hold any belief in God as an 'externalized, individualized, personal being.' When we speak the word God, it is purely in the poetical meaning, and as a symbol for the idea. I have defined God as 'the advancing totality of our highest ideals.' We speak of religion as the search for life's meanings, the 'interpretation of human life with idealism.' Our view of religion is solely humanistic, and in no way

---

[20] "The God of Modern Israel," *New Palestine*, June 7, 1929.

> theistic. We deal with man and not with God. Our great difficulty is to find in Jewish life and literature any expression of this view, and we are compelled to interpret even the 'Sh'ma Yisrael' in order to enable us to voice the one expression which every Jew uses as a watchword."

Rabbi Lissauer blunders because he apparently lacks philosophic and psychologic perspicacity. A philosophic study of Judaism will reveal the fact that in it miracles did not play the rôle which it did, for example, in Christianity. Christian theologians have deemed the performance of miracles, in the present as well as the past, as absolute evidence of the veracity of a doctrine and divine credibility of man. That was not so in Judaism, at least to the same degree as in Christianity. As early as the Book of Deuteronomy we are warned by Moses that if a prophet comes and exhorts the people to worship strange gods and offers as proof his ability to perform signs and wonders, his teachings should be rejected. The rabbis refused to permit the "Bath-Kol"—Heavenly Voice—to swerve them from any decision which their reason or best judgment suggested to them. Jewish seers and sages were indisposed to pin their faith on the unerring reliability of miraculous claims or even evidences. They adjusted the validity and sanctity of doctrines or deeds on the basis of their inner tenor and tendency.

The natural and the supernatural did not have the connotation to them that it has to us. Nature and law are categories of thought which we have acquired recently. They are hypotheses of modern science. A miracle meant to them a phenomenon that was uncommon and extraordinary and in or through which they perceived the workings of God. The Psalmist expresses it in the verse: "This was the Lord's doing—it is therefore marvellous in our eyes." When the rabbis and Maimonides assert that the occurrence of miracles was ordained at the very creation,[21] they in reality deny the likeliness, if not possibility, of any divine intrusion or interruption of natural law. With reference to the Sinaitic theophany, one rabbi openly states that God never descended on Mount Sinai, nor did Moses go up to heaven.[22]

---

[21] See Gen. R. V., Aboth 5[6] and Morch 11[25], [29].
[22] Sukkah 5[a].

Such acceptance of scientific postulates, however, did not imply to them the rejection of the belief or conviction that "our whole physical life," as William James expresses it, "lies soaking in a spiritual atmosphere; a dimension of being that we at present have no organ for apprehending. The so-called world of nature, which constitutes this world's experience, is only one portion of the total universe, and that there stretches beyond this visible world an unseen world of which we now know nothing positive, but in its relation to which the true significance of our present mundane life consists."[23]

Judaism asserts two doctrines which exempts it from humanistic attacks. It believes in the doctrine of progressive revelation. Just as God discloses Himself through nature, though He does not confine Himself to it, so does He manifest Himself through man, and to us particularly through Israel's sublimest actions and aspirations. (That, however, must not be construed in implying that He has no objective reality except in Israel's thought and life.)

It was not necessary that these actions and aspirations should be accompanied by any superphysical manifestations. If they tended to bring out the highest and best in man, then they were deemed to be divine. "When wise men sit together and try to reason out the moral implication of an event or situation, though they arrive at diverse conclusions, the One God moves them all," say the rabbis.[24]

When Moses implored God to permit him to behold His Face, He replied, "Wherever you find the footprints of man, there am I."[25] Succinctly put, they believed that the Moral Law of man revealed the Divine Will. When they termed the Torah (Moral Laws) to have emanated from Heaven, they meant nothing more than what G. R. Elliott, the neo-humanist, said, "that they are supernatural

[23] *Will to Believe*, p. 51.

[24] תלמידי חכמים שיושבין אסופות ועוסקין בתורה הללו מטמאין והללו מטהרין, הללו אוסרין והללו מתירין, הללו פוסלין והללו מכשירין . . . כולם נתנו מרועה אחד אל אחד נתנן, פרנס אחד אמרן.

Hag 3[b]

[25] 'הנני עומד לפניך שם' אמר לו הב"ה מכל מקום שאתה מוצא רושם רגלי אדם שם אני לפניך.

without being ever unnatural, always immanent in us and yet, in a mystery beyond the reach of our science, always transcendent of us."[26]

It is this doctrine that made us averse to put a seal of finality to the last page of the Bible, the Mishna, or the Talmud. *Israel's ideal life was Israel's Scripture.* It is the window through which he beholds God.

Secondly, Judaism, unlike Christianity, has consistently avoided prescribing a metaphysical creed to its devotees. It may have doctrines, as Schechter rightly contends, but not transcendental dogmas. Its monotheism was not intended as a philosophic ultimate, but more as an ethical means. I cannot stop here and discuss the difference between the two. Now the Jewish humanists make much of this. They invoke this fact as a warrant for their theistic negations. If they would, however, probe deeper into the cause of this phenomenon, they would discover that it is due to Judaism's humanistic outlook and orientation. Judaism focused its attention upon man, life and this world. "Seek me and live," is its motto. Of course when it said "live," it connoted a plane of life different from that which the moderns stipulate. It advocated controlled and consecrated living, and not the free and unbridled satisfaction of all our impulses. In this postulate Judaism discloses no difference of attitude from that of Humanism, except that its religious beliefs and background save it from being vague and indefinite and criterion-less.[27]

The mistake which the Jewish humanists have made in their protest is that they conceived Judaism to be identical in nature with Christianity, and therefore supposed that the transcendental and

---

[26] "The human task is to clarify and obey, as well as we can, Laws which we did not invent; which no man, except when stupefied by pride—either his own pride or the pride of his teachers, relentlessly visited upon him to the third and fourth generation—can conceive to be merely human inventions." (G. R. Elliott in N. Foerster's Symposium *Humanism and America*, p. 96.)

[27] "Humanism conceives that the power of restraint is peculiarly human, and that those who throw down the reins are simply abandoning their humanity to the course of animal life or the complacency of vegetables. It conceives, further, that the attainment of the ideal of completeness of life, of a human nature rounded and perfect on all its sides, is fatally frustrated at the start unless the ideal of centrality or self-control is introduced as the

other-worldly tendencies of the latter were equally present and fundamental to the former. *The humanistic protest is valid when directed against dogmatic theology of the Church. It is out of order when made in the Synagog.*

As I said above, the version of the Jewish humanists constitutes a perversion of the doctrines of New Humanism. While the exponents of this new humanistic movement do not agree among themselves in details, nevertheless one need not be a subtle logician to detect the contrary tenor and tendencies between the two.

The Jewish humanists completely capitulate to the radical scientist. They accept his most extravagant claims. The neo-humanists, on the other hand, begin their creed and career by denying the assumption and presumption of those scientists who think that the materialistic and mechanistic method of explanation offer us the key to the complete understanding of the essence of Nature and Man. The absolute character of things, say they, still lies beyond the veil of mystery. Science has not and cannot rend this veil. What it does is merely give us a quantitative reduction of the universe. It ignores completely the qualitative side of things, which we experientially feel to be more real than physical ultimates and the symbolic equation of mathematics. Science traffics not with facts, but with fictions. At best their account is but a portrait of a thing or being which they imagine, but have never seen face to face. I shall quote copiously from the writings of the humanists because the charge that I made that Jewish humanists unjustly appropriated and distorted their teachings is a serious one.

> "The man of science is attempting to picture things which can never be seen, for atoms lie in the realm of the infinitely small, whose very existence is problematical. Models of atoms, of ethers, or of space have about the same degree of authenticity as the posthumous portrait of a person whom no one then alive had ever seen. Men of science are too

---

regulating principle. The substitution of intensity as the regulating principle, which is proposed by many modernists, such as Aldous Huxley, provides for quantity but not quality of life, and tends to defeat the ideal of completeness, because certain parts of human nature, if not disciplined, will always thrive at the expense of other parts." (Norman Foerster, Symposium on *Humanism and America,* Preface, p. xiv.)

prone to confuse the thing and the model in their own minds, and they have certainly been so careless in their teaching that even very highly educated laymen accept these hypotheses as facts." [28]

"There was indeed at first sight a seductive simplicity about the theories of Huxley and his militant brothers. It is so easy to say that the world is nothing but a machine nicely constructed of atoms, running smoothly and undeviatingly under the mechanical laws of motion; to deny that anything new or incalculable ever breaks in to disarrange the regularity demanded by science; to dispose of the passions and appetites and the very consciousness of men as mere products of atomical reaction. It was the kind of simplification that promised to solve for us all the annoying problems of life, exactly the kind of bait that the Demon of the Absolute loves to dangle before a mind unprotected by the humility of common sense. Certainly if ever any group of men had a cosmic footrule in their pockets, it was this particular group of mid-Victorians who married the atheistical philosophy of the Eighteenth Century to the physical discoveries of the Nineteenth." [29]

"The (quantum) hypothesis affirms action without specifying something to act, unless the word energy is given all the physical attributes of matter. In which case a quantum of radiant energy is merely our old friend, a corpuscle of light, masquerading under a new name. Again it substitutes the principle of discontinuity of action for continuity, and one is puzzled to know from what the quantum originates and in what it ends. And again, it creates the dilemma that light is simultaneously corpuscular and vibrational, since without the latter quality none of the phenomena of interference is explicable. Lastly, it drifts into a pure philosophy of idealism." [30]

"Science as an accumulation and classification and utilization of observed facts may go on from victory to victory, but science as a name for such hypothetical theories of time and space, matter and motion and life, as those broached by the Darwinians of the Nineteenth Century or the Einsteinian relativists of the Twentieth is not a progress in in-

[28] Louis Trenchard More, *Humanism and America,* p. 16.
[29] Paul Elmer More, *Humanism and America,* p. 86.
[30] Louis Trenchard More, *Humanism and America,* p. 21.

sight, but a lapse from one naïve assumption to another in a vicious circle of self-contradicting monism." [31]

"If the phenomena of life are to be classed as an exact science, it is necessary to postulate that the living organism also is a machine—a thing of various material parts, acting on each other by mechanical forces. Such a postulate is pure fiat, for we have found no common factors between what we call vital actions and mechanical and physical forces." [32]

"We are worse confused than the Deists of the Eighteenth Century who believed that the mind of God could be defined by learning the facts and laws of nature; we now propose that the intellectual and spiritual attributes of man be framed in the hypotheses of dogmatic Science." [33]

"An effective procedure is, as I have said, to meet the mechanist on his own ground and point out to him that he is unduly dogmatic if he holds that his hypothesis is absolutely valid even for the natural order, and that if he goes further and seeks to make it cover the whole of experience, to impose a deterministic nightmare on the human spirit itself, he is abandoning the experimental attitude for an even more objectionable form of dogmatism." [34]

Secondly, the Jewish humanists are inclined to identify the good life with a program of social action which takes into account the material cravings of man. Practices and procedures are sufficient to be considered as ethical when they are useful and lead to happiness. They do not stress so much the quality of such usefulness and happiness. They are in reality but positivists, defying man and his wants and desires. The humanists, however, posit the presence in man of a higher self. They may be weak in the definition of what this self is, but they are certain of its reality. A line of conduct is ethical, not when it conforms to the wills and the whims of an individual or a group, but when it conforms to the imperatives of that higher self in man. The humanist speaks with derogation, if not contempt, of the positivists whom he calls humanitarians.

---

[31] Paul Elmer More, *Humanism and America*, pp. 72–73.
[32] Louis Trenchard More, *Humanism and America*, p. 7.
[33] Louis Trenchard More, *Humanism and America*, p. 17.
[34] Irving Babbitt, *Humanism and America*, p. 45.

The ideal of the humanitarian is physical contentment and the obtainment of power. His model is Bacon. The ideal of the humanist is the elevation and exaltation of the spiritual side of man. His model is not Bacon, but Socrates.

> "The humanitarians in particular, whether of the utilitarian or of the sentimental type, have put slight emphasis on the inner control of the appetite. They have encouraged either directly or through the ineffectiveness of the substitutes they have offered for this control, a multiplication and complication of desires that is in flat contradiction with the wisdom of the ages. Judged by the standards of the great traditional faiths, the religion of 'progress' or 'service' or humanity, merely illustrated on a vast scale the truth of the old Latin adage that the world wishes to be deceived. The various naturalistic philosophies that have been built up on the ruins of tradition should, at all events, whatever their merits or demerits, be made to stand on their own feet. It should be one's ambition to develop so keen a Socratic dialectic, supported by such a wealth of historical illustration, that it will not be easy for the Walter Lippmanns of the future to propose some form of naturalism as the equivalent of 'humanism' and 'high religion.'"[35]

> "The humanitarian has favored not only temperamental expansion; he has also, as a rule, favored the utmost expansion of scientific knowledge with a view to realizing the Baconian ideal. Perhaps indeed the chief driving power behind the humanitarian movement has been the confidence inspired in man by the progressive control physical science has enabled him to acquire over the forces of nature. It goes without saying that the humanist is not hostile to science as such, but only to a science that has overstepped its due bounds, and in general to every form of naturalism, whether rationalistic or emotional, that sets up as a substitute for humanism or religion. In the case of such encroachments, there is not only a quarrel between the naturalist and the humanist, but a quarrel of first principles. When first principles are involved, the law of measure is no longer applicable. One should not be moderate in dealing with error. I have pointed out elsewhere the danger of confounding the humanistic attitude with that of the Laodicean."[36]

---

[35] Irving Babbitt, *Humanism and America*, p. 48.
[36] Irving Babbitt, *Humanism and America*, pp. 31–32.

The Jewish humanists, together with Dr. Charles Francis Potter, fail to distinguish between the humanists' contention that man possesses an inner moral dignity and the positivists' creed that man is deity.

> "No excuse remains for muddle-headed critics, for example, the saccharine simplicity of that Dr. Charles Francis Potter, who recently has acquired a kind of newspaper notoriety (extending, to my knowledge, as far as Lahore, India) by launching a 'new religion' of 'humanism' wherein humanity is to be enthroned in the place of God, and who, in his initial address, mentioned Mr. Babbitt and myself, among others, as associates in the foundation. The *Commonweal* of October 16, 1929, made the proper reply to such impertinence: 'Whoever may have said that man is inherently good, it was certainly not Professor Babbitt; the diverse negators of the supernatural have many names, but that of More is not among them." [37]

Thirdly, the Jewish humanists, because of their emphasis on nationalism, not only place the interest and the dignity of the group above that of the individual, but in their search for ideals and inspirations they are parochial. As humanists their sweep ought to be universal. They should not consistently confine themselves to the wisdom and values of their own people.

> "Cultural movements," writes Norman Foerster, the humanist, "have two sexes, so to speak, one native and one foreign, and the native expresses itself in the main unconsciously under the incitement of the foreign. The native for the most part takes care of itself, the foreign must be sedulously cultivated. Humanism believes with Goethe that 'everyone must form himself as a particular being, seeking, however, to attain that general idea of which all mankind are constituents.' " [38]

Fourthly, the Jewish humanists conceive Humanism to be antagonistic to the attitudes and affirmations of Religion. This is not the case. It is true that a few humanists hint that the philosophy of

---

[37] *The Bookman*, March, 1930, p. 5.
[38] Norman Foerster, *Humanism and America*, p. xiv.

Humanism and Religion do not chime together. The great majority, however, feel and increasingly so, that Humanism and Religion not only run parallel to each other, but that they are interdependent and supplement and support one another. Some humanists invoke not only the general principle of Religion, but ally themselves with definite and particular religious traditions and denominations. There are humanists who feel themselves at home even in the Church of Rome. To them the pursuit of private judgment and individualistic whims in religion as in ethics are fraught with evil. The wise institutions and mellowed traditions of a church that has to its credit the experience of ages and the visions of extraordinary saints and seers is more likely to give to the individual the standards and sublimities which the humanist is in search of.

> "For my own part, I range myself unhesitatingly on the side of the supernaturalists. Though I see no evidence that humanism is necessarily ineffective apart from dogmatic and revealed religion, there is, as it seems to me, evidence that it gains immensely in effectiveness when it has as a background religious insight."[39]

> "It is an error to hold that Humanism can take the place of religion. Religion indeed may more readily dispense with humanism than humanism with religion. Humanism gains greatly by having a religious background in the sense I have indicated: whereas religion, for the man who has actually renounced the world, may very conceivably be all in all. On the other hand, the man who sets out to live religiously in the secular order without having recourse to the wisdom of the humanist is likely to fall into vicious confusions—notably into a confusion between the things of God and the things of Caesar. The Catholic Church has therefore been well inspired in rounding out its religious doctrine with the teaching of Aristotle and other masters of the law of measure. It can scarcely fail to recognize that the position of the positive and critical humanist is sound as far as it goes. It follows that the Catholic and the non-Catholic should be able to co-operate on the humanistic level. A like co-operation should be possible between the humanist and the members of other Christian communions, who have not as yet succumbed

---

[39] Irving Babbitt, *Humanism and America*, p. 39.

entirely to humanitarianism. Religion, not merely today, but always, has been subject to extraordinary perversions. It has ever been the chosen domain of self-deception and 'wishful' thinking. When one reflects on the fanaticism, casuistry, obscurantism, and hypocrisy that have defaced the history of Christianity itself, one is tempted at times to acquiesce in the famous exclamation of Lucretius 'Tantum religio potuit suadere malorum.' Yet one must insist that religion is in its purity the very height of man. As to where this pure religion is to be found, we should keep in mind the saying of Joubert that in matters religious it is a bad sign when one differs from the saints." [40]

"Humanism is in the end futile without religion." [41]

"In surrendering dogmatic faith they are at the same time surrendering their humanism. It is from such people that we hear most about 'science and religion': It is such people who pay and lead the flock to pay, that exaggerated devotion to 'science' which the true humanist deplores." [42]

"They (Von Hugel and Babbitt) agree in the conviction that now, for the sake of religion itself, the way of humanism must be clearly discriminated from the way of religion. Mr. Babbitt has urged that religion at its best is far above, and at its worst far below a sound humanism. Baron Von Hugel has urged that Christians should face now, more frankly and fully than they have ever faced before, the fact that the ethical or humane way has a distinct and divinely ordained validity of its own for those who cannot honestly follow the religious way; and that the full health of each way depends upon the health of the other." [43]

"The fresh humility that we need must be built up patiently by religion and by humanism, each working in its own way and carefully respectful of the other, even (perhaps especially) when these two approaches are equally employed by one person." [44]

"The great achievement of modern times is the general realization that life is of necessity experimental, that change

---

[40] Irving Babbitt, *Humanism and America,* pp. 45–46
[41] T. S. Eliot, *Humanism and America,* p. 105.
[42] T. S. Eliot, *Humanism and America,* p. 108.
[43] G. R. Elliott, *Humanism and America,* p. 100.
[44] G. R. Elliott, *Humanism and America,* p. 97.

is a constant law for us and that the human spirit is more important than human customs and institutions, however sacrosanct. Hence our pride of freedom, freedom from the past. And this pride is proper and sound in so far as it is a proud gratitude for the general dissemination of a truth that the great saints and sages, under all dispensations, knew —the experimentality of life. But our pride is rank and noxious when we imagine we know this truth as well as the saints knew it, if not better. To be sure, we know it, more widely in a certain sense than they did, having discovered with the aid of science many exterior illustrations of it which were unknown to them. We know it with a wide and superficial immediacy. But they knew it with a profound immediacy. They knew the basal experimentality of life because they knew it was basifixed. They knew the depth and height of change because they knew the permanency below and above it. They knew the permanency that does the experimenting, the changeless that enables us to know change. Of this we have lost hold." [45]

"This pride means a false emphasis on 'personal religion' over against institutional religion. 'Personal religion' now comprises a vast variety of creeds. Many of these are asserted by their proponents, sometimes angrily asserted, to be not religious at all, but they really are religious in the broadest or lowest extension of the term. A few years ago, newspaper reporters discovered in a western state a not insane man who claimed that the earth was flat. As to the long story of *geodesy*, he said it meant little to him, for he had 'a science of my own.' Nowadays many persons have in the same way a 'religion of my own.' But this phenomenon, unlike the other, is too popular, just at present, to have any comic news value. It would start a public laugh only in the thirteenth, or who knows, the thirtieth century. Today many persons who religiously swallow the authority of science, who religiously believe that Einsteinism is true and wish they could understand what it means, reject all authority on religion." [46]

It is interesting to note that these misnamed Jewish humanists of the clerical variety maintain an allegiance, despite their radical-

[45] G. R. Elliott, *Humanism and America*, p. 84.
[46] G. R. Elliott, *Humanism and America*, pp. 84-85.

ism, to the more orthodox or conservative brand of Judaism. They deny or are skeptical of the reality of God, but yet they put on "tefilin" and wear "arba kanfos." They remind me of the Christian atheist who averred that "there is no God, but Jesus was His son."

The phenomenon is as tragic as it is ludicrous. It discloses to us the lack of independence and the utter spiritual impoverishment of the Jew of today. He is critical of the beliefs of his seers and sages, but he gullibly assents to the dogmas and orthodoxies of the rash scientist. He boasts of being courageous and independent, but yet he apes in a monkey-like fashion every move of the Gentile. Christian Science bobs up and immediately a Jewish Science movement comes into existence. A Potter raises his voice against the transcendentalism and other-worldliness of Christianity, and erroneously labels it as Humanism, and lo and behold, we find rabbis dancing to the same tune and mumbling the same words and phrases.

Beholding such antics, I at times feel that the reproach of Carlyle was not unmerited. "The Jews," he wrote in one of his anti-Semitic fits, "are always dealing in old clothes, spiritual or material."

Judaism has had a long and checkered career. Its course was never smooth and easy. The oppositions and the obstacles which it encountered were innumerable. Assimilation and imitation, however, never yielded it safety and salvation. If its history has to teach us anything, it is not to commit the two evils which Jeremiah described, when he said:

> "They have forsaken Me, the fountain of living waters, and hewed out for themselves cisterns, broken cisterns, that can hold no water."

III

The ways that lead to a knowledge of God are many. The one that was pursued by traditional theologians and philosophers was the one of deduction. These men felt that they could prove the existence and reality of God by the process of ratiocination. Man and nature were to them premises which inescapably led to the conclusion that God is. Once His existence was established, they, with the further aid of reason and tradition, deduced all the dogmas and doctrines which were to them indispensable to a religious outlook and life. I shall not burden you with the classical proofs of the existence of God (cosmological, ontological, teleological, etc.). You know as well as I do that these proofs have been shown by Kant and later thinkers to be not invulnerable. Personally, I believe that with the exception of the cosmological proof, much can be still said for their validity. I am, however, strongly disinclined to place much reliance upon the syllogistic method of establishing a faith in God. In the first place, a God who is arrived at through such deduction is a God who does not warm our souls and raise our spirits. He is a pure abstraction, cold and aloof and transcendental. If that god is a living God, it is not because of the subtle dialectics used, but because there is in back of the believer a desire or instinctive urge for God, or what William James called "the will to believe." A man who by nature is inclined in the opposite direction could muster up as much of wishful thinking to show that atheistic philosophy is most logical. We need not resort to the deductive method of teaching God in our religious schools. God to youngsters is a fact, if He is anything at all. It may, however, be advisable to acquaint high-school pupils with the traditional proofs and especially with those which modern thinkers still believe to be valid. (See the writings of J. E. Turner, *Personality and Reality,* and Pupin, *The New Reformation.*)

The second method is that of the more critical and pragmatic philosophers and also religious scientists. To them God is an assumption, an hypothesis, rather than a conclusion. This hypothesis they accept because it works in an intellectual and ethical sense. It helps some to understand and explain the meaning of nature and man. They also feel it is indispensable in raising and placing human action upon a high moral plane. Since the contrary or atheistic hypothesis does not possess merits over or even equal the postulate of theism, they feel that the assumption that God is, ought to be accepted. It verifies itself, say they. We ought to avoid the use of this method more than that of deduction in our religious schools. The strictly pragmatic argument has too much of an element of doubt in it, which may be useful in the period of late adolescence, but not to the tender minds and souls of children. Doubts must not be awakened until they arise of their own accord. Secondly, it is too much complicated by appraisals of expediency and relative values.

The third method of arriving at the consciousness of God is that of intuition. By intuition I mean that mystic feeling which is more potent that even the perceptions of the eye and the conceptions of the mind. Professor Montague has recently published a book entitled *The Ways of Knowing,* wherein he shows that the intuitive approach is legitimate and is not to be disparaged. You will recall that I quoted in my paper Havelock Ellis, who told us that not only do the fine arts spring from such intuitions, but the very sciences have been born therefrom. Science grows out of the intuition that the world and truth are objectively real and that our sense impressions and cogitations reveal more than our mere physiological states and changes. Science and religion both, Mr. Ellis contends, come from that consciousness of man that he, through his thoughts and actions can not only know but even control nature. They differ only in method, but not in meaning and motive. Morals and ethics are possible because of man's mystic faith that the universe is responsive to our highest hopes and strivings.

> "Truly, all we know of good and duty proceeds from nature; but none the less so all we know of evil. Visible nature is all plasticity and indifference—a moral multiverse, as one might call it, and not a moral universe. To such a harlot, we owe no allegiance; with her as a whole we can establish no moral communion; and we are free in our dealings with her several parts to obey or destroy, and to follow no law but that of prudence in coming to terms with such of her particular features as will help us to our private ends. If there be a divine Spirit of the universe, nature, such as we know her, cannot possibly be its ultimate word to man. Either there is no Spirit revealed in nature, or else it is inadequately revealed there; and (as all the higher religions have assumed) what we call visible nature, or this world, must be but a veil and surface whose full meaning resides in a supplementary unseen or other world." [47]

[47] William James, *Will to Believe,* pp. 43, 44.

This method, I believe, is most fruitful and effective, and it is the one we ought to utilize primarily in our religious schools. Do not waste your time with abstruse proofs of the existence of God in the religious schools. Do not calculate values and advantages with your children when you speak of God. Help them to cultivate that faculty which will make them see with the eyes of their souls what should be to them the fact that God is. That is of primal importance. Avoid giving them any final and fixed picture of the nature of God. Stress to them the Biblical injunction that no man, not even a Moses, can behold the face of God. Tell them the story of the emperor who aspired to see God clearly, and how the rabbi showed him his limitation by pointing out to him that he could not even look at one of His creations—the sun. Tell him about the rabbi who rebuked his colleague who used more than the traditional number of adjectives in his prayers, thinking that thus he fully described God. Explain to him why the Jewish medieval philosopher preferred negative to positive attributes. Remember that the word God is but a symbol, not, as the Jewish humanists contend, of a Being that does not exist, but of a Power and a Soul that is so infinite and so sublime that to attempt to define Him is to limit and to degrade Him. Let the child's imagination has free play. Do not worry about his childlike notions. Remember that the most sophisticated concepts of God, even of the naturalists and humanists (when they have one) are personal and defective. If the teacher will stress the conviction and not the contour of God, the child's faith in God's reality will remain, but his notion of Him and His wants will grow and develop with age, wisdom and insight.

If the metaphysical concept of God which we impart to the child seems vague and incomplete to you, which I maintain is an advantage rather than a disadvantage, in that it fascinates and challenges speculation, the concept of the active nature of God, namely, His Will, should be made more distinct and definite. The child must be taught to see the manifestation of God in the ethical experience and strivings of his own person, his people and humanity. The child must be made to feel that God not only exists, but that He is ascertainable in and through such ideal aspirations. That constituted a burning conviction with the founders and the expounders of Judaism. They saw God in the sublime odyssey of man, and especially Israel, more so than in the phenomenon of nature, which in places and phases seems so repugnant to our higher and finer instincts. This conviction made the prophets link up God with every significant event in the life of Israel.

That God is a concept that becomes manifest in the progressive experience of Israel is voiced in the statement of the rabbi who, in explaining the seemingly superfluous word אֱלֹהֶיךָ "Thy God," in the verse "I am the Lord, Thy God," said: "Its use was necessitated because the Holy One, blessed be He, revealed Himself to Israel at the Red Sea, like a warrior engaged in battle, and at Sinai like a Scribe, teaching Torah, and in the days of Solomon like a blithe young man, and in the days of Daniel, like a venerable old man, full of mercy. Therefore, said the Holy One, blessed be He, —think not because ye see Me in diverse forms and appearances, I am different. I am the same One who was at the Red Sea and at Sinai, in fact every place—I am the Lord, THY God."[48]

If the child is to be made aware of God by intuition and not by logical deductions and pragmatic suppositions, we must realize then that our schools *alone* cannot evoke and establish in the heart of the child the consciousness of God. It is utter folly to believe that intuitive faculty can be made to blossom forth by homeopathic doses of Sunday school instruction, splendid as may be its faculties, textbooks and teaching staff. In the first place, such instruction is brief and not continuous and little related to the everyday life of the child. Secondly, the home plays a much greater rôle in his life. The child has continuous contact with his parents. If the child therefore is to possess the faith and feeling that God is, it must be planted in his soul by the parents, and in the home. All that the school can do is to foster its growth.

Whether in school or at home, the consciousness of God will come if the child will be made to see, first, that spiritual qualities are to

---

48

„אנכי ה׳ אלהיך לפי שנראה להם הק׳ב׳ה בים כגבור עושה מלחמה ובסיני כסופר מלמד תורה, ונראה להם בימי שלמה כבחור וימי דניאל כזקן מלא רחמים. אמר להם הק׳ב׳ה: לא בשביל שאתם רואים אותי דמויות הרבה, אלא אני הוא שבים, אני הוא שבסיני, אני הוא שבכל מקום —— אנכי ה׳ אלהיך (תנה״ק).

be esteemed above material things. If the child sees that the parents and teachers idolize wealth and material power above that of wisdom and virtue, it has very little chance of growing up with the consciousness that spiritual things are real and supremely worth while.

Secondly, the home and the school must make the child perceive that beauty and divinity are everywhere, in the blade of grass, in the sunset, in the coming of a new babe, as well as in acts of kindness and noble impulse, no less than in the things and events which in the past were deemed to be celestial and supernatural.

Thirdly, the child must be trained by example and habit to seek contact and communion with that Being who is the living source and embodiment of our spiritual and ethical ideals. To the theist it is God, and not a metaphysical abstraction or a mere symbol.

In helping the child to obtain such a God concept, we shall give him strength to bear, power to strive, and vision to see things that are ineffably noble and satisfying.

THE ASSAULT ON REASON

by
JACOB KOHN

The Assault on Reason

By JACOB KOHN

THERE are two divergent attitudes toward religious thought today which seem to clear the way for new depth of religious insight and to define with imaginative vividness new areas of religious experience. They are stimulating to the religious imagination because they hint at the promise of liberating theology from scholastic rationalism, from the need of empirical verification and from the cold embrace of objectivity and disinterestedness, which the thinker had previously sought to attain in search of the truth which he cherished above his desires.

They may arouse suspicion, however, because they promise this liberation all too easily by simply denying the relevance of logic, reason and conceptual thought in general to all the deeper phases of religious life. The process of objectification, especially of making man or God the object of contemplation, is sometimes spoken of in bated breath as though it were, in the realm of philosophy, the parallel of original sin.

Positivism and Existentialism

One of these trends to which I refer is logical positivism. This is not so well known as the other which goes usually by the name of existentialism. The positivists are, for the most part, more deeply concerned with their own specialty, logic, than with theology or metaphysics in general. They sometimes confess admiration for the structural beauty of deductive systems but assert that the reference of such systems is not to reality. Statements concerning infinity, eternity, value, divinity, spirituality, are neither true nor false, they say. What the philosophical systems are really doing, is weaving a kind of spell. They belong to the world of fantasy. This is true not because their logic is necessarily fantastic, for their logic may be sound, but it reveals a world of fantasy not a world of reality. Existentialism, on the other hand—and the word is usually spoken by those who profess it with a kind of supressed excitement, as if now at last new vistas are to open up before us — can, I am sure, make a great contribution to religious philosophy, but only if we do not take it to be a philosophy. It will require a searching metaphysics to distill from it whatever stimulus to our religious thinking it has to offer.

Spinoza and Positivism

Important for the understanding of both positivism and existentialism is the part that Spinoza is made to play in the claims and counterclaims of these recent claimants to philosophical dominance. Thus, Ruth Lydia Saw of the University of London writes a penetrating little book on the philosophy of Spinoza but entitles it the *Vindication of Metaphysics,* for Spinoza's *Ethics* may well be recognized, by both friends and foes of its method, as one of the most ambitious attempts in the history of human thought to develop a deductive system. But many contemporary positivists assure their disciples that, apart from being given some verifiable statements belonging properly to psychology and ethics (never to metaphysics), they are being bemused by meaningless words or regaled esthetically by the beautifully embroidered syllogisms of a deductive system in reading Spinoza. What Spinoza meant for statements are pseudo-statements since they employ affirmations containing words such as space, eternity, necessary existence, which cannot

JACOB KOHN is the author of *The Moral Life of Man.* He is dean of the graduate school of the University of Judaism in Los Angeles.

possibly be verified scientifically or be tested by sense perception. Such judgments are neither true nor false. They are alike meaningless as far as their truth values are concerned. Dr. Saw writes:

"The strength of the verification theory of truth lies in the apparent modesty of its demands. It looks as though we are simply being asked to agree to certain observations, but we are also being asked to give intellectual assent to a piece of reasoning. To take Carnap's example of verifying the hypothesis: this key is made of iron.

"Hypothesis, previously verified. Magnets attract iron.

"Hypothesis, previously verified. This is a magnet.

"Deduction. If this key is made of iron, this magnet will attract it.

"Observation. The key is placed near the magnet.

"Observation. The key moves towards the magnet.

"Therefore, the key is made of iron."

Dr. Saw wants to know why, if she is asked to give assent to the above piece of reasoning, she may not give assent to a series of reasoned statements leading to the conclusion that a true statement is one which occurs in a reasoned system of coherent statements. Such a statement cannot be tested by an appeal to sense perception, and, says Dr. Saw, "neither can any statement."

Before examining the last remark, which has all the earmarks of unwarranted dogmatism but which, I think will be found to be perfectly reasonable and sensible, let me state that Dr. Saw believes the *Ethics* to be a meaningful reasoned system. Some of the statements of Spinoza can be judged true or false or partially true, adequate or inadequate, but none can be dismissed offhand as dealing with anything but the most meaningful aspects of life and being.

Let us, in our own way, examine Carnap's verification of his hypothesis. It does not follow at all that, if magnets attract iron, and this key is so attracted and we actually witness its being so attracted, this key, is therefore, made of iron. The first hypothesis would have to read 'magnets attract iron and *only* iron.' There may be metals somewhere in the universe, as yet unknown or undiscovered, that have some of the properties we now ascribe to iron.

No general statement qualifying the whole of physical nature, of life, or being as such, can be verified by observation because the *whole* can never be confined to any area of nature or being for purposes of such observation. Nor can man so live that he can accept two contradictory judgments concerning the world as equally true. You cannot behave as though the universe was all mind and all mindless matter. It can be partly one or the other but not wholly one or the other. The degree in which one or the other prevails will depend upon certain observations and *the logical and conceptual interpretation of these observations.* The foregoing analysis underlies all metaphysical reasoning.

Spinoza and Existentialism

Spinoza meets us again in Buber's fine treatise on *The Eclipse of God.* It may, from my point of view, be doing Buber an injustice to call him an existentialist. His existentialist dogmatism nevertheless flames forth when, speaking of Herman Cohen and tracing his alleged spiritual pilgrimage, to which Rosenzweig already alludes, from love of the idea of God to the love of God. "Whoever professes to love God the Father of man," Buber claims, "has renounced in his innermost heart the God of the philosophers even though he may not confess it to himself. Spinoza began with the proposition stating that God is, that he exists not as a piritual principle which has no being except in the mind that thinks it, but as a self-subsistent reality absolutely independent of our existence. This he expresses in the concept of Substance. But he concluded with a purpose implying that God stands in a living relationship to us and we in a living relationship to Him.

"Spinoza includes these two aspects in the one concept of the intellectual love of God and the adjective 'intellectual' is to be construed in the light of the anti-anthropomorphic tendency of the philosophy. Thus he aimed to give greater stringency to the Biblical prohibition" (against images, I suppose) "without however impairing the reality of the relationship between God and man. *He failed to avoid this impairment* solely because he recognized the supreme aspect of the relation but not its core—the dialogue between God and man—the divine voice speaking in what befalls man and man answering in what he does or forbears to do. However, Spinoza clearly stated his intention."

We need not enter into the validation of Spinoza's philosophy or even the question whether Buber appraises it correctly in every detail. Buber, for example, does not discuss, in reference to the above statement, the concept of "blessedness" through the intellectual love of God. He abides by the existentialist affirmation that the love of God drew Spinoza out of the strangulating web of his metaphysical speculation to meet the reality that is God and, as with Cohen, he ended by renouncing the God of the philosophers, and hence his own philosophical system, in the culminating pages of his great work.

It is difficult to penetrate such confusion. To say that Spinoza's idea of God and his preoccupation with truth, and his laborious attempt to show that the substance which he calls God is worthier of a wise man's love than the God of the scholastics—that all this had nothing to do with and bore no relation to his actual love of God, but that it had to be consciously or unconsciously renounced the moment he asserted that love—seems nothing short of the ridiculous. He knew the intellectual love of God because his intellect was engaged in discovering a rational pathway to God, one which was not to be obstructed by ancient and anthropomorphic myths. For himself, I think, he succeeded. In the thinking of others, he remained a clarifying and stimulating influence. All subsequent builders of philosophical systems confess themselves indebted to him.

A Dangerous Fallacy

We come now to the most dangerous fallacy of existentialist thinking—that the love of God is an encounter with reality but that the passion for truth is an unholy love because it may lead to prolonged speculation. We may have to objectify and conceptualize the God whom we love. Granted for a moment that God is a subject and not an object, it is quite possible and sometimes necessary to think *objectively* of one's neighbor or one's God that one may do justice to either.

The idea of God is, of course, never God but it is quite possible to love both God and the idea of Him. The philosophy of esthetics is never a work of art and theology cannot substitute for God—it can only attempt to show that faith in Him and the serving of Him is a rational occupation for thinking men. Philosophy will then have done its task. It demands one primal postulate and will always demand this—that reason has an advantage in the pursuit of truth over unreason.

The existentialists are both profilic and insistent. It would not profit theology to be deaf to what they have to say, for they offer some useful material, but it would be an end to theology if it gave uncritical assent. We shall, therefore, examine certain affirmations that crop up again and again in the writings of men whose views otherwise and whose religious identification often differ.

First, there is the emphasis upon existence rather than essence, upon the concrete rather than the abstract in dealing with God, upon truth through living rather than thinking, upon the horror of nothingness which man constanty faces. I find, in reading the literature, that assertions such as the above are often spoken with a kind of confidence that the advantages of the former over the latter, in each separate case, in self-evident. I cannot help feeling that this is the mood of existentialist polemics rather than its content.

Thus it is said by one of Kierkegaard's admirers that he takes personal existence as the clue to being, just as idealists take thought with idea, empiricists experience with its sense data, and vitalists life. That all the clues of being find their place in personal existence seems to me self-evident. We reach out with all the tentacles of personal experience to take hold of reality. Thought and reason are among these, feeling and emotion and insight are forms of personal existence. That which we call philosophy is a metaphor for reality as grasped in thought and logic. When we assign to thinking an inferior role in the search for truth or would eliminate it, as though it were not integral to or had no essential place in human personality, we are consigning metaphysics and philosophy in general to the dustpile of useless and abandoned furnishings of which the human mind was once rather proud. Truth is not only mirrored in ideas but it is especially mirrored in ideas thoughtfully and carefully arrived at. There is something very contradictory in a philosophy that begins with contempt for Reason. We may concede that we can only truly experience our own concreteness and grant that universals and essences have no existence in themselves except as they enter into concrete entities or are ascribed to concrete objects as definitions of their being. What is dangerous to thought in this sniffing at abstractions lies in the simple truth that *concreteness itself is an abstraction* and not a thing, even as is abstractness. Is it not strange that, whereas modern art has substituted abstractness for representative concreteness, modern theology should now look askance at abstractions?

Buber's Contribution

If we approach God through living rather than thinking, we find the relation of "Thou and I" to be subject to subject and never subject to object, say the existentialists. The whole universe of matter and of history, and assuredly of revelation, becomes a dialogue, it is claimed, between God and man and man and God. In such dialogue alone, not in a speculative system, can we find God in His glory as the absolute Thou. God confronts man and man confronts God in this existentialist position. In such confrontation, man acquires knowledge of God and only in such confrontation. This I consider to be Buber's great contribution to existentialist philosophy. His writings as well as those of Professor Heschel often contain exquisite, significant and striking analyses of religious experience and attitudes.

One might be quite ready to agree with the proposition that without experiencing this inner relationship, some form of reciprocal communication between man and God, a man's philosophical assent to the *idea* of God has not yet evoked religious acceptance. Even the soundest theology may not be able to arouse in a particular person the impulse to such dialogic relationship because of certain blind spots in the area of the will and the emotions which make him hesitate or falter. What makes such startling religious insight barren for philosophic thinking is, first, the fallacy that nothing can be an experiencing subject entering into relation with another subject without becoming at once an object of experience to that subject. Even Buber is sometimes almost aware of this difficulty. When we say that God is only a subject we are really objectifying God by the concept of His absolute subjectivity and I have a right to ask: "How do you know that this is indeed a divine object whose essence is pure subjection?" The answer might be "I do not have to know, I experience it through actual communication." The failure to recognize that no fact of experience ever validates itself is perhaps the most dangerous threat to logical inference and analogy. A fact is neither true nor false. Only a statement or a proposition emerging out of the experience is true or false.

What is true or false about a scientific experiment is not usually the fact that it took place but the statement that it proves one thing or another. This exaggeration of experimental magic is a crude empiricism which was natural in an age when many believed in miracles but which we have in this more sophisticated age illegitimately transferred to religious philosophy. The judgment evoked in any existentialist experience, religious or scientific, must always be questioned and tested by logical probing and reasonably controlled experimentation that it may yield a consistent statement concerning the value and meaning of the experiment in question. No matter what the happening may be, attraction of iron by the magnet or the creation of a universe, whether a man insists "I saw it happen" as in the case of the experiment or "My ancestors saw it happen," as in the traditional account of revelation, it still remains the duty of speculative philosophy to determine whether the event could have happened as reported.

The reports may be truthful or they may be erroneous. No one will deny that something has happened—a fact was involved, physical or psychological—unless someone wishes to impute deliberate falsification to the experiment or to the ancestor. So, when a man claims that he carried on a dialogue with God, that God confronts him as absolute subject, that He comes forth to meet him in love, philosophers ought to reply, "This is all very fascinating but it cannot be true because I have come to the conclusion that there is no God, since the idea of God is in complete contradiction to my idea of nature upon which you and I both depend and the self-consistency of whose laws once we discover them, we cannot rationally deny." Or, on the other hand, the philosopher may say: "I quite agree with you, for such attitudes are perfectly rational in a world which would utterly lack meaning and lucidity without an idea of God supplementing nature or involved in nature, for these two are contrasting phases of experience not contradictory ones." Again, a theologian may say: "The Thou and I relationship is inadequate if you have come to believe in a God who is the infinite unity of all being, as with Spinoza, and in whom all subjects and all objects are contained and transmuted. God then is every object I seek and every subject seeking Him."

There is a final phrase that shocks us occasionally as we peruse the existentialist literature. It amounts to the *apotheosis of nothingness.* Existentialism is sometimes called by its opponents a philosophy of crisis or of despair. It was undoubtedly influenced and stimulated by the horror and excitement of the war years and the war experience. In France, especially in the entourage of Sartre, many had emerged from the ranks of the French underground, the guerilla fighters, the desperados for freedom's sake, who had been, in the day of Vichy and even shortly after the liberation, not alone champions of liberty but judge, jury and executioner of many Frenchmen suspected of co-existence with the Germans when it became pleasant or profitable. The values by which these liberated intellectuals had previously lived, including the military values, they had now been forced, in the fact if not in theory, to repudiate. There was a void to be filled and they sought a way of life by which they could fill that void. Indeed, filling the void, overcoming the nothingness of being, triumphing in the free exercise of will over his own vacuity, became the only way of life for many.

Again you have the emphasis on conduct, uninhibited by conscience or the search for rational standards. The nothingness of man's being, the nothingness that is characteristic of all being, the fear and horror of nothingness is said to be the root of all human anxiety and, in some way, man's salvation depends on the triumph over this nothingness, of learning to live with it in a kind of ecstatic dance of victory.

It is to the credit of existentialists that they do not minimize the agonies of life or its mysteries. They do not envisage human destiny as an inevitable, biologically assured, progressivism. They allow for the pains and ecstacies of living, for the victories and the frustrations which are man's lot. The Christian existentialists somehow bind all this up with "original sin" with the doctrine of the fall of man, with the need for salvation by the transformation and transvaluation of the inner life through the mysticism and magic of faith, much in the sense in which Paul uses the word. Even one of the Jewish existentialists employs the term "scandal" to recommend the faith in revelation such as Christians use in reference to the incarnation and passion of Christ —as something that you dare not believe and therefore *must.*

Of Mythology and Theology

But here again we are presented with a mythological construct described in theological terminology. We speak of nothingness, as though it were a thing. We meet with phrases "the being of nothingness," "nothingness belongs to being," or "nothingness sleeps at the heart of being." Nothingness, I should have thought, is just nothing. According to Heidegger, on the other hand, man is obsessed with a total anxiety which is the fear of death and springs from man's consciousness that he is headed for nothingness. Now, the fear of death in most cases, is either the disinclination to relinquish life, or the fear of dying—old age, helplessness and possibly pain. The fear of death itself was brought on by the ancient myths which made death a state of being after life, and filled that state of being with Stygian darkness, or fire and brimstone, or at least a final judgment in which ultimate fate was to be decided. Modern philosophy, on the whole, has tended to assuage human anxiety by dissolving these myths, by pointing out that death was not a state of being after life but simply the limit to finite existence. Life contains many sorrows including the loss of loved ones, but man has to resign himself to suffering he cannot avoid, to a span of life which cannot be extended beyond certain limits even as he reaches out his arms to life's joys.

Being is a plenum. It involves all that exists and all that can possibly exist. The moment you take for granted that when you speak of nothing you may possibly be delivering a lecture on nothingness instead of just remaining silent, you are doing more than misusing language—you are creating a mythological monster to unsettle man's reason and conscience, the most fragile of his possessions, since they appeared so late in the evolution of life. As sin was thought to spring from the devil instead of from man's will and the freedom which God had bestowed upon him, so now, all our anxieties are but the fiery breath of the dragon of nothingness instead of the combined inadequacies of ignorance and superstition with which we face life and existence. One of these inadequacies may be the present flight from objective thought and conceptual lucidity, and the contempt for contemplative wisdom.

THE DESIRE FOR IMMORTALITY

by
C[LAUDE] G. MONTEFIORE

THE DESIRE FOR IMMORTALITY.

IN the *Fortnightly Review* for October there appeared a fresh and interesting article, by Mr. F. C. S. Schiller, called, "Do men desire Immortality?" The writer attempts to show that at the present day among cultivated and semi-cultivated persons in Europe and America, there is no real longing for a future life. It is still considered the proper thing to assume that we all desire it and frequently think about it, but Mr. Schiller believes that it is not difficult to show that this assumption has little or no basis in reality.

Men live their lives without reference to death or to the life which death may bring: when "the ordinary man for the first time truly realizes that *his* days are numbered," it is usually a "tremendous shock." The future life and its conditions are seldom written or talked about; it is bad form to dwell on death in conversation, except in a most casual and distant way; the Society for Psychical Research has a very limited number of subscribers; "Spiritism," which, unlike all other religions, "treats the future life as a hard (and somewhat crude) fact, and not as a mere dogma of faith," has not become a success. "Christian Science" may be foolish, fraudulent, or false, but its vogue shows that it answers to a want. The failure of "Spiritism" shows that it does not.

To what is this supposed lack of interest in the chance or prospect of a future life really due? Mr. Schiller is not wholly clear about this part of his subject. First of all, so far as I understand him, men actually believe less. A future life is not exactly denied, but it is a mere vision which floats before the eye of faith at certain seasons of unhappiness or pain, and is then comfortably forgotten. "Men no longer dream themselves in Heaven nor dread themselves in Hell." But, secondly, men on the whole like this life on earth so well that they do not *want* even to think of another. They wish to postpone death as long as possible, and meanwhile to ignore it. This feeling, Mr. Schiller holds, grows stronger with age, and he even goes so far as to say that "the only sort of future life which would have any attraction for the old would be one in which they could go on very much as on earth"[1]. Thirdly, we are told that men do not want to know the truth about a future life because, while it would not make them die the sooner, it would be *inconvenient*. People would have to "act on their knowledge, and that might upset the habits of a lifetime." It is not clear what is meant by this. Are we to suppose that if I *knew* that my personal consciousness would continue or be revived after death, I should live a nobler life? Or is Mr. Schiller referring to future punishments and rewards? He does not say. Fourthly,

[1] Jowett says: "The wicked man, when old, is not, as Plato supposes, more agitated by the terrors of another world when he is nearer to them, nor the good in an ecstasy at the joys of which he is soon to be the partaker. Age numbs the sense of both worlds; and the habit of life is strongest in death. Even the dying mother is dreaming of her lost children as they were forty or fifty years before, 'pattering over the boards,' not of reunion with them in another state of being. Most persons, when the last hour comes, are resigned to the order of nature and the will of God. . . . Nature, like a kind mother or nurse, lays us to sleep without frightening us; physicians, who are the witnesses of such scenes, say that, under ordinary circumstances, there is no fear of the future. Often, as Plato tells us, death is accompanied 'with pleasure.' When the end is still uncertain, the cry of many a one has been, 'Pray that I may be taken.' The last thoughts even of the best men depend chiefly on the accidents of their bodily state. Pain soon overpowers the desire of life; old age, like the child, is laid to sleep almost in a moment. The long experience of life will often destroy the interest which mankind have in it." (*Dialogues of Plato*, vol. II, pp. 176, 181, 3rd ed.) The feelings of old people towards the future life are surely more subtle and various than Mr. Schiller would seem to allow.

there still half-unconsciously lurks over the whole subject a certain discomfort or uneasiness. It is uncanny. In regard to it, it is especially true that "Society entertains a fierce fear of knowledge, a savage suspicion that to eat of the fruits of the tree of knowledge is a sin deserving of death." Hence the subject is guarded and kept away by a vigorous social taboo. Hence too, as Mr. Schiller supposes, the real reasons, which man is partly ashamed and partly afraid to confess (and partly, too, he successfully deceives himself) have engendered a number of mock reasons and pretences. To inquire into these things is said to be a "morbid craving." It may lead to insanity. It encourages fraud. It is unscientific, because you are dealing with a subject which lies outside the boundaries of legitimate science. It is irreligious, because religion says that you are to take the future life upon trust, as a dogma of faith or an assurance of revelation. It is irrational because you are asking the answer to a question which on earth can never be known.

In its issue of September 7 the *Spectator* makes, to my mind, various powerful replies to Mr. Schiller's arguments. I will quote much of what the *Spectator* says in lieu of saying some of the same things less cogently myself:—

Mr. Schiller forgets, we think, that there are questions about which men are silent because they are too deeply interested to discuss them, and that reverence produces in this respect precisely the same result as indifference. Nobody in Germany, or at least none of the educated class, would publicly discuss the character of the Emperor, much less make it the subject of free newspaper discussion, least of all move for a Committee to investigate it by cross-examination or otherwise, yet to every politician it is matter of the deepest interest, of much thought, and of perpetual inquiry. That an enormous number of men try to avoid thinking of the future life is true, and has been true in all ages, but that is because they are afraid of it as too weighty, too absorbing, too fatal to immersion in the business of daily life, not because they think it of second-rate importance. If it is not so, how does it happen that religion, which is only the study of what is to follow after death, and how to make the state which succeeds death pleasant or unpleasant, is of all subjects that which most deeply divides mankind, and on which opinion is considered most important, not only as regards the future but as regards the present? What else but interest in the future state, or things directly connected therewith, divides Catholic and Protestant? We should say, in exact opposition to Mr. Schiller, that an immense majority have the greatest difficulty in turning their thoughts from it, and that anybody who brought them any fresh and clear light about it, or even professed to bring it, would receive the most eager attention. The real reason why men do not investigate the question of what follows after death, as they investigate secular problems, is that they are convinced that investigation can have no result, that light can come only from revelation, and that consequently the thing to investigate is the truth or falsehood of whatever professes to contain that revelation. Surely there is interest enough in that; why all society, all the systems of life prevalent throughout the world, are based on that, and the conclusions deduced from that. That men do not inquire carefully enough into the phenomena of spiritualism may be true—the present writer thinks it is true—but the reason is hopelessness of obtaining light by that method, not indifference to light if obtainable. Let men but see a reasonable hope, and till the hope was dispelled nothing else would attract their attention at all. Politics, business, pleasure, all would be forgotten in the presence of so absorbing an interest. The thing has happened in history several times, and whenever it has occurred the moving force governing the peoples and constantly producing religious wars has been interest in the "Whither."

Some things in this long quotation might be contested, and others might be differently expressed, but I venture to think that in the first sentence there is a great deal of truth. "There are questions about which men are silent because they are too deeply interested to discuss them." And there is even more than this involved. The late Master of Balliol truly observed: "At the approach of death there is not much said: good men are too honest to go out of the world professing more than they know. There is perhaps no important subject about which, at any time, even religious people speak so little to one another." Why do they, however, Mr. Schiller would say, not *want* to know? Mr. Schiller seems rather disposed to laugh at the way in which the religions, responsive to man's fears and apprehensions, have expressly disavowed the obligation of raising the dogma of faith to positive knowledge. But it may be questioned whether the disavowal does not correspond to a higher feeling than fear or inconvenience. Do we not regard immortality much in the same way as we regard God? God is not a fact among other facts. He is not an object of knowledge. He is the condition of knowledge. We believe in him; we do not "know" him, as we know that wool comes from the sheep's back. To search for God or to prove him by ordinary scientific processes seems absurd and vulgar. And with the future life the same feeling holds good. If I *knew* that there was a future life, it would not be inconvenient to me. The *kind* of life I lead at present on earth would not be changed: I doubt whether scientific knowledge would influence my life otherwise than my present mental condition, which may be said to oscillate between hope and faith, affects it, but if it did, it could only affect me (I suppose) in making me live better or yield less often to temptation. And in that case knowledge would be not inconvenient but useful and welcome. But how can one have a *knowledge* of the future life that is not vulgarizing? For whatever that life may be, it seems obvious that it is not lived under conditions of sense. Whatever knowledge could be obtained about it here, must be dragged down and accommodated to sensuous limitations. I do not by any means deny that there have been real communications from the spirit world, but if these communications were real they have (so far as I am aware) also been cheap and unsatisfying. And how can this be otherwise so long as our earthly conditions continue? Mr. Schiller seems to think that if you do not care to *try* to communicate with the beloved dead, this must be due either to the fact that you do not really and intensely believe that they are still alive and conscious, or that your love has grown cold. The cynical story which he tells with some satisfaction on p. 436 seems to show that this is his meaning. Forcing myself to be truthful, so far as I can, I still disagree with him. I know of a lady who in a state of trance speaks words and gives messages which no theory of chance or fraud can apparently explain. Why was I disinclined to be taken to see her? So far as I can read my own mind, it was not because I disbelieved in her trances and thought them rubbish and fraudulent (though I did not intensely believe in them), not because I thought such communications with the dead sinful or harmful, not because my interest in and love for certain dead persons had waxed cold, and finally not because I did not believe that they were still "conscious" and alive, but because the whole thing seemed to me so vulgar and demeaning. What could I hear that would be *really* spiritual? The conditions made that impossible. I could not bear the idea that a third person, even in a trance (and I fully believed that the medium was unconscious of what she said) should be the bearer of unsatisfying communications between the beloved and me. The noble words of Mr. Browning seemed applicable in quite another sense than that in which he wrote them:—

Is the remainder of the way so long,
Thou need'st the little solace, thou the strong?
Watch out thy watch, let weak ones doze and dream.

I preferred to wait for the time, when, if God see well, spirit may draw nigh to spirit without intermediary or interruption. If death mean the destruction of consciousness, then indeed the results of those trances must be, one would suppose, either accidental or fraudulent. If death be not the destruction of consciousness, I can afford to wait. Just in proportion as the belief in a future life is closely connected with the belief in God, does our faith in it share the qualities of our faith in him. To *know* would deprive faith of its rapture and its glory—there is a glory of knowledge and there is a glory of faith,—and as with our belief in God, so with our belief in immortality.

That educated persons desire a future life seems to me more certain than to Mr. Schiller. Here again I will first quote the *Spectator* :—

At present, when new creeds are manufactured every year, they all profess to affirm a future; and true agnosticism, though it spreads among the educated, takes little hold upon the body of any people. The hope of a better world may be vague, but it *is* always a hope, and a hope implies a wish. The hope, indeed, seems to increase rather than decrease as belief in dogma dies away, the truth being, we fancy, that as the supreme dogma, the existence of a personal God, becomes more lonely, the confidence in God as necessarily good increases, and produces the belief, so startlingly strong among the masses, that he will grant compensation for the injustices of this world. There must be a wish to live again behind that faith. The writer would be inclined to say, as the result of his personal observation, that the doubt of a future state is strongest among the happy, the unhappy clinging to it as their only consolation. As those who are unhappy, at least at intervals, are infinitely the more numerous, Mr. Schiller's question on his theory answers itself. Moreover, human instincts, bad or good, are facts to be always taken account of, and it is difficult to imagine that the universally diffused fear of death can exist without, what is really an extension of it, the fear of extinction. The answer that men do not dread sleep, but rather seek it as a refuge, is no answer at all, for we all instinctively think of sleep as a condition sure to have an awakening. It is often assumed that suicides must expect death to be the end, but the evidence is directly to the contrary, for suicides die every day hoping or praying that God will forgive them, though, if death is extinction, prayer and hope are alike absurd formulas. We cannot but think that the great majority of men expect a future state, and would gladly, if they knew how, pierce the veil which God for some purpose we none of us perceive has dropped between our minds and any knowledge of our *kind* of future condition.

The last sentence of this quotation seems to me to need modification in accordance with what has previously been said. I am also not quite sure as to what the *Spectator* says about the fear of death. Mr. Schiller has, I think, left that fear too much out of account in speaking of the common disinclination to talk and think about death except in an external sort of way. What is feared is not so much extinction as the *process* of death. Will it hurt? What does it feel like? Even if we fully believe that there will be a continuance or revival of consciousness, still to get to this new life we must pass through the gates of death. And it is this passing through of which every now and then we feel a dread. We sometimes shrink from the thought of death not because we care so intensely for our present life, not because we fear non-existence, and certainly not because we are afraid of "punishment" (that feeling might perhaps even wisely be less dormant than it is!), but because we are frightened of the actual process or moments of dying.

In order "to test and bring out the feelings with which the prospect of a future life is actually regarded at the present day," the American branch of the Society for Psychical Research has issued "a circular or *questionnaire*," dealing with the subject in some detail. The answers to the circular are, for England, to be sent to Mr. Schiller at Corpus Christi College, Oxford, and "all names will be regarded as strictly confidential." In the remainder of this paper I shall attempt to answer the *questionnaire*, and the appearance of my article in this REVIEW means that I can answer it with sincerity. It is quite true that I may sometimes be self-deceived. The *Spectator* says: "People are not truthful enough to themselves to make such a return of much value." All I can say is, I have done my best.

The text of the circular runs as follows:—

I. Would you prefer (*a*) to live after "death" or (*b*) not?

II. (*a*) If I (*a*), do you desire a future life whatever the conditions may be?

(*b*) If not, what would have to be its character to make the prospect seem tolerable? Would you, e.g., be content with a life more or less like your present life?

(*c*) Can you say what elements in life (if any) are felt by you to call for its perpetuity?

III. Can you state *why* you feel in this way, as regards questions I and II?

IV. Do you NOW feel the question of a future life to be of urgent importance to your mental comfort?

V. Have your feelings on questions I, II, and IV undergone change? If so, when and in what ways?

VI. (*a*) Would you like to *know for certain* about the future life, or (*b*) would you prefer to leave it a *matter of faith*?

To the first question: "Would you prefer to live after death or not?" I reply in the affirmative. To the first part of question II the answer seems to be as clear. If, for instance, I were supernaturally informed that for my unorthodoxy and other defects I was either to be annihilated at death or condemned to perpetual torments, it is obvious that annihilation would be preferable.

Difficulties begin with II (*b*). The character of the future life is, and must always be, wholly unknown to us. Whatever else it may be, it must be utterly (and not merely "more or less") unlike the present life. Therefore I am totally unable to make up a "character" for it which would make its "prospect ... tolerable." One can of course speak in generalities and negatives, and say that for another life to be desired there must be moral and mental development, or an increasing love of God; but, after all, such wide conditions carry one a very little way. Because it seems to me that "the truest conception which we can form of a future life is a state of progress or education," therefore doubtless these conditions suggest themselves to my mind. But one's habitual attitude is rather to leave the matter in the hands of God. We earnestly hope that it may please him to grant unto us the chance of deeper love and fuller knowledge, but beyond this we do not go.

I am not sure that I understand the meaning of II (*c*). I find it difficult to believe in an all-wise and all-good God without clinging also to the doctrine of immortality. The problem of sin, of idiocy, of madness and of misery press otherwise too heavily upon me. A future life seems more necessary for the bad than for the good, not that they may be punished, but that they may have "a better chance."

I am also influenced by the usual arguments about human reason and human love, though in a less degree. I sometimes venture to hope that the intense puzzles about savages, about the Australian aborigines for instance, may find their solution in another life. I believe in "immortality," not because I desire it, but because it seems to be the necessary corollary of my belief in a righteous God. If a divine voice should say: "There is no immortality for you, but God is righteous all the same," I sometimes feel as if I should be satisfied and at rest.

Perhaps it may seem strange that I have said nothing about meeting again those whom we have loved and lost upon earth. But it does not seem to me as if the desire for reunion, however strong or legitimate, is one of the "elements in life" which "call for its perpetuity." Divine righteousness *must*, as it seems to me, grant "another life" to the idiot, or to the woman who by man's intolerable villany has been condemned to a life on earth of agonizing shame, misery and ruin, but I cannot see that this perfect righteousness *must* grant *me* a conscious reunion with the beloved dead, though I earnestly hope that such may be the case.

I find it extremely difficult to answer III. I observe that in the remarks which precede the *questionnaire* it is stated that there "may be a marked divergence between conviction or belief and *sentiment*." It is, however, personal "preferences, *sentiments*, or desires" which are to be elicited by the circular, quite irrespective of religious faith or[1] reasoned convictions, "the influence of which, where it exists, may be recorded in answer to question III." But in my own case faith and sentiment correspond. In other words, my "sentiments" are not suffered to grow beyond my "faith." Hence "why I feel in this way, as regards I and II," so far as I can extract any intelligible

[1] The *Fortnightly Review*, p. 440, has "religious faith of reasoned convictions," but I conclude that "of" is a mere misprint for "or."

and intelligent answers from my mind, has practically been mentioned already. Perhaps I ought to add that I do not desire to live after death because I am unhappy on earth. Nor does it seem to me that such a desire, based on the wish for fuller knowledge, for self-purification, for continued progress, and for reunion with the beloved dead, is inconsistent with a very vividly felt regret for the life on earth. Mr. Schiller has hardly taken this dual feeling into account. If I have to leave a home where I have spent many years of mingled joy and sorrow for another, I may leave it full of hope and interest in the new and unknown future, but yet also with feelings of wistful sadness. If I were stricken to-day with a mortal disease and knew that I had only a year to live, I should feel a regret that does not seem to me inconsistent with a very real faith in a desire for immortality. The question, Would you prefer to die now or in (say) ten years' time? and the question, Would you prefer, whenever you do die, to live again or to become extinct? must surely be kept apart. The life of the butterfly may be higher than the caterpillar's, but the caterpillar's life may contain joys peculiarly its own. And not merely joys, but even tender sorrows, quaintnesses, humours, which cannot possibly recur. One sometimes thinks: Shall we laugh in another life? Surely it is consonant with the goodness and wisdom of God, that he has made us, under normal circumstances, like and be interested in *this* life, even though it be *also* the preparation for another.

Question IV, by implication, has been answered already. If I can imagine that a divine revelation informed me that individual consciousness did continue after death, I should, I suppose, rejoice that my faith was confirmed; but somehow or other the supposition of something which I believe to be impossible (i. e. the authenticated divine revelation) produces no effect upon my mind. I cannot clearly imagine how I should feel if something happened which I do not believe could happen. Again, if the supposed divine revelation informed me that God in his infinite wisdom and goodness did not grant individual consciousness after death, it would not, I think, make any marked difference to my manner of life. It would still seem best, and most in accordance with the divine will, to live worthily to-day, though we are utterly extinguished to-morrow. One would be less ready to die, sorrier to lose what was to be one's only chance of consciousness, of knowledge, of love. But though one's own life, which has been formed under the stimulus of the belief in immortality, might not be greatly changed, I should feel that mankind had received a blow from which it could hardly hope to recover. Jowett said: "The denial of the belief takes the heart out of human life: it lowers men to the level of the material." "Mental comfort" is such an odd phrase; but what I have already said proves that the question of a future life does enter greatly into my working conception of the world. It is so closely connected with my faith in a righteous God that the one seems to follow from the other. And if, *per impossibile*, I make the supposition that I have learned from a divine and certain source that the righteous God is, but that there is no survival after death, then, though my own life might not be changed, yet life's most precious hope and consolation would be gone. My own self would seem unutterably poorer. Therefore I think I may truthfully answer IV in the affirmative.

But here I wish to make a remark which may seem utterly inconsistent with all that has hitherto been said. I hope that I may retain my identity at death, and that I may enjoy a conscious reunion with the beloved dead. But I am not prepared to say that I always and absolutely identify a future life with the survival of individual consciousness and memory. Jowett has said:—

> We must also acknowledge that there are degrees of the belief in immortality, and many forms in which it presents itself to the mind. Some persons will say no more than that they trust in God, and that they leave all to him. It is a great part of true religion

not to pretend to know more than we do. Others when they quit this world are comforted with the hope "that they will see and know their friends in heaven." But it is better to leave them in the hands of God, and to be assured that "no evil shall touch them." There are others again to whom the belief in a divine personality has ceased to have any longer a meaning; yet they are satisfied that the end of all is not here, but that something still remains to us, "and some better thing for the good than for the evil." They are persuaded, in spite of their theological nihilism, that the ideas of justice and truth and holiness and love are realities. They cherish an enthusiastic devotion to the first principles of morality. Through these they see, or seem to see, darkly, and in a figure, that the soul is immortal.—*Dialogues of Plato*, vol. II, p. 180, 3rd ed.

I do not understand how the righteous God can grant us immortality without continuity of individual consciousness, but how can *I* understand the methods of God? For "we acknowledge that these are the things which eye hath not seen nor ear heard, and therefore it hath not entered into the heart of man in any sensible manner to conceive them" (Jowett, ibid., p. 182). But whatever immortality may mean, the belief in it rests (to my mind) on the belief in God. "If there is a good and wise God, then there is a progress of mankind towards perfection; and if there is no progress of men towards perfection, then there is no good and wise God. We cannot suppose that the moral government of God, of which we see the beginnings in the world and in ourselves, will cease when we pass out of life" (Jowett, ibid., p. 180).

I have nothing much to say in answer to V. In my own family we were very wholesomely brought up in regard to these matters. We were told that God was good and forgiving. He might indeed punish us for our sins, but only as a loving father would punish his sons. Such punishments would be temporary and disciplinal. The notion of eternal punishment and of a material hell was openly scouted. Rightly or wrongly, it was called un-Jewish. The future life never had any terrors for us, only attractions. Yet so far as I remember, we did not dwell on it very greatly. As I grew up the usual doubts began, but these doubts seldom or ever extended to the fundamental doctrine of the righteous God and to that which ever seemed its corollary, the doctrine of a future life. Just before or just after I went to Oxford, I read Jowett's essay on the Immortality of the Soul, and it seemed to me then, as it seems to me now, the truest and wisest thing that ever had been, or could be, said upon the subject. Since I read it, my opinions have never changed, and if I have read it once, I have read it fifty times. The exquisite final sections (added in the *third* edition of the Plato) are quoted in full in my *florilegium*, "The Religious Teaching of Jowett" (*J. Q. R.*, vol. XII, pp. 372–374).

I had already dealt with question VI before I attempted the *questionnaire*. How am I to "know for certain" about the future life? I imagine the implied answer is by investigation and inquiry, not by fresh and novel revelation. How investigation and inquiry can "make me know for certain," I do not at present understand. Even beyond accident and fraud, there may still conceivably be explanations of supposed proofs which would deprive them of all validity. The notion of seeking sensuous proofs for spiritual truths seems to me incongruous and unsatisfactory. It has the incurable taint of cheapening and of vulgarity. It is, as I said before, something like "proving" the existence of God. Though in moments of gloom, one might be glad to have such doubts put finally to rest, still one would feel that life had lost a certain peculiar joy. That joy is not uncertainty, but the joy of *believing* in God, the joy of *believing* that the souls of the righteous (yes, and of all mankind) are safe in his hands. Belief may be subject to ups and downs: it is now stronger, now weaker; but it yields an added richness to existence; life, on earth at any rate, would be the poorer if there were nothing but knowledge. Hence if I must answer VI without qualification one way or the other, I vote without hesitation for leaving the "future life a *matter of faith.*"

I have sought to answer the circular as truly and as simply as I can. It would be a matter of great surprise to me if the majority of the replies bear out Mr. Schiller's anticipations. They will rather, I think, tend to show that our belief in the immortality of the soul has become inseparably connected with our belief in God, and that the future life is still desired both for its own sake and as the pledge and guarantee of the Eternal Righteousness.

C. G. MONTEFIORE.

MORALIZATION AND DEMORALIZATION IN JEWISH ETHICS

by
LEON ROTH

MORALIZATION AND DEMORALIZATION IN JEWISH ETHICS

LEON ROTH

To EXPLAIN MY TITLE, I offer two illustrations. The first is well-known, and I adduce it only because its significance is often overlooked.

The Mishnah in Sanhedrin recounts the way in which the old Jewish court tried to bring home to witnesses in a capital case the uniqueness of human life and the consequent responsibility of their position. The court would have them brought in, we read, and would admonish them as follows:

> You are not to speak from guesswork or from gossip or from reliance on a third party however trustworthy in your eyes. You must understand that cases involving the death penalty are not like those which involve only money. In money cases a false witness can atone for the damage he has caused by a money payment. In capital cases there rests on his head the blood of the condemned man and the blood of the descendants [who may have yet to be born to him] to the end of days.

The Mishnah then goes on:

> It is for this that man was created one, to instruct us that whoever destroys one life, it is accounted to him by Scripture as if he had destroyed a whole world, and whoever preserves one life, it is accounted to him by Scripture as if he had preserved a whole world.

As it stands thus, this statement is completely general. The original creation was of one man, and from that one man came the life of all human beings. To preserve one life is thus to preserve a whole world of humanity: to destroy one life is to destroy a whole world. This is obviously the sense meant, and this is obviously the proper text; and so we find it—I am quoting the late Professor J. N. Epstein—in all exact manuscripts and early references. Our printed texts however insert the word *me-Yisrael,* and therefore read *not* "whoever preserves or destroys one *life,*" *but* "whoever preserves or destroys one *Jew.*" The addition of the word *me-Yisrael* produces a sudden, and ludicrous, deflation.

A similar point may be noted in our text of a verse (21) in the last chapter of Isaiah. According to the Septuagint and most modern translations, and with explicit emphasis in the Targum, the verse says that "some of the Gentiles also will

LEON ROTH, a Fellow of the British Academy since 1948, served as professor of philosophy at the Hebrew University in Jerusalem from 1928 till his retirement in 1953. Author (in English) of books on Descartes and other 17th-century thinkers, and (in Hebrew) on ancient and modern philosophy and on the theory of education and politics he recently published *Judaism, A Portrait* (Faber and Faber, London 1960; Viking Press, New York 1961), which has now appeared in a paperback edition (Compass Books, 1962). The above essay was delivered, in a slightly different form, by Dr. Roth last year in London as the Leo Baeck Memorial Lecture for 1961, under the auspices of the London Society for Jewish Study and the Leo Baeck Lodge of the Independent Order of B'nai B'rith.

I take for Priests and for Levites, saith the Lord."[1] This could be expressed, however, by *le-Kohanim,* with a *Sheva* under the *Lamed,* not, as in the Masoretic text, *la-Kohanim,* with a *Patach.* Now this *Patach,* which belongs ot course to the sphere not of text but of exegesis (the independent vowel-system in our text of the Hebrew Bible being, as is well-known, of late date), allows a different translation altogether, *not* "for priests" *but* (as in the American Jewish Publication Society version of 1917) "for *the* priests," that is, for the already existing priests. The persons referred to are not to be priests themselves; they are to be "for," that is, for the use of, the priests already there. Like the Gibeonites of old,[2] they are to do the menial jobs.

I am not decrying this kind of service: "He also serves who only stands and waits." I am only pointing out the nature of the change of meaning which is made possible by the choice of vowel. Instead of what at first sight looks like the widest throwing open, to "all nations and tongues," of the presumed privilege of being priests on the holy mountain, we have, or we seem to have, only the admission of the non-Jew to the offices of hewers of wood and drawers of water. When the repentant Gentile comes to the restored Temple with the assured expectation of being offered, and performing, honorable office, he runs the risk of being told that he has not read the text accurately. The text has a *Patach* and not a *Sheva,* and therefore his place is (as it were) not in the drawing-room but the kitchen.

[1] The significant references to understand the peculiar interpretation offered by the Jewish commentators are *Midrash Shohar Tob* on Psalm 87; *Yalkut* 207 end.

[2] So Joseph Kimchi, as quoted by his son.

II

These instances of "deflation," or even "debasement," in Jewish Ethics will suffice to explain and illustrate my title. They also reveal its insufficiency. For it is obvious that what they teach us is not so much that such instances exist in Jewish Ethics as that we seem to have no Jewish Ethics to tell us how we may recognize them. The insertion of the word *me-Yisrael* in the Mishnah passage, or the reading the verse from Isaiah with a *Patach,* represents a change in moral conception, yet I do not notice it remarked on as such by our commentators; and this suggests the reflection that having noticed it, they think it of no significance. This would seem to be a monstrous situation. The fact that the latest editor of the Mishnah can allow the printed text to remain with the word *me-Yisrael* in, and only in his *second* set of additional Notes and Afterthoughts to remark that its omission would be superior, makes one think that our greatest scholars, so sensitive to the minutest points of history and philology, are singularly *in*sensitive to points of moral concern.

Yet these instances cut very deep. Each pair of readings involves a contrary moral attitude; and it is imperative for us, in the normal workings of our lives, to receive guidance between them. Is the view of Judaism on the subject of the place of the non-Jew in the restored Jerusalem that indicated by the Masorah and the American Jewish version; or can we follow the Septuagint and, most explicitly, the Targum, and read our text with a *Sheva* and not a *Patach?* Is the view of Judaism on the subject of the sacredness of life that indicated by the printed text of our Mishnah,[3] i.e., apparently, that only Jews count; or can we, with the manuscripts and early authorities and Professor Albeck's second Afterthoughts, omit the word *me-Yisrael?* These are important issues, and we need to know which of the contrary views we are to account as Judaism.

III

It is the consideration of this sort of problem which is the province of the science of Ethics; and in the light of the instances I have given it will not be unfair to say that Jewish Ethics, or more properly an Ethics of Judaism, does not exist.[4] I am not saying that Jewish *morality* does not exist, or that Judaism has no *morals.* It is Jewish *Ethics,* or more properly, as I have said, an Ethics of Judaism, which does not exist. Ethics is the *theory of* morals. It is the reflective enquiry into the *nature of* morals. It is the reasoned attempt to see, or (possibly) to introduce, order and principle in moral ideas. An Ethics *of Judaism* would be the theory of the morals of *Judaism,* the attempt to see, or (possibly) to introduce, order and principle in the moral ideas of Judaism. Thus we need two things: the first, a plain statement of the moral ideas of Judaism; the second, the bringing of them together into one intelligible and coherent view. The order of enquiry is important: the statement first, the theory second. So many attempts at an Ethics of Judaism have failed because of the mistaken assumption that Ethics is a deductive science and that (ideally at least) moral ideas can be excogitated from the blue.

I say that the creation of an Ethics of Judaism is an urgent need, but I do not mean that it can be produced by authority. Even the smaller points of morals cannot be determined in this way. It is of no use convening a Rabbinical Synod in order to change that *Patach* into a *Sheva,* or to decide that the next official edition of the Mishnah should print the original and not the falsified text. Moral attitudes cannot be changed by acts of Synods. I am pleading for something else. I am begging our wise men to turn their attention towards the erection of a coherent set of ideas about the values of Judaism; and by a coherent set of ideas I mean a reasoned account, not a series of oracular pronouncements. It is *a reasoned account of the values of Judaism* which constitutes what I have called an Ethics of Judaism. It may necessitate some hard words and severe wrenches. Not everything printed in Hebrew, not even everything printed in some editions of our Prayerbooks, is Judaism; and I recall to the reader's attention the fact that Maimonides, giving his

3 See the note of Edels (the Maharshah, 1555–1631), in the Romm (Vilna) edition of the Talmud, Sanhedrin, Appendix, p. 10a, col. 2, l. 4 ff., mercifully omitted in the excerpts given in the current editions of the *Eyn Yaakov.*

4 I regretfully hold to this opinion in spite of the great and justly honored names of Hermann Cohen and Moritz Lazarus (of which the managing editor of Judaism has reminded me). Both of these were too immersed in Kant, and Kantian modes of thought and expression, to be able to do independent justice to our subject. This does not mean that the study of their writings is unprofitable. Very much to the contrary. They are often richly suggestive, as are, too, the essays of Ahad Ha-am, Klausner, Neumark, Shai Ish Hurwitz, and many another writing in Hebrew; and there is much to be learned from books like the posthumous *Be-Malchut Ha-Yahadut* of the late Rabbi Abraham Chen. But no one of these offers the reasoned account of the values of Judaism which our subject calls for. For the same reason the *Mussar* literature, both medieval and modern, is inadequate. It does not contain a coherent set of ideas knit together by thought-out principles.

reasons, felt compelled to dismiss an early Kabbalistic classic as sheer idolatry, to be not wondered at as a sublime mystery but, simply, destroyed.

IV

We are sometimes told that the interest in theory, the seeking after principles, the desire for order and coherence, is a heresy of the Greeks, and alien to Judaism. I do not find this so. On the contrary, I find traces in the oldest tradition of just that of which we are in search. Indeed, what I am going to suggest is that questions of principle and, in particular, questions concerning the *principles of morals,* that is, questions of *Ethics,* occupied the minds of the creators and upholders of historical Judaism much as they do ours, and in much the same fashion.

I offer a preliminary and simple example:

There is an elementary distinction, basic to all discussions about morals, between the two uses of the word "can." Let me turn to the Greeks. Socrates, after his condemnation at the hands of the court, is told by his friends that he can walk out of prison: arrangements have been made and the jailer will look the other way. Socrates retorts: "I can; but *can* I?" *Physically,* of course he can. He can flex the muscles of his legs and walk out. But "can" he *morally? Ought* he? Is it not perhaps his duty as a citizen to obey the law and to stay? Just as in the one sense, the physical sense, he *can,* so in the other, the *moral* sense, he can *not.*

We find this ambiguity of the word "can" in the Hebrew of the Pentateuch itself. We are told that if we see our neighbor's animal astray in the fields, we *can not* shut our eyes. But *can* we not? Of course we can—in one sense. A famous cartoon in *Punch* once showed a cross-Channel passenger in the middle of a rough passage taking refuge in a freshly carpeted private cabin. A steward comes up to him and says: "But, sir, you can't be sick here." To which he retorts: "O, *can't* I?"—and *is.* Of course we can keep our eyes shut. There is nothing easier—physically. But *morally? Ought* we? Perhaps, after all, morally, we can *not.*

This distinction was noticed specifically in Rabbinic literature. We read in Deuteronomy 12:7: "Thou canst not eat in thy gates." Canst not? Of course we can; we can eat anywhere. But as Rabbi Joshua b. Korchah remarks explicitly: *"Yachol ani aval ain ani rashai"* ("I can, but I am not *allowed"*); and he quotes in support Joshua 15:63, where the children of Judah "could not" drive the Jebusites out. Could not? Of course they could—*physically*; but *morally* they could not because of their oath, and therefore *"yecholim hayyu aval ainom rashaim."*

The distinction is simple but fundamental. It is that between the "is" and the "ought." But the important thing to observe is that the distinction was not only recognized in our literature. It had its special terminology assigned to it—in our instance, the physical *yachol* is distinguished from the moral *rashai*; and this suggests that it was discussed, which means that people had developed a sense not only for moral fact but for ethical theory.

V

We are used to the idea of discussion in matters of Halachah; and we are used to the pronouncements of the Agadists, both among themselves and in controversy with non-Jews, on matters of morals and religion. But these latter are as a rule pronouncements, dicta, supported by verses, not by argument. This is the rule, but there are exceptions; and these exceptions would seem to testify to the existence of regular argument, that is, of rational reflection, on these matters. The theological argumentation with the neighboring idolaters is well-known and is certainly based on a reasoned review of the issues discussed, however meagerly the theoretical basis survives in the short reports preserved in the existing literature. But let us consider the implications of the no less well-known *internal* confrontation of some of the great 1st- and 2nd-century Rabbis.

I take a famous, but to my mind imperfectly understood, instance both for its intrinsic importance and because it illustrates further my plea that our printers and scholars pay insufficient attention to the moral significance of our classical literature.

I start with the conventional text of the well-known passage of the Sifra on Leviticus 19:18:

> Rabbi Akiba said: " ' And thou shalt love thy neighbor as thyself'—this is a great principle in the Law." Ben Azzai said: " 'This is the book of the generations of man'—this is a greater principle than that."

On the face of it we have here a confrontation not of reasoned arguments but of Biblical verses, the verses being arbitrarily chosen and set one against the other. Akiba gives us no reason for his choice of verse; and Ben Azzai gives no reason for his assertion that his verse embodies a greater principle than Akiba's. We are not even told in what sense one principle is "greater" than the other, or for that matter what a "principle" *(k'lal)* is. So far as this report is concerned we may make any guess we like. The accepted explanation of Ben Azzai's statement that his verse embodies a greater principle than Akiba's is that Akiba's verse speaks only of neighbor, Ben Azzai's of man in general; and if we happen ourselves to think that concern with all men is superior to concern with the man next door (though obviously Akiba did not mean that restriction at all), we approve Ben Azzai and accept his valuation.

But this, as I say, is guesswork. For reasoned argument we need *reasons,* a considered statement in the light of a comprehensive principle; and this fortunately is preserved for us, although in a mutilated form, in the Midrash of Ben Azzai's verse *in situ.*

I translate the conventional text:

> Ben Azzai said: " 'This is the book of the generations of man'—this is a great principle in the Law." Rabbi Akiba said: " 'And thou shalt love thy neighbor as thyself'—this is a great principle in the Law. For thou shouldst not say: 'Seeing that I have been treated contemptuously, let my fellow be treated contemptuously with me; seeing that I have been cursed, let my fellow be cursed with me.' " Rabbi Tanhumah said: "If thou actest thus, know who it is thou dost contemn. 'In the likeness of God he made him.' "

THE KEY to the understanding of this passage as a whole is to be found in an acute remark of the brilliant (and concise) 17th-century commentator on the Midrash, the Mathnoth Kehunah, who saw that an "etc." *(ve-gomer)* had dropped out of our conventional text, and in order to understand Ben Azzai's point we have to see the whole of the verse he quotes, and not its first words only. In its entirety it reads: "This is the book of the generations of man (or Adam): when God created man (or Adam), it is in the likeness of God that he made him." If this remark of the Mathnoth Kehunah is accepted (as it clearly must be; incidentally, the addition of such an "etc." to many other difficult passages would help solve many mysteries), all we have to do is to see that the words "for thou shouldst not say" belong to Ben Azzai and not to Akiba. The whole passage then becomes:

> Rabbi Akiba said: " 'And thou shalt love thy neighbor as thyself'—this is a great principle in the Law." Ben Azzai said: "The verse 'This is the book of the generations of man; in the day that God created man, in the likeness of God made he him' is a greater principle. It teaches us that we must not say [as we might if we only loved our neighbor *as* ourselves]: 'Since *I* have been contemned, let *my fellow too* be contemned just as I was; since *I* have been cursed, let *my fellow too* be cursed just as I was.' "
>
> Rabbi Tanhumah [a later teacher] explained: "If you do that, know who it is whom you contemn—you contemn God in whose likeness man was made."

(In order to anticipate any objection that this a "subjective" and doubtful reconstruction of my own, I point out in passing that I am quoting the *ipsissima verba* of the Rabad, not however the philosopher of that appellation but the 12th-century French Talmudist, anti-Maimunist and Kabbalist, in his commentary on the Sifra, a commentary first published by I. H. Weiss in 1862, that is, a couple of centuries or so *after* the death of the Mathnoth Kehunah. See too Theodor's note in his edition of the Bereshith Rabbah.[5])

THESE TEXTUAL CONSIDERATIONS are trying, but they are important, for they demonstrate again the insensitivity of our scholars to questions of morals: two recent so-called "critical" editions of the Midrash Rabbah on Genesis reprint without comment the conventional text! But apart from this regrettable fact, one should note the genuine importance of our results. We have uncovered in our classical literature a regular argument on a point of morals conducted on rational lines. Ben Azzai does not just produce a verse and make an *ex cathedra* statement about it. He gives a sound reason for his assertion that his principle is greater than Akiba's. If Akiba's principle is to be the determining principle in morals, moral action (Ben Azzai argues) would disappear. It would result in passive acquiescence in the face of wrong. A person who had himself suffered would shrug his shoulders at the suffering of others. He would say, and on Akiba's principles say rightly: "What then? *I* have been treated badly. Why should not others be treated badly too?" It is to this that Ben Azzai objects. He says: "Each and every man *in himself* has his dignity. He bears within him the likeness of God. And *therefore*, even though we may have been treated badly ourselves, we should strive that others should be treated properly."

Ben Azzai is thus more than an empty universalist. He is not only extending the boundaries of moral concern from neighbor to man. He is repudiating the view expressed in that most abominable of modern phrases: "It's one of those things," or "It's the same everywhere." For Ben Azzai the moral claim is independent of our personal situation, or the human situation as such, *because* it derives from the *self-transcendent* character of man.

But what of Akiba? I think he accepted Ben Azzai's argument. We know that he was big enough to change his mind on points of Halachah. I suggest that he changed his mind on this point of morals too. Recall the great saying preserved in that book of great sayings, the *Pirkei Aboth:* "Beloved is man in that he was created in the likeness, and even greater love was shown him in making him conscious of the fact that

[5] [Cf. also Hermann Cohen, *Religion der Vernunft*, p. 137 ff.—Ed.]

he was created in the likeness." We have no mention here of fellow-Jew (this comes in his next sentence) or even neighbor, but *man,* and man (in accordance with Ben Azzai's principle) as "created in the likeness." We would seem thus to have unearthed in the literature not only a reasoned argument on morals between our early teachers but that most unusual of all things, an argument in which one of the disputants was convinced by the other and changed his views accordingly.

VI

THE VALUE of such a principle as Ben Azzai's, a principle not just asserted but supported by reasoning and tested in discussion, is that it offers a standard. It gives a criterion by which we can determine the comparative quality of our actions. We now know, for example, that to sit passive in the face of wrong, a wrong which we may indeed have suffered ourselves but which is for all that wrong, is to deny morality. We dare not say: "Oh, it is just one of those things." Things have nothing to do with persons, and each man is a person, created in the likeness. It is respect for the likeness, not love of neighbor which is only an instance of it and possibly in some cases a misleading or at least misguided instance of it, which in Ben Azzai's view (and in Akiba's later view) is the spring and criterion of morality. Actions which proceed from it are therefore moral actions and right; actions which deny it or contradict it, immoral and wrong. I have no doubt at all what Ben Azzai would have thought of that *Patach* in the verse from Isaiah or the insertion of that word *me-Yisrael* in the text from the Mishnah with which I started; but my point is that he would have judged, as he would in my view undoubtedly *have* judged, not from whim or emotion but from a clearly articulated first principle, that is, rationally.

A principle, clearly articulated and firmly grasped, enables us not only to judge. It enables us to correct and improve. It enables us, out of the multifarious material accumulated by time, to select. I have pointed out elsewhere[6] that the great service to Judaism performed by Maimonides was to show us how to master the indiscriminate mass of Aggadah, the great *dis*service of the Kabbalists and their modern followers to attempt to subject us to it again. Basically, the problem is that of the *translation of Aggadah into Halachah;* but whereas much attention has been given by our scholars to the rules of hermeneutics by which new guidance was found in (or extracted from) reluctant, or recalcitrant, texts in the sphere of Halachah, little, if any, has been paid, apart from the work of Heinemann, to the similar activity engaged in the sphere of Aggadah. Yet I think it can be shown that part of the conscious energy of the Talmudic Rabbis was devoted to increasing and developing the higher elements in Jewish morality, and depressing or obliterating the lower.

We have here a most inviting field of research for our sociologists, and I welcome with all my heart and all possible encouragement such studies as Professor Jacob Katz's recent *Exclusiveness and Tolerance* (Oxford University Press, 1961). This book opens up almost unlimited fields of enquiry into these important matters and conceptions, and it is particularly valuable in that it treats of them from the point of view of history and of the Halachah. Since we are

[6] In my book on Maimonides (*The Guide for the Perplexed, Moses Maimonides,* Hutchinson's University Library, London 1948).

dealing now with the problem of an *Ethics* of Judaism, our concern is with Aggadah, in the sense of the preliminary molding of men's minds to accept ideas which produce finally the concrete practical ruling which is Halachah; and it is sufficient for this purpose to note the existence of the process of what may broadly be called *moralization.*

The meaning of this word will appear from definite examples. Its need is only emphasized by the often violent methods adopted in order to effect it. The Rabbis' hands were tied. They were bound to an inviolable text. But they limited, extended, broadened, narrowed, ignored, blandly changed, even in some striking cases perverted, the plain sense, in order to achieve their aim. They knew that philology is a good servant. They knew even better that it is a bad master; and they had grasped the truth that the determining factor in all exegesis is the whole context and not the isolated word or sentence or even paragraph.

By a "whole context" I mean here something wider than Professor Barr's, in his recent admirable *Semantics of Biblical Language* (O. U. P., 1961), or in my own Montefiore Memorial Lecture *(Some Reflections on the Interpretation of Scripture,* 1955) of some years ago. I mean a general framework of interpretation, consciously adopted and consistently carried through. For example, the Prayerbook speaks of God as having given the Jewish people, "in the light of His countenance," *Torath hayyim ve-ahavath hessed u-tzedakah u-berachah ve-rahamim ve-hayyim ve-shalom,* i.e., a Law of life and a love of kindness, and righteousness and blessing and pity and life and peace. True, the early text of Saadia, which is pretty much that of Maimonides and (with minor variants) of the Spanish and Italian rites in general, reads: *Torah ve-hayyim, ahavah va-hessed,* i.e., Law *and* life, love *and* kindness, etc. But verbal minutiae apart, the collocation of terms, each one of which, and in some cases the pairs of words together, can be documented by countless references both in Holy Writ and in the Rabbinical writings—the collocation of words itself expresses succinctly a complete framework of ideas or what I call a "whole context."

For traditional Jewry the Torah—that is, please remember, *Judaism*—was essentially and primarily a doctrine of life and love and kindness and fair-dealing and pity. It is no use anybody saying anything to the contrary, be he anthropologist or theologian or moral philosopher or mythologist. *For Jewry* the Law, the Torah, is a law of life and kindness and love and decency and pity. This being the guiding principle, whatever appears contrary to it must be explained away.

And it *was* explained away. For example, in the case of a whole city going idolatrous we read (Deuteronomy 13): "And ye shall gather all its spoil into the midst of its open square, and burn the city and all its spoil with fire." Its open square? Here is an opportunity for modifying the judgment, and we are told: "If it has not got a square, you do not do this." True, the contrary opinion is also expressed that if the city has no square, you should make one and carry the sentence out; but the point is that openings for moralization were sought for. The guiding principle was encouraged to squeeze out the narrower views.

THIS PARTICULAR CASE would be an instance of conscious limitation, and we have the natural consequence in the dictum: "The case of a condemned city never occurred nor ever will occur." In the same way the problem of the savage treatment of the "seven nations" is met by the observation that they have long disappeared and therefore the regulations affecting them are of antiquarian interest only; though even so we are told, on the legal principle that there is no punishment without previous warning, both that, unless proper warning had been issued, the sentence did not hold and that, if the inhabitants changed their ways, no sentence was imposed at all.

The audacity, both philological and historical, by which the process of moralization was effected shows vividly the intense feeling with which a way out was sought. I love that Mishnah which relates how an Ammonite, against the express prohibition of the Pentateuch and the explicit opposition of the official Patriarchate, was admitted into the congregation. The ground was that there were no longer any Ammonites (or indeed any other "pure" races) in existence because Nebuchadnezzar, with his policy of transferring populations, mixed us all up! But in the same way as the early authorities could on occasion get around the obvious sense of the Pentateuch,[7] so later authorities could on occasion change the clear ruling of the Mishnah. Maimonides, for example, against the explicit ruling of the Mishnah, directed a convert to Judaism to use the full text of the Prayerbook blessings and say "the God of our fathers," and "Who brought us out of the land of Egypt," etc.; and his ruling is so important in its general attitude, and so helpful for our needs of today, that it is worth recalling and pondering. I draw particular attention to its calm conviction and its serene good sense:

> Thou hast asked about the blessings and the prayers, and whether thou shouldst say "Our God and the God of our fathers" and "Who sanctified us with his commandments" and so on.
>
> Thou shouldst use them all and change nothing but shouldst pray as any born Jew, whether thou prayest in private or whether thou leadest the congregation in prayer.
>
> The root of the matter is that Abraham our father taught the whole people and made them acquainted with the religion of truth and the uniqueness of God, and spurned idolatry and destroyed its worship and brought many under the wings of the Divine Presence. . . . Therefore any stranger who joins us till the end of time, and everyone who recognizes the unity of God as taught in Scripture, is a disciple of Abraham our father; and they are all of them members of his household, and he it is who brought them to the right path.
>
> And therefore thou art to say "Our God and the God of our fathers," because Abraham is thy father; . . . there is no difference between us and thee in any thing. Thou mayest certainly say in thy prayers "Who has chosen us," "Who has given us the Law," and "Who has caused us to inherit" and "Who has separated us," because God hath indeed chosen thee and separated thee from the peoples and given thee the Law; for the Law is given alike to us and to the stranger, as it is written: "One law and one judgment is there for ye and for the stranger who sojourneth with thee."
>
> Know this: Our fathers who went up from Egypt were, in Egypt, idolaters for the most part; they had mixed with the nations and learned of their ways; until God sent Moses our teacher and brought them under the wings of the Divine Presence, us and the strangers together, and gave us all one statute.
>
> Let not then thy descent be light in thine eyes. If our descent is from Abraham, Isaac and Jacob, thy descent is from God himself.

---

[7] It will be remembered that an Ammonite *woman* was in any case "admitted into the congregation" on the ground that the prohibiting text says "Ammonite" in the *masculine*.

VII

Maimonides's ruling on the subject of the proselyte is not an instance of limitation but of broadening. The term "Jew" is widened to include people who would naturally be considered to be excluded; and it has a curious parallel in the United States of today where one can still hear immigrants, and sons of immigrants, sing lustily: "Land where our fathers died." The point is that in the case of Maimonides the position taken is a reasoned one and based on the fundamental, and deeply felt, theological position that Jews are definable as members of the household of Abraham which is the household of God. The proselyte is therefore even nearer to God than the born Jew because he is a member of God's household by original conviction like Abraham himself, not merely by the fact of birth.

I take now a more subtle instance affecting primarily theology, but (as always in Judaism) theology, as we shall see especially later, involves morality.

We pray: "O God the great, the powerful, and the awesome," and according to the Talmud even these epithets would not have been allowed but for the fact that they are recorded as having been used of God by Moses. But what do they *mean?* As the Aggadists themselves asked: "Where now is His greatness; where now His awesome deeds?" On the face of it, "greatness" means presumably "power," *physical* power; but is the greatness of God just that of a super-scientist or super-politician, that of the hundred-times-a-hundred megaton bomb? The Rabbis say flatly, No! Deuteronomy 3:24 reads: "O Lord God, Thou hast begun to show Thy servant Thy greatness and Thy Mighty hand"; and the Sifré (Pinhas §134) says:

> *Thy greatness:* this means Thy goodness, as in the verse (Num. 14:17): "And now I pray Thee let the power of the Lord be great."
>
> *Thy hand:* this means the hand which is stretched out [i.e., in mercy and pardon] to all those who come into the world.
>
> *Thy might:* this refers to the might Thou showest when Thou dost in mercy repress the attribute of justice; as it is written, "Who is a God like unto Thee, forgiving sin and passing over transgression."

The point of interest is the complete moralization of the idea of power. Power has been transmuted from the physical to the moral; and that this is not a casual eccentricity but a purposeful and deliberate change is clear from the note of the same Sifré on the verse of Deuteronomy *in situ* (§27 with Friedmann's note 11, p. 71); "This is the universal meaning of the word 'greatness' when applied to God."

That the greatness of God lies in His goodness and His power to forgive, that is, in the words of the Sifré we have referred to, in His control of justice by pity, is one of the commonplaces of traditional Judaism, and it is thrust home in the Prayerbook by one of the most striking instances of moralization which any purposeful exegesis could offer. In the list of the "thirteen attributes" of God repeatedly appealed to in the liturgy of the New Year and Day of Atonement the last is *ve-nakeh,* "and acquitting," that is, "and acquitting the guilty." But this, of course, is the very opposite of the original text which reads: *ve-nakeh* lo *yenakeh,* that is, "and *not* acquitting the guilty." It would be difficult to find a more blatant, and more instructive, instance of conscious moralization.

From the point of view of the science of Ethics, as distinguished from, and as giving strength and confirmation to, the code of morals, the point of interest is the way in which the supreme principle —let us call it summarily *Torath hayyim ve-ahavath hessed:* Judaism as a doctrine of life and love of kindness—is followed consistently throughout and creates an integral pattern. Moralization in this specific direction, explicit and conscious, was going on all the time in the expansion and development of the tradition. Indeed, I should say myself that the moralization *constituted* the expansion and development of the tradition.

VIII

We can descry, I think, some of the main lines of the emerging pattern: in the warp, the increasing warmth and confidence of the universalism; in the woof, the recession of justice before pity (not, of course, that these are new elements but that they are seen to cohere more with the old and give them support and consistence). But these are delicate matters, and concern the future science of Ethics. On the practical side, within the sphere of living morality, it is sufficient to indicate the deliberate attempt on the part of the Talmudic Rabbis, under the guise of Biblical exegesis, to promote the emergence of a new type of man. The instance I am to give is remarkable because of its very absurdity, absurdity, that is, as exegesis. In intention it is so far from being absurd as to raise vividly the most modern of all issues.

In II Samuel 23 we are given an account of David's "mighty men" and their deeds of valor. Benaiah the son of Jehoiadah, the son of a valiant man of Kabzeel who had done mighty deeds, slew the two "Ariel of Moab," and slew a lion in the midst of a pit in time of snow; on which we have the comment in Babli Berachoth:

> *A valiant man*—this means that he increased and assembled workers for the Law;
>
> *He smote the two Ariel of Moab*—this means that he left no one like him [i.e., for scholarship] whether in the First or the Second Temple;
>
> *He slew a lion*—that is, he learned the Sifra of the school of Rav.

You will agree that the comment is astounding. As exegesis it is nonsense. But for that very reason it merits special attention. After all, the author of the comment, and its recorders and preservers, were presumably as intelligent as we are, and they would not have wasted time and space for a foolish remark if indeed it were just foolish. But it is far from that. In its sphere it gives expression to exactly the same idea (and here is this unity of pattern so interesting and important for Ethics) as the theological statement to which I referred earlier. God's greatness, we were told then, does not lie in the exercise of physical power. His mighty hand is mighty because it exercises the moral virtue of pity. Here we have the parallel for man. Man's greatness, too, does not lie in physical power. Soldiers are not the ideal man. Generals are not the ideal man. Even athletes are not the ideal man. It is the moral qualities which count and which constitute man's power. It is those who "although themselves treated with arrogance, do not treat others with arrogance, who bear humiliation but do not humiliate others, who fulfill God's will in love and put up with adversity" whom "Scripture calls the lovers of God and whom it declares to be like the sun when it goes forth *in its power (gevuratho!)*." (Bab. Sabb. 88b on Judges 5:31)

It is usually said that the Talmudists, or some of them, were so afraid of the civil authorities that they allegorized away all mention of military acts. Indeed, we are often told that the suppression, or apparent suppression, of the military achievements of the Maccabees in our editions of the classical Rabbinic literature—as is well-known, Hanukah is mentioned only sparingly and in connection with the miracle of the oil— was due to fear of the police, whether the Roman or the Parthian or the Arab, or, later, of the censors of Christian Europe. *I wonder*; and in spite of the modern school of Jewish history represented prominently by the late Gedaliah Allon, I even doubt whether it was true of the historical Pharisees themselves. If, as a principle of universal application, *God's* power is to be equated with His goodness, perhaps, in the Rabbinic mind and as a principle of equally universal application, *man's power also* is to be equated with his goodness. Perhaps they thought sincerely, apart altogether from the fear of the policeman and other considerations of the higher diplomacy, that there are virtues superior to the military. They made great use of the doctrine of the Imitation of God and constantly urge us to follow God in His moral attributes: "As He is merciful, be thou merciful." I am not aware of any passage in which we are urged to follow God in His *military* capacity.

If this contention is sound, we seem to have one instance of a society where the soldier was not held up to admiration as the highest type of man; as indeed, in Rabbinic idea, he was not (the supreme type was the student of the "Law of life and the love of kindness").

BUT HERE INDEED the question which I raised earlier becomes insistent: which is the higher type and which is the lower? The studious life of scholarship and learning; the practical life of kindness and pity; the religious pursuit of holiness ever beckoning us on and ever far away; or the life of the soldier with its Roman ideal of *parcere subjectis et debellare superbos* ("sparing those who are at your feet and destroying by war those who are not")? A recent speaker on the British Broadcasting Corporation, a schoolmaster, observed that a principal cause of war in our societies is the idealization of the military life and the submission of the Churches to the military ideal. Perhaps the Rabbis of the Talmud also noticed something of this kind and tried to turn men's minds away, not from the *fact* of war—that, alas, would be impossible—but from the regarding of war, and of the warrior, as an ideal. As they said of the tanner and the perfumer: "Both are required, but better be a perfumer." It may be that soldiers, like tanners, are necessary; but that is no reason for our considering them, *pace* Ruskin, as the highest type of human being. "Forgive Thy people Israel whom Thou hast redeemed," says the Deuteronomist, "and suffer not innocent blood to remain in the midst of Thy people"; and the Sifré comments: "It was for this Thou didst redeem us, that there should not be among us men who spill blood."

But (again!) which *is* the highest type of human being; which, in the scale of virtues, is the high and which the low? And what constitutes their high-ness and low-ness? Wherein does it lie and how do we recognize it? By reason of what can we say that any one kind of activity is *better* than another, "better," that is, not in any utilitarian or pleasurable sense, but *morally?* Aristotle says somewhere that if there is a better, there is a best. I rather fancy that Judaism would say that, since there is a Best, there is a better. But I am beginning to approach my subject and shall therefore, after the fashion of the learned, stop.

THE DOGMAS OF JUDAISM

by

S[olomon] Schechter

THE DOGMAS OF JUDAISM.

THE object of this article is to say about the dogmas of Judaism a word which I think ought not to be left unsaid.

In speaking of dogmas it must be understood that Judaism does not ascribe to them any saving power. The belief in a dogma or a doctrine without abiding by its real or supposed consequences (*e.g.* the belief in *creatio ex nihilo* without keeping the Sabbath) is of no value. And the discussion about certain doctrines is not whether they possess or do not possess the desired charm against certain diseases of the soul, but whether they ought to be considered as characteristics of Judaism or not.

It must again be premised that the subject, which occupied the thoughts of the greatest and noblest Jewish minds for so many centuries, has been neglected for a comparatively long time. And this for various reasons. First, there is Mendelssohn's assertion, or supposed assertion, in his *Jerusalem* that Judaism has no dogmas—an assertion which has been accepted by the majority of modern Jewish theologians as the only dogma Judaism possesses. You can hear it pronounced in scores of Jewish pulpits; you can read it written in scores of Jewish books. To admit the possibility that Mendelssohn was in error was hardly permissible, especially for those with whom he enjoys a certain infallibility. Nay, even the fact that he himself was not consistent in his theory, and on another occasion declared that Judaism *has* dogmas, only that they are purer and more in harmony with reason than those of other religions; or even the more important fact, that he published a school-book for children, in which the so-called Thirteen Articles were embodied, only that instead of the formula "I believe," &c., he substituted "I am convinced,"—even such patent facts did not produce much effect upon many of our modern theologians. They were either overlooked or explained away so as to make them harmonise with the great dogma of dogmalessness. For it is one of the attributes of infallibility that the words of its happy proprietor must always be reconcilable even when they appear to the eye of the unbeliever as gross contradictions.[1]

Another cause of the neglect into which the subject has fallen is that our century is an *historical* one. It is not only books that have their fate, but also whole sciences and literatures. In past times it was religious speculation that formed the favourite study of scholars, in our time it is history with its critical foundation on a sound philology. Now as these two most important branches of Jewish science were so long neglected—were perhaps never cultivated in the true meaning of the word, and as Jewish literature is so vast and Jewish history so far-reaching and eventful, we cannot wonder that these studies have absorbed the time and the labour of the greatest and best Jewish writers in this century. Indeed, we cannot be grateful enough to such scholars as Zunz and Graetz, who have furnished us with the history of the Jewish literature and people. For what use is it to have a literature embracing all branches of human thought without understanding it in the right way, and how shall we recognise Judaism in all its glory and significance for the world so long as its history remains a secret to us?

There is, besides, a certain tendency in historical studies that is hostile to mere theological speculation. The historian deals with realities, the theologian with abstractions. The latter likes to shape the universe after his system, and tells us how things *ought to be*, the former teaches us how they *are* or *have been*, and the explanation he gives for their being so and not otherwise includes in most cases also a kind of justification for their existence. There is also the *odium theologicum*, which has been the cause of so much misfortune in the history of the world that it is hated by the historian, whilst the superficial, rationalistic way in which the theologian manages to explain every thing which does not suit his system is most repulsive to the critical spirit.

But it cannot be denied that this neglect has caused much confusion. Especially is this noticeable in England, which is essentially a theological country, and where people are but little prone to give up speculation about things which concern their most sacred interest and greatest happiness. Thus

---

1 *Jerusalem*, in Mendelssohn's *Sämmtliche Werke* (Vienna, 1838), especially from page 264 onwards, and a letter by him published in the *Monatsschrift*, 1859, p. 173. For Mendelssohn's position, see Graetz, *Geschichte*, xi. 86 *seq.*, especially p. 88 and note 1; Kayserling, *Leben und Wirken* of M., 2nd ed., p. 394; Steinheim, *Moses Mendelssohn* (Hamburg, 1840), p. 30 *seq.*; Holdheim, *Moses Mendelssohn* (Berlin, 1859), p. 18 *seq.*; L. Löwe's pamphlet, *Jüdische Dogmen* (Pest, 1871).

whilst we are exceedingly poor in all other branches of Jewish learning, we are comparatively rich in productions of a theological character. We have a superfluity of essays on such delicate subjects as eternal punishment, immortality of the soul, the day of judgment, &c., and many treatises on the definition of Judaism. But knowing little or nothing of the progress recently made in Jewish theology, of the many protests against all kinds of infallibility, whether canonised in this century or in olden times, we in England still maintain that Judaism has no dogmas as if nothing to the contrary had ever been said. We seek the foundation of Judaism in national economy, in hygiene, in everything except religion. Following the fashion of the day to esteem religion in proportion to its ability to adapt itself to every possible and impossible metaphysical and social system, we are anxious to squeeze out of Judaism the last drop of faith and hope, and strive to make it so flexible that we can turn it in every direction which it is our pleasure to follow. But alas! the flexibility has progressed so far as to classify Judaism among the invertebrate species, the lowest order of living things. It strongly resembles a certain Christian school which addresses itself to the world in general and claims to satisfy everybody alike. It claims to be socialism for the adherents of Karl Marx and Lassalle, worship of men for the followers of Comte and St. Simon; it carefully avoids the word "God" for the comfort of agnostics and sceptics, whilst on the other hand it pretends to hold sway over paradise, hell, and immortality for the edification of believers. In such illusions many of our theologians delight. For illusions they are; you cannot be everything if you want to be anything. Moreover illusions in themselves are bad enough, but we are menaced with what is still worse. Judaism, divested of every higher religious motive, is in danger of falling into gross materialism. For what else is the meaning of such declarations as "Believe what you like, but conform to this or that mode of life," what else does it mean but "We cannot expect you to believe that the things you are bidden to do are commanded by a higher authority; there is not such a thing as belief, but you ought to do them for conventionalism or for your own convenience."

But both these motives—the good opinion of our neighbours, as well as our bodily health—have nothing to do with our nobler and higher sentiments, and degrade Judaism to a matter of expediency or diplomacy. Indeed, things have advanced so far that well-meaning but ill-advised writers even think to render a service to Judaism by declaring it to be a kind of enlightened Hedonism, or rather a moderate Epicureanism.[1]

I have no intention of here answering the question, What is Judaism? This question is not less perplexing than the problem, What is God's world? Judaism is also a great Infinite, composed of as many endless Units, the Jews. And these Unit-Jews have been, and are still, scattered through all the world, and have passed under an immensity of influences, good and bad. If so, how can we give an exact definition of the Infinite, called Judaism?

But if there is anything sure, it is that the highest motives which worked through the history of Judaism are the strong belief in God and the unshaken confidence that at last this God, the God of Israel, will be the God of the whole world[2]; or, in other words, Faith and Hope are the two most prominent characteristics of Judaism.

In the following pages I shall try to give a short account of the manner in which these two principles of Judaism found expression, from earliest times up to the age of Mendelssohn; that is, to present an outline of the history of Jewish Dogmas. First a few observations on the position of the Bible and the Talmud in relation to our theme. Insufficient and poor as they may be in proportion to the importance of these two fundamental documents of Judaism, these remarks may nevertheless suggest a connecting link between

---

[1] This hygienic explanation of the dietary laws is not at all modern. It is refuted already by an author who wrote at about the end of the 13th century. See Jellinek's Appendix to the Dialogue of R. Shem-Tob Palquera (Vienna, 1875). As a modern refutation, we shall only mention here that of Reggio, in his book התורה והפילוסופיאה (Vienna, 1827), p. 156 *seq.* See also Joel's *Beiträge*, I., p. 99, note 2. We cannot here enlarge on this subject, which deserves a special study, but shall only direct attention to two passages in works of the 13th century. The *Zohar*, IV. 221a (ed. Krotoschin), runs as follows:—אנן (הגוים) אכלינן כל מה דבעינן ואנן תקיפין בחילא בבריאותא ····ואתון דלא אכלין חלשין כלכו במרעין בישין ובתבירו יתיר מכל שאר עמין: Compare the commentaries on the Haggadoth by R. Salomon ben Addereth, edited by Dr. Perles, in his biography of that Rabbi (Breslau, 1863), p. 31a, where the following passage occurs:—וחלק הקדושה שאמרת גם המניעה מן המאכלים האסורים נכנסת באותו חלק ועליו אנו נקראים קדושים:

[2] This is the explanation given by the *Sifré* (ed. Friedmann, p. 73a) on the verse "Hear, O Israel," Deut. vi. 4. Compare Rashi's remark on this verse. We venture to suggest that on this passage from the Sifré, is founded the prayer from the תנא דבי אליהו (I. 21), which forms part of the daily Liturgy, and in which occur passages relating to the belief in the final recognition of God by all mankind, and also to the sanctification of His name throughout the world. See Oppenheim in *Beth Talmud*, I., p. 373, on the high antiquity of this prayer.

the teachings of Jewish antiquity and those of Maimonides and his successors.

We begin with the Scriptures.

The Bible itself hardly contains a command bidding us *to believe.* We are hardly ordered, *e.g.*, to believe in the existence of God. I say hardly, but I do not altogether deny the existence of such a command. It is true that we do not find in the Scripture such words as: "You are commanded to believe in the existence of God." Nor is any punishment assigned as awaiting him who denies it. Notwithstanding these facts, many Jewish authorities—among them such important men as Maimonides, R. Jehuda Halevy, Nachmanides—perceive, in the first words of the Ten Commandments, "I am the Lord thy God," the command to believe in His existence.[1]

Be this as it may, there cannot be the shadow of a doubt that the Bible, in which every command is dictated by God, and in which all its heroes are the servants, the friends, or the ambassadors of God, presumes such a belief in every one to whom those laws are dictated, and these heroes address themselves. Nay, I think that the word "belief" is not even adequate. In a world with so many visible facts and invisible causes, as life and death, growth and decay, light and darkness; in a world where the sun rises and sets; where the stars appear regularly; where heavy rains pour down from the sky, often accompanied by such grand phenomena as thunder and lightning; in a world full of such marvels, but into which no notion has entered of all our modern true or false explanations—who but God is behind all these things? "Have the gates," asks God, "have the gates of death been open to thee? or hast thou seen the doors of the shadow of death? . . . Where is the way where light dwelleth? and as for darkness, where is the place thereof? . . . Hath the rain a father? or who hath begotten the drops of dew? . . . Canst thou bind the sweet influences of Pleiades, or loose the bands of Orion? . . . Canst thou send lightnings, that they may go, and say unto thee, Here we are?" (Job xxxviii.) Of all these wonders, God was not merely the *prima causa;* they were the result of his direct action, without any intermediary causes. And it is as absurd to say that the ancient world believed in God, as for a future historian to assert of the nineteenth century that it believed

[1] See commentaries to Maimonides' ספר המצות, I., especially R. Simon Duran in his זוהר הרקיע; cf. also old and modern commentaries to Ex. xx. 2, and the treatises on the division of the Decalogue.

in the effects of electricity. We see them, and so antiquity *saw* God. If there was any danger, it lay not in the denial of the existence of a God, but in having a wrong belief. Belief in as many gods as there are manifestations in nature, investing them with false attributes, misunderstanding God's relation to men, lead to immorality. Thus the greater part of the laws and teachings of the Bible are either directed against polytheism, with all its low ideas of God, or rather of gods; or they are directed towards regulating God's relation to men. Man is a servant of God, or his prophet, or even his friend. But this relationship, man obtains only by his conduct. Nay, all man's actions are carefully regulated by God, and connected with his holiness. The 19th chapter of Leviticus, which is considered by the Rabbis as the portion of the Law in which the most important articles of the Torah are embodied, is headed, "Ye shall be holy, for I the Lord your God am holy." And every law therein occurring, even those which concern our relations to each other, is *not* founded on utilitarian reasons, but is ordained because the opposite of it is an offence to the holiness of God, and profanes his creatures, whom he desired to be as holy as he is.[1]

Thus the whole structure of the Bible is built upon the visible fact of the existence of a God, and upon the belief in the relation of God to men, especially to Israel. In spite of all that has been said to the contrary, the Bible *does* lay stress upon belief, where belief is required. The unbelievers are rebuked again and again. "For all this they sinned still, and believed not for His wondrous work," complains Asaph. (Ps. lxxviii. 32.) And belief is praised in such exalted words as, "Thus saith the Lord, I remember thee, the kindness of thy youth, the love of thine espousals, when thou wentest after me in the wilderness, in a land that was not sown." (Jer. ii. 2.) The Bible, especially the books of the prophets, consists, in great part, of promises for the future, which the Rabbis justly termed the "Consolations."[2] For our purpose, it is of no great consequence to examine what future the prophets had in view, whether an immediate future or one more remote, at the end of days. At any rate, they inculcated hope and confidence that God would bring to pass a better time. I think that even the most advanced Bible-critic — provided he is not guided by some modern Aryan reasons—must perceive in such passages as, "The Lord will reign for ever and ever," "The Lord shall

---

[1] *Sifra* (ed. Weiss), pp. 86b and 93b.

[2] *Baba Bathra*, 14b. Compare Fürst, *Kanon*, p. 15.

rejoice in his works," and many others, a hope for more than the establishment of the "national Deity among his votaries in Palestine."

We have now to pass over an interval of many centuries, the length of which depends upon the views held as to the date of the conclusion of the canon, and examine what the Rabbis, the representatives of the prophets, thought on this subject. Not that the views of the author of the "Wisdom of Solomon," of Philo and Aristobulus, and many others of the Judæo-Alexandrian school would be uninteresting for us. But somehow their influence on Judaism was only a passing one, and their doctrines never became authoritative in the Synagogue. We must here confine ourselves to those who, even by the testimony of their bitterest enemies, occupied the seat of Moses.

The successors of the prophets had to deal with new circumstances, and accordingly their teachings were adapted to the wants of their times. As the result of manifold foreign influences, the visible fact of the existence of God as manifested in the Bible had been somewhat obscured. Prophecy, as the highest degree of direct communion of God with man, ceased, and the Holy Spirit (רוח הקדש) which inspired a few chosen ones took its place. Afterwards this influence was reduced to the hearing of a Voice from Heaven, which was audible to still fewer. On the other hand the Rabbis had this advantage that they were not called upon to fight against idolatry as their predecessors the prophets had been. The evil inclination to worship idols was, as the Talmud expresses it allegorically, killed by the Men of the Great Synagogue, or, as we should put it, it was suppressed by the sufferings of the captivity in Babylon. This change of circumstances is marked by the following fact:—Whilst the prophets mostly considered idolatry as the cause of all sin, the Rabbis show a strong tendency to ascribe sin to a defect in, or a want of, belief on the part of the sinner. They teach that Adam would not have sinned unless he had first denied the "Root of all" (or the main principle), namely, the belief in the Omnipresence of God.[1] Of Cain they say that before murdering his brother he declared: "There is no judgment, there is no judge, there

[1] *Synhedrin*, 38b. The phrase כפר בעיקר occurs for the first time in the *Sifra*, 111b. See also *Pesikta* (ed. Buber), 163b, and *Mechilta* (ed. Friedmann), 22b. In this last case it is doubtful whether we should read כפר or וכפר. In another version of this Baraitha, the whole passage is wanting. Compare Hofmann, *Magazine*, xiii. 192.

is no world to come, and there is no reward for the just, and no punishment for the wicked."[1]

In another place we read that the commission of a sin in secret is an impertinent attempt by the doer to oust God from the world. But if unbelief is considered as the root of all evil, we may expect that the reverse of it, a perfect faith, would be praised in the most exalted terms. So we read: Faith is so great that the man who possesses it may hope to become a worthy vessel of the Holy Spirit, or, as we should express it, that he may hope to obtain by this power the highest degree of communion with his Maker. The Patriarch Abraham, notwithstanding all his other virtues, only became "the possessor of both worlds" by the merit of his strong faith. Nay, even the fulfilment of a single law when accompanied by true faith is, according to the Rabbis, sufficient to bring man nigh to God. And the future redemption is also conditional on the degree of faith which will be shown by Israel.[2]

It has often been asked what the Rabbis would have thought of a man who fulfils every commandment of the Torah, but does not believe that this Torah was given by God, or that there exists a God at all. It is indeed very difficult to answer this question with any degree of certainty. In the time of the Rabbis people were still too simple for such a diplomatic religion, and conformity in the modern sense was quite an unknown thing. But from the foregoing remarks it would seem that the Rabbis could not conceive such a monstrosity as atheistic orthodoxy. For, as we have seen, the Rabbis thought that unbelief must needs end in sin, for faith is the origin of all good. Accordingly, in the case just supposed, they would have either suspected the man's orthodoxy, or would have denied that his views were really what he professed them to be.

Still more important than the above cited Aggadic passages is one which we are about to quote from the Tractate Synhedrin. This tractate deals with the constitution of the supreme law-court, the examination of the witnesses, the functions of the judges, and the different punishment to be inflicted on the transgressors of the law. After having enumerated various kinds of capital punishment, the Mishnah adds the following words: "These are (the men) who are excluded from the life to come: He who says there is no

---

[1] *Targum Jerushalmi*, Gen. iv. 8.

[2] *Mechilta*, 33b. Innumerable passages of a similar character occur in the Rabbinic literature.

resurrection from death; he who says there is no Torah given from heaven, and the Epikoros."[1] This Mishnah was considered by the Rabbis of the Middle Ages, as well as by modern scholars, the *locus classicus* for the dogma question. There are many passages in the Rabbinic literature which exclude man from the world to come for this or that sin. But these are more or less of a poetic legendary (Aggadic) character, and thus lend themselves to exaggeration and hyperbolic language. They cannot, therefore, be considered as serious legal dicta, or as the general opinion of the Rabbis.[2]

The Mishnah in Synhedrin, however, has, if only by its position in a legal tractate, a certain Halachic character. And the fact that so early an authority as R. Akiba made additions to it guarantees its high antiquity. The first two sentences of this Mishnah are clear enough. In modern language, and, positively speaking, they would represent articles of belief in Resurrection and Revelation. Great difficulty is found in defining what was meant by the word *Epikoros*. The authorities of the middle ages, to whom we shall again have to refer, explain the Epikoros to be a man who denies the belief in reward and punishment; others identify him with one who denies the belief in Providence; while others again think the Epikoros one who denies Tradition. But the parallel passages in which it occurs incline one rather to think that this word cannot be defined by one kind of heresy. It implies rather a frivolous treatment of the words of Scripture or of Tradition. In the case of the latter (Tradition) it is certainly not honest difference of opinion that is condemned; for the Rabbis themselves differed very often from each other, and even mediæval authorities did not feel any compunction against explaining Scripture in variance with the Midrash, and sometimes they even went so far as to declare that the view of this or that great authority was only to be considered as an isolated opinion not deserving particular attention. What they did blame was, as already said, scoffing and impiety. We may thus

---

[1] The words מן התורה are undoubtedly a later interpolation, though it is not impossible that Rashi had them in his text of the Mishnah. See Rabbinowitz, *Variae Lectiones*, IX., p. 247, note 1. The Cambridge MS., published by Mr. Lowe, also omits these two words. See also Weiss, *Beth Talmud*, II., p. 287.

[2] A collection of such passages may be found in Schlesinger's notes to his German translation of the *Ikkarim* (Frankfurt, 1844), p. 677 *seq.*; but his list is incomplete, and might be largely extended by quotations from the *Sifré*, etc.

safely assert that reverence for the teachers of Israel formed the third essential principle of Judaism.[1]

I have still to remark that there occur in the Talmud such passages as "the Jew, even if he has sinned, is still a Jew," or "He who denies idolatry is called a Jew." These and similar passages have been used to prove that Judaism was not a positive religion, but only involved the negation of idolatry. But it has been overlooked that the statements quoted have more a legal than a theological character. The Jew belonged to his nationality even after having committed the greatest sin, just as the Englishman does not cease to be an Englishman—in regard to treason and the like—by having committed a heinous crime. But he has certainly acted in a very un-English way, and having outraged the feelings of the whole nation will have to suffer for his misconduct. The Rabbis also did not maintain that he who gave up the belief in Revelation and Resurrection, and treated irreverently the teachers of Israel, severed his connection with the Jewish nation, but that, for his crime, he was going to suffer the heaviest punishment. He was to be excluded from the world to come.

Still, important as is the passage quoted from Synhedrin, it would be erroneous to think that it exhausted the creed of the Rabbis. The liturgy and innumerable passages in the Midrashim show that they ardently clung to the belief in the advent of the Messiah. All their hope was turned to the future redemption and the final establishment of the Kingdom of Heaven on earth. Judaism, stripped of this belief, would have been for them devoid of meaning. The belief in reward and punishment is also repeated again and again in the old Rabbinic literature. A more emphatic declaration of the belief in Providence than is conveyed by the following passages is hardly conceivable. "Everything is foreseen, and free will is given. And the world is judged by grace."[2] Or "the born are to die, and the dead to revive, and the living to be judged. For to know and to notify, and that it may be known that He (God) is the framer and He the Creator, and He the Discerner, and He the Judge, and He the Witness," etc.[3]

---

[1] Besides the ordinary commentaries to the Mishnah, account must be taken of the remarks of Chasdai Crescas, Duran, Albo, and Abarbanel on the subject. Of modern writers, I mention Kämpf, in the *Monatsschrift*, 1863, pp. 144 and 376; Oppenheim, *ibid.*, 1864, p. 144; Friedmann, *Beth Talmud*, I., pp. 210 and 296. Compare also Rapoport, *Erech Millin*, p. 181, and Talm. dicts. sub voce אפיקורוס. The explanation I have adopted agrees partly with Friedmann's, partly with Oppenheim's view.

[2] *Aboth*, III., 9.

[3] *Aboth*, IV., 22.

But it must not be forgotten that it was not the habit of the Rabbis to lay down either for conduct or doctrine rules which were commonly known. When they urged the three points stated above there must have been some historical reason for it. Probably these principles were controverted by some heretics. Indeed, the whole tone of the Mishnah is a protest against certain unbelievers who are threatened with punishment. Other beliefs, not less essential, but less disputed, remain unmentioned, because there was no necessity to assert them.

It was not till a much later time, when the Jews came into closer contact with new philosophical schools, and also new creeds, that were more liable than heathenism was to be confused with Judaism, that this necessity was felt. And thus we are led at once to the period when the Jews became acquainted with the teachings of the Mohammedan schools. The Karaites came very early into contact with non-Jewish systems. And so we find that they were also the first to formulate Jewish dogmas in a fixed number, and in a systematic order. It is also possible that their separation from the Tradition, and their early division into little sects among themselves, compelled them to take this step, in order to avoid further sectarianism.

The number of their dogmas amounts to ten. According to Jehuda Hadassi (1150), who would appear to have derived them from his predecessors, their dogmas include the following articles:—1. *Creatio ex nihilo;* 2. The existence of a Creator, God; 3. This God is an absolute unity as well as incorporeal; 4. Moses and the other prophets were sent by God; 5. God has given to us the Torah, which is true and complete in every respect, not wanting the addition of the so-called Oral Law; 6. The Torah must be studied by every Jew in the original (Hebrew) language; 7. The Holy Temple was a place elected by God for His manifestation; 8. Resurrection of the dead; 9. Punishment and reward after death; 10. The Coming of the Messiah, the son of David.[1]

How far the predecessors of Hadassi were influenced by a certain Joseph Albashir (about 950), of whom there exists a manuscript work, "Rudiments of Faith," I am unable to say. The little we know of him reveals more of his intimacy with Arabic thoughts than of his importance for his sect in particular and for Judaism in general.[2] After Hadassi I shall mention

[1] I have followed the exposition of the late Dr. Frankl, the greatest Karaitic scholar of our time. See his article "Karaiten" in the *Encyclopädie* of Ersch and Gruber, section II., vol. 33, p. 18. Compare Jost's *Geschichte*, II., ch. 13, where the articles of Bashazi are given.

[2] Concerning this author see Frankl's *Ein Mutazilitischer Kalam*, and his *Beiträge zur Literaturgeschichte der Karäer* (Berlin, 1887).

here Elijah Bashazi, a Karaite writer of the end of the 15th century. This author, who was much influenced by Maimonides, omits the second and the seventh articles. In order to make up the ten he numbers the belief in the eternity of God as an article, and divides the fourth article into two.[1] In the fifth article Bashazi does not emphasize so strongly the completeness of the Torah as Hadassi, and omits the portion which is directed against Tradition. It is interesting to see the distinction which Bashazi draws between the Pentateuch and the Prophets. While he thinks that the five books of Moses can never be altered, he regards the words of the Prophets as only relating to their contemporaries, and thus subject to changes.[2] As I do not want to anticipate Maimonides' system we must refrain from giving here the articles laid down by Solomon Troki in the beginning of the 18th century. For the articles of Maimonides are copied by this writer with a few slight alterations so as to dress them in a Karaite garb.[3]

We must dismiss the Karaites with these few remarks, my object being chiefly to discuss the dogmas of the Synagogue from which they had separated themselves. Besides, as in everything Karaitic, there is no further development of the question. As Bashazi laid them down, they are still taught by the Karaites of to-day. We return to the Rabbanites.

As is well known Maimonides (1130—1205) was the first Rabbanite who formulated the dogmas of the Synagogue. But there are indications of earlier attempts. R. Saadjah Gaon's (892—942) work, "Creeds and Opinions," shows such traces. He says in his preface, "My heart sickens to see that the belief of my co-religionists is impure and that their theological views are confused." The subjects he treats in this book, such as creation, unity of God, resurrection of the dead, the future redemption of Israel, reward and punishment, and other kindred theological subjects might thus, perhaps, be considered as the essentials of the creed that the Gaon desired to present in a pure and rational form. R. Chananel, of Kairowan, in the first half of the 11th century, says in one of his commentaries that to deserve the eternal life one must believe in *four* things: in God, in the prophets, in a future world where the just will be rewarded, and in the advent of the Redeemer.[4] From R. Jehuda Halevy's "Kusari,"

---

1 See אדרת אליהו, (Goslow, 1835) p. 48, where whole passages are verbally copied from Maimonides.

2 *Encyclopädie*, p. 16.

3 See אפריון, p. 17a, edited by Dr. Neubauer, and our Appendices A and B.

4 Rapoport, *Bikkure Haittim*, XII., p. 48.

written in the beginning of the 12th century, we might argue that the belief in the election of Israel by God was the cardinal dogma of the author. Abraham Ibn Daud, a contemporary of Maimonides, in his book "Emuna Ramah," speaks of *rudiments*, among which, besides such metaphysical principles as unity, rational conception of God's attributes, &c., the belief in the immutability of the Law, &c., is included.[1] Still, all these works are intended to furnish evidence from philosophy or history for the truth of religion rather than to give a definition of this truth. The latter task was undertaken by Maimonides.

I refer to the thirteen articles embodied in his first work, "The Commentary to the Mishnah." They are appended to the Mishnah in Synhedrin, with which we dealt above. But though they do not form an independent treatise, Maimonides' remarks must not be considered as merely incidental.

That Maimonides was quite conscious of the importance of this exposition can be gathered from the concluding words addressed to the reader: "Know these (words) and repeat them many times, and think them over in the proper way. God knows that you would be deceiving yourself if you think you have understood them by having read them once or even ten times. Be not, therefore, hasty in perusing them. I have not composed them without deep study and earnest reflection."

The result of this deep study was that the following Thirteen Articles constitute the creed of Judaism. They are:—

1. The belief in the existence of a Creator. 2. The belief in his Unity. 3. The belief in his Incorporeality. 4. The belief in his Eternity. 5. The belief that all worship and adoration are due to him alone. 6. The belief in Prophecy. 7. The belief that Moses was the greatest of all Prophets, both before and after him. 8. The belief that the Law was revealed to Moses on Mount Sinai. 9. The belief in the Immutability of this revealed Torah. 10. The belief that God knows the acts of men. 11. The belief in Reward and Punishment. 12. The belief in the coming of the Messiah. 13. The belief in the Resurrection of the dead.[2]

---

[1] See אמונה רמה, pp. 44 and 69. Compare Gutmann's essay on this author in the *Monatsschrift*, 1877-8, especially 1878, p. 304.

[2] For the various translations of the Thirteen Articles, which were originally composed in Arabic, see Steinschneider, *Cat. Bod.*, p. 1887, where references to modern literature may be found. Compare Rosin, *Ethik des Maimonides*, p. 30, note 4. In Appendix A will be given the version of Alcharizi from an Oxford MS. See also Chajoth, תורת נביאים, and his תפארת למשה, p. 17a. His reading of Article 13, given on De Rossi's authority, is an interpolation from Maimonides' מאמר תחיית המתים. See מאור עינים ed. *Cassel*, p. 93. Compare Weiss, *Beth Talmud*, I., p. 330. *Ben Chananjah*, 1863, p. 942, and 1864, pp. 648 and 697. See also Dr. N. M. Adler's Introduction to נתינה לגר, ch. 4.

The impulse given by the great philosopher and still greater Jew was eagerly followed by succeeding generations, and Judaism thus came into possession of a dogmatic literature such as it never knew before Maimonides. Maimonides is the centre of this literature, and I shall accordingly speak in the remainder of this essay of Maimonists and Anti-Maimonists. These terms really apply to the great controversy that raged round Maimonides' "Guide of the Perplexed," but I shall, chiefly for brevity sake, employ them in these pages in a restricted sense to refer to the dispute concerning the Thirteen Articles.

Among the Maimonists we may probably include the great majority of Jews, who accepted the Thirteen Articles without further question. Maimonides must indeed have filled up a great gap in Jewish theology, a gap, moreover, the existence of which was very generally perceived. A century had hardly elapsed before the Thirteen Articles had become a theme for the poets of the Synagogue. And almost every country where Jews lived can show a poem or a prayer founded on these Articles.[1] R. Jacob Molin (1420) speaks of metrical and rhymed songs in the German language, the contents of which were the Thirteen Articles, and which were read by the common people with great devotion.[2] The numerous commentaries and homilies written on the same topic would form a small library in themselves. But on the other hand it must not be denied that the Anti-Maimonists, that is to say those Jewish writers who did not agree with the creed formulated by Maimonides, or agreed only in part with him, form also a very strong and respectable minority. They deserve our attention the more as it is their works which brought life into the subject and deepened it. It is not by a perpetual Amen to every utterance of a great authority that truth or literature gains anything.

S. SCHECHTER.

[*To be concluded.*]

---

[1] In Appendix B will be given a collection of such poems both from MSS and rare printed books. Appendix A will contain a bibliographical account of the commentaries on the Thirteen Articles from similar sources.

[2] See Maharil, ed. *Sabionetta*, 113a. Compare Landshut, *Amude Ha-Aboda*, p. 231.

THE DOGMAS OF JUDAISM.

[*Concluded from page* 61.]

THE Anti-Maimonists can be divided into two classes. The one class categorically denies that Judaism has dogmas. I shall have occasion to touch on this view when I come to speak of Abarbanel. Here I pass at once to the second class of Anti-Maimonists. This consists of those who agree with Maimonides as to the existence of dogmas in Judaism, but who differ from him as to what these dogmas are, or who give a different enumeration of them.

As the first of these Anti-Maimonists we may regard Nachmanides, who, in his famous "Sermon in the Presence of the King," speaks of three fundamental principles: Creation, Omniscience of God, and Providence. Next comes R. Abba Mari ben Moses, of Montepellier. He wrote at the beginning of the 14th century, and is famous in Jewish history for his zeal against the study of philosophy. We possess a small pamphlet by him dealing with our subject, and it forms a kind of prologue to his collection of controversial letters against the rationalists of his time. He lays down three articles as the fundamental teachings of Religion: 1. Metaphysical: The existence of God, including His Unity and Incorporeality; 2. Mosaic: *Creatio ex nihilo* by God—a consequence of this principle is the belief that God is capable of altering the laws of nature at His pleasure; 3. Ethical: Special Providence—*i.e.*, God knows all our actions in all their details. Abba Mari does not mention Maimonides' Thirteen Articles. But it would be false to conclude that he rejected the belief in the coming of the Messiah, or any other article of Maimonides. The whole tone and tendency of this pamphlet is polemical, and it is therefore probable that he only urged those points which were either doubted or explained in an unorthodox way by the sceptics of his time.[1]

---

[1] See pages 1—19 of his polemical work מנחת קנאות (Presburg, 1838). Compare Renan-Neubauer, *Les Rabbins Français*, p. 679.

Another scholar, of Provence, who wrote but twenty years later than Abba Mari—R. David ben Samuel d'Estella (1320)—speaks of the seven pillars of religion. They are: Revelation, Providence, Reward and Punishment, the Coming of the Messiah, Resurrection of the Dead, *Creatio ex nihilo*, and Free Will.[1]

Of authors living in other countries, I have to mention here R. Shemarjah, of Crete, who flourished at about the same time as R. David d'Estella, and is known from his efforts to reconcile the Karaites with the Rabbanites. This author wrote a book for the purpose of furnishing Jewish students with evidence for what he considered the five fundamental teachings of Judaism, viz.: 1. The Existence of God; 2. Incorporeality of God; 3. His Absolute Unity; 4. That God created heaven and earth; 5. That God created the world after His will 5106 years ago—the latter (1346) being the year in which Shemarjah wrote these words.[2]

In Portugal, at about the same time, we find R. David ben Jom Tob Bilia adding to the articles of Maimonides thirteen of his own, which he calls the "Fundamentals of the Thinking Man." Five of these articles relate to the functions of the human soul, that, according to him, emanated from God, and to the way in which this divine soul receives its punishment and reward. The other eight articles are as follows: 1. The belief in the existence of spiritual beings—angels; 2. *Creatio ex nihilo*; 3. The belief in the existence of another world, and that this other world is only a spiritual one; 4. The Torah is above philosophy; 5. The Torah has an outward (literary) meaning and an inward (allegorical) meaning; 6. The text of the Torah is not subject to any emendation; 7. The reward of a good action is the good work itself, and the doer must not expect any other reward; 8. It is only by the "commands relating to the heart," for instance, the belief in one eternal God, the loving and fearing him, and not through good actions that man attains the highest degree of perfection.[3] Perhaps it would be suitable to mention here another contemporaneous writer, who also numbers twenty-six articles. The name of this writer is unknown, and his articles are only

---

[1] *Hebräische Bibliographie* (VIII., 63 and 103). Compare Neubauer, *Revue des Etudes Juives*, IX., 215. See also Appendix A.

[2] See אוצר הספרים, p. 41, No. 781, and Steinschneider, *Cat. München*, No. 210. But from the ליקוטי ר׳ יוחנן אלימנו, p. 133a (Cat. Neubauer 2,243) it would seem that R. Shemarjah considers the belief in *Creatio ex nihilo* as the most important article. Compare also Graetz, *History*, VII., 299, where the date 5106 is questioned; Neubauer, *Revue*, X. 68.

[3] See the collection דברי חכמים, by Ashkenasi, pp. 56b, etc.

gathered from quotations by later authors. It would seem from these quotations that the articles of this unknown author consisted mostly of statements emphasizing the belief in the attributes of God: as, His Eternity, His Wisdom and Omnipotence, and the like.[1]

More important for our subject are the productions of the 15th century, especially those of Spanish authors. The fifteen articles of R. Lipman Mulhausen, in the preface to his well-known *Sefer Nizzachon* (1410), differ but slightly from those of Maimonides. In accordance with the anti-Christian tendency of his polemical book, he lays more stress on the two articles of Unity and Incorporeality, and makes of them four. We can therefore dismiss him with this short remark, and pass at once to the Spanish Rabbis.

The first of these is R. Chasdai Ibn Crescas, who composed his famous treatise, "The Light of God," about 1405. Chasdai's book is well known for its attacks on Aristotle, and also for its influence on Spinoza. But Chasdai deals also with Maimonides' Thirteen Articles, to which he was very strongly opposed. Already in his preface he attacks Maimonides for speaking, in his "Book of the Commandments," of the belief in the existence of God as an "affirmative precept." Chasdai thinks it absurd; for every commandment must be dictated by some authority, but on whose authority can we dictate the acceptance of this authority? His general objection to the Thirteen Articles is that Maimonides confounded dogmas or *fundamental* beliefs of Judaism, without which Judaism is inconceivable, with beliefs or *doctrines* which Judaism inculcates, but the denial of which, though involving a strong heresy, does not make Judaism impossible. He maintains that if Maimonides meant only to count fundamental teachings, there are not more than seven; but that if he intended also to include doctrines, he ought to have enumerated sixteen. As beliefs of the first class—namely, fundamental beliefs—he considers the following articles: 1. God's knowledge of our actions; 2. Providence; 3. God's omnipotence—even to act against the laws of nature; 4. Prophecy; 5. Free will; 6. The aim of the Torah is to make man long after the closest communion with God. The belief in the existence of God, Chasdai thinks, is an axiom with which every religion must begin, and he is therefore uncertain whether to include it as a dogma or not. As to the doctrines which every Jew is bound to believe, but without which Judaism is not im-

[1] Albo, *Ikkarim*, ch. iii.; probably the same author that is mentioned by Duran in his book אוהב משפט, 13b.

possible, Chasdai divides them into two sections: (A.) 1. *Creatio ex nihilo*; 2. Immortality of the soul; 3. Reward and Punishment; 4. Resurrection of the dead; 5. Immutability of the Torah; 6. Superiority of the prophecy of Moses; 7. That the High Priest received the instructions sought for from God, when he put his questions through the medium of the Urim and Tummim; 8. The coming of the Messiah. (B.) Doctrines which are expressed by certain religious ceremonies, and on which belief these ceremonies are conditioned: 1. The belief in the efficacy of prayer—as well as that the benediction of the priests has the power of conveying to us the blessing of God; 2. God is merciful to the penitent; 3. Certain days in the year—for instance, the Day of Atonement—are especially qualified to bring us near to God, if we keep them in the way we are commanded. That Chasdai is a little arbitrary in the choice of his "doctrines," I need hardly say. Indeed, Chasdai's importance for the dogma-question consists more in his critical suggestions than in his positive results. He was, as we have seen, the first to make the distinction between fundamental teachings, which form the basis of Judaism, and those other simple Jewish doctrines, without which Judaism is not impossible. Very daring is his remark, when proving that Reward and Punishment, Immortality of the soul, and Resurrection of the dead must not be considered as the basis of Judaism, that the highest ideal of religion is to serve God without any hope of reward. Even more daring are his words concerning the Immutability of the Law. He says: "Some have argued that, since God is perfection, so must also His law be perfect, and thus unsusceptible of improvement." But he does not think this argument conclusive, though the fact in itself (the Immutability of the Law) is true. For one might answer that this perfection of the Torah could only be in accordance with the intelligence of those for whom it was meant; but as soon as the recipients of the Torah have advanced to a higher state of perfection, the Torah must also be altered to suit their advanced intelligence. A pupil of Chasdai illustrates the words of his master by a medical parallel. The physician has to adapt his medicaments to the various stages through which his patient has to pass. That he changes his prescription does not, however, imply that his medical knowledge is imperfect, or that his earlier remedies were ignorantly chosen; the varying condition of the invalid was the cause of the variation in the doctor's treatment. Similarly, were not the Immutability of the Torah a "doctrine," one might maintain that the perfection of the Torah would not be inconsistent with the assumption that it was susceptible of modification, in accordance with our changing and progressive circumstances. But all these arguments are purely of a theoretic character; for, practically, every Jew, according to Chasdai, has to accept all these beliefs, whether he terms them fundamental teachings or only Jewish doctrines.[1]

Some years later, though he finished his work in the same year as Chasdai, R. Simon ben Duran (1366-1444), a younger contemporary of the former, made his researches on dogmas. His studies on this subject form a kind of introduction to his commentary on Job, which he finished in the year 1405. Duran is not so strongly opposed to the Thirteen Articles as Chasdai, or as another "thinker of our people," who thought them an arbitrary imitation of the thirteen attributes of God. Duran tries to justify Maimonides; but nevertheless he agrees with "earlier authorities," who formulated the Jewish creed in Three Articles—The Existence of God, Revelation, and Reward and Punishment, under which Duran thinks the Thirteen Articles of Maimonides may be easily classified. Most interesting are his remarks concerning the validity of dogmas. He tells us that only those are to be considered as heretics who stick to their own opinions, though they know that they are contradictory to the views of the Torah. But those who accept the fundamental teachings of Judaism, but are led by their deep studies and earnest reflection to differ in details from the opinions current among their co-religionists, and explain certain passages in the Scripture in their own way, must by no means be considered as heretics. We must therefore, Duran proceeds to say, not blame such men as Maimonides, who gave an allegorical interpretation to certain passages in the Bible about miracles, or R. Levi ben Gershon, who followed certain un-Jewish views in relation to the belief in *Creatio ex nihilo*. It is only the views that are condemnable, but not those who cherish them. God forbid, says Duran, that such a thing should happen in Israel as to condemn honest inquirers on account of their differing opinions. It would be interesting to know of how many divines, as tolerant as this persecuted Jew, the 15th century can boast.[2]

---

[1] See אור ה׳, Ed. Johannisberg, in the preface, pp. 20a, 44b, 59b, and 61a and 62b. The style of the author is very obscure, and the book is full of misprints. See also Joel's essay on this author (Breslau, 1866).

[2] Of Duran's many works, we have here to consider his commentary אוהב משפט on Job, pp. 13 *seq.*, and the first pages of his book מגן אבות (Leghorn, 1758). See also Dr. Jaulus' essay in the *Monatsschrift*, 1874.

We can now pass to a more popular but less original writer on our theme. I refer to R. Joseph Albo, the author of the Ikkarim, who was the pupil of Chasdai, a younger contemporary of Duran, and wrote at a much later period than these authors. Graetz has justly denied him much originality. The chief merit of Albo consists in popularising other people's thoughts, though he does not always care to mention their names. And the student who is a little familiar with the contents of the book Ikkarim will easily find that Albo has taken his best ideas either from Chasdai or from Duran.[1] As it is of little consequence to us whether an article of faith is called "stem," or "root," or "branch," there is scarcely anything fresh left to quote in the name of Albo. Dr. Löw, of Szegedin, was indeed right, when he answered an adversary who challenged him—"Who would dare to declare me as an heretic as long as I confess the three Articles laid down by Albo?" with the words "Albo himself." For, after all the subtle distinctions Albo makes between different classes of dogmas, he declares that every one who denies even the immutability of the Law or the coming of the Messiah, which are, according to him, articles of minor importance, is a heretic who will be excluded from the world to come.[2] But there is one point in his book which is worth noticing. It was suggested to him by Maimonides. Still Albo has the merit of having emphasised it as it deserves. Among the articles which he calls branches, Albo counts the belief that the perfection of man, which leads to eternal life, can be obtained by the fulfilling of *one* commandment. But this command must be, as Maimonides points out, done without any worldly regard, and only for the sake of the love of God.[3] When one considers how many platitudes are repeated year by year by certain theologians on the subject of Jewish legalism we cannot lay enough stress on this article of Albo, and we ought to make it better known than it hitherto has been.

Though I cannot enter here into the enumeration of the Maimonists, I must not leave unmentioned the name of R. Nissim ben Moses of Marseilles, the first great Maimonist, who flourished about the end of the thirteenth century, and

---

[1] See Schlesinger's introduction and notes to *Ikkarim*, and Dr. S. Back's lecture on Joseph Albo. For the relations of Chasdai and Duran, see Joel's Essay, p. 82, and Jaulus, *Monatsschrift*, p. 463. For his plagiarisms from Rabbi Nissim, see Brüll, *Jahrbuch*, IV. 52.

[2] *Ikkarim*, I., ch. 23.

[3] Ibid., I., 23, and III., 29, and Maimonides' Commentary to Mishnah, end of tractate Makkoth.

was considered as one of the most enlightened thinkers of his age. From the extracts I shall publish in Appendix A from his *Sepher Hanissim*, contained in MS. in Oxford and the British Museum, it will be seen that he greatly influenced his successors, and perhaps also suggested their systems to them, though he himself adhered to the Thirteen Articles of Maimonides. Another great Maimonist deserving special attention is R. Abraham ben Shem Tob Bibago, who may perhaps be regarded as the most prominent among those who undertook to defend Maimonides against the attacks of Chasdai and others. Bibago wrote "The Path of Belief" in the second half of the 15th century, and was, as Dr. Steinschneider aptly describes him, a *Denkgläubiger*. But, above all, he was a believing Jew. When he was once asked, at the table of King John II., of Aragon, by a Christian scholar, "Are you the Jewish philosopher?" he answered, "I am a Jew who believes in the Law given to us by our teacher Moses, though I have studied philosophy." Bibago was such a devoted admirer of Maimonides that he could not tolerate any opposition against him. He speaks in one passage of the prudent people of his time who, in desiring to be looked upon as orthodox by the great mob, calumniated the teacher (Maimonides), and depreciated his merits. Bibago's book is very interesting, especially in its controversial parts; but in respect to dogmas he is, as already said, a Maimonist, and does not contribute any new point on our subject.[1] To return to the Anti-Maimonists of the second half of the 15th century. As such may be considered R. Isaac Aramah, who speaks of three foundations of religion: *Creatio ex nihilo*, Revelation (?), and the belief in a world to come.[2] Next to be mentioned is R. Joseph Jabez, who also accepts only three articles: *Creatio ex nihilo*, Individual Providence, and the Unity of God. Under these three heads he tries to classify the Thirteen Articles of Maimonides.[3]

The last Spanish writer on our subject is R. Isaac Abarbanel. His treatise on the subject is known under the title "Rosh Amanah," and was finished in the year 1495. The greatest part of this treatise forms a defence of Maimonides, many points in which are taken from Bibago.[4] But in spite of this fact, Abarbanel must not be considered a Maimonist. It is

---

[1] Part 5 of Bibago's דרך אמונה (Constantinople, 1521), treats exclusively of the Thirteen Articles. Compare Steinschneider in *Monatsschrift*, 1883, p. 79.

[2] See עקידת יצחק, section 55. The meaning of the word תורה in this passage is not quite clear.

[3] See his יסוד האמונה and מאמר האחדות.

[4] Steinschneider, *Monatsschrift*, etc., p. 95.

only a feeling of piety towards Maimonides, or perhaps rather a fondness for argument that made him defend Maimonides against Chasdai and others. His own view is that it is a mistake to formulate dogmas of Judaism, since every word in the Torah has to be considered as a dogma for itself.[1] It was only, says Abarbanel, by following the example of non-Jewish scholars that Maimonides and others were induced to lay down dogmas. The non-Jewish philosophers are in the habit of accepting in every science certain indisputable axioms from which they deduce the propositions which are less evident. The Jewish philosophers in a similar way sought for first principles in religion from which the whole of the Torah ought to be considered as a deduction. But, thinks Abarbanel, the Torah as a revealed code is under no necessity of deducing things from each other, for all the commands came from the same divine authority, and, therefore, all are alike evident, and have the same certainty. On this and similar grounds Abarbanel refused to accept dogmatic articles for Judaism, and he thus became the head of the school that forms a class by itself among the Anti-Maimonists to which many of the greatest Cabbalists also belong. But it is idle talk to cite this school in aid of the modern theory that Judaism has no dogmas. As we have seen it was rather an *embarras de richesse* that prevented Abarbanel from accepting the Thirteen Articles of Maimonides. To him and to the Cabbalists the Torah consists of at least 613 Articles.

Abarbanel wrote his book with which we have just dealt at Naples. And it is Italy to which, after the expulsion of the Jews from Spain, we have to look chiefly for religious speculation. But the philosophers of Italy are still less independent of Maimonides than their predecessors in Spain. Thus we find that R. David Messir Leon, R. David Vital, and others were Maimonists.[2] Even the otherwise refined and original thinker, R. Elijah Del Medigo (who died about

---

[1] See Duran אוהב מ״שפט, 14b, where this view is already hinted at, Compare R. Solomon ben Addereth, as quoted above, where he speaks of שלמה תורה תרי״ג העיקרים מן כוללת ; but it is not probable that he uses עיקרים in the philosophical sense.

[2] A list of the Maimonists will be found in Appendices A and B. But I must remark that, owing to the kindness of Dr. Gaster, who allowed me to have a glance at the library of the Ramsgate College, I was able to examine there a MS. by R. David Messir Leon, which throws a fresh light on the life and views of this scholar. His views on dogmas, as given in this MS., are widely at variance from his opinion, known to us from his printed book תהלה לדוד. His relation to Abarbanel deserves closer examination. Hoping to publish soon a monograph on this author, I defer the treatment of these points for that occasion.

the end of the 15th century) becomes almost rude when he speaks of the adversaries of Maimonides in respect to dogmas. "It was only," he says, "the would-be philosopher that dared to question the articles of Maimonides. Our people have always the bad habit of thinking themselves competent to attack the greatest authorities as soon as they have got some knowledge of the subject. Genuine thinkers, however, attach very little importance to their objections."[1]

Indeed, it seems as if the energetic protests of Del Medigo scared away the Anti-Maimonists for more than a century. Even in the following 17th century we have to notice only two Anti-Maimonists. The one is Rabbi Tobjah, the priest (1652), who was of Polish descent, studied in Italy, and lived as a medical man in France. He seems to refuse to accept the belief in the Immutability of the Torah, and in the coming of the Messiah as fundamental teachings of Judaism.[2] The other, at the end of the 17th century (1695), is R. Abraham Chayim Viterabo, of Italy. He accepts only six articles: 1. Existence of God. 2. Unity. 3. Incorporeality. 4. That God was revealed to Moses on Mount Sinai, and that the prophecy of Moses is true. 5. Revelation (including the historical parts of the Torah). 6. Reward and Punishment. As to the other articles of Maimonides, Viterabo, in opposition to other half-hearted Anti-Maimonists, declares that the man who denies them is *not* to be considered as a heretic; though he ought to believe them.[3]

I have now arrived at the limit I set to myself at the beginning of this essay. For there is, between the times of Viterabo and those of Mendelssohn, hardly to be found any serious opposition to Maimonides worth noticing here. Still I must mention the name of R. Saul Berlin (died 1794); there is much in his opinions on dogmas which will help us the better to understand the Thirteen Articles of Maimonides. As the reader has seen, I have refrained so far from reproducing here the apologies which were made by many Maimonists in behalf of the Thirteen Articles. For, after all their elaborate pleas, none of them was able to clear Maimonides of the charge of having confounded dogmas or fundamental teachings with doctrines. It is also true that the Fifth Article—that prayer and worship must only be

---

[1] See בחינת הדת, ed. Reggio, p. 28.

[2] See מעשה טוביה (Venice, 1707), 16a and 23a. His language is very vague.

[3] See אמונת חכמים in collection טעם זקנים, by Ashkenasi, p. 29b. We think this a very important work, and we must strongly recommend it to the reader.

afforded to God—cannot be considered even as a doctrine, but as a simple precept. And there are other difficulties which all the distinctions of the Maimonists will never be able to solve. The only possible justification is, I think, that suggested by a remark of R. Saul. This author, who was himself like his friend and older contemporary—Mendelssohn, a strong Anti-Maimonist, among other remarks, maintains that dogmas must never be laid down but with regard to the necessities of the time.[1]

Now R. Saul certainly did not doubt that Judaism is based on eternal truths which can in no way be shaken by new modes of thinking or changed circumstances. What he meant was that there are in every age certain beliefs which ought to be asserted more emphatically than others, without regard to their theological or rather logical importance. It is by this maxim that we shall be able to explain the articles of Maimonides. He asserted them, because they were necessary for his time. We know, for instance, from a letter of his son and other contemporaries, that it was just at his time that the belief in the incorporeality of God was, in the opinion of Maimonides, a little relaxed.[2] Maimonides, who thought such low notions of the Deity dangerous to Judaism, therefore laid down an article against them. He tells us in his "Guide" that it was far from him to condemn anyone who was not able to demonstrate the Incorporeality of God, but he stigmatised as a heretic one who refused to believe it.[3] This position might be paralleled by that of a modern astronomer who, while considering it unreasonable to expect a mathematical demonstration of the movements of the earth from an ordinary unscientific man, would yet regard the person who refused to believe in such movements as an ignorant faddist.

Again, Maimonides undoubtedly knew that there may be found in the Talmud—that bottomless sea with its innumerable undercurrents—passages that are not quite in harmony with his articles; for instance, the well-known dictum of R. Hillel, who said, there is no Messiah for Israel—a passage which has already been quoted *ad nauseam* by every opponent of Maimonides from the earliest times down to the year of grace 1888. Maimonides was well aware of the existence of this and similar passages. But, being deeply convinced of the necessity of the belief in a future redemption of *Israel*—in opposition to other creeds who claim this redemp-

[1] See בשמים ראש, p. 251.
[2] Weiss, *Beth Talmud*, I., 291.
[3] *Guide*, I., 35, 36.

tion solely for themselves—Maimonides simply ignored the saying of R. Hillel, as an isolated opinion which contradicts all the feelings and traditions of the Jews as expressed in thousands of other passages, and especially in the liturgy. Most interesting is Maimonides' view about such isolated opinions in a letter to the wise men of Marseilles. He deals there with the question of free will and other theological subjects. After having stated his own view he goes on to say: "I know that it is possible to find in the Talmud or in the Midrash this or that saying in contradiction to the views you have heard from me. But you must not be troubled by them. One must not refuse to accept a doctrine, the truth of which has been proved, on account of its being in opposition to some isolated opinion held by this or that great authority. Is it not possible that he overlooked some important considerations when he uttered this strange opinion? It is also possible that his words must not be taken literally, and have to be explained in an allegorical way. We can also think that his words were only to be applied with regard to certain circumstances of his time, but never intended as permanent truths . . . . No man must discard his own opinions. The eyes are not directed backwards but forwards." In another place Maimonides calls the suppression of one's own opinions—for the reason of their being irreconcilable with the isolated views of some great authority—a moral suicide. By such motives Maimonides was guided when he left certain views hazarded in the Rabbinic literature unheeded, and followed what we may perhaps call the religious common-sense of his own time. We may again be certain that Maimonides was clear-headed enough to see that the words of the Torah: "And there arose no prophet since in Israel like unto Moses" (Deut. xxxiv. 10), were as little intended to imply a doctrine as the passage relating to the king Josiah, "And like unto him was there no king that turned to the Lord with all his heart . . . . neither after him there arose any like him" (2 Kings, xxiii. 25). And none would think of declaring him a heretic who should believe another king as pious as Josiah. But living among the "imitating confessions," who claimed that their religion had superseded the law of Moses, Maimonides, consciously or unconsciously, felt himself compelled to assert the superiority of the prophecy of Moses. And so we may guess that every article of Maimonides which seems to offer difficulties to us, contains an assertion of some relaxed belief, or a protest against the pretensions of other creeds, though we are not always able to discover the exact necessity for them. On the other hand, Maimonides did not assert the belief in free will, for which he argued so earnestly in his "Guide." The "common man," with his simple unspeculative mind, for whom these Thirteen Articles were intended,[1] "never dreamed that the will was not free," and there was no necessity of impressing on his mind things which he had never doubted.

So much about Maimonides. As to the Anti-Maimonists it could hardly escape the reader that in some of the quoted systems the difference from the view of Maimonides, is only a logical one not a theological. Of some authors again, especially those of the 13th and 14th centuries, it is not at all certain whether they intended to oppose Maimonides. Others again, as for instance R. Abba Mari, R. Lipman, and R. Joseph Jabez, acted on the same principle as Maimonides urging only those teachings of Judaism which they thought endangered. One could now, indeed, animated by the praiseworthy example given to us by Maimonides, also propose some articles of faith which are suggested to us by the necessities of our own time. One might, for instance, insert the article, "I believe that Judaism is, in the first instance, a divine religion, *not* a mere complex of racial peculiarities and tribal customs." One might again propose an article to the effect that Judaism is a proselytising religion, having the mission to bring God's kingdom on earth, and to include in that kingdom all mankind. One might also submit for consideration whether it would not be advisable to urge a little more the principle that religion means chiefly a *Weltanschauung* and worship of God by means of holiness both in thought and in action. One would even not object to accept the article laid down by R. Saul, that we have to look upon ourselves as sinners. Morbid as such a belief may be, it would, if properly impressed on our mind, have perhaps the wholesome effect of cooling down a little our self-importance and our mutual admiration that makes every progress among us almost impossible.

But it was not my purpose here to ventilate the question whether Maimonides' articles are sufficient for us, or whether we ought not to add new ones to them. Nor did I try to decide what system we ought to prefer for recitation in the Synagogue—that of Maimonides or that of Chasdai, or of any other writer. I do not think that such a recital is of much use. What I intended by this sketch is rather to make the reader *think* about Judaism, by proving that it

---

[1] Abarbanel, ראש אמנה, ch. 21.

does not only regulate our actions, but also our thoughts. We usually urge that in Judaism religion means life; but we forget that a life without guiding principles and thoughts is an existence not worth living. At least it was so considered by our greatest thinkers, and hence their efforts to formulate the creed of Judaism, so that men would not only be able to do the right thing, but also to think the right thing. Whether they succeeded in their attempts towards formulating the creed of Judaism or not will always remain a question. This concerns the logician more than the theologian. But surely Maimonides and his successors *did* succeed in having a religion depending directly on God, with the most ideal and highest aspirations for the future; whilst the Judaism of a great part of our modern theologians reminds one very much of the words with which the author of "Marius the Epicurean" characterises the Roman religion in the days of her decline: a religion which had been always something to be done rather than something to be thought, or believed, or to be loved.

Political economy, hygiene, statistics, are very fine things. But no sane man would for them make those sacrifices which Judaism requires from us. It is only for God's sake, to fulfil his commands and to accomplish his purpose, that religion becomes worth living and dying for. And this can only be possible with a religion which possesses dogmas.

It is true that every great religion is "a concentration of many ideas and ideals," which make this religion able to adapt itself to various modes of thinking and living. But there must always be a point round which all these ideas concentrate themselves. This centre is Dogma.

S. Schechter.

KIERKEGAARD AND JUDAISM

by
Milton Steinberg

Kierkegaard and Judaism

By Milton Steinberg

As a thorough Christian—or, as he would have put it, infinitely interested in becoming one—Soren Kierkegaard (1813-1855) addressed himself neither to Jews nor to Judaism. But they have overheard him. In part because they could not help it. Is not Kierkegaard the begetter of Existentialism? Is not the school he fathered all the vogue of late? Are Jews less submissive than others to the tyrannies of fashion?

But Kierkegaard, though made into a fad, was himself a highly original and richly endowed spirit, the author of various fresh critical judgments and insights. But every new truth, every reformulation of an old one, constitutes a challenge to all inhabitants of the universe of discourse on which it bears. In effect then, even if not by intention, Kierkegaard has confronted Jews with a twofold *mai ko mashmo lon*: "What has this to teach us?"

He needs to be considered first of all for his theses of which Judaism has been inadequately aware heretofore. "From all my teachers have I derived understanding"—that is a norm for traditions as well as individuals. Kierkegaard demands appraisal also in still another frame of reference. If Fichte is to be believed, it is from the non-Ego that the Ego becomes conscious of its own nature. Now whatever else Kierkegaard may have been, he was a Christian, marginal and idiosyncratic perhaps, but a Christian none the less. For each of his positions, no matter how eccentric, some authoritative warrant can be found, whether in his immediate Lutheran-Calvinist heritage, or in such a tangential Catholic as Pascal and before him in Duns Scotus and Augustine, or, as is to be expected in a Christian theologian, in Paul, the fountainhead of all Christian doctrine But if so, if in Kierkegaard we have an *anima totaliter Christiana,* then he constitutes a non-Ego against which the Jewish Ego may whet its self-awareness.

Nor, to this end, is his extremism an impediment. To the contrary, it is an advantage. Just because Kierkegaard represents Christianity at its most intense and distinctive, his evocative effect on the Jewish spirit is all the more pronounced. Approaching him, therefore, Jews are well advised to be on the alert for what they can learn not only about him but about themselves also.

AMONG the more consequential of Kierkegaard's affirmations are these:

A. That man's plight is desperate, beset as he is by sin and bewilderment, dreading his freedom, shrinking from death, confronting Eternity; forever seeking, never finding, mitigation of his dire lot in the pleasures of the body, the conceptions of the mind.

B. That among human delusions none is more common and baseless than the belief that reason is capable of grasping reality at all, let alone achieving certainty. In this connection Kierkegaard criticizes conceptual thought with such acumen and thoroughness as to win for himself a place in the high tradition of anti-intellectualism stretching from Pyrrho of Elis and Sextus Empiricus to William James and Henri Bergson.

C. That of all conceptualist errors none is more bizarre than the notion of man as a thought-machine who cannot say *sum* ("I am") until he has first asserted *cogito* ("I think"); or the notion of man as a depersonalized, devitalized "something in general" into which philosophy loves to congeal him; whereas, in fact, he is always something particular, dynamic and passionate, more *sentiens* (emotional) than *sapiens* (intellectual).

D. That the crucial determinations of the human soul are reached in privacy and in decisive instants, not in the public domain and the unfolding of events. This thesis, aimed at Hegel, constitutes the first sortie in modern thought against "historicism," the doctrine that the social and the temporal are somehow involved in salvation.

Such are Kierkegaard's premises, from which flow as consequences:

A. An importunate appeal for subjectivity, for the soul's turning away from the outer world and externalized ideas to its own immediacy.

B. The renunciation of the hope of finality, of attaining to a resting place. To the contrary, man's destiny is to be always "on the way," that dialectical ingress and progress penetrating without end to ever deeper levels of inwardness.

C. And finally—or, more accurately, first of all—a revolutionary reenvisagement, in the light of the foregoing, of the religious life.

The sole principle of religious truth, according to Kierkegaard, is subjectivity. For Christianity is "spirit, spirit is inwardness, inwardness is subjectivity, subjectivity is essentially passion, and in its maximum and infinite, personal, passionate interest in one's eternal happiness." Whence it follows that externality, intellectuality, objectivity—call them what you will—are all obstructive to the religious purpose. Scholarship, biblical and doctrinal, may be an appealing and sometimes illuminating enterprise; but so far as salvation is concerned—and that is man's only serious business—of no account. So also with formal creeds and rituals; so also with the church as an institution; so even with ethics and all its apparatus of rules and principles.

The religious quest, Kierkegaard insists, is neither so easy, so impersonal, mechanical or self-limiting. It demands within man a burning with what Pater called "a hard gem-like flame." Even that does not suffice. For God must respond, and who can commit or compel Him? That, too, if granted, is not enough. For salvation and grace are not "things" to be given once and thereafter owned by their recipients. They are not possessions to be held in fee simple: they are ever-receding goals which, once won, must be won again. Hence the most stupid of all complacencies is that of "believers" who suppose that no more is asked of them than the performance of the right commandments or the recitation of the proper confessions. And the most arrogant of offenses is to cease, out of religious pride and self-assurance, from that anguished striving which is the mark of the human soul and its hope of salvation.

Man's freedom therefore is his peril, his misery and his grandeur. His peril, since all depends on it; his misery, since it consigns him to an infinitely toilsome and ultimately endless task; his grandeur, for its goal is nothing less than eternal bliss in God.

BUT there is more to Kierkegaard, much of which is philosophically questionable and some, from the Jewish point of view, nothing short of perilous.

Consider, first, Kierkegaard's radical anti-rationalism. This, to be sure, is far from total. For Socrates his admiration is as warm as his antagonism to Hegel is deep; and if he has no high regard for the physical sciences, he recognizes them as legitimate fields of human interest, with the intellect as the proper tool for their exploration. But though he pays obeisance to reason and gives abundant evidence of expertness in it, on the climactic issues of living—religion and human salvation—he repudiates reason totally, radically, with zest.

Faith for Kierkegaard is not supplementary to the intellect but its antagonist. This, be it noted, is something different from the usual conflict between faith and reason, whether in religion or philosophy. Here we are not dealing with the *noesis* of Plato or the *theoria* of Aristotle, which, reaching beyond the discursive intellect or *logos,* nevertheless carry it along in their very transcendence of it. Nor are we handling here that more commonplace collision between religious dogma on one side and science on the other.

Kierkegaard makes a different and much more radical point. He argues not merely the conventional thesis that faith and reason can have no traffic with each other, operating as they do in different realms, separated as they are by a "disjuncture" which may be "leaped" but not bridged. His is the revolutionary contention—and it is the core of his doctrine—that faith *of necessity* must "affront" reason, must "spurn" and "scandalize" it. Nor could it be otherwise when faith's climax is the twin declaration (a) that God became man and (b) that His death on the cross, an event in time, is the occasion of eternal salvation.

Can any assertion, Kierkegaard queries again and again, be more paradoxical and absurd? But if the supreme affirmations of faith be absurdities and paradoxes, then manifestly reason is not only insufficient to faith, reason must be faith's natural enemy.

AN anti-rationalist, Kierkegaard turns out something of a non-moralist also. As in logic, so in ethics, he discloses great forensic virtuosity. Witness the case for marriage and traditional morality in general, which he sets forth in the latter half of *Either-Or.*

But again it is another tack he takes once the issue becomes salvation. As before he sprang from reason to faith, spurning the intellect and trampling it down in his leap, so now he springs above morality. Goodness, he asserts, whatever its other utilities, does not save; it cannot even help to salvation. What is more, when God asks it as He may, or faith requires it as it sometimes does, moral principle must be jettisoned. This is the "teleological suspension of the ethical," propounded by Kierkegaard in his *Fear and Trembling* as the final meaning of Abraham's readiness to sacrifice Isaac at God's behest. This, be it observed, is such a *midrash* on the *Akedah* as no rabbi in two thousand years ventured to put forth.

Closely related to such "secondarizing" of the ethical is that aspect of Kierkegaard's thinking which Buber has analyzed in *The Question to the Single One*—its near-solipsism. This is no morally neutral solipsism (the metaphysical view that the self is the only knowable, or the only existent, thing) such as might derive from the epistemological question of how one can know anything. It is rather a projection of self-centeredness, so total a concentration on one's private existence and salvation as to leave no room for concern over anyone else. Indeed, in Kierkegaard's writings "others" simply do not exist as objects of solicitude. There is no community, no society. There is only the soul alone with God.

But if the relation between the individual soul and God be all, then "horizontal" history—the succession of happenings in time—embraces only one true event, the self-revelation of the Eternal. Obviously, however, a history composed of a single and unique episode is not history at all. As for internal or "vertical" history—the soul's confrontation by God—not only is this not history in the usual sense, Kierkegaard, in addition, leaves unresolved whether this is the culmination of a progress in which time is involved or of an instantaneity, a "leap," in which time is not involved. But what manner of history can it be in which the status of time is left questionable? In sum: nothing, or at most next to nothing, remains of history when Kierkegaard is through.

Consistently, therefore, he strikes the study of history from the roster of earnest concerns. Historical research is not only an irrelevance to the quest after salvation: it can be a hindrance, interposing a "century-long parenthesis" into the urgent business of faith. Indeed, it may prove an active peril, a "most dangerous enemy," eventuating as it does in objective knowledge rather than inwardness and passion.

The main point however remains, that history effects nothing toward man's salvation. As Kierkegaard puts it in his *Philosophical Fragments*: "The first and last [generations] are essentially on the same plane. . . . Immediate contemporaneity is merely an occasion. . . . "

FROM all the foregoing, the anti-clericalism and anti-ecclesiasticism of Kierkegaard's last phase, his attacks on institutional Christendom, follow inevitably. That is not an expression of mere unsociability or eccentricity, not even of an ambivalence to the world's esteem which he affected to despise, though all these were factors in the case. Given his points of departure and the direction of his tending, he can arrive at no other terminus. His logic gives him no choice but to reject all churches, regardless of character and denomination. Are they not institutions, externalizations of faith, and so objectivity incarnate? Are they not, further, social entities existing in time, whereas both the social and the temporal are alien to essential religion? So it came to pass that this ardent Christian ended up as Christendom's intransigent critic.

Finally, it should be recorded that when Kierkegaard speaks of the desperateness of man's plight he is indulging in no rhetorical exaggerations. To him the human condition is one of desperation in the most literal denotation of the word. It is, so far as man's own capacities are concerned, simply and starkly hopeless.

For what is it that man can achieve for himself? As all the historic religions have agreed, esthetic gratifications, whether crude or refined, are unlikely to effect tranquility in this world, let alone eternal life in the next. And if one seek his salvation in virtue, what man is there on earth who doeth only good and sinneth not, whose righteousness is sufficient to redemption? What can remain then except to transcend pleasure and the good alike, perhaps even—and here Kierkegaard leaves the main road of religious affirmation—to spurn and repudiate them, and go seeking elsewhere?

Only now does the true desperateness of man's plight become apparent. For his very desire and ability to seek belong not to him but to God. As much as the finding is a gift of divine grace, so much is even the setting out to find. Or, to put it in the figure employed by Kierkegaard himself in his *Philosophical Fragments*: Man is not only "destitute of the Truth up to the very moment of his learning it; he cannot even have possessed it in the form of ignorance . . ."; the teacher, that is, God, "gives the learner not only the Truth but also the condition for understanding it. . . ." Which means that facing the alternatives of eternal salvation and damnation, man is all dependence, all impotence; for what he can do for himself is of no avail, and of what avails he can do nothing. Was ever a plight more "dreadful"?

THE essence of Kierkegaard, then, at least in so far as he constitutes a non-Ego to Judaism's Ego, consists of the five following antinomies, in each of which the first term is affirmed as against the second:

1. Faith *versus* Reason
2. The Religious *versus* the Ethical
3. The Individual *versus* Society
4. The Moment *versus* History
5. Man's Need *versus* his Powers

It is important that these positions be seen for what they are, not the eccentricities of an individual but the expressions—extreme perhaps, and certainly not exclusive, but none the less authentic—of the Christian *Weltanschauung*. Kierkegaard is not properly understood unless he be taken for the Christian he claimed to be. Nor does our discussion center on anything so unequal as a single person *vis à vis* a historic tradition. What concerns us here is nothing less than the timeless dialectical interchange between the Jewish and Christian faiths.

That it should be necessary to argue now what was asserted earlier in this essay—namely, the Christian character of Kierkegaard—is itself astounding. Few authors have been more explicit about their purposes. He was forever declaring and underscoring his Christian intentions and temper. Of his expositors, however, many have simply refused to take him at his word, some because they have come to him with special interests of their own, others because they were not themselves Christians, or else not Christians of his stripe. Whatever the reason, the role of Protestant doctrine and spirit in Kierkegaard has been consistently underestimated.

The fact is that Kierkegaard was a Christian *ab ovo*. He was raised in a devout Lutheran society, steeped in Christian learning, schooled in Reformation theology, attracted as well as repelled by the prospect of becoming a pastor. The issues of Christian faith and practice burned in him, all the more fiercely for the fierce troubled piety of his guilt-ridden father. Under such influences, under the dynamism of his own genius, Christianity became for Kierkegaard in the end—though not without a terrible struggle—the living heart of his thought, the *pathos* and *telos* of his entire existence.

As for the antinomies above listed, there is no accounting for them in terms of the idiosyncratic or capricious, nor as reactions to Hegel nor as responses to Kant or Schelling or Schleiermacher. They can be explained adequately only as Christian affirmations, restatements in individualistic phrases and insights, of the key assertions of Protestant Christendom in its Lutheran version.

That subordination of reason to faith, that denial of one for the sake of the other, what is it except an exultant obeisance to the mysteries of the Christian faith, the Incarnation foremost among them? On this article the less steadfast believer turns apologist or rationalizer. Not Kierkegaard. Recognizing that any attempt to make sense of it is foredoomed to failure, foreseeing that the sole sure result is to strip away its supernatural power, he elects the bolder course. He sets forth faith not only as beyond, but as radically opposed to reason. His repudiation of the intellect turns out, then, neither wanton nor philosophically motivated, but rather a doctrinal necessity.

It is also impelled by another, equally weighty consideration. Within Christianity, within all theisms, there have always been two states of mind as to the nature of the divine essence. One holds it to consist in reason and the rational. To this school the Christian

Platonists and Thomists belong and, in a drastic metamorphosis, the Hegelian idealists also. In the alternative view, God is Will before He is Reason. What He determines, by the very fact that He determines it, becomes the reasonable and the good. In this line stands Duns Scotus, Calvin and Luther. This is the foundation-stone of all those theologies which teach that salvation is of God's election only.

The logic behind this doctrine is clear. On two grounds salvation cannot be by man's merit. First, all men are sinners and, if the dogma of "total depravity" be granted, none is consequentially better than any other. Shall they then be saved by a righteousness no one of them possesses?

Second, were salvation by merit, God would be *bound* to confer it on those who had earned it, in which case God would not be free; which is a palpable absurdity. This is the classic Augustinian-Lutheran-Calvinist argument. Its effect is to present God as arbitrary in His bestowal of grace. He saves whom He pleases, and for no other reason than that He pleases. But if so God is not only intellectually absurd but morally irrational also.

Little wonder that it comes easy to Kierkegaard, who was reared in such conceptions, that indeed he finds it necessary, to make faith the antagonist of reason; for such, in his scheme, it is.

IN his non-moralism, too, Kierkegaard voices an authoritative Christian judgment, one as ancient as the Pauline Epistles.

Having asserted Christ to be the sole medium of salvation, Paul found himself confronted by a dilemma. Obviously, none but the good man should or could be saved. Yet salvation was now a matter not of morality but of faith. But suppose a man had faith but not goodness? The problem was too much for Paul, who ended up by insisting that if the believer were truly a believer he would inevitably be good also. But on the choice between faith and morality, on the issue of what it is on which salvation ultimately depends, Paul was all explicitness. "He who believeth shall be saved; he who disbelieveth shall be condemned."

The "secondarization of the moral" in Kierkegaard, therefore —his "teleological suspension of the ethical," about which such a fuss has been made—that is basically no more than a restatement of a doctrine as old as Paul. Revived by the Reformationists in their rebellion against the "works" of the Catholic Church, it was a conviction imbibed by Kierkegaard with his father's first instruction.

Nor is it otherwise with his near-solipsism. In the Pauline-Protestant tradition the crucial tension is always between the individual and God, to which relation other persons and the community are irrelevant. This conception of primitive Christendom, interrupted for centuries by the Catholic Church with its communalizing of the anchorite and its theologizing of society, was revived in an extreme form by Luther. That was indeed, so far as practical consequences went, one of the major differences between the German and Swiss Reformationists: the former yielded up politics and economics to the secular powers and so arrived, by simple subtraction, to a religious life centered on the private soul. Eventually, in the nineteenth century, Lutheranism turned from Luther's precedent toward Calvin's. Some of its communicants evolved a "social gospel." Revealingly enough, to achieve this they had to reach beyond Luther, beyond Paul, beyond even Jesus, to the Hebrew Prophets for sanction and content. But though in the end a rebellion arose against the non-sociality of the Lutheran way, it came after Kierkegaard's time and too late to affect him.

To confirm the already marked individualism of the Reformation religion went its doctrine of the Church. Under the Catholic dispensation the Church was conceived as indispensable to the soul, there being no salvation outside it and the dogmas and sacraments it administered. Religion then, even though it might seek the salvation of the individual, was necessarily social in its expression. With the Reformation, however, that theory was displaced by a congregational conception whereunder redemption became a transaction between each individual man and God. It was Christ directly, immediately, who was the mediator. As for the Church, its proper function was now to serve, before the saving moment, as a guide in its direction; and, after, as an assembly of the Elect in the eyes of men. But since even this limited role could be construed as an invasion by a human institution into the redemptive prerogatives of the Christ, among some Protestant sects the Church was whittled down further until it all but ceased to exist.

Thus, when Kierkegaard ended up an anti-ecclesiast, he was doing no more than traveling the same road to the same goal which other tangential Protestant groups had arrived before him.

IN the case of his next antinomy—the Moment *versus* History—its traditional Christian derivation, while less obvious than with the others, is nevertheless not difficult to trace. The prevailing Christian tradition has always been strongly historicist. How could it be otherwise with a faith which reaches its apogee in an event regarded as the fulfillment of the ages, and expects an even higher climax in a second event at the end of days? The Augustinian schematization of history as an interplay through the centuries between the City of God and the City of Man—Apocalypse, Millenarianism, Eschatology—these are all expressions of the deep Christian preoccupation with time. But against that there is another, a narrower yet no less authentic stream of Christian thought, which flows not downward through the succession of incidents but circularly about one, which considers as consequential not time and its episodes but a single Moment only, that of the Cross. These were the waters of Kierkegaard's baptism.

As for the texture of man's temperament, as Kierkegaard described it, dread is the warp, powerlessness the woof. A dark fabric to begin with, it is rendered darker still when interwoven with such threads of Christian dogma as Original Sin and *sola gratia*. Under these doctrines man, born in corruption and predestined to damnation, is altogether without the power to save himself. Which is the meaning of the anti-Pelagianism of the Catholic Church, and of the anti-Arminianism of the Protestant. Under the former, Christendom rejected as heresy the suggestion that man can achieve anything toward his salvation outside the Church. Under the latter, he is conceived as standing in even a more parlous pass, first because he is now adjudged a creature of total depravity, without a single merit, and second because not even the Church can aid him. Only God can save; and, since man is deserving of naught, God can save only as an act of pure grace.

This is original Protestantism. Witness the repudiation by the Protestant world of Melanchthon's proposal of Synergism: the thesis that man may cooperate with God in his own deliverance. This is the teaching of the neo-Reformation school in our own time. Witness Barth's insistence that man, the drowning swimmer, is incapable of even a single feeble stroke to keep afloat; that the rescue is to the last effort God's.

Here, then, is the root of Kierkegaard's despair as to man's capacities. It is a despair deriving in part from the precariousness of the human situation, but even more from the inability of the individual to do anything about it—a despair, in a word, which, like the rest of the antinomies, comes to him from the Lutheranism of his rearing.

NOW historic Judaism and historic Christianity, being kindred religions, share all sorts of presuppositions. The fact that a thesis is Christian does not exclude it from the possibility of being Jewish. The probabilities, in fact, are quite the reverse. Yet the distinctive points of Kierkegaard's position, those caught in the antinomies, are one and all, non-Jewish; indeed, so far as they go, they are the crucial issues at stake between catholic Judaism and universal Christianity. But in varying degrees.

Least clearly definable is the position of Judaism on the first of the five antinomies, that between faith and reason. Of conflicts on the philosophy-*versus*-religion or science-*versus*-religion level Jewish thought has its quota. Such is the purport of the first chapter of Saadyah's *Emunoth v'Deoth* and of the entire Maimunist controversy. Like other men professing a revealed religion, Jews have debated whether speculative inquiry is necessary or permissible and, if so, what may be the status of its conclusions *vis à vis* religious verities. But the possibility that faith and reason should be ideally exclusive of each other has little troubled traditionally minded Jewish thinkers.

They neglected to consider that possibility for one simple reason: they had no reason to. Paradox may inhere in all religious affirmation; but where Christianity must glory in it, Judaism need not. Its central position is neither "absurd" nor an "affront" to reason. It is involved in no mysteries like that of the Trinity-Unity, of which one has no choice but to say *credo quia absurdum est* ("I believe because it is absurd"). It sets forth no Gods who are yet mortals. It does not rest on the premise that the death of one man can atone for the sins of other men. All these are notions truly impenetrable to reason. Against them Jewish theology is purely of God, an object of faith to be sure, but by no means of faith against reason; of revelation, miraculous of course, but scarcely a scandal to rationality; of the election of Israel and human redeemability by moral effort, positions complex and difficult enough, and undemonstrable to boot; but, in every case, compared to Christian dogma, comprehensibility itself. As is attested by the fact that "natural religion" approaches many of these basic Jewish positions.

Historic Judaism does include some elements totally impenetrable to the intellect; such a tenet, for example, as Resurrection; such a ritual as the *Parah Adumah* (the red heifer, Numbers XIX). But even with these, neither virtue nor principle is made of obscurity or mystery. To the contrary, the prevailing effort has always been to rationalize.

Not that such efforts were regarded with universal favor. Some of the ancient rabbis objected to inquiring into the *taame ha-mitzvoth,* the purpose of the commandments. The anti-Maimunists sought to ban all philosophical inquiry. But these rabbis, whether ancient or the medieval, were motivated by a kind of anti-rationalism worlds apart from Kierkegaard's. Their objection to speculation was pragmatic: that with revelation available it is superfluous; or, by its stubborn questioning, disturbing to faith; or, given human limitations, foredoomed to failure. No Jewish thinker is on record as advancing Kierkegaard's contention of the radical incompatibility of religious truth and reason. To the contrary, the common Jewish assumption has always been that the two for God are one, as they would be one for man were his powers of comprehension equal to the theme.

NOR is the Jewish conception of God at all conducive to anti-intellectualism along the lines of the Lutheran-Calvinist.

Kierkegaard, we have already seen, was predisposed to such

a conclusion by, among other things, the notion of a God who is Will rather than Reason. Admittedly, the Jewish tradition shows traces of a similar position on the part of some Jewish thinkers: such a characterization of God as in Exodus XXXIII, 19: "I will be gracious to whom I will be gracious, and will show mercy on whom I will show mercy"; such ideas as the *En-Sof* of Kabbalism, whereunder God is pure Being before He unfolds moral or intellectual qualities. Notions of this sort, however, are the exception.

The prime distinction among God's attributes drawn in rabbinic literature is between His justice and His mercy. Medieval Jewish philosophers as a rule demonstrate first the existence of God and then His other attributes, intellectual and moral. That is a matter of forensics almost altogether. The fact is that those thinkers agree one and all, whatever their argumentative procedures, that God is simultaneously and co-essentially existent, moral and free; that, in sum, whatever He is or does or ordains, all makes equal intellectual and moral sense.

From the Jewish viewpoint, God remains beyond man's reason, perhaps beyond all reason. He cannot be counter to it, rationality pertaining to His nature.

Kierkegaard's anti-rationalism is thus altogether a Christian, more exactly a Lutheran-Calvinist, but not in the slightest degree a Jewish, necessity. Nor does anything in Judaism correspond to Kierkegaard's teleological suspension of the ethical.

From the Jewish viewpoint—and this is one of its highest dignities—the ethical is never suspended, not under any circumstance and not for anyone, not even for God. *Especially not for God!* Are not supreme Reality and supreme Goodness one and co-essential to the Divine nature? If so, every act wherein the Good is put aside is more than a breach of His will; it is in effect a denial of His existence. Wherefore the rabbis define sin as constituting not merely rebellion but atheism as well.

What Kierkegaard asserts to be the glory of God is Jewishly regarded as unmitigated sacrilege. Which indeed is the true point of the *Akedah*, missed so perversely by Kierkegaard. While it was a merit in Abraham to be willing to sacrifice his only son to his God, it was God's nature and merit that He would not accept an immoral tribute. And it was His purpose, among other things, to establish that truth.

In sum, the secondary antinomy of Kierkegaard turns out, like the first, alien to Judaism.

SO equally with the third, disjoining the individual from others and society.

In the Jewish view, as Buber has demonstrated, it is a false exclusion of which Kierkegaard has here been guilty. The fulfilled human life requires, in both theory and fact, the simultaneous affirmation and sanctification of both the self and the community. "If I be not for myself," asked Hillel, "who will be for me? But if I be for myself alone, what am I?" Each man, the tradition insists, must seek the redemption of his own soul; but at the same time the "perfecting of the world under the Kingdom of the Almighty."

In his fourth antinomy, the negation of history, Kierkegaard, as we have observed, is out of harmony with the dominant Christian tradition itself. As to Judaism, the discrepancy is total. Contemplating a Creation and Revelation in the past and a Resurrection and Kingdom of God in the future, the Jewish tradition is historical throughout. This is not to say that it is "historicist." Judaism does not hold that mere time regenerates men, or history by itself redeems society. Only the decisions of the human spirit are determinative—of the individual to his own salvation, of all men to the achievement of the Kingdom; and neither, of course, ever without God. Yet time and history, like the air men breathe and the space in which they move, are the necessary preconditions for the working out of their destiny.

They are not merely inert, environmental media. They are living, even if not crucial factors, both in the career of the soul (here Kierkegaard might assent) and in that of society (here he would disagree altogether). Indeed, no sharper contrast than on this score can be found between Judaism and Christianity in its Kierkegaardian version. On the latter side is the insistence that "the history of the race" is a merely "quantitative accumulation," that is, a meaningless piling up of more and more of the same thing. On the other hand we have such teachings as Isaiah's "end of days," the rabbinic "future to come" and the "merits of the fathers," and the Kabbalist schema whereunder each soul that lives hastens or retards, by the tempo of its return to its Primal Source, the descent and ascent of the last soul, the Messiah's.

Poles apart on whether the Moment is all, Judaism and Kierkegaard are if possible even further apart on the fifth antinomy—the issue of man's own ability to do anything of consequence towards the alleviation of his plight. The plight is one of anguished intensity, Judaism agrees. But that the human condition is beyond hope Judaism denies, with fourfold warrant.

In the first place Judaism does not, like Kierkegaard, set up a disjuncture between the esthetic and ethical, and again between the two of them together and the religious. Nor is this a matter of theoretical import only. Kierkegaard is thereby impelled to regard all pleasures, whether sensual or esthetic, as at best spiritually indifferent, more likely deleterious; all principled morality as at the most a preparation for something else, rather than as anything in itself; all scientific and speculative thought as a diversion from the religious encounter. Once so much that contributes to the joy and meaning of life has been depreciated or rejected—in any case, ruled out as a field of God's service—little wonder that the human prospect comes to appear inordinately limited and bleak.

Judaism takes a stand of clear opposition to all that. It maintains that God can be encountered, and accordingly salvation can be furthered, in anything man feels and does, so long as it is felt and done "in holiness," that is, in obedience to God's will.

With its pleasures and activities legitimized, its opportunities for service of the divine multiplied times beyond number, life very naturally takes on another, a brighter guise. If the evil in it is still as grave as in the Kierkegaardian view, its good is larger, more variegated, more readily accessible.

Secondly, where Kierkegaard can discern but one hope for man, the deliverance of his soul, Judaism espies another also, the regeneration of society. This is no little thing, this goal of the Kingdom. It throws a second light and warmth on all human existence.

Third and fourth, Judaism has greater confidence than has Kierkegaard in God and in man.

THIS is the Deity which Kierkegaard, after the pattern of Paul and the Reformationists, depicts: a God who first made men imperfect and then demands sinlessness from them—wherefore he took on flesh and died as an atonement for them—who offers them deliverance but on the condition that they believe, a capacity however which lies not in their power but in His to give or withhold. The greatest thing of all, Salvation, is altogether by Grace, since no man has the least shred of righteousness to plead for him. Does not this account of God's administration of His world make Him out as questionably just, incontrovertibly unmerciful?

Judaism's appraisal of man's powers is far more generous. They are not unlimited, to be sure; they are often severely circumscribed, as we too well know. But always, the Jewish tradition insists, there is some margin of self-determination. Always a man can do something, no matter how little, with his own soul. And that something may suffice to transform him into a *b'riah hadashah,* a new regenerated creature. If nothing else, a man can do *teshuvah,* he can repent—repent of the evil which heretofore he has loved and affirm the good which up to now he has scorned. By that the whole import of his life may be remade. He may even thereby, and thereby alone, come to merit salvation, according to the rabbinic teaching concerning those who "acquire Eternity in one moment."

How can this be? First because man is a free agent. Everything may be pre-ordained for him, said the sages of old, but not whether he will be righteous. That crucial issue is left to his own decision. It is a determination which not God Himself will coerce. A man's failure to attain perfection is no insuperable obstacle to his vindication. For, being just, God asks but does not exact perfection from one whom He made frail and fallible. "He remembers that we are dust." Not impeccability is required of man, but earnestness of striving toward it. "Not thine to finish the work, but neither art thou free to quit it."

Then is man not in need of God's grace? Of course; all the time and in everything. But that grace is not to be supposed as only exceptional and crucial, as it were, a lightning flash of redemptive mercy breaking unpredictably into and through normality. There is that grace described in the *Siddur* as the "miracles which are daily with us, the wonders and goodnesses which are at all times, evening, morn and noon." This is the grace manifest in the Torah's guidance and in "the merits of the fathers," the examples and admonitions of the righteous, in the *yezer tov* (good instinct), conscience and aspiration toward the good, and, above all, in the uninterrupted magnetic pull of God. It is a grace always at work, ever available, never failing. All a man need do to have it is to call for it in truth. Even as it is said: "he who setteth out to be purified, from heaven do they help him."

This is the supreme and ultimate reason why Judaism, conscious with Kierkegaard of the human ordeal and peril, does not yield to his despair. It knows that man is stronger, and God is greater in justice and mercy, than he allowed.

ANALOGIES in history are never exact. Yet in many respects Existentialism of the Kierkegaardian stripe is to Judaism in our day what Gnosticism was at the beginning of the Common Era—an alluring but dangerous heresy. There were virtues in that doctrine as in this: inwardness, mystical sensibility, a passion and groping for truths but coldly or imperfectly comprehended by conventional religion, a returning to the primary experiences from which all formal faith stems, and a penetrating feeling for the dilemmas and torments of human existence.

But there were grave failings also. Gnosticism, like Existentialism, abandoned natural reason, the one for esotericism, the other for faith. Like the latter the former also suspended and secondarized and so, in the end, perverted moral values; abandoned the group in its concern for the self; considered only the saving moment but not history, personal salvation but not the Kingdom of God; and, out of despair, surrendered the world to the demiurge, looking for salvation in flight.

To one doctrine as to the other the proper Jewish response is that of Rabbi Meir when he said, concerning the teachings of his heretic master Elisha ben Abuyah, "As with a pomegranate, one eats the seed and throws the rind away."

THE IDEA OF HUMANITY IN JUDAISM

by
KURT WILHELM

14

The Idea of Humanity in Judaism*

KURT WILHELM

[I]

The unity of the human race is a doctrine of Judaism. The Bible opens with a sole God, creator of Adam, Man, the father of all men; and the God of Israel is not only God of humanity, but God for humanity, what may be termed 'monanthropy' being the logical consequence of monotheism.[1] For even though the notion of Adam's having been created as a single individual is cardinal to all Jewish thinking about humanity, yet more decisive still is the circumstance of his having been created by a uniquely sole God. The Babylonian epic of creation likewise knows of a solitary man as the source of all his kind: but its gods are a plurality. It is the unity of God which points inexorably towards the unity of man, and *vice versa*. In his posthumous work *Religion der Vernunft aus den Quellen des Judentums*,[2] Hermann Cohen represents this conditioned reciprocity by the term *Korrelation* or correspondence (*Entsprechung*); the concept by means of which the co-relativity of God and man realises itself being the concept of moral discernment – a quality common to both parties. The correlation is, moreover, absolutely reciprocal, so that man, in virtue of his God-given perceptivity, is not merely the creature but the discoverer of God. It necessarily follows that God is one if, and only if mankind is one; or in other words, that the completion of that correlation falls within the Utopia of Judaism's messianic future. 'And the Lord shall be king over all the earth; in that day shall God be one, and His name one.'[3] In Cohen's own words, the divine Name is equivalent in meaning to the divine kingdom.[4]

The doctrine that the unity of mankind will find its completion in a messianic age yet to come has produced, within Jewish speculative theology of the last hundred years, a belief in progress – a belief to which other movements of social and political philosophy as well as the religious liberalism of western Europe and America have also come to subscribe. The final significance of Judaism would then lie in its sense of development from Peculiar People to Mankind, from the sum total of all individuals to the revelation of true Humanity within the messianic union of all men. The Bible purports to describe – or rather to anticipate – this historical process, in which a personal God at the final stage of a long development chooses for Himself humanity as a whole: and it hints that this development corresponds to the spiritual and moral nature of man himself. But within the doctrine of the moral progress of humanity there is to be found a wide range of tones.

In his *Wesen des Judentums* – not, strictly speaking, a theologically orientated book – Leo Baeck did not fall for this kind of formal ethical monotheism. More than any of the theologians who were his contemporaries, Baeck traced out the paradoxes in the religious ideas and institutions of Judaism, and remained on his guard against the making of messianism into an abstract ideal in which the unity of humanity should be achieved. In any theological formulation of a Jewish belief in progress the concept of the Messiah becomes distorted: for Jewish messianism is something more than a mere symbol for a belief in the moral progress of humanity. To quote Max Wiener, who is one of the few modern liberal theologians to pose the whole problem correctly, the hall-mark of traditional Jewish messianism is 'miracle in its most stupendous proportions – the transcendental intervention of a living, personal God in the fate of man.'[5] Like creation, messianism is unique in its wondrous quality; whereas the extensive speculations of the rabbis concerning the coming of the Messiah have little to say on the subject of the moral development of mankind. On the contrary: the so-called 'footsteps of the Messiah' – the days that will precede his arrival – are to be distinguished by a godlessness and a negation of morality that will form, so to speak, the shadows heralding the appearance of the Redeemer. A whole series of speculations regarding these fateful forerunners is to be found in the Talmud, for example the following[6]: 'With the footprints of the Messiah presumption shall increase and dearth shall reach its height . . . the empire shall fall into heresy and there shall be none to utter reproof. The council-chamber shall be given to fornication. . . . The face of this generation is as the face of a dog, and the son will not be put to shame by his father. On whom can we stay ourselves? On our Father in heaven.' In talmudic Judaism the messianic epoch stands in connection with the so-called 'weeks', i.e. *aeons* into which world history is divided, itself constituting the climax of them. Even though the 'weeks' originally ordained to precede the messianic period have now all elapsed, the Messiah has nevertheless not yet appeared: his coming will materialise when Israel merits the messianic age, or else in God's own good time. The actual date of his coming is one of the seven things that remains concealed from all.[7] Eschatological speculation is unanimous to the effect that at the onset of the messianic kingdom God will bring about a visible miracle analogous to the miracles associated with creation and revelation. Jewish excitement concerning the miraculous aspect of messianic redemption may be descried in the fever of anticipation that has invariably gripped Jewry on the occasion of each successive pseudo-messianic phenomenon. The days of the Messiah signify the rendering visible, in an experience of overwhelming emotional intensity, of God's own very Act – or, in the words of a familiar messianic prayer, 'in His loving-kindness He will yet again cause us to hear, before the eyes of all that live, [His promise] "to be to you for a God".'[8]

Nevertheless, traditional Jewish expectation of the Messiah's coming has the following in common with modern Jewish messianic notions, *viz.* that it is here, on earth, that the divinely intended messianic kingdom of the future will find its implementation. The time of the messianic *eschata* is historical time, and the kingdom *is* of this world. Furthermore – and this appears to be of fundamental importance for the presentation of the concept of humanity in Judaism – it is God's purpose to unify the whole of mankind in the messianic period into a single community that is morally one. The messianic kingdom is the kingdom of justice and of moral order. And yet, together with this aspect of messianic expectation, belief in the special position of the people of Israel never disappears. Israel's redemption coincides with the redemption of mankind – or rather, it introduces it alongside itself. On the other hand modern Jewish theology, in representing Judaism as the simplest and most direct method of implementing moral good with the messianic concept as its guarantor, makes use of traditional Jewish messianism as a foundation for a universal ethical creed of mankind – a Judaism set free from religious law.

The contradiction has often been sensed, and the attempt made to overcome it by representing Judaism as a world-religion in tension, between universalism and particularism or universalism and nationalism; it being claimed that in times of persecution or oppression it is particularism that has been the centre of interest, and universalism in times of external freedom. Precisely so, the Jewish concept of election is alleged to have both its particularistic and its universalistic traits, Israel's own domestic election falling in the here and now and the election of humanity at the end of days. Universalism and particularism are, however, inextricably interwoven in Judaism, and it is in the perpetual interpenetration of national and universal religious elements that Judaism itself both consists, and asserts its own specific God-idea, *viz.* that the God of Israel is the God of all humanity.

These preliminary remarks are necessary, in order that the concept of humanity in Judaism may be represented without resort to apologetics. Meagre are the attempts that have been made to prepare the way for a statement of the concept of humanity in Judaism, if we are to disregard (as, for reasons already stated, we have to) Jewish theological writing of the last hundred years. We may limit ourselves to reference to the outline by Max Wiener, who was a rabbi and lecturer at the Berlin Hochschule für die Wissenschaft des Judentums, entitled *Aufriss einer jüdischen Theologie*.[9] As his starting-point for an appreciation of the Jewish concept of humanity Wiener no longer postulated a polarity between universalism and particularism; for him it is '*people* and *history* [that] are the two poles between which the particular life of our religion moves.' God is, from the outset, the God of history, who creates the world as the stage on which the human drama is to be played out. Human events can be individual or ethnic ones. In Christianity, as already in Stoicism and the thought of late antiquity in general, history is a process that moves from individual to humanity, whilst in Judaism history predominantly means happenings as between one people and another and as between God's people and the community of peoples. The peoplehood of Israel is consequently an indispensable component of the religion of Israel; and this is the reason for the election of Israel *qua* people. The chosen people is Israel because of considerations that are neither racial nor statistical, but because it occupies a special position *vis-à-vis* the God of history. It has chosen the God who chose it for Himself.

[II]

To assert that the early chapters of *Genesis* had, right from their earliest beginnings, the unity of mankind in view might be regarded as a debatable claim. The narratives of the creation of the world and of the first human pair, if taken in themselves, evince rather a cosmological and anthropological interest, into the fabric of which a religious concern has been woven.[10] Be that as it may, these chapters have been not merely inserted into the Bible, but rather stand as a preface to *Genesis* as being documents of Israel's pre-history, and form with it a self-contained unity: and this circumstance lifts the biblical history of man's creation on to the ethical plane, providing Judaism with a *locus classicus* for the idea of the unity of the human race. Deutero-Isaiah, too, recognises that the chronological process of the time-span of human history begins in the very moment of the transcendent act of creation effected by the God of the cosmos, 'calling the generations from the beginning it is I, the Lord, who am first, and with the last I am the same as I ever was.'[11] The idea of humanity orientated on the future is here indicated as being implicit in the story of the creation of one single man in the beginning.

The doctrine of the unity of mankind runs through the whole of *Genesis*. After the flood, it is Noah who stands for the whole human race as Adam had done in the creation narrative. Jewish tradition finds in the covenant contracted with Noah by God the basis of its conviction of man's perpetual continuance, which no flood will ever again come to annihilate. Noah thus becomes the guarantor of mankind; in place of the biblical description of which as 'children of Adam', rabbinic Hebrew prefers to speak of 'children of Noah' when it is referring to humanity as a moral entity. The so-called Seven Commandments of the sons of Noah[12] constitute a formula whereby recognition becomes possible of a wider humanity, into relations with which of a moral and lawful kind Jewry can enter without requiring of its environment any avowal of Judaism. The 'seven commandments' are, of course, but an artificial postulate which, as affording a minimum programme of human morality, are subsumed in what is binding upon the Jew himself, just as if the seven had once been 'revealed' to the whole non-Jewish (or rather, pre-Jewish) world. But it is specifically as precepts incumbent upon mankind in general that they could provide the basis of a moral order affecting all: and that is why the first of the seven is deemed to be the obligation to administer justice.[13] The Noachides' dispensation belongs to the pre-history of revelation in Judaism, but those still subject to it are reckoned nonetheless amongst 'the righteous of the Gentiles'. Maimonides (1135–1204) writes as follows in his great codification of the religious law of Judaism: 'Whosoever [of the Gentiles] acknowledges the Seven Commandments and is circumspect in fulfilling them is one of the pious ones of the Gentiles and has a portion in the world to come, provided always that such acknowledgement is on grounds of their divine origin and revelational transmission.'[14] In Dante's *Divine Comedy* the unbaptised, together with many of the philosophers and poets of classical antiquity, find themselves in the uppermost region of Inferno, albeit immune from the torments of Hell. In the Hebrew imitation of Dante by Immanuel of Rome, poet and exegete (1265–1330), entitled *Hell and Paradise* (*Hat-topheth we-ha-'edhen*), in Paradise the Jew meets the righteous of the Gentiles: 'and it came to pass, as we were strolling along Eden's ways, observing the eminence of men distinguished by reason of their wisdom. . . . And forasmuch as I knew not one of them, I asked my guide about them: he said unto me, "these be the righteous of the peoples of the earth, every one of them a hero by reason of his wisdom and understanding".'[15]

W. Eichrodt[16] observes that the genealogical table of *Gen.* 10 is without parallel in the literature of the ancient Orient; and in this chapter Israel's concept of humanity again finds expression. By its inclusion of this genealogical tree the Bible renders racialism as a basis of political theory untenable, since the table knows of no people that was not worthy of being embraced within a definition of mankind. Greek concepts of humanity did not acknowledge the notion of mankind implicit in this table of *Genesis* – for Aristotle there are Hellenes and barbarians, those born to be masters and those born to be slaves. It is from the genealogy of *Genesis* that there derives the rabbinic idea of the 'Seventy Nations of the world' as comprising between them all mankind, and the parallel concept of the 'Seventy Tongues' – notwithstanding sundry difficulties of arithmetical equation with the text of *Gen.* 10 as it has come down to us. The number 70 – itself the symbol of completeness – has been laid under contribution by religious thinking on the subject of the inherent unity of mankind as running through the multiplicity of nations. And indeed the Pentateuch does not regard their sum of seventy as being a mere coincidence. In Moses' valedictory song – at any rate in the Hebrew text authenticated by the Massoretes[17] – we read 'When the Most High divided to the nations their inheritance, when he separated the sons of Adam, he set the bounds of the peoples *according to the number of the children of Israel.*' The traditional number of the issue of Jacob-Israel was 70, and the allusion in the song to the genealogy of the peoples is obvious enough: the sum of the peoples, themselves each the issue of its own founding father, corresponds to the number of the issue of Israel's own eponymous ancestor. Moreover, *Genesis* places the peoples of the world into a position of responsibility for themselves *vis-à-vis* God like that occupied by Israel, the key word being in each case the *covenant* – *berith*: a term more decisive than any other with regard to Israel's relationship with God.[18] The first of the post-diluvians (apart from Noah himself and his immediate progeny)[19] with whom God contracted a covenant – a covenant that had in mind an as yet non-existent people of Israel – was Abraham. His own story, and consequently the history of Israel itself, begins with the divine summons to leave his own country and his father's house, to launch out into the unknown where God will contract an everlasting covenant with him. The call to face something new, the full implications of which he could not know, concludes with the words[20] 'and in thee shall all the families of the earth be blessed'. It is in virtue of his being the ancestor of Israel that Abraham's connection with the entire human race is effected.

The biblical notion of humanity avoided the danger to which the universalism of post-classical civilisation succumbed: it did not lose itself in a facile cosmopolitanism. Stoic notions of mankind recognise nought but individual and world-polity, with no middle term between individuality and totality.[21] *Per contra*, Judaism's Utopia of a mankind united at the end of days by an acknowledgement of the one sole God consists of a world-wide fellowship of peoples:

> And it shall come to pass in the last days that the mountain of the Lord's house shall be established so as to be at the top of the mountains, and shall be exalted above the hills; and all nations shall flow to it. And the peoples in great numbers shall go and say, Come ye, and let us go up to the mountain of the

> Lord, to the house of the God of Jacob, that he may teach us of His ways, and that we may walk in His paths: for it is from Zion that shall go forth Torah, and the word of the Lord from Jerusalem. And he shall judge between the nations, and shall adjust all differences between the peoples in their crowds: and they shall beat their swords into ploughshares, and their spears into pruning-hooks: nation shall not lift up sword against nation, neither shall they learn war any more.[22]

Thus can Isaiah, the contemporary of kings whose faithlessness evoked disillusionment after disillusionment, portray the future of mankind. The prophecy is again taken up, but with slight alterations, in the collection of Micah's prophetic utterances.[23] The temple mount at Jerusalem is the stage towards which the peoples stream in order to find, at God's mountain, their own unification. At present, the temple hill stands lower than the Mount of Olives and the other hills that surround it. The end of days will bring with it the miraculous transfiguration of the physical landscape of the spot where the peoples are destined to meet. Since they will then recognise the one God alone, all barriers that now separate the peoples will fall. As ethnic entities they continue, indeed, to exist; but their contests bring them all alike before the one Lord and Judge for settlement. They will therefore have no need any longer to resolve their disputes by force of arms, and will consequently not learn war any more. In the Holy City there will hold sway a judge of right on whom there will 'rest the breath of God's spirit, the spirit of wisdom and discernment, the spirit of counsel and heroic courage, the spirit of knowledge and fear of the Lord; and it shall be the fear of the Lord that shall inspire him.'[24]

It is the circumstance that through him there breathes the spirit of God that serves to characterise the ideal lord and judge of all. Quite typically, the Messiah is not priest, but judge or king; and as such, he is no less and no more like to God than is any other man. Precisely because Jewish eschatological notions of a united humanity do not reveal a vista of some crowning achievement to consummate the higher development of religious thinking, but signify rather the concrete realisation of the rule of God on earth and in every single department of life, the Messiah's governance of Israel and the nations which comprise the world is a political governance in the fullest sense.[25] The messianic age is one in which the peace of God embraces creation as a whole, the very wild beasts being transformed and changing their relationships towards each other and towards man.[26] A whole series of prophets proclaimed that the ideals implicit in the concept of humanity would find their practical implementation in an international peace founded upon justice; and in the Babylonian exile the second Isaiah was to draw the logical conclusion to the thinking of his great predecessors. It is that the historic charge of leading a unified mankind on to the stage devolves upon Israel. Israel's own redemption is bound up with that of the nations, and *vice versa*. Israel is summoned, from a state of being God's people, to become a 'covenant of the peoples' (*berith 'am*) – a people standing as intermediary between God and the human kind. 'I, the Lord, call thee by way of confirming something as right and do grasp thee by the hand, and will keep thee and assign thee as a people's covenant, as a light for the national families of the world: to lighten the eyes that are blind, to bring out the prisoners from the dungeon, from the prison-house them that sit in darkness.'[27] Such is the role for which Deutero-Isaiah casts his own people while it is itself confined in the prison-house of exile. The comforting of Israel is tied to the comforting of mankind, or rather, as Martin Buber has put it, the redemption of Israel and that of the gentile peoples are but different stages of one single redemptive act that concerns the whole world of man.[28]

Rabbinic Judaism sees in the messianic age the great contrast to the epoch in which, following the Tower of Babel, mankind has fallen apart into the seventy nations. It is the Evil Inclination which, in this world, has divided the peoples into seventy: but in the world to come they will find themselves unanimous in the service of God alone. It is in this connection that *Zeph.* 3: 9 is quoted[29] – 'For then will I change the peoples to a pure language, so that they will all call upon the name of the Lord, to serve Him with a united shoulder.' The 'clear lip' or pure language is the image, in prophetical and midrashic literature alike, for purity of heart and thought; and pure speech here means the mutual understanding of the peoples. But implicit in the thinking here there is also the idea of a linguistic idiom that bonds the peoples into one; and it is no coincidence that the rabbis connect the verse with the story in *Gen.* 11 of the confusion of tongues. The original language of humanity – according to rabbinic notions Hebrew, the speech of Eber (*Gen.* 10: 21) – will in messianic times take the place, as a universal language, of the present seventy. In rabbinic literature there is to be found a rich store of imagery regarding the messianic age, from the overcoming of war to the overcoming of death; and in it thinking about the unification of humanity revolves normally round the role therein that will fall to Israel. This may conceivably be but a passive role, and as such it was formulated by Mar Samuel (*c.* 180–253 C.E.), the most important talmudic scholar of his time, when he declared that 'the only difference between this world and the days of the Messiah is enslavement to the world powers'[30]; i.e., in the messianic age Israel will no longer be subjected by the world-kingdoms to slavery. Maimonides took up this dictum into his code of halakhic Judaism,[31] and states expressly that no alteration in the laws of nature will mark the messianic age, nor any renovation of the act by which the world was created; the world will pursue its normal course. Nevertheless, 'at that time there will be neither hunger, jealousy, nor competitiveness, since good things will be available in prodigious amplitude, luxuries being as common as dust, and the whole world will be engaged in no other pursuit than that of knowing the Lord alone.'[32] Thus the great canonist of Jewish law: But the *'Aggadha* can find scope for the elaboration of a fantastic imagery of the end of days and of a mankind united in them. It may suffice to refer to the vision conjured up for it by *Isa.* 60, *Arise, shine, for thy light is come.*[33] A great light will burst over Jerusalem to attract the Gentiles by its powerful brilliance. On the basis of a decision all their own, they move towards it in streams – mankind coming to the light, and not the light to mankind. Jerusalem will be the metropolis of all humanity; but the idea that the Gentiles will then find it possible to profess Judaism plays no crucial part in this picture.

It is towards a redeemed tomorrow that all our unredeemed todays must orientate themselves. The ideas of redemption and yearning for Utopia consequently form an important theme of the Jewish liturgy, particularly on the days of exalted solemnity, *viz.* the New Year festival and the Day of Atonement. The special prayers for these occasions are distinguished by petitions regarding the Kingdom – that is, the kingdom of the Messiah, scion of David, which is at once the Kingdom of God ruling over a united humanity:

> Now therefore, O Lord our God, impose Thine awe upon all Thy works, and Thy dread upon all that Thou hast created, that all works may fear Thee and all creatures prostrate themselves before Thee, that they may all form a single band to do Thy will with a perfect heart, even as we know, O Lord our God, that dominion is Thine, strength is in Thy hand, and might in Thy right hand, and that Thy name is to be feared above all that Thou hast created.
>
> Give then glory, O Lord, unto Thy people, praise to them that fear Thee, hope to them that seek Thee, and free speech to them that wait for Thee, joy to Thy land, gladness to Thy city, a flourishing horn unto David Thy servant, and a clear shining light unto the son of Jesse, Thine anointed, speedily in our days.
>
> Then shall the just also see and be glad, and the upright shall exult, and the pious triumphantly rejoice, while iniquity shall close her mouth, and all wickedness shall be wholly consumed like smoke, when Thou makest the dominion of arrogance to pass away from the earth.
>
> And Thou, O Lord, shalt reign, Thou alone over all Thy works on Mount Zion, the dwelling place of Thy glory, and in Jerusalem, Thy holy city, as it is written in Thy holy words, 'The Lord shall reign for ever, Thy God, O Zion, unto all generations. Praise ye the Lord.'[34]

The foregoing prayer originates from the early talmudic period. Like other prayers that have the Kingdom of God as their main concern, it is characterised by the universal hope that the peoples of the world may bind themselves into a community of mankind in order to acknowledge none but God. No man, no people is excluded from God's Kingdom, which knows neither national nor geographical boundaries: the one condition is that the peoples should renounce their false gods and ascribe honour to God alone.[35] A somewhat later variation on this same theme of prayer forms the latter part of the introduction to the so-called *Malkiyyoth*, or prayers for the inauguration of the divine Kingdom ('Our God and the God of our fathers, do Thou reign in Thy glory over the whole universe . . .'),[36] in the Additional Service for the New Year Festival, whence it has been taken over in the majority of liturgical rights for daily use as a closing prayer:

> We therefore hope in Thee, O Lord our God, that we may speedily behold the glory of Thy might, when Thou wilt remove the abominations from the earth, and the idols will be utterly cut off, when the world will be perfected under the Kingdom of the Almighty, and all the children of flesh will call upon Thy name, when Thou wilt turn unto Thyself all the wicked of the earth. Let all the inhabitants of the world perceive and know that unto Thee every knee must bow, every tongue must swear. Before Thee, O Lord our God, let them bow and fall; and unto Thy glorious name let them give honour; let them all accept the yoke of Thy Kingdom, and do Thou reign over them speedily, and for ever and ever. For the Kingdom is Thine, and to all eternity Thou wilt reign in glory; as it is written in Thy Law, 'The Lord shall reign for ever and ever'. And it is said, 'in that day shall the Lord be One, and His name One'.[37]

It is with this citation from *Zechariah* which, as stated above (pp. 289 f.), is of major importance for Hermann Cohen's theory of Correspondence (*Korrelation*) and its complete implementation in the utopian thinking of Judaism, that the Jewish divine office draws to a close.

[III]

Mankind united at the end of days is a Utopia; but Judaism has been able to develop the Utopia of a *Humanitas* precisely because it has also made its own certain definite notions, not conceived of utopianism, regarding the *Societas* from which the true oneness of mankind inevitably follows. It is only the essential principles of a Jewish social theory that will be touched upon here.

The Hebrew language can boast of a marked richness in its vocabulary for expressing the idea of entirety. Conversely, the language does not distinguish between the notions of *entirety* and *totality*, and the same word, *kol*, is applied to mean *the whole* when reference is to a *unit* and to mean *each* or *all* where what is in view is a *plurality*. Characteristic of this double application is the 145th psalm, in which it is this little word that as *leitmotif* binds the various themes of the psalm together and renders it a sublime hymn of universalism. All works of the divine love, all works of the divine justice are manifest to mankind as a whole, and all flesh sings God's praise in melodious unison.[38] Where Hebrew wishes to express individual entirety, it usually employs the root of *tam*, the other meanings of which are *ingenuous* (Latin *integer*), (morally) *perfect*, *complete* – and so, *whole*. The word for collective entirety, on the other hand, is *shalem*, and is thus intimately related to *shalom*, the word for 'peace'. *Peace* in Hebrew is thus not – or not merely – the opposite of war, and that which overcomes it, but rather a symbol for everything, divine and human alike, that is complete. The last note of the priestly benediction (*Num.* 6: 26) is 'peace' in this deeper sense: the Jew prays for the protection of God's tabernacle of 'peace'[39]; and so *shalom* is the natural word wherewith he extends his greeting. It is by 'peace' that the human race effects its own completeness, and 'peace' is the true token of the messianic age – the Messiah himself being once styled[40] *prince of peace*.

This chain of moral ideals – entirety, totality, completeness and 'peace' – points further (in virtue of their being both social ideals and presuppositions of thinking about mankind) towards notions of human unity. In the tractate *Sanhedrin* – in which the Mishnah deals with judicial processes – there is discussed at length the testimony of witnesses and their interrogation before criminal courts. The following caution is prescribed against carelessness in the witness-box that may involve the deposition of false evidence. After impressing on witnesses (in a capital case) the tremendous responsibility which they bear, the clerk of the court is to continue thus[41]:

> Therefore but a single man was created in the world, to teach that if any man has caused a single soul to perish[42] Scripture imputes it to him as though he had caused a whole world to perish; and if any man saves alive a single soul[42] Scripture imputes it to him as though he had saved alive a whole world. Again [but a single man was created] for the sake of peace among mankind, that none should say to his fellow, 'My father was greater than thy father'; also that the heretics should not say, 'There are many ruling powers in heaven.' Again [but a single man was created] to proclaim the greatness of the Holy One, blessed is He; for man stamps many coins with the one seal and they are all like one another; but the King of Kings, the Holy One, blessed is He, has stamped every man with the seal of the first man, yet not one of them is like his fellow. Therefore everyone must say, for my sake was the world created.

In this passage of the Mishnah the oneness of mankind is elevated into a matter of principle in connection with the creation story that records the forming of one solitary man. The idea of it being monotheism which is the principle whereon the unity of humanity rests has now had injected into it the further assertion that the unity of man is, for that reason, also the refutation of all gnostic systems – 'in order that the heretics (*minim*, i.e. sectarians) should not say . . .'. The final proposition is divided by the Mishnah into two parts. In the first, it is the fact of the derivation of all men from the single Adam that is raised into the principle of the *equality* of all men: each individual represents mankind as a whole, and no one can say to his fellow man, my ancestor was greater than yours. In the second part, the same circumstance is elevated into the principle of the *diversity* of men. True though it be that God fashions every man in the form of Adam, no two men are ever alike in the way that one penny piece is like another. Men are differentiated, physically as well as in matters of the mind, and the peoples, too, are differentiated. This latter doctrine Judaism had, indeed, to maintain in its own interests: for Israel is, in point of fact, something other than the nations of the world. The two clauses of the Mishnah constitute no contradiction; the equality of men and peoples rests on the right of each to be different and on the divine charge to eliminate all social inequalities and asocial differentiations. Those passages of the Bible that speak of *thy brother* or *thy neighbour* or the *brother thou knowest not*[43] are not merely elegant declamatory flourishes, but commandments. And where the commandment requires that there be 'one manner of law, as well for the stranger as for the native',[44] it is followed immediately by the foundation for that one law for all – 'for I am the Lord your God'. And examples could be adduced from elsewhere in the Pentateuch for what *Deut.* (1: 17) means when it declares 'for judgment is God's'.

Judaism has no place for any ideology founded on race, and it knows of no sagas regarding aristocracy of blood wherewith to support the concept of Israel's election. Quite the contrary: the prophet Amos, in a bold picture, can place on the same level with Israel both her neighbouring peoples and peoples from afar. 'Are ye not as the children of the Ethiopians unto me, O children of Israel ('tis the Lord's own word)? Have I not brought up Israel out of the land of Egypt? And the Philistines from Capthor, and the Syrians from Kir?'[45] It is a calculated gesture in which Amos sees to it that the feature shared by the Chosen People with the children of the dark-skinned Kush, Ethiopia, a people held by his contemporaries in universal contempt, is that both are styled *children* (or rather, *sons*); of set purpose it is the uncircumcised Philistine to whom there is compared the people with which God has contracted a covenant itself symbolised by circumcision: and it has to be the Aramaic-speaking people of Syria, traditionally the enemy of Israel, that must put up with being mentioned by God in the same breath as Israel itself. In God's sight they are all equal, inasmuch as it is God who directs the destiny of each. Amos' message had his own contemporary world in view. Looking into the future, Isaiah saw the salvation of the nations in the circumstance that Assyria would one day be linked with Egypt by a road running through Israel. The three peoples would constitute themselves a triad specifically bonded together by covenant, and vouchsafed God's blessing: 'Blessed be Egypt My people, and Assyria the work of My hands, and Israel Mine inheritance.'[46] Egypt, for Israel, meant the house of bondage and the epitome of every aspect of enslavement; and yet, salvation for Israel is to consist in there being a covenantal state between itself and this one arch-enemy and the other that had led Israel's northern kingdom into exile. The terms of affection that have hitherto been applied to Israel alone are the very ones in which God now sees fit to address Egypt, 'My people', and Assyria, 'the work of My hands'. The peoples are to knot themselves together – not to merge themselves in each other beyond all identification. In the Midrash, it is the diversity of the peoples to which reference is made as corresponding with the divine plan: 'God explained the details regarding the frontiers of each several nation, in order that they should not become mixed up in each other.'[47]

That which puts the seal on the recognition of the same rights for diverse groups is love; for the commandment to love one's neighbour is the logical consequence of this attitude towards one's brother and fellow. 'Thou shalt love thy neighbour as thyself' – or rather, to translate it in true accord with both the canons of Hebrew syntax and the essence of Judaism, 'Thou shalt love thy neighbour, he being like thee'[48]; and once again the basis of the commandment follows immediately – 'I am the Lord'. Quite characteristically, rabbinic Judaism has set this commandment regarding loving one's neighbour alongside a verse of *Genesis* (5: 1), 'This is the book of the generations of Adam.'[49] According to Ben 'Azzai, one of the mishnaic scholars of the second generation (*c.* 90–130 C.E.), this latter verse affords a basic principle of Judaism of even wider purview than that covered by the commandment to love one's neighbour, which his contemporary, Rabbi 'Aqiba (*c.* 50–135), defended as being an all-embracing statement of what Judaism means. All that Ben 'Azzai is doing, fundamentally, is merely to use the *Genesis* text to underscore the commandment to love one's neighbour. The obligation to love one's fellow man is founded upon the brotherhood of all men, each of whom – as the continuation of the verse in *Genesis* explicitly states – was created by God in His own likeness.[50] Ben 'Azzai's exegetical emphasis accords with the circumstance that post-biblical Judaism has introduced a new term for 'fellow man' – or rather, has reminted an old word in this sense (*beriyyoth*, creatures)[51] – and indeed makes use of it in a rabbinic restatement of the commandment to love one's neighbour. In the *Ethics of the Fathers*[52] Hillel (*c.* 30 B.C.E. – 10 C.E.) is recorded to have said 'be among [those who] . . . love [their fellow-] creatures'. The word *beri'ah* occurs once in the Hebrew Bible[53] in the sense of creation, or rather of a phenomenon newly created; it occurs once, in the sense of *creature*, in the Aphorisms of Ben Sira,[54] and it is in this sense – but restricted contextually to human beings – that it is common in midrashic literature in the form *biryah*, the less frequent singular form *beriyyah* referring still to the divine act of creation.

The final – as well as the primary – requirement of Jewish morality for any common life of humanity is justice. Law is the principle upon which all social existence must rest, but (as the Bible never tires of reminding us) law has to be applied with justice (*ṣedaqah*). This Jewish 'justice' (the inverted commas may serve to emphasise the inadequacy of the translation) is something more than a general principle formally stated in the sense of *suum cuique*, no matter whether the latter be taken to mean 'to each his own task in society' or 'let each enjoy what is his own'. To be sure, the equality of all before the law goes without saying in Judaism: and the commandment not to countenance a poor man in his cause,[55] or 'Ye shall do no unrighteousness in judgment, thou shalt not respect the person of the poor'[56] is an injunction regarding which Geiger could remark[57] that as a warning against the perversion of justice expressed within the context of a legal code, it is probably not to be paralleled. But this in itself does not suffice to characterise what is essential in the Jewish notion of 'justice', which is a dynamic and active principle even as is love. For both Philo and the Midrash the twin cherubim above the ark of the covenant represent 'love' and 'justice'.[58] This 'justice' – *ṣedaqah* – constitutes in Judaism the *imitatio Dei*, it being said of God[59] that 'all His ways are judgment' (*mishpaṭ*); and it was to Abraham that there was addressed the demand, for himself and those who should come after him, that 'they will keep the way of the Lord, to do "justice" (*ṣedaqah*) and judgment' (*mishpaṭ*).[60] God is 'the Just' – *ṣaddiq* – and it is as *'El ṣaddiq* that He effects a just settlement between nations.[61] And where man is described as *saddiq* he is, quite simply, piously God-fearing and his doings are doings of beneficence (*ṣedaqah*).

A presupposition of the existence of human society is the acknowledgment of a humanity the members of which are actively concerned in manifesting 'acts of piety' (*gemiluth ḥasadhim*) each towards the other. According to the Talmud[62] it is this spirit of humanity that constitutes the beginning and the end of the Torah. At the beginning of the Pentateuch[63] God clothes man's nakedness as he goes forth from Eden, and at the end of it, it is God again who, according to a bold midrashic interpretation,[64] Himself buries Moses in the fields of Moab. Thus the Torah begins and concludes with examples of God's own evincing of 'acts of piety', in order to teach that man may learn from them to imitate God.

It is through maintaining this attitude towards human society that Judaism has been able to pave the way for its own Utopia of a united mankind at the end of days. For the concept of humanity has never been, for Judaism, a matter for the intellect alone; and Hermann Cohen rightly observes[65] that it is no accident that Herder, the author of *Ideen zur Philosophie der Geschichte der Menschheit*, also wrote a book entitled *Vom Geist der ebräischen Poesie*.

NOTES

* An article entitled *Der Menschheitsgedanke im Judentum* appeared in *Studium Generale* 15, 9, 1962, pp. 571 f., over the name of (the late) Dr Kurt Wilhelm, who suggested to the Editor of the present volume that an English version of it might be a fitting contribution to a volume in memory of Leon Roth. In accordance with a freedom of treatment which he gave the Editor, it has here been slightly abridged in a few places; unfortunately Dr Wilhelm died before the English draft could be submitted to him.

For the biblical passages cited in the German original Dr Wilhelm had quoted the translation of M. Buber and F. Rosenzweig. Where this version differs from King James' either in emphasis or in exegesis, the Editor has, in translating the article into English, endeavoured to follow it closely.

1 M. Guttmann, *Das Judentum und seine Umwelt*, Berlin, 1927, p. 2 f.
2 2nd edition (reprinted Cologne, 1959), pp. 95, 154.
3 *Zechariah* 14: 9.
4 *Op. cit.* (note 2), p. 403.
5 'Der Messiasgedanke und seine Umbiegung im modernen Liberalismus', in *Festgabe für Claude G. Montefiore*, Berlin, 1928, pp. 151 f.
6 Mishnah, *Soṭah* 9, 15, H. Danby's translation, p. 306.
7 *Baraita* in T.B. *Pesaḥim* 54b, *supra*.
8 S. Singer, *Authorised Daily Prayer Book* (1929 ed.), p. 161.
9 *Hebrew Union College Annual* 18, 1943–4, Cincinnati, pp. 353 f.
10 G. von Rad, *Theologie des Alten Testaments*, i, p. 144.
11 *Isaiah* 41: 4.
12 On the Noachide Commandments see more fully R. Loewe, *supra*, pp. 125 f., and S. H. Bergman, *supra*, pp. 52 f.
13 Guttmann, *op. cit.* (note 1), pp. 98 f; S. H. Bergman, *supra*, p. 56 f.
14 *Hilekhoth Melakhim*, 8, 11. For the significance of the concluding proviso, see R. Loewe, *supra*, pp. 143 f.
15 *Maḥbereth* 28, part ii (*ha-'edhen*), ed. Dov Yarden, Jerusalem, 1957, vol. 2, p. 542, l. 715 f; L. Goldschmidt's edition, p. 45.
16 *Das Menschenverständnis des Alten Testaments*, p. 35.
17 *Deut.* 32: 8; but the Septuagint, in which the verse ends *according to the number of angels of God* (i.e. *beney 'elohim* instead of *beney yisra'el*) quite possibly preserves an earlier text, according to which the number of the peoples tallies with that of their respective champion or guardian angels. For the traditional figure of 70 for the sons of Jacob, reflected in the massoretic text here, cf. *Ex.* 1: 5, *Deut.* 10: 22, and the arithmetical and syntactical gymnastics of *Gen.* 46: 26–7 that are resorted to in order to achieve this total.

18 Eichrodt, *op. cit.* (note 16), p. 36.
19 *Gen.* 9: 8 f.
20 *Gen.* 12: 3.
21 I. Heinemann, 'Die geschichtlichen Wurzeln des neuzeitlichen Humanitätsgedankens', *Der Morgen*, 6, 1930, pp. 112 f.
22 *Isaiah* 2: 2–4.
23 *Micah* 4: 1–3.
24 *Isaiah* 11: 2–3.
25 M. Buber, *Der Glaube der Propheten*, pp. 218 f.
26 *Isaiah* 11: 9.
27 *Isaiah* 42: 6–7.
28 *Op. cit.* (note 25), p. 309.
29 T.B. *'Abhodhah Zarah* 24a. For the linking of the verse with the story of Babel in *Genesis* cf. *Yalquṭ Shim'oni* to *Zephaniah* (ii, 567; R. Yosē).
30 T.B. *Berakhoth* 34a.
31 *Hilekhoth Melakhim* 12, 1–2.
32 *Ibid.* 12, 5.
33 T.B. *Babha Bathra* 75a, *Exodus Rabbah*, 23, 10, ed. Wilna, f. 43b, col. ii. Cf. also *Pesiqta Rabbathi*, 36, *end*, ed. M. Friedmann, f. 162b. The basic text is of course *Isaiah* 60: 1–3.
34 S. Singer, *op. cit.* (note 8), p. 239a.
35 I. Elbogen, 'Die messianische Idee in den alten jüdischen Gebeten', *Judaica* (*Hermann Cohen Festschrift*, 1922), p. 669.
36 S. Singer, *op. cit.* (note 8), p. 249.
37 *Ibid.*, p. 37 f.
38 Leon J. Liebreich, 'Psalms 34 and 145 in the light of their key words', *Hebrew Union College Annual*, 27, 1956, p. 190. Cf. also C. G. Montefiore and H. Loewe, *A Rabbinic Anthology*, 1938, p. lxxxvii.
39 S. Singer, *op. cit.* (note 8), p. 99 f., *infra*.
40 *Isaiah* 9: 5.
41 *Sanhedrin* 4, 5, H. Danby's translation, p. 388.
42 Some texts add, at both these points, 'from Israel'. In regard to the comparative lack of modern Jewish attention to the ethical question raised by the insertion or omission of these words, see Leon Roth's remarks in his 'Moralization and Demoralization in Jewish Ethics', *Judaism*, 11, no. 4, Fall, 1962, p. 292.
43 *Deut.* 22: 2.
44 *Lev.* 24: 22.
45 *Amos* 9: 7.
46 *Isaiah* 19: 25.
47 *Siphrē, Deut.* 311 (to 32: 8), ed. L. Finkelstein, p. 352, l. 1.
48 *Lev.* 19: 18. Cf. E. Ullendorff's article, *supra*, pp. 276 f.

49 *Siphra, Qedoshim* 4 (on. *Lev.* 19: 18), ed. I. H. Weiss f. 89a, col. ii, (12).

50 See Leon Roth's illuminating analysis of the passage, *op. cit.* (note 42), pp. 295 f.

51 See further on this term R. Loewe, *supra*, pp. 127 f.

52 1, 12, Danby's translation, p. 447.

53 *Numbers* 16: 30.

54 *Ecclesiasticus* 16: 16 (*biryothaw* parallel to *beney 'adham*); but the verse – which is omitted by nearly all MSS of the Greek version – is regarded by many as a later insertion. Cf. W. O. E. Oesterley's commentary, Cambridge, 1912, p. 111.

55 *Exodus* 23: 3.

56 *Lev.* 19: 15.

57 A. Geiger, *Das Judentum und seine Geschichte*, 1864, p. 25. Cf. Z. Diesendruck's Hebrew article on 'The perfection of society according to the teaching of Judaism', *H. N. Bialik Festschrift*, Tel Aviv, 1934, 3, p. 51, a study to which I am indebted for a number of references.

58 Philo, *Cherubim*, 9, 27, 144, ed. Cohn-Wendland, i, p. 176, Loeb translation by F. H. Colson and G. H. Whitaker, ii, p. 24. Cf. *Midrash Tadeshē*, A. Jellinek, *Beth Ham-midrash*, 3, p. 164, *infra*.

59 *Deut.* 32: 4.

60 *Gen.* 18: 19.

61 *Isaiah* 45: 21.

62 T.B. *Soṭah* 14a (R. Simla'i); cf. *Tanḥuma*, ed. Buber, *Genesis*, *Way-yera'*, 4, f. 43b, note 30.

63 *Gen.* 3: 21.

64 *Deut.* 34: 6.

65 *Op cit.* (note 2), p. 282.

THE JEWISH PEOPLE

HISTORY • RELIGION • LITERATURE

AN ARNO PRESS COLLECTION

Agus, Jacob B. **The Evolution of Jewish Thought:** From Biblical Times to the Opening of the Modern Era. 1959

Ber of Bolechow. **The Memoirs of Ber of Bolechow (1723-1805).** Translated from the Original Hebrew MS. with an Introduction, Notes and a Map by M[ark] Vishnitzer. 1922

Berachya. **The Ethical Treatises of Berachya, Son of Rabbi Natronai Ha-Nakdan:** Being the Compendium and the Masref. Now edited for the First Time from MSS. at Parma and Munich with an English Translation, Introduction, Notes, etc. by Hermann Gollancz. 1902

Bloch, Joseph S. **My Reminiscences.** 1923

Bokser, Ben Zion, **Pharisaic Judaism in Transition:** R. Eliezer the Great and Jewish Reconstruction After the War with Rome. 1935

Dalman, Gustaf. **Jesus Christ in the Talmud, Midrash, Zohar, and the Liturgy of the Synagogue.** Together with an Introductory Essay by Heinrich Laible. Translated and Edited by A. W. Streane. 1893

Daube, David. **The New Testament and Rabbinic Judaism.** 1956

Davies, W. D. **Christian Origins and Judaism.** 1962

Engelman, Uriah Zevi. **The Rise of the Jew in the Western World:** A Social and Economic History of the Jewish People of Europe. Foreword by Niles Carpenter. 1944

Epstein, Louis M. **The Jewish Marriage Contract:** A Study in the Status of the Woman in Jewish Law. 1927

Facets of Medieval Judaism. 1973. New Introduction by Seymour Siegel

The Foundations of Jewish Life: Three Studies. 1973

Franck, Adolph. **The Kabbalah, or, The Religious Philosophy of the Hebrews.** Revised and Enlarged Translation [from the French] by Dr. I. Sossnitz. 1926

Goldman, Solomon. **The Jew and The Universe.** 1936

Gordon, A. D. **Selected Essays.** Translated by Frances Burnce from the Hebrew Edition by N. Teradyon and A. Shohat, with a Biographical Sketch by E. Silberschlag. 1938

Ha-Am, Achad (Asher Ginzberg). **Ten Essays on Zionism and Judaism.** Translated from the Hebrew by Leon Simon. 1922. New Introduction by Louis Jacobs

Halevi, Jehudah. **Selected Poems of Jehudah Halevi.** Translated into English by Nina Salaman, Chiefly from the Critical Text Edited by Heinrich Brody. 1924

Heine, Heinrich. **Heinrich Heine's Memoir:** From His Works, Letters, and Conversations. Edited by Gustav Karpeles; English Translation by Gilbert Cannan. 1910. Two volumes in one

Heine, Heinrich. **The Prose Writings of Heinrich Heine.** Edited, with an Introduction, by Havelock Ellis. 1887

Hirsch, Emil G[ustav]. **My Religion.** Compilation and Biographical Introduction by Gerson B. Levi. **Including The Crucifixion Viewed from a Jewish Standpoint:** A Lecture Delivered by Invitation Before the "Chicago Institute for Morals, Religion and Letters." 1925/1908

Hirsch, W. **Rabbinic Psychology:** Beliefs about the Soul in Rabbinic Literature of the Talmudic Period. 1947

Historical Views of Judaism: Four Selections. 1973

Ibn Gabirol, Solomon. **Selected Religious Poems of Solomon Ibn Gabirol.** Translated into English Verse by Israel Zangwill from a Critical Text Edited by Israel Davidson. 1923

Jacobs, Joseph. **Jesus as Others Saw Him:** A Retrospect A. D. 54. Preface by Israel Abrahams; Introductory Essay by Harry A. Wolfson. 1925

Judaism and Christianity: Selected Accounts, 1892-1962. 1973. New Preface and Introduction by Jacob B. Agus

Kohler, Kaufmann. **The Origins of the Synagogue and The Church.** Edited, with a Biographical Essay by H. G. Enelow. 1929

Maimonides Octocentennial Series, Numbers I-IV. 1935

Mann, Jacob. **The Responsa of the Babylonian Geonim as a Source of Jewish History.** 1917-1921

Maritain, Jacques. **A Christian Looks at the Jewish Question.** 1939

Marx, Alexander. **Essays in Jewish Biography.** 1947

Mendelssohn, Moses. **Phaedon; or, The Death of Socrates.** Translated from the German [by Charles Cullen]. 1789

Modern Jewish Thought: Selected Issues, 1889-1966. 1973. New Introduction by Louis Jacobs

Montefiore, C[laude] G. **Judaism and St. Paul:** Two Essays. 1914

Montefiore, C[laude] G. **Some Elements of the Religious Teaching of Jesus According to the Synoptic Gospels.** Being the Jowett Lectures for 1910. 1910

Radin, Max. **The Jews Amongs the Greeks and Romans.** 1915

Ruppin, Arthur. **The Jews in the Modern World.** With an Introduction by L. B. Namier. 1934

Smith, Henry Preserved. **The Bible and Islam;** or, The Influence of the Old and New Testaments on the Religion of Mohammed. Being the Ely Lectures for 1897. 1897

Stern, Nathan. **The Jewish Historico-Critical School of the Nineteenth Century.** 1901

Walker, Thomas [T.] **Jewish Views of Jesus:** An Introduction and an Appreciation. 1931. New Introduction by Seymour Siegel

Walter, H. **Moses Mendelssohn:** Critic and Philosopher. 1930

Wiener, Leo. **The History of Yiddish Literature in the Nineteenth Century.** 1899

Wise, Isaac M. **Reminiscences.** Translated from the German and Edited, with an Introduction by David Philipson. 1901